W9-AWH-696

Dedication

This book is dedicated to two very important groups of people in my life. First to my family: Michael, my son, who at age 18 still trusts me as an editor and who has given me endless hours of pleasure watching him work his magic on the pitching mound; to Nikki, my talented and witty daughter who makes me laugh from my very soul, and who shares both writing and coffee with me; and to Jerry, my husband and lifelong friend, without whose patience and support I could not have traveled these millions of miles.

Second, to the thousands of teachers who have so graciously and selflessly invited me into their hearts and lives, sharing their ideas, inspiration, and students' work. Thank you for the time and trust you have so generously given me, but even more, for the hours you have spent helping students become writers, even when the path felt very steep. Thank you for refusing to give up and for believing that students can, indeed, write.

CONTENTS

CHAPTER 9:   TEACHER TALK: LEARNING FROM OTHER TEACHERS   256

CHAPTER 10:   ADAPTING THE 6-TRAIT GUIDE TO FIT YOU   271

CHAPTER 11:   THE WORLD OF BEGINNING WRITERS   318

CHAPTER 12:   **COMMUNICATING: THROUGH COMMENTS, CONFERENCES, PEER REVIEW, AND GRADES   359**

EPILOGUE: **REFLECTING AND BELIEVING   383**

FOREWORD

by Richard J. Stiggins

As my Assessment Training Institute colleagues and I travel the land demonstrating the power of student-involved classroom assessment, we encourage teachers to see that we must always address our assessment challenges with a clear sense of what is to be assessed. Assessment literacy—with a very well-defined vision of success—is our goal.

Our assessment lessons cover an ever broadening range of achievement targets: mastery of content knowledge, patterns of reasoning, performance skills and product development capabilities. Through this necessarily generic vision, we start them down the road to building sound assessment environments. From there, others more experienced in teaching a given content area must add their wisdom.

Creating Writers (1st and 2nd Ed.) has been at the top of our list of follow-up references for a decade. We consistently hold this book up as the "bible" for anyone who wishes to help students come to believe in themselves as writers. But the fact is (I must admit meekly), this recommendation used to be somewhat self-serving. I was the second author of those first two editions. However (I hasten to add in my own defense), I have always pointed out that this is Vicki's book. I informed my listeners that I have built my career around associating myself with really smart people, hoping that some of their competence would rub off on me. Vicki is one of those people. She has been one of the two or three most important teachers in my professional life.

We grew up together in the realm of writing assessment. We first collaborated on a monograph entitled *Direct Writing Assessment* published by the Northwest Regional Educational Laboratory in 1982. At that time, I was the large-scale assessment expert and Vicki began working on me to focus in another direction: "Rick, we have to pay much greater attention to the needs of teachers and students in the classroom . . ."

After a second edition of this monograph in 1986, our paths diverged. Vicki continued her headlong rush into understanding classroom applications of writing assessment. I branched into other applications of performance assessment—still not understanding that my headlights were misdirected.

Soon Vicki began to draft the first edition of *Creating Writers.* I couldn't resist her invitation to renew our partnership. That experience represented a personal epiphany for me. I was jolted into the realization that, in fact, it is not the once-a-year standardized test that paves the path to effectiveness of schools. Rather it is the other 99.9% of the assessments that happen in a student's life that determine if schools work for students—those assessments developed and conducted day to day in the classroom by teachers. As we brought *Creating Writers* to its first incarnation (1990), I watched with rapt attention as Vicki wove our classroom assessment ideas together into a wonderful vision of assessment wisdom.

At about that time in my career, I decided to devote the remainder of my professional life to understanding and improving classroom assessment. Not that periodic summative assessments are unimportant. Indeed, they serve many valuable purposes. But through my work with Vicki and others, I came to realize that as visible and politically important as they are, standardized tests represent only a tiny segment of the total assessments that must be of high quality if our students are to succeed.

In 1997, Vicki wrote the second edition of *Creating Writers,* permitting me to contribute a chapter or two. Is this sufficient involvement to justify second authorship? But nevertheless, once again, she welcomed me as a partner on her title page.

Now, as this third edition of *Creating Writers* appears, Vicki stands alone. This time I remain merely to introduce her—my teacher. This is as it should be. It is my joy to recommend to you that you study her continually growing and enriching ideas and strategies. In my opinion, Vicki has emerged as the nation's leading advocate of student-involved classroom applications of writing assessment.

In the chapters that follow, you will learn many valuable lessons. For instance, you will read about the need to *remain in balance* in all matters related to assessment, including our use of classroom and standardized writing assessment, our use of different assessment methods within the classroom and our classroom assessment procedures. Even in these times of obsessive concern for high-stakes standardized testing at local, state, national and international levels, we must attend to the day-to-day informational needs of students, teachers and parents.

Further, while many seem to believe that the power that can be brought to bear on behalf of learning is finite, Vicki reveals that it is, in fact, infinite. The more power we share with our students, the more absolute power is harnessed in the service of helping them become confident, competent writers. She instructs us to take the risk and reap the harvest of *sharing the power to assess with our students.*

Vicki shows us how to radically reduce, if not eliminate, the paralyzing hopelessness that can beset those of our students who don't write well at first. If we can help those students see where they are now in relation to where we want them to be, we can *reveal to them a path to their own success.* Then our challenge is to keep them believing that they are in control of their own destiny as they move to achieve their goal—strong writing.

Ultimately, she helps us see that *our job is to teach ourselves out of a job*—to take our students to a place where they don't need us anymore to tell them that they have done well. Students who cannot monitor the quality of their own writing and fix it when it isn't working cannot yet function as independent writers. By helping our students to monitor and fix their own writing, therefore, we help them to become the independently functioning life-long writers they need to be.

Within *Creating Writers* we find a highly refined vision of excellence in writing—a vision that comes from teachers and continues to be improved by teachers (and their students!). The six-trait analytical scoring scheme, whether cast in adult or student-friendly language, and when accompanied by examples of student work, represents a sharply focused road map to high levels of student performance in writing. Moreover, the six traits are closely connected to state standards virtually everywhere. This vision of writing knows no geographic boundaries; and think of the implications for student success when we share with them the very keys to that success.

Consider the power of a learning environment in which everyone, including students, can accurately predict his or her writing assessment results before the assessment is ever administered. If you can, try to imagine schools in which everyone faces a pending assessment with the confidence that comes from knowledge (knowledge of writing and knowledge of one's own abilities).

We do not have to live with uncertainty. Our current understanding of writing is clear, expansive, and ready to share with students, in language meaningful to them. *Creating Writers* shows us the way.

Richard J. Stiggins, President
Assessment Training Institute
Portland, Oregon

PREFACE

This is a book about assessing to learn. It is based on the premise that, in order to assess writing performance effectively, we have to teach ourselves to think like writers. That means developing a working vocabulary that defines, in very explicit terms, what it means to write well.

For many of us, such a vocabulary comes as a welcome and long overdue gift. As student writers, we had only a limited language with which to analyze, discuss, or describe our own writing—or any writing. Assessment, after all, was not our responsibility; we waited for external evaluation to know how we had performed. We struggled to write things that would win us attention, praise, kind comments, and, of course, high grades; but often such rewards came as a total surprise or were withheld for reasons that were, to us, equally mysterious.

How different writing instruction—and assessment—can be when teachers of writing and their students share a common vocabulary that allows them to think, speak, assess, and plan like writers. Suddenly, there is no more mystery.

The underlying foundation of this book is simple: What students can assess they can revise. Clear, specific criteria that define writing along a continuum from beginning through developing to skilled performance levels give students realistic, understandable guidelines both for drafting and for revising their work. This is particularly good news to writing teachers, many of whom find revision among the most difficult steps in the writing process to teach effectively. Explicit criteria simplify both teaching and learning by making the goals of writing clear and by laying out for students precisely what they must do to succeed.

THE INTENDED AUDIENCE

This book is written for both current and future teachers of writing—from first-year beginners to veterans—who are seeking a way to help their students truly find writing success, and who would also like (added bonus) a way of talking about writing to students, colleagues, and parents.

This book will also benefit teachers who are weaving more writing into the curriculum as a way of encouraging creative and logical thinking in math, science, social studies, history, art, or any content area.

The assessment model and approach shared here has proven its worth through use in hundreds of writing assessments and thousands of classrooms across the country. It is highly adaptable, and it can be used in some form (as we shall attempt to show) at virtually any grade level, from primary- through college-level writing—and beyond. It can be used with any form of prose writing, including narrative, expository/informational, persuasive, descriptive, business, and technical. And it can even be used, with limitations, in assessing poetry (see Chapter 4 for an example). Best of all, it does not require teachers to abandon *any* good process-based practice. It offers enough structure to lean on—like a good rail fence—but not so much you feel boxed in or forced to change your current successful practices.

Want your students to taste success? Success you can see and measure? This is your book.

This revised edition includes numerous new teaching ideas, a greatly expanded section on working with primary/beginning writers, thoughts on helping struggling writers, things you can do when working with students who have already had training in the six traits, and several brand new scoring scales, including simplified scales based on *both* 5-point and 6-point assessment. In short, every effort has been made to meet the needs of the classroom teacher who says, "I want to do this—show me how."

THOSE MEMORABLE MOMENTS FROM STUDENTS' WRITING

The miscellaneous bits and pieces—whimsical, outrageous, striking, poignant, insightful—that close most chapters come from district and state writing assessments across the country.

These "moments" (many of which *could* be from my own writing—or yours!) make us smile or chuckle, pause and reflect, and sometimes shake our heads as we recognize serendipitous wit—or, alternatively, the very problems of logic and conventional befuddlement that all of us, as writers, encounter in our work. Writing is, after all, largely problem solving. There will be comedic blunders. There will be flashes of insight. It's never easy getting all the ducks in a row. Ask anyone who writes.

ACKNOWLEDGMENTS

Countless people have contributed to the development of this book. First and foremost, I wish to acknowledge how much I—indeed, all teachers—owe to the tens of thousands of student writers who, through their writings, have taught all of us so much. Without their voices, this book could not exist. Not just the best of the writing but *all* of the writing has contributed to our understanding of what makes writing work.

Every effort has been made to contact every student writer whose work appears in this book. We have not knowingly included any work without the author's explicit written permission. If any work has inadvertently been included without such permission, we will gladly remedy that inclusion with the next publication.

Special thanks to the following students for their willingness to share insights, invaluable student perspectives and, in many cases, the samples of their work that are the very heart and soul of this text: Aaron Bartels, Amber Burbage, Shannon Carter, Kallie Ciechomski, Jocelyn Coats, Courtney Cunningham, Zack Day, Brian Deckelmann, Katie Ehly, Veronica D'Aprile, Robert Graisbery, Alyssa Gutmeir, Leah Hauser, Jessica Hemmerly, Kristin Hess, Kirsten Heydel-Knorr, Andrew Hicks, Tiffany Jensen, Kevin Karetsky, Trisha Kilgus, Andrew Koster, Donald LaDue, Amanda Lien, Amy Lippert, Claire Lopez, Matt McCammon, Billy McClaskey, Sarah McClure, Joshua Mohr, Megan Oxton, Tony Pratt, Rhonda Riley, Rocky Ross, Lauren Rothrock, Connor Scott, Nancy Shapiro, Cody Simon, Michael Spandel, Nikki Spandel, Jimmy Tatalias, Nicholas Tatalias, Jacob Vankeirsbilck, Jessica Woodbridge, Curtis Wackerle, Randy Wainwright, Katy White, Jana Yenser, and Andrea Zengion. Your contribution to our learning is incalculable, and I am extremely honored to share your writing. I hope you will continue to be writers. Thanks also to those writers who shared their work anonymously. I am equally honored by your contributions. Finally, thank you to those writers whose work we did not have space to include. It was wonderful; we simply ran out of room.

I am particularly indebted to Ronda Woodruff, a member of the original Analytical Writing Assessment Model Committee and a former fourth- and sixth-grade teacher at West Tualatin View Elementary School in the Beaverton (Oregon) School District, who taught me what I was so hungry to know: how to teach writing *in a way that works*. Ronda, a treasured friend and teacher of teachers, generously shared countless lessons and student papers upon which much of this text is based. She also opened her classroom to me, serving as my mentor and allowing me to work with her student writers. Ronda was one of a kind and irreplaceable. Her spirit lives on every page of this book.

Special thanks to the following remarkably talented teachers, who offered extended opportunities to work with their students and to teach lessons and/or who provided ideas, materials, and suggestions that greatly enriched the classroom perspectives of this book: Faith Arsanis, Roseann Comfort, Darle Fearl, Barbara Ann Galler, Sammie Garnett, Christine Guenther, Lenore Hay, Jeff Hicks, Karen Verti Hungate, Sue McClung, Arlene Moore, Wendy Pruiett, Lynn Radcliffe, Jeanne Richards, Lynne Shapiro, Sally Shorr, Ellen Tatalias, Jennifer Wallace, and Fred Wolff. Thank you *all*.

My deepest thanks to those persons who have been my personal teachers: to the phenomenally talented Lois Burdett, who taught me to "take the lid off" because there are no limits to what children of any age or ability can accomplish;

to the inimitable Barry Lane, perhaps the finest teacher of revision skills I have yet to encounter—and unquestionably the wittiest (thanks for making me laugh when I needed it most); to my dear friend Donna Flood, who has supported this project in a thousand ways through her own teaching and writing, and who continues to share her considerable wisdom, acute and gentle humor, sensitivity toward students, and vast knowledge of writing assessment with fortunate teachers and student writers everywhere; to Patrick Sebranek, Dave Kemper, and Verne Meyer of Write Source Publishing, my writing/editing heroes—and especially Dave, for teaching me you really *can* fit it all on one page (no whining); to Tommy Thomason and Sneed B. Collard, my writer/teacher friends who do not just talk writing but who *do* it; to my Great Source friends Al Bursma, Phil LaLeike, Lisa Bingen, Shannon Murphy and Tina Miller (to name but a few), who have given my own voice and spirit new life; and to Richard J. Stiggins, who so generously refers to me as "his teacher," showing that even assessment visionaries can have a sense of humor. Thank you, Rick, for *everything.*

I'd also like to thank the rather thorny reviewer who suggested none too gently that I read *his* book to gain some insights. I did. And though I can't commend the book for its voice, it was definitely rich with ideas, and I believe—at least hope—that my book is the better for my having read it.

My continued appreciation to those who started the ball rolling so long ago (who knew?). In particular, thanks to the wonderful, generous, and talented Carol Meyer, Evaluation Specialist for the Beaverton, Oregon School District, and to the Analytical Writing Assessment Model Committee, a group of seventeen teachers (grades 3–12) from the Beaverton District, with whom, in August 1984, I was privileged to work in designing the original scoring guide upon which those in this book are based.

Many thanks are due the excellent team of editors whose meticulous attention to detail transformed this manuscript into a book. A good editor *is* hard to find, as editor Michael Korda (1999) reminds us, and I have been fortunate.

And finally, personal thanks for hundreds of hours of entertaining, enlightening instruction to Margery Stricker Durham, from whom I took seven undergraduate and graduate courses (*different* classes—I did pass them all), and who remains my all-time favorite teacher. I'm often asked why, and it was more than her dynamic personality—though she had that in abundance. Margery had the gift of insight. She taught us not just to analyze literature, but to analyze life—to synthesize ideas and to value reflection over speed. She taught us that all books, poems, essays, moments of epiphany, paintings, pieces of music, and other extensions of the mind and soul were interconnected, part of a larger record of intelligent thought. She taught us to think, and to dare to speak what we thought. It is the finest, most unselfish gift we give one another—for a piece of ourselves goes with it. And this gift is the reason teachers are so loved. I think of her daily, and always will.

CREATING A VISION

Good teaching is inseparable from good assessing.

Grant Wiggins

Good assessment always begins with a vision of success.

Richard J. Stiggins

THROUGH TEACHERS' EYES AND EARS

On a cool, early fall morning, I wake early, and lie in bed listening for the familiar scuff of shoes on the pavement, the thud of a car door, water running in the kitchen, the fridge opening and closing. My children are grown and most often gone, but I continue to listen with a mother's ears for signs that they are nearby and safe. I expect I always will. It strikes me that this is what teachers of writing do. They listen with a teacher's ear and look with a teacher's eye for the smallest signs of the person they know within the words. This book is about making their search a little easier.

A VISION—NOT A WHOLE NEW CURRICULUM

Easier is good. No teacher anywhere these days is saying, "I don't know what it is—with this skimpy curriculum, I simply *cannot* fill the days." Teachers are treading water faster than ever, and the tide continues to rise. Six-trait assessment and instruction cannot make classes smaller or make testing go away. It can, however, ease writing teachers' stress by showing them how to help students

- Take charge of their own writing process
- Understand the difference between strong and weak writing—and use that knowledge to write stronger drafts

- Revise and edit their own writing because they can "read" it and know what to do to make it better

All this sounds a little like magic, but really, it's logic. The key has been right before us the whole time; we had only to put it into the lock. The key is language. *Writers'* language. And that key unlocks the door to revision.

Consider for a moment the power of language to influence thinking: What medical intern can diagnose or treat patients without knowing terms like *hypoglycemia, myotonia,* or *toxemia?* Would we place much faith in an investment advisor who could not speak with ease about *market risk, return on equity* or *price to earnings ratios?* Similarly, writers must know about leads, transitions, brevity, clarity, development, detail, fluency, conventional correctness, conclusions and so much more—and must use these terms with ease in discussing their own and others' work. I am not talking about a superficial vocabulary list of the week approach here, but an in-depth understanding of how to write, how to revise, and how to assess.

Not a Replacement

By the way, trait-based instruction is intended to *enhance* a process-based approach to writing instruction, not to replace it. You will not need to give up *any* of the good instructional things you are now doing, including modeling, use of writer's workshop, direct intervention through individual or group teaching, integration of literature, sharing in response groups, or sharing your own writing. Each of these components will be strengthened by your use and your students' use of writers' vocabulary—six-trait language. Further, because the traits and the criteria that define them at various levels of performance are already developed, you will not need to invent them yourself. (You *could*—and that would be a very good use of your students' time and yours, for you would learn much through the process—but you won't *have* to.) And so you'll find yourself—once you've taught the traits to students—saving time.

Paul Diederich (1974) demonstrated the practical value of good criteria when he and some colleagues analyzed how long teachers were spending grading student essays. Results of his study showed that teachers who marked student essays line by line spent, on average, a remarkable eight minutes per essay. That means a teacher with 130 students (a much smaller class load than many have these days) could spend nearly eighteen hours per assignment *just responding to students' work.* (As a teacher, you might wish to have this figure handy the next time someone asks, "Why don't teachers assign more writing?") But here's the interesting part: When teachers abandoned their old ways of grading, stopped functioning as editors for their students, used consistent criteria that were familiar to student writers, and kept their comments to a minimum (brief marginal notes on what the student had done well plus one short suggestion), that time dropped to just two minutes per paper—*one-fourth the time they had been spending.*

I will create a class culture of questioning . . . . If I have 120 students, I will have 120 teacher's aides. I will train students to assess and reflect on their own work daily and take charge of their learning.

Barry Lane (1999, 194)

Don't get discouraged when you first begin to use the six traits and find it takes you ten minutes to score one paper. Speed comes with practice, and if you score one paper per day for a month, your efficiency and knowledge of the traits will astound and encourage you; you will be able to read and score a double-spaced two-page paper on all six traits in about three minutes—add one minute for a brief comment, and you're done.

ASSESSING TO LEARN

When we think *assessment,* we usually think *grading.* But while assessment feeds our grading system, its most important function *by far* is to help us understand those things, like writing, that are too complex to teach through mini lessons and worksheets. As Lucy Calkins (1994) so eloquently points out in her revised edition of *The Art of Teaching Writing,* we assess to learn: "If . . . children can't talk easily about texts, they will have a hard time being critical readers of their own or anyone else's writing" (p. 326). They will also have a difficult time revising. How can you revise something if you do not know whether it is any good or not?

Learning to look deep within (for that's what assessment is, after all) is essential not only to students' understanding of their own writing, but to the very act of writing itself. "We teach [students] how to read books," Donald Graves (1994) points out, "but not how to read their own writing. Unless we show children to read their own writing, their work will not improve." This, then, in a nutshell is our vision of success: Students who can read their own writing, and who know what to do to make it stronger.

It's easier to see this link to learning if we take assessment out of the classroom altogether and consider how we use it in everyday life.

If you're a World Series fan, you watch the pitchers and the batters closely, and over time, you learn what to look for, don't you? If you've been a pitcher or batter yourself, you watch with an even keener eye. As you drive down the freeway, you watch the drivers "performing" all around you, and you figure out what to look for there, too. If asked, you could list the traits of good driving right now, probably—could you not? In fact, you probably applied those criteria and made some judgments about others' driving the very last time you were out in traffic. The truth is, we use assessment criteria all the time: in choosing books to read, clothes to wear, candidates to vote for, or even people to marry. Assessment is the key to understanding almost anything; to say we can write and revise without learning to assess is like saying a surgeon can operate without first making a diagnosis. Yes, technically, she *can,* but . . .

Knowing What to Assess

In writing, as with anything, the trick lies in figuring out *what* to assess in order to make the most accurate judgments without overlooking anything important. If someone had asked me during my first years of teaching whether I used criteria to assess my students' work, I would have said, "Yes, certainly. Doesn't *every* good teacher do that?" The "six traits" had yet to be written down, and I had never held a rubric in my hand—nor, to my knowledge, ever even heard the word. Yet, I was quite sure that my own criteria for assessing writing existed in my head, and that I applied them consistently and fairly in judging students' work.

To some extent, I was probably right. I look at my own library, filled with the works of Sandra Cisneros, Wallace Stegner, Larry McMurtry, Maya Angelou, Tim O'Brien, Mark Twain, Carl Sagan—and more recently, Walter Dean Myers, E. Annie Proulx, Janet Fitch, Karen Hesse, and Toni Morrison. And it seems to me I have always treasured strong, independent voice, and a gift for finding significance in the tiniest of details. Surely I looked for those qualities in my students' writing, too. Or did I? Did I recognize detail and voice when I saw them? Did I reward those things with praise—or teach my students to look for those things in others' work or in their own? Sometimes, probably. Maybe. *Possibly.* One thing I know for sure, though: I did *not* provide my students with any written description of what I was looking for in their writing. If they had a vision of success, they made it up themselves through inference.

It had not yet occurred to me as a beginning teacher how powerful sharing criteria with students could be. For one thing, I still thought (unfortunately) that assessment criteria were for *me*, the assessor. I didn't know yet that we assessed to learn; I was still assessing to grade, and so did not see any reason to involve students in the process.

But beyond that, putting expectations in writing, especially writing that makes sense to students (and by the way, criteria that do not speak to students are all but worthless) is hard—as anyone who has tried it will tell you. It demands that you come face to face with what you value in writing, and that you *understand* it, for if you don't, you won't be able to describe it in anything but the vaguest of terms. Had I tried it, I would probably have discovered what most people discover the first time they attempt to put their own criteria in writing: that I really did *not* know precisely what I was looking for from my students, even though I thought I did. Later, when I worked with a teacher team in putting the original six-trait model together, we discovered language that described things we'd been trying to teach, *struggling* to teach all along, only we did not know what to call them—things like *voice* and *fluency*. There they were, like old friends, speaking to us from the page; in the words of Yogi Berra, "It was déjà vu all over again" (Lederer, 1994).

Once *we* had figured out what we were looking for, the next step was to share it with students, so they would know too. We would put our scoring guides, our rubrics, right into their hands, from day one. We would say, "Here it is. Here's the goal. Now we're going to help you achieve it." No more mystery. No more black box. As clear and open book as you can make assessment: That is what six-trait writing is about. You get the *answers* first.

If we look at most report cards, there is no explanation of the measurements superior, good, average, below average, and failing.

Strickland and Strickland
(1998, 103)

GOOD ASSESSMENT: HELPING STUDENTS HIT THE TARGET

It's easy to make the teaching of writing sound simple. It's not simple. Not even if you are a champion in the art of process-based writing. Not even if you write yourself. Not even if your room is awash in six-trait posters and rubrics. The teaching of writing is extraordinary in its demands—but also in its rewards.

Similarly, good writing assessment (which is an important component of instruction, not a separate activity) does not come about by accident. It's planned. When we judge the quality of our writing assessment, here are seven critical things we should be looking for all the time (Stiggins, 1996).

Key 1: Making the Target Visible

Students who have their own rubrics know precisely what criteria will be used to assess their work. Then the target is visible—and thus much easier to hit. Further, they get immediate feedback on their performance, not from the teacher, but from *themselves*. Students who can self-assess do not have to wait for some outside authority to tell them whether their performance is all right. They "read" their writing, as Donald Graves has suggested, and they know.

"A student who remains dependent on the teacher's grades for evaluation," declares Peter Elbow (1986), "is defectively taught in a simple, functional sense. He cannot, strictly speaking, do what he was supposedly taught to do because he cannot do it alone; without help, he cannot tell whether he did it right" (p. 167). Students who are taught to use criteria know when they are doing well, without waiting for outside confirmation, and when things go wrong, they know what to do about it.

When we present students with clear criteria, we turn on the lights.

Instead of simply saying "Be specific" or "Include more detail," we define what we mean by "detailed writing":

- Details are carefully, selectively chosen to go beyond common knowledge.
- The reader learns something.
- The writing is visual; the reader can picture what the writer is talking about and feels he/she is right at the scene.
- The reader's questions are answered.
- The writer's knowledge and experience lend the writing authenticity.

Now let's round out the picture with an example that helps the student understand what we're talking about. With younger writers, you might use this one from Roald Dahl's classic *Matilda*:

When she marched—Miss Trunchbull never walked, she always marched like a storm-trooper with long strides and arms aswinging—when she marched along a corridor you could actually hear her snorting as she went, and if a group of children happened to be in her path, she ploughed right on through them like a tank, with small people bouncing off her to left and right.

(1988, 67)

Do you see Miss Trunchbull? Of course. A woman who ploughs through small children like a tank is hard to miss. With older writers, a good example might be this short excerpt from Rick Bragg's *All Over But the Shoutin'*:

You begged the sky for a single cloud. The sun did not shine down, it bored into you, through your hat and hair and skull, until you could feel it inside your very brain, till little specks of that sun seemed to break away and dance around, just outside your eyes.

(1997, 100)

Feel the heat? Examples—whether written by professionals or by students themselves—help make criteria complete.

Key 2: Ensuring That What We Assess Is Important

We should be *very* careful what we assess because what we assess is what we will get. I often think of my friend and colleague Barry Lane (author of *After THE END* and *The Reviser's Toolbox*) whose high school teacher commented on one piece of his writing "It's nice to read typewritten work." We have to wonder how much time that teacher had spent pondering what she really wanted to see from her students. Was it *really* typewriting, or was that just the obvious trait?

As teachers, we usually mean well. We start out intending to teach knowledge of foreign capitals, but wind up assessing another thing altogether—whether the names of the capitals are written horizontally on the page. Or, we may intend to teach the importance of content and delivery in public speaking skills, but wind up assessing the length of the speech: Did it run the full four minutes? This tendency to assess the obvious, the readily observable, happens more often than we might like to think. In *Reflections on Assessment*, Kathleen and James Strickland caution that "Many rubrics we use are invalid because we don't score what's important in the real-world application of the content being assessed. Instead we design rubrics to assess what's easiest to describe rather than what really matters" (81).

As teachers of writing, we may start out meaning to assess content, voice, fluency, or organization (and even go so far as to tell students this is what we will be looking for) but wind up basing a grade on neatness, choice of topic, use of a pen rather than a pencil, perceived effort, length, or close adherence to the assignment. In short, the *easy* things to spot. One teacher actually gave an F to a third-grade student who had written a clever, original fairy tale—in purple ink; the teacher did not consider this color appropriate for a serious writing assignment. We might counter that giving a low grade for such a superficial reason is not appropriate in serious assessment.

The scoring criteria should be authentic, with points awarded or taken off for essential successes and errors, not for what is easy to count or observe.
Grant Wiggins (1992, 27)

Students are more engaged when indicators of success are clearly spelled out.
Judith Zorfass and Harriet Copel (1995)

Key 3: Ensuring That the Task Matches the Assessment Method

Possible assessment methods include **selected response** (multiple choice, true-false, matching, and fill-in); **essays** (which show in-depth understanding sometimes backed by factual knowledge); **performance assessments** (in which students actually do something, such as make a speech, or write a persuasive essay); and **direct personal communication** with the student (through conferences, interviews, and questionnaires). No one method is inherently better than another—and often a combination of approaches over time yields the most complete picture of what a student knows and can do. Although this book obviously focuses on one specific kind of performance assessment—six-trait analytical writing assessment—other kinds of assessment work for other purposes.

If we want to know whether students can punctuate copy correctly, for instance, we could give them a short editing task: two punctuation-free paragraphs to prepare for publication. We could also use a multiple-choice test, but it would not give us as much information about students' ability to apply rules.

If we wish to know whether students can write a critique of a film or craft a short narrative or prepare a persuasive argument about a newly proposed law, we must give them opportunities to gather information, to write, and to revise and edit their work.

Since performance assessment does not involve "right" or "wrong" answers but *degrees of proficiency,* it requires definitions of performance along a continuum ranging from beginning levels through proficient. Use of an analytical scoring guide such as the one presented in Chapter 3 helps ensure consistency among ratings of students' work.

Key 4: Sampling Enough to Trust Results

Sampling repeatedly over time instead of hoping one writing sample will "tell all" gives us a more accurate picture and helps minimize bias. The value of this approach is confirmed by Alan Purves's (1992) ten-year study of primary and secondary writing within fourteen international school systems, including those in the United States, England, Finland, Wales, Italy, Chile, Nigeria, and New Zealand. Among this study's many intriguing findings is this conclusion: "To make any assessment of students' [overall] writing ability, one at least needs multiple samples across the domain" (p. 112). Most of us would agree without thinking twice, but the "one sample tells all" approach is widely used at district and state levels where funding is scarce and time short; and at the classroom level, though we know instinctively we need as much information as possible, the reality of huge class loads makes us ask, "What's reasonable?"

No teacher can reasonably hope to assess dozens of samples of writing per year per student, however much we might wish to have such thorough information. But on the other hand, a teacher who assessed only one or two samples could not possibly count on such a small snapshot to tell her whether Mike's writing was strong in voice or whether Emily could plan and conduct sound research. Somewhere between these hypothetical extremes lies a realistic and valid compromise: a representative sample of all possibilities small enough to manage, yet large enough to yield strong inferences about how well students write.

Probably, because each classroom is different, we'll never come up with a magic formula to tell us precisely how many samples we need. Yet, there are guidelines to help us. First, we can look at what is being emphasized in the classroom—say narrative writing or business writing. Then we might say, well, it would be good to have at least two examples of each form of writing to assess. More (say three to four), if we wish to show growth over time in one specific form. Smaller assignments mean less to assess and so, if we wish to look at more than one or two samples per grading period, we should minimize assignment length in favor of more opportunities to write.

Time must play a factor, too. What is reasonable to demand of student writers and of ourselves as assessors over a 9- or 10-week period? Students may write daily, but formal assessment is not likely to occur more than once in two weeks, and even that is asking a lot of a teacher who has 150+ students to whom he/she must respond.

From four to six samples per grading period will offer us a good *minimum* (a small body of work) on which to base conclusions about student performance, and teachers who are able to do more will receive a proportionately more accurate picture of students' writing skills.

> Careful research shows us what common sense tells us is obvious: no matter how trustworthily we may evaluate any sample of a student's writing, we lose all that trustworthiness if we go on to infer from just that one sample the student's actual skill in writing.
>
> Peter Elbow (1986)

Key 5: Finding Ways to Limit Bias

In performance assessments, many things, including test content and structure, can bias results. Raters' expectations and cultural preferences are factors, too. Imagine, for instance, an assessment of public speaking skills administered to two very different groups of children: one culturally predisposed to freely sharing ideas and readily questioning adult authority, the other predisposed to exhibiting a quiet demeanor and never challenging an adult speaker. If raters look for a strong, confident delivery and plenty of eye contact, it is not difficult to imagine which group will be favored—regardless of the quality of content in their presentations.

In writing assessment, raters (who most often are teachers but sometimes professional writers or editors) may fail to use criteria, misinterpret those criteria, place too much emphasis on one factor while disregarding others, or ignore criteria altogether in favor of some personal basis for making a judgment (e.g., "This student wrote a science fiction piece, and I just don't like science fiction").

Research cited by Brian Huot (1990) indicates that raters often do not know the reasons behind their responses to a piece of writing or that they may believe they are responding to such factors as ideas and organization when in truth it is the voice of the piece or even the rater's own tendency to agree with the writer's point of view that determines the score. Researcher and writing instructor Paul Diederich (1974) discovered that raters actually scored the very same essays higher when told they had been written by honors English students. We might also ask ourselves, *How often do similar expectations influence our assessments within the classroom?*

A LITTLE SUBJECTIVITY WON'T HURT YOU

We must be cautious about taking the position that subjectivity is somehow inherently wrong, or that it invalidates the assessment process. There's nothing wrong with subjectivity if it's applied with consistency and intelligence. After all, lots of things in this world—films, books, restaurants, and performers in the Olympics—are rated subjectively, but we trust those ratings when they are given by persons with the training, insight, or experience required to make the ratings meaningful. We wouldn't want writing teachers to judge Olympic skating competition, and we would not ask professional skaters to judge writing samples.

At the same time, our judgments must be defensible. If I say, "Emily's writing in this piece about quarter horses isn't very good. It just feels—I don't know—kind of two-ish to me," that judgment comes from the sort of intuition-based, crystal ball approach that has made many teachers suspicious of writing assessment—and rightly so. But suppose I say, "Well, Emily spells well and punctuates correctly, but her paper lacks development and shifts in focus here . . . and here. Emily's voice shines through with this humorous anecdote on page 1 but fades on page 3 with these generalizations about the importance of animals in a person's life." Now my subjectivity is grounded in defensible points that match Emily's text to explicit criteria. Emily (or anyone else for that matter) has a right to disagree, but at least we have good beginning points for useful discussion.

Further, as Peter Elbow (1986) points out, our subjective reactions can be just what student writers value most. "When we give our students our frankly acknowledged subjective reactions," says Elbow, "we are treating them with more respect: 'Here are my reactions; here's the data; you decide what to do with them' " (p. 230).

Key 6: Making Students an Integral Part of the Assessment

Research by Paulette Wasserstein (1995) shows that students learn best when they are challenged, actively engaged, and asked to be self-reflective: "Hard work does not turn students away, but busywork destroys them" (p. 43). With six-trait assessment, students are elevated in status; they become part of a writing community in which their opinions about the quality of writing are frequently, actively sought. It is a good feeling to have your opinion valued. It teaches you to think, and it makes you feel as if your presence in the classroom might have purpose.

Key 7: Bringing Parents Into the Process, Too

A six-trait, criterion-based assessment model can look suspiciously lenient to parents haunted by memories of the good old days, when sentences were stretched on racks and the red ink flowed. Too often parents have not had the opportunity—or the invitation—to question what was *truly* being assessed in those classrooms of long ago, or to question whether writing instruction should cover thinking and presentation skills, not just mechanics.

As teachers, we can show them how six-trait assessment works by sharing rubrics, and inviting parents into our classrooms to observe and work with student writers using writers' language. We can even ask them to write, and to identify the strengths and weaknesses, trait by trait, within their own writing: an enlightening experience for anyone.

RELIABILITY AND VALIDITY

Degree of consistency (sometimes called *reliability*) depends on the specificity of the scoring criteria and the quality of the rater training. When the criteria are highly refined and very explicit, and when the raters are very thoroughly trained and feel confident in applying those criteria (so confident they could score a paper without even looking at the criteria, *but they look at the criteria anyway*), the likelihood of their scoring consistently rater to rater or paper to paper increases dramatically. This is important not only in large-scale assessment, but in the classroom as well. More so there, in fact, because so much more assessment occurs at the classroom level.

A good assessment of writing is also said to have **validity,** the closest possible connection with the knowledge or skills we wish to assess. Four kinds of validity are possible (and you should consider them all as you use the six-trait model we present in this text):

> *Predictive validity:* The extent to which performance on the assessment will be a good predictor of performance in a related context (e.g., in a writing course or a job that requires writing)
>
> *Concurrent validity:* The extent to which performance on one assessment will be a good predictor of performance on another assessment
>
> *Construct validity:* The extent to which the assessment measures skills and abilities truly essential to writing competence
>
> *Face validity:* The extent to which the assessment measures skills and abilities that teachers of writing (and employers who require writing) deem important

FROSTING ON THE CAKE: STUDENT MOTIVATION

Wouldn't it be terrific—as long as we're creating a vision here—if our students could feel engaged, motivated, inspired to write, and confident enough to take risks? Many students simply do not like to write, are afraid to write, or feel they have nothing important to say. Perhaps engagement is too much to hope for—or is it?

When we ask students to be critics, to use criteria in assessing the work of others, we show respect for their opinions and their thinking. And we discover something interesting: Students *like* being assessors. They like being the ones to say for a change what works and what doesn't. The result? Not only do writing and revising skills improve, but motivation and enthusiasm go up as well.

In a recent analysis of this question, Richard Strong and others (Strong, Silver, and Robinson, 1995) suggest three factors essential to student motivation.

- *We must clearly articulate the criteria for success and provide clear, immediate and constructive feedback.*
- *We must show students that the skills they need to be successful are within their grasp by clearly and systematically modeling those skills.*
- *We must help students see success as a valuable aspect of their personalities.* *(p. 10)*

We do all three with six-trait assessment. Rubrics define success in student friendly language. The immediate feedback is there if students are taught to understand the criteria within the rubric and look for features like fluency or a strong lead in their work. As we'll see when we talk about weaving traits into instruction, modeling is key. We recommend not only sharing strong and weak pieces of writing, but modeling the writing process itself through the sharing of your own writing and your thinking about that writing. And finally, analytical scoring offers *every* student an opportunity for success. Instead of assessing just one big "whole"—writing—we offer six traits, six chances to do well.

Multiple Chances for Success

This multiple-trait scoring and the performance profile it generates are important because every writer's work is so different. We're not all crackerjack editors; we do not all have powerhouse voices. But we all do *something* well. Rocky is a case in point. Rocky had not experienced much success with writing in his early years of school, and had not enjoyed many positive comments from teachers. Negative comments and multiple corrections taught Rocky an important lesson: Don't write too much. Keep it short. Get in and get out; then, they can't hurt you too much.

Then, he had an opportunity to make friends with Harry, the school custodian. From all indications, this was an enormous boost to Rocky's spirit. In addition, Rocky encountered a teacher who encouraged him to write, to express himself. From this kernel of success grew the courage to write more than a line or two—to actually express himself on paper and, not surprisingly, he chose the topic that was important to him at the time: his friend, Harry.

When students actively and co-operatively develop knowledge, understanding, and ethical attitudes and behaviors, they are more apt to retain these attributes than if they had received them passively.

Linda Tredway (1995)

Every student ought to have the equivalent of a baseball card—many different kinds of abilities measured and brief narrative report—if we are seriously interested in accurately documenting and improving complex performance.

Grant Wiggins (1993, 33)

Teachers should focus on students' strengths rather than on deficiencies.

Strickland and Strickland (1998, 25)

Harry is the one that made me stop fighting help me focus and do my work.

Ever sense I've been friends with Harry I've got all As & Bs on my reportcards. He's brought me to his camp, brought me fishing, let me sleep over his house I think hes the best friend a kid could have.

He brought me to eat at a resteront in Wiscasset. He bouht me an carereokey isn't that so nice. Harry and I play the gutar together my gutar is alatrek his I have know idea. Harry plays like the greatest singer there is. I help Harry at lunch time he let's me help him dump trays.

The day Harry and I stop being friends is the day I die, and that's along time from now.

from Rocky, Grade 4

Rocky's paper contains a number of conventional errors. But this is not what his teacher chose to focus on. She chose to focus on the details and the voice. Her positive comments let Rocky know that in two important ways, sharing a complete story and letting the reader in to share his feelings, he had indeed succeeded. "I can write," was his response. He certainly can. And we hope he continues.

NOT EXPECTING TOO MUCH

No assessment can answer *all* our questions, yet we often act as if it could. We expect assessment, especially large-scale assessment, to magically improve performance, when the reality is that only instruction can do that. If assessment alone were the key, we would need only to weigh ourselves daily to lose weight. Would that it were so. If you think this sounds silly, ask yourself what it is we do when our student writers do not perform as we feel they should. That's right. We assess more *often,* make our standards more rigorous, heighten our expectations. Well, then, perhaps if we weighed ourselves *hourly* . . .

As we look at the results from large-scale writing assessment, we should also keep in mind that while they can be good—even excellent—*indicators* of how students as a group (all fourth graders in a district or state, for instance) are performing, they are of limited value in determining either overall quality of instruction across a group or the nature of individual performance. Only a pre-post format can determine whether quality instruction is occurring across a given group, since too many factors prior to one isolated assessment will determine how students perform on *that particular test* of writing—just as prior events determine how we cook or drive or speak publicly on a given day.

A pre-post assessment—assuming it is well-conceived, carefully administered, and not overly restrictive in terms of prompt choice or time restraints—will show a very great deal about growth in writing across a

> Feedback has been shown to improve learning when it gives each pupil specific guidance on strengths and weaknesses, preferably without any overall marks.
>
> Paul Black and Dylan Wiliam
> (1998)

group, and if it is quality of instruction we wish to look at, we must stop trying to do that with single-assessment indicators and get serious about setting up the kind of pre-post assessment that will provide the information we need. We must look at where students (as a group) begin in their writing performance (the pre-test)—and then at how far instruction across a given period takes them (growth, as measured by the post-test). We must be sure that our assessment process matches—at least in a general way—the writing process within the classroom, that students have opportunity for revision (the heart and soul of good writing), and that the prompts are both clear and relevant to students' experience.

As for individual performance, a single measure gives us a good guess about overall performance—nothing more. And this is so *even when all the essential components are in place:* good prompts, choice of prompts, time to write and revise, time between writing and revision, sound criteria tested and retested over time, criteria provided to students during the assessment, access to writing tools such as dictionaries or handbooks during the assessment, prior related instruction, outstanding training for highly qualified raters, review training during the assessment, a knowledgeable and qualified scoring director, and frequent, repeated checks for rater bias (beginning with review of the prompt and all assessment procedures).

We must also be willing to recognize that even under ideal conditions, countless factors other than writing proficiency can influence individual performance—making our interpretation of results tricky at best. Here are just a handful: a student's understanding of or personal response to the prompt, his or her attitude toward the teacher administering the test, time allotted for writing and revision, what may be happening in that child's personal life, attitudes of the raters, quality of the criteria, a good match between the prompt and the criteria, skill of the raters in interpreting the criteria accurately, time allowed for thorough assessment, absence of distractions (e.g., noise) during assessment, absence of *any* bias (racial, ethnic, content, contextual, experiential, etc.) on the part of raters and prompt writers, and far from least, the general philosophy of the scoring director, or the person who trains the raters.

This person can literally cause the whole atmosphere of an assessment scoring session to shift—through such things as an overly heavy or minimal emphasis on conventions, over-attention to word choice, under-valuation of content and detail, or scoring based on factors that have nothing to do with writing ability per se, such as the child's perceived adherence to the precise requirements of the prompt. I say *perceived* because many papers (*way* too many) judged as "off topic" are in reality highly individual, even ingenious, responses to a topic that was hopelessly unclear or needed some serious tweaking in the first place to hold anyone's attention. Prompts are not holy writ. They're invitations to write, nothing more. Often, students who wander "off topic" are penalized for interpreting a prompt in an individual way or for thinking in an original manner, the very thing our instruction seeks (or should seek) to promote.

> Before presenting a case, don't lawyers spend hours poring over texts and researching? Would anyone tell a lawyer he couldn't use his notes at a trial?
>
> Strickland and Strickland (1998, 75)

No wonder teachers so often say, when they receive their students' writing samples back from scoring, "These samples do not reflect my students' best writing." They are right. Their students may have been inhibited by mind-numbing topics or perhaps had to complete all their writing within a fixed time that was ridiculously short. It's highly unlikely they had time to research or explore a topic in a way that would do it justice, or to talk with other writers about their work. "Revision," while often encouraged or even required, is usually, in reality, simply recopying to make the piece neater, longer, or both.

Over a very large group of test takers, or over a series of writing performances by a single test taker, factors (other than writing skill per se) that influence performance tend to balance out because all students have "good" writing days and "bad" writing days. But it is risky—highly risky—to make major judgments, such as whether a student should go to the next academic level, on the basis of a single sample.

We must not ask more of our assessments than they can give. They are snapshots and cannot be more. Let us not award them the status of biographical documentaries.

The Difference 6 Traits Can Make

Six-trait assessment and instruction can make a difference in students' writing performance not only at the classroom level but on large-scale measures of writing proficiency. This is so because students who know what writing is all about feel confident, know how to plan both a draft and a revision of that draft, and are likely to be a little speedier in doing both. These days, speed seems to be a common criterion for judging writing proficiency—perhaps because we do *everything* faster now, including shopping, eating, talking, and driving. How this came about, this reverence for speed, I am not sure, but I do not feel its overall impact on assessment is a good one. It creates stress, for one thing. But beyond this, writing is not by nature a speedy activity, but a reflective one. Until we recognize that, our measurements cannot dip beneath the superficial. That being said, though, it's time for practicality: The tests are here. They are upon us. And we must find ways to help our students survive. We must teach them to

- Interpret prompts thoughtfully
- Understand differences among modes of writing (e.g., narrative vs. informational), so they know what is being asked of them
- Assemble their thoughts and respond quickly to the question being asked
- Understand what good writing is (through the six traits), so they will have the best possible shot at creating something readable

Notice, please: This is *not* my recipe for high quality writing instruction; it is a recipe for surviving when you're thrown into the pool at the deep end and someone is watching to see how you do.

Someday

When we speak of a "vision of success," we generally mean a vision we share with students so they will know what we mean by quality writing performance. Just for a moment, though, let's broaden the definition to include our own vision of the seamless integration of assessment and instruction, especially how that integration might look if student success were the driving force behind it. Someday—in the world of Ideal Assessment—

1. Criteria will be clear, written in student friendly language, and carefully aligned with the traits or qualities teachers and professional writers value in good text.
2. Those criteria will be shared with teachers at all grade levels and taught to students from kindergarten on up—not three or six weeks prior to testing, but *all the time,* as an integral part of the curriculum.
3. Criteria will be consistent from grade to grade, class to class, teacher to teacher—and will *not be alarmingly different from what is emphasized on any district, state or national test of writing.*
4. Criteria will be shared with parents, too, so they can support a system that teaches their students to think critically about writing and to revise their writing for audience and purpose.
5. Self-assessment will be a major focus of the writing curriculum, making revision a logical step, not an imposed torture.
6. Students will self-assess *during* the writing process—not wait for the teacher to assess after the fact when it is too late to do anything about identified problems in the writing.
7. Grades or scores will almost *never* be a surprise because students will know without any outside intervention whether their writing is good.
8. Formal writing assessment will model classroom writing instruction, with time for gathering information, shaping thoughts, drafting, sharing, revising, editing, and proofreading.
9. In the classroom, students will write sometimes on topics of their choosing, but will also learn to interpret and personalize (as appropriate) assigned topics. In large-scale assessment, students will have choices among prompts and will be encouraged to come to an assessment with a preaccepted prompt of their own choosing, if they prefer.
10. Ability to present coherent ideas in a logical fashion and to address the informational needs of an audience will be valued above following directions, and the concept of "off-topic" will go the way of the Dodo bird.
11. *Everyone* who participates in the creation of a large-scale assessment or the use of its results will also participate by submitting an anonymous writing sample to be assessed. I do mean *everyone,* including teachers, administrators, prompt writers, and legislators. How can we possibly presume to judge whether an assessment is reliable and valid, or whether our assessment procedures are sound, unless we undergo the assessment process ourselves and allow our own performance to come under scrutiny?

12. All large-scale assessment results will be reviewed by an interpretive panel comprising classroom teachers, teacher-raters, administrators, curriculum specialists, prompt writers, parents, and the scoring director for the assessment. Together, these people will discuss how the assessment process worked, whether and how it could be improved, what the results meant, and how curriculum within the building or district or state could better serve student writers.

13. High stakes conclusions—e.g., *How well writing teachers or schools are performing*—will be based on the careful assessment of *multiple* writing samples collected over the duration of the instructional year. (Additional factors, including teacher observation, will naturally be included in any such evaluation.)

14. Teachers will focus on making students lifelong learners and writers—not just on helping them survive the "writing test."

15. Students will not lie awake the night prior to a writing assessment or cry when they stare at a sheet of blank paper or glaze over in bewilderment when they cannot figure out what a poorly worded prompt is asking of them. Instead, they will walk into any assessment situation, any time, any place, with the confidence that only comes from knowing that you write well enough to meet head on any assessment they can throw at you.

REFLECTING ON CHAPTER 1

1. Have you ever had a really bad experience with assessment, as a student or as a teacher? A really good experience? What did you learn from each experience?

2. Have you ever used a rubric (scoring guide) to assess performance in writing or any area? Did you think the guide created a clear "vision of success"? Why or why not? Was it easy to use? What could have improved it?

3. What is your personal vision of quality assessment?

4. What is your vision of success for student writers? If you are currently teaching, what methods or materials do you use within your classroom to share this vision with your students?

ACTIVITIES

1. Make a list of decisions you think could be fairly made on the basis of large-scale assessment. Make a list of decisions that could not fairly be made on the basis of such assessment.

2. Design a rubric (as a group or in your classroom) for something simple outside the academic world: say, a rubric for judging a good film, book, or place to eat.

First, list the factors (traits) that are important, and then see if you can define one or two traits on a continuum of performance ranging from beginning or weak (wouldn't bother to see this film) to strong (a great film I'd recommend to anyone).

LOOKING AHEAD

In Chapter 2, we will take a closer look at the link between writing assessment and instruction, considering how large-scale and classroom assessment affect each other, and what lessons each has to offer the other. We will also consider why analytical assessment has thrived in the classroom while holistic and primary trait assessment have been less widely used.

MEMORABLE MOMENTS FROM STUDENT WRITING

- Grandma and Grandpa have plenty of love in their worn out hearts.
- I hate reading books more than wrinkled pants.
- Her hair just seemed to pop from her head like the ends of a broken spring.
- I'm pretty occult, myself.
- Sandals don't come with a lifetime guarantee, and neither does life.

2

A QUICK WALK THROUGH THE WORLD OF WRITING ASSESSMENT

Good, honest assessment necessarily involves risk; call it danger. It demands patience and faith.

Kathleen and James Strickland (1998)

To assess is to question—constantly, honestly—where you are going and why you are going there.

Jim Burke (1999)

AN ANCIENT HISTORY

With all our emphasis on "authentic" (close to real world demands) assessment today, it is easy to imagine that we have just now adopted this approach to assessing writing. Far from it. Actually, "authentic" writing assessment is ancient. It goes back at least to sixth-century China, where it was used in the Sui dynasty as a means of competition for government positions (Lederman, 1986).

In nineteenth-century China, it is recorded, some unfortunate applicants, apparently plagued by unusually persistent writer's block, actually repeated their writing exams for as long as thirty years, or more. One wonders if the prompts changed much during this period—or if the rubrics were exceptionally unclear. At any rate, the stress of all this testing produced great anxiety among those assessed, who sometimes reverted to sewing notes into the hems of their garments or baking them right into their pastries and smuggling them into the assessment center. This suggests, of course, that the Chinese officials were looking for some sort of right or wrong answers for which notes would be helpful.

Direct assessment, the kind that requires students to actually *write*, is not about rights and wrongs, though. It is about writing to fit an audience, clarifying ideas, knowing when to shrink or stretch an idea, knowing how to begin and where to end, and so much more. It is not the sort of task for which little notes sewn into hems will usually be very helpful—as we will see shortly.

As we move into the twenty-first century, direct assessment (which re-quires students to craft stories, business pieces, essays, or persuasive argu-ments, usually to a prompt they're given) has easily displaced indirect (multiple choice, fill-in) in most writing assessment contexts. The old argu-ments that direct assessment takes too long, is too costly, or will not allow for fair, accurate assessment have not disappeared, but have been largely overridden by the widespread recognition of how much information is gained by looking at actual samples of writing. This difference is immedi-ately apparent to anyone who participates in a writing assessment. A mul-tiple choice test on subject-verb agreement or comma placement tells us a little about a student's *knowledge* of writing; an essay shows what she can *do*. It's the difference between reciting a recipe and whipping up a mean Caesar salad.

As of late 1999, roughly 42 states include writing samples as part of their statewide writing assessment programs, with six more under development (Thomason and York, 2000, 72). By the time you read this, that number (42) will likely have increased.

What is more, teachers who participate as raters in these (or district level) assessments quickly discover that being a rater is not what they ex-pected. They expected to be buried alive with paperwork. They expected to be bored. They *are* buried (that part's not a myth)—but under the mounds of student essays, they grow inspired. They develop perspective from seeing hundreds of writing samples at the grade level they teach; they encounter papers that rock the very foundations of what they previ-ously thought students could do; they gain a very solid picture of how well their own students are doing; and they learn things about what makes writing work or not work that they can take back into the class-room and use—immediately.

Good assessments—of the sort I'll show you in this book—guide and en-hance instruction. Good assessment is never about entrapment of students (or teachers, for that matter); it's about giving students an opportunity to show what they *can* do. It's also about giving teachers an instructional spark. It all begins with—in fact, almost everything hinges upon—solid, sound, clear criteria. Without that piece of the puzzle, the whole picture never comes together.

The only way to raise the quality of writing in a school is to create, share, and celebrate the specific criteria for that quality with everybody on a regular basis.

Barry Lane (1996)

CRITERIA: WHAT ARE THEY? WHERE DO THEY COME FROM?

Time was that if you needed a scoring guide to measure, say, math problem solving proficiency, you would have to build it yourself. These days, we are awash in rubrics—for playing the violin, diving, driving, cooking, sitting up straight—you name it. On the one hand, this is a very good thing. It shows a tremendous collective educational conscience about the importance of consistent, fair ratings based on the most thoughtful judgment of persons experienced in the field.

The problem is, not all scoring guides are good. Many are vague, ill-focused, wordy, redundant, incomprehensible—or worst of all, insulting to those unfortunate assessees who fall (in the assessors' minds, at least) at the lower end of the rating scale. More about this in a moment, but for now let's return to our opening questions: What are criteria? And where do they come from?

What Are Criteria?

When you hear the word *criteria,* what do you think of? These days, probably, standards. Also, expectations, requirements, measurement, goals, assessment and testing. All valid associations. But perhaps the most important association we can make with criteria is—*language.* Criteria are all about language. Language used to describe performance at various levels of proficiency along a continuum.

This connection becomes more clear once we recognize that analytical writing assessment is one example of *performance assessment.* Such assessment is quite different from, say, multiple-choice, fill-in, or true-false testing, in which there may be a best or correct answer. While individual patterns of grammar or marks of punctuation may be right or wrong, there is no "best" or "correct" way to write in the broader sense. This is why any *performance,* including writing, dancing, or diving, is so challenging to assess at all. With any human behavior, the indicators of success are numerous, often subtle, and therefore tricky both to define and to observe.

To see how criteria can help us define successful performance, let's focus for a moment on just one writing trait—say, organization. Most people would agree, without even thinking about it, that organization is important to good writing. But what exactly *is* organization? If we're going to teach it to students, we cannot simply say, "Get organized." That's about as helpful as "Write well. Good luck." To really teach a concept like organization, we have to figure out what it looks like along a performance continuum (see Figure 2.1), ranging from beginning to strong levels, then describe it level by level.

START WITH A DEFINITION
It's often best to start by defining the trait itself—then we can move on to how that trait looks at different levels of proficiency (the various level definitions being the criteria).

Organization is often defined as "having a beginning, middle, and end." As a teacher, I find this definition slightly clichéd. As a writer, I find it downright annoying, and confusing as well. Everything from watermelons to elevator rides has a beginning, middle, and end. Surely we can dig deeper to find language we can learn from and teach from.

Here's a start: Think of organization as internal structure, the skeleton of a piece—like the framework of a building under construction. It's more than this, of course. It's also finding a lead that hooks the reader and provides a foundation for what comes next. It is separating the significant from the trivial so that filler can be tossed aside. It is putting details in an order that shapes meaning and entertains or educates the reader—or does both. It is also finding the words and phrases that provide smooth transitions from point to point. Finally, it is crafting a showstopper conclusion that ties up loose ends.

FIGURE 2.1. Sample performance continuum

NEXT—DEFINE PERFORMANCE AT DIFFERENT LEVELS

Now we have only to define performance at different levels, translate these definitions into language that speaks to *student* writers, and voilà: See Figure 2.2. We have a language for teaching students to think about, talk about, and assess organization. That assessment is the key to revision. (In the chapters that follow—notably 5, 6 and 7—you will learn just how to use this tool in the classroom.) For now, just remember this: When you hear the word criteria, think *language.*

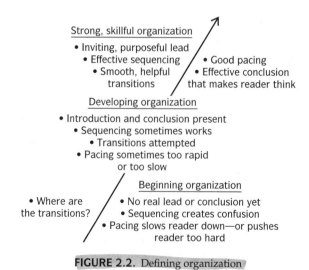

FIGURE 2.2. Defining organization

By the way, the terms *traits* and *criteria* are often confused; they *are* related, but are not precisely the same thing. Traits are the qualities—ideas, organization, voice, etc.—that define good writing. Criteria are the language we use to define how those traits look at various levels—beginning, developing, proficient—along a continuum of performance.

Where Do Criteria Come From?

Criteria sometimes come from would-be assessors who put together a list of things they currently feel are important—to writing, reading, architectural drafting, or any other kind of performance. I call these "arm-chair criteria" because they are developed from afar without a close-up look at actual performance. The armchair approach to criteria development is very dangerous. First, it can lead us to focus on things—say, margins—that sound worthy enough when we jot them on our list, but in truth have remarkably little bearing on readers' response to writing. It can also cause us to overlook things like voice that make the ultimate difference in whether a piece of writing is even read.

Now, to clarify, I am not for a moment minimizing the importance of margins, or any other writing convention. It is a matter of balance. Look at the margins in this book, for instance. Do you like them? I do. Nice and wide—a style that cuts down on the text your eyes need to traverse and makes space for the graceful insertion of sidebars. They're visually pleasing and useful as well. I would truly hate to think, however, that someone would actually buy this book or *any* book for its margins. That's the point; good criteria development demands that we identify what is *most* important, and we can only figure that out when we look at performance after performance and ask ourselves, "Which performances are strong? Which ones aren't? Why do we think so?" The answer to "why" will give us our most important criteria.

Expect Surprises

When we as teachers analyze student performance systematically, a curious thing happens: we often discover that in real life, good performance doesn't look quite the way we'd imagined it in our heads, and that the problems we'd originally thought would be most significant are not really as troublesome as others.

We may start out, for instance, believing that correctness is what we'd most like to see in a strong piece of writing, but then we crash head on into reality. When I curl up to read Annie Proulx's *Close Range*, I cannot really say I do not *care* about the punctuation and spelling. Of course I do. Still, I don't put the book down and say to myself, "Wow. Now *that* was exciting use of commas." But you can believe the eloquent word choice gives me pause when Proulx (1999) writes, "In the long unfurling of his life, from tight-wound kid hustler in a wool suit riding the train out of Cheyenne to geriatric limper in this spooled-out year, Mero had kicked down thoughts of the place where he began, a so-called ranch on strange ground at the south hinge of the Big Horns" (p. 19). I read this compelling line over and over, thinking what a fine choice "unfurling" is and how well the contrast of "tight-wound kid" and "geriatric limper" works, how often I feel I am living in a "spooled-out year" myself, and how we all "kick down" thoughts of the past. We read to learn about life and about ourselves, and so only writing that teaches us and touches us can, ultimately, be successful.

Because criteria teach us what is important in a content area (such as the importance of word choice in writing), they form the basis not only of quality assessment but also of quality instruction. Criteria literally create for us a vision of what makes writing work—and it's a vision that changes over time. Look at a student handbook from the 1800s, for instance, and you're likely to find language of this sort:

> *We heartily trust that our young writers will commence the perusal of our pages with pleasure equal to that which we feel in sitting down to write them, and that we shall go pleasantly together through our work.*
>
> (Clarke, 1829, 7)

Well, you can "heartily trust" all you wish, but write in this sort of ponderous style now and you'll likely find yourself going pleasantly *alone* through whatever work lies ahead. The rest of us will be off doing something else. We no longer speak or write this way because our expectations and preferences have evolved.

Similarly, our experience over the past few years has helped us see how a trait such as voice changes remarkably from one form of writing to another; we may write in a friendly, professional voice in a business letter or in a satirical, comic voice in an essay on choosing a new computer. Criteria can and *must* change over time and must also shift with context (audience and purpose).

What Do Good Criteria Look Like?

Criteria are *not* all created equal. Some are much better written than others. How will you be able to sort the gemstones from the mica and agates? Here are a few guidelines to help you. Good criteria

- *are clearly written;* that is, they are easy to understand, specific, explicit and, in the best of all possible worlds, complemented by samples of strong and weak performance (in this case, writing samples) that model what is described;
- *focus on significant aspects* of performance (organization), not on trivia (size of margins);
- *create clear distinctions* among performance levels so that raters have little difficulty agreeing on whether a paper should receive a score of 1, 2, 3, 4, or 5 on a given trait (or 6, if the scale goes that high);
- *thoroughly cover what is important* to quality performance; they do not pass over key qualities (such as *voice*) just because they're difficult to define;
- *use positive language,* even to describe beginning performance levels, a factor that is critical because we use criteria to teach students to think about themselves and their work and we want them to think in positive terms;

are easy to teach from because they are written in student-friendly language;

are generalizable across tasks, so that it is not necessary to invent brand-new criteria for every new assignment; and

are forever changing as experience in analyzing and assessing student performance refines our thinking about what good performance looks like.

I believe the analytical models presented in this book more than meet these specifications, but I invite you to put them to the test. Check out the thoroughness, the positive quality of the language, the significance of the key descriptors, the generalizability, and the friendliness to teachers and students.

FORMS OF DIRECT ASSESSMENT

Once we have made the decision to assess writing directly—to ask students to write, then analyze and assess what they have written—the next question becomes, how should we best go about this?

As Andrea Lunsford (1986) points out in her essay "The Past—and Future—of Writing Assessment," many approaches are possible, and assessors have searched for years for some formulaic method of assessing writing that would eliminate pain, time and expense. Some methods have included things like counting numbers of words per sentence (think how high legal contracts would score on that one) or comparing complex sentence structure to simple (imagine an eighth grade Ernest Hemingway's scores or a rater's response—"Ernest writes clearly, but needs to vary his sentences more"). Unfortunately for those who favor the quick approach, no one, as yet, has been able to pinpoint any definitive relationship between writing quality and something so superficial as words per sentence or numbers of interlinked independent clauses (Huot, 1990).

Among the many scoring methods tried over the past few decades, three approaches survived into the 1990s: holistic, primary trait, and analytical scoring. Of these three, analytical scoring has been the overwhelming favorite (and will likely remain so through the beginning of the twenty-first century) because it provides the most information for the time invested, and because it fits with writing process instruction so nicely. Still, it is worth looking at all three in order to better appreciate the benefits of analytical scoring.

Primary Trait Scoring

Primary trait scoring is based on the premise that all writing is done for an audience and that successful writing will have the desired effect upon the audience, mainly due to the impact of the primary, or most important, trait within that piece of writing. The primary trait varies with context—primarily audience and purpose.

Let's say a writer is putting together a set of directions on assembling a bicycle, which will be included with the bicycle components shipped to customers. Of course it is important to write clearly, to use terms correctly, and to have sound mechanics, but perhaps the most critical trait of all is to organize the steps correctly, to tell the customer exactly how to begin and precisely what to do next and after that. We can say then that, in this case, organization is the primary trait.

Primary trait assessment has never really caught on in large-scale state or district writing assessments because many educators feel it is too limited in scope to provide all the feedback they want about their students' writing. Even if one or two secondary traits are assessed, each paper still receives only two or three scores, and one of those (the primary trait score) will usually be weighted to reflect its importance.

Further, both teachers and assessment specialists point out the inherent difficulty in scoring just one trait while attempting to put others on the back burner. If a person unfolds a set of bicycle directions that are full of spelling errors, or that contain faulty capitalization or punctuation, it may be hard for her to see beyond that. If she is not an experienced biker, and if the instructions contain numerous unexplained references to things like *tension*, *heavy-duty forks*, *rapid-fire shifting*, and *quick-release wheels*, she may spend so much time just figuring out what the writer is telling her that she winds up boxing the whole thing up and relegating it to a dark corner of the attic—at which time the fine points of organization become irrelevant.

On the other hand, primary trait scoring can be useful at the classroom level where teachers may wish to focus on a particular skill. For instance, let's say a teacher is helping his students learn to write good business letters. He might wish to focus on such primary traits as conciseness, business tone, or appropriate format. Primary trait scoring is perfect for such focused instruction/assessment.

Holistic Scoring

Holistic scoring is based on the premise that the whole is more than the sum of its parts and that the most valid assessment of writing will consider how all components—ideas, mechanics, voice, and so forth—work in harmony to achieve an overall effect. Holistic scoring is usually based on explicit criteria, in which case it is termed *focused holistic scoring*. When raters assign scores by matching students' papers to exemplars (aka anchor papers), samples that typify performance at various score points, the process is called *general impression scoring.*

Holistic scoring is an efficient method of selecting students who are likely candidates for special help in writing or who show promise of being successful in a more challenging writing course. Because each paper receives only one score, however, holistic assessment has limited effectiveness in diagnosing writing skills. One paper that receives a score of 3 on a five-point rating scale may have powerful voice but weak mechanics, while another may receive a 3 because, although fluent and mechanically sound, it says little. Because so many different interpretations are possible, holistic scores are often frustrating to both students and teachers, who wonder what the scores actually mean.

In short, holistic scoring is useful when a quick, overall assessment fits the bill; it is of far less value in a situation where students want and need to know specifically what components of their writing need work—and that's nearly always the case in the classroom.

Analytical Scoring

Because of its strong, natural link to writing instruction, analytical assessment has virtually swept the popularity polls over the past ten years, becoming far and away the most preferred form of direct writing assessment at classroom, building, district, and state levels.

Like its holistic counterpart, analytical scoring acknowledges the underlying premise that, in writing, the whole is more than the sum of its parts, but it adds that, if we are to teach students to write, we must take writing apart—temporarily—in order to focus on one skill at a time. Thus, writing is described in terms of its key components, often called *traits*. An analytical scale or scoring guide is an attempt to define these traits and to describe, using language or *criteria*, what each one would look like at various levels of proficiency, ranging from beginning performance through strong performance.

In order for analytical scoring to work well, the traits must be significant: e.g., use of voice appropriate to purpose and audience would seem important to most readers; placement of a title in the center of a page less so. Traits must also be distinct enough from one another that each can be individually scored. In addition, traits must reunite to form a cohesive whole, a full definition of quality writing. We must not leave out anything important; nor must we make any one trait overly dominant. An analytical model that omits conventions—or focuses so heavily on conventions that ideas and organization are swept aside—must be considered incomplete at best.

How Many Traits Are There?

The model in this book uses six traits, but there is nothing magical about that number; it simply reflects the six qualities most often cited by teachers and writers themselves as significant:

Ideas and Development (Details)
Organization
Voice & Tone
Word choice
Fluency
Conventions and Presentation (How it looks on the page)

Other models of analytical assessment include anywhere from two to ten or more traits. Analytical scoring systems that include only two or three traits probably do not cover all bases. Some may group multiple traits to-gether so that the effect is really a modified holistic model. It is possible, for instance, to group voice, word choice and fluency together into something called "style," but this trait would be so huge, so complex, and so unwieldy that, while scorable at district or state levels, it would be all but impossible to teach in the classroom. And after all, what is the point of using traits that cannot be taught to students?

On the other hand, ten traits would be quite a few. It is hard to internalize that many, or really make them our own so that we can use them and reflect on them, as we write and revise. Further, it's hard to be sure that we are not simply using different terms—say, *organization* and *internal structure*—to de-fine what is essentially the same thing or that we are not including as "traits" things like "inclusion of a title," a concern that is not global enough to be a trait; it's only a component of conventions.

Similarly, format and layout (what we call "presentation") are sometimes viewed as a "seventh trait." I have no real problem with this, since presenta-tion is a critical factor, especially in informational, business and technical writing—not to mention children's writing, if we wish to consider, for in-stance, the importance of interweaving text and illustrations in picture books. In this book, though, I have included it under the trait of conventions in the *Informational Scoring Guide* in Chapter 8. I tend to view it as a special component of conventions since, like conventions, it has to do with shaping the text for readability; but if you prefer to break it out and score it as a sep-arate trait, that is up to you.

Of the three scoring approaches we have discussed, analytical scoring provides the strongest foundation for instruction because it both affords a complete picture of writing (which primary trait scoring often does not) and allows students to focus their revision on particular problems, such as orga-nizing information, providing more detail, or strengthening vocabulary (something holistic cannot do). This is not to say that these traits actually function independently of one another—or that they will never come together in one unified whole. Of course they will. Writing is by nature holistic. An analytical approach simply makes revision manageable.

Think of a good baseball coach working with his players: "Really plant that back foot," you'll hear him say. He doesn't worry about shoulder posi-tion, grip on the bat or follow-through—yet. All those will come later, one by one. The coach knows this, and he is patient. One by one, trait by trait, we coach—till the writer hits a home run.

LARGE-SCALE AND CLASSROOM ASSESSMENT: BUILDING THE BRIDGE

As teachers, we sometimes tend to think of classroom assessment as friendly and comfortable, and of large-scale as threatening and intimidating—mostly because it is sometimes (often inappropriately) wielded as a weapon to judge teacher performance. The truth is, though, large-scale assessment has brought attention to writing as never before in history. And while both large-scale assessment and classroom assessment have limitations, each offers numerous strengths, and numerous lessons to teach us about quality instruction and assessment. We can improve both by using those lessons wisely.

Lessons From the Large-Scale Perspective

In large-scale assessment, students usually write on one prompt (or a choice between two), which is pre-selected and often cannot be fully explained by the teacher during the assessment because such explaining is considered unfair coaching. (Isn't this interesting? Picture a hospital administrator saying with a straight face, "I can't explain the appropriate surgical procedures once the operation begins. You will need to figure those out as best you can. And please do not consult a medical textbook or talk to other doctors while you are operating.")

Students must complete their work in a prescribed time frame, as little as 25 minutes total or as much as two or three 45-minute periods (a few forward-thinking states and districts allow as much time as the student reasonably requires). Once students turn in their work, their papers are read and scored by two trained raters (usually teachers) working separately.

Teachers are sometimes horrified by this scenario, given its differences from what usually occurs in writing classrooms—until they participate in it as raters. Through that participation, they see what is invisible from the outside looking in: that teachers who assess students' work, who struggle to bring a touch of humanity to a process that demands speed and efficiency, are giving themselves an education both in how to write and in how to assess and teach writing. Then the tone of their comments changes: "This is the most valuable experience I have had as a teacher of writing," and, "I will never see assessment, or my own students' writing, in the same way again."

ON THE POSITIVE SIDE

Large-scale writing assessment, for all the furor and anxiety it produces, performs several good writing deeds. First, it keeps writing in the public eye, reminding everyone of its importance in education. Second, it encourages the development and use of sound scoring criteria, which make the assessment of writing more valid and consistent. And third, it offers teachers who may work for years in one building or at one grade level an opportunity to gain a broader perspective: seeing several hundred samples of student writing from throughout a state or district is very different from seeing only the writing of your own students.

Few people outside the teaching profession can realize how isolated a teacher often feels. Opportunities for teacher-to-teacher sharing are more rare than most people might think, and many teachers are troubled by a persistent, sometimes daunting perception that much of what we do as teachers—including assessment and grading—we must do alone. It is incredibly gratifying, comforting even, to share reactions and insights with colleagues.

Fourth, large-scale assessment has taught us the infinite value of an interpretive community: people who openly create, shape, discuss, and live by criteria that influence their thinking and their performance, whether in writing or in any academic area. This idea, transported to the classroom, has power that can scarcely be measured. In sharing and developing criteria, not only do we take the mystery out of writing, but we encourage students to be active members of our writing community.

Large-scale assessment does one more thing, too, and this (excepting the promotion of criteria) is perhaps the primary contribution that this form of writing assessment has made to the world of writing instruction in the past ten years: it raises expectations about student performance.

Little more than a decade ago, the premise that student writers of all ages were sadly deficient in writing skill was widely accepted as truth. Now we know better. There are problems, yes. For many students, getting one coherent sentence on paper is a victory. But there are also students who write with power and grace, and move us to laughter—or tears. They write better than many of us did at the same age. This does not make for good press, though, so you won't see headlines that read "Student Writers Startle Teacher Raters With Their Eloquence." It happens all the time, but no one prints it.

Instead, you'll see "Most students stumble on writing exam" (*The Oregonian*, September 29, 1999). The article begins by telling us that "only one in four U.S. students is able to write reports, narratives and persuasive pieces at a proficient level, according to the U.S. Department of Education." This "proficient level" is not defined, but we are told that the results are based on two writing samples, with 25 minutes of writing time allowed for each. We are also given one of the prompts: "Imagine this situation! A noise outside awakens you one night. You look out the window and see a spaceship. The door of the spaceship opens, and out walks a space creature. What does the space creature look like? What do you do? Write a story about what happens next" (Source: National Assessment of Educational Progress).

Do you see anything wrong with this picture—this so-called test of writing proficiency? The 25-minute time limit says clearly to students: "Writing is a quick activity that requires little thinking or reflection. If you cannot do it quickly, you are not 'proficient.' Revision is not important; if it were, we would have provided time for it." The prompt itself says, "Your ability to think up an imaginary story is of more value to us than your ability to perform a real-life writing task—such as writing a business letter or explaining a process."

This prompt, I suggest, would make almost *any* thinking person "stumble." Written for eighth graders, it does not take into account what might interest or intrigue them, nor is it written at their level. Notice the short, simple sentences; it's almost a parody of a basal reader: Open, space-ship, open. Walk, space creature, walk. I can only be thankful that *I* do not have to respond to this prompt, especially in the tiny space of only 25 minutes. I do not like "space creature" stories, films—*or* prompts (mostly because so many are based on the unsubstantiated assumption that aliens are ugly, creepy, and out to get us). I especially do not like *this* prompt, which is borderline disrespectful about the whole notion of interplanetary life, and surely begins with an unlikely premise: a space ship landing right outside someone's window. Come on.

My response here reflects a personal bias, I realize, and while some students for whom imaginative writing comes easily may have *loved* this prompt, I suspect that for others it was a prescription for writer's block. Also, notice the wording of the prompt: It calls for *both* a description *and* a story (the prompt writer being unsure which he/she wanted); this is a lot to ask in a short timeframe. Notice the opening line: "Imagine this situation!" Apparently, student writers are supposed to be excited (the prompt itself sounds downright bouncy), but many writers find prompts that are not linked to reality baffling—or just plain boring.

Wait, though—I'm getting a vision here: Let's see . . . Perhaps the space person descends from a spaceship inscribed "Intergalactic Assessment, Inc." She has criteria tattooed to her arms. She is an interplanetary rater. She has no hair to comb, no teeth to brush—big time savers there. Her eyes are enormous and never blink; she can take in whole pages of student text at a glance, translate inventive spelling, word strings, full-cap writing, loopy letters, punctuation-free text, and the tiny print that causes others to go mad—all at lightning speed. She has a dictionary computer chip implanted behind her left ear, a handbook chip behind the right. Her fingernails are made of graphite for quick recording of scores. The glow emanating from her face enables her to see light pencil-written papers even in dark spaces. She has a thin body that requires no food, and through her veins flows an amber-colored blood high in natural caffeine—the result of hundreds of years of rater evolution. She tells me in a cheery but compassionate voice, "We've been watching your struggle. I've been sent to help you with your prompts."

We should be careful—much more careful than we now are—about the conclusions we draw based on tests of "writing proficiency." Let's ask what we're *really* measuring, and how we're doing it. What *this* prompt really measures is my ability to second-guess the prompt writer and to string together enough coherent sentences (some descriptive, some narrative) in 25 short minutes to appear far more engaged in this writing task than I really am. Let me suggest, at the risk of sounding insolent, that this kind of game playing is not an appropriate response from an educated person, and we should stop encouraging it, even if it does earn the person points on this kind of assessment.

The appropriate response in this situation, from a strong and educated writer, would be a brief essay on a topic of that writer's choice, with an explanation of why this prompt did not work for him/her. Would we dare encourage this sort of response? Not yet. We feel protective of our students and the sad truth is, we do not yet trust raters who work for a testing company to have a sense of humor or to be open minded in thinking through what might constitute a good response. We don't know for sure, in short, whether they are writers—or only critics of writing. We will get there, though. As Kathleen and James Strickland suggest, "Once teachers begin to question behaviors that accompany traditional testing, other alternatives . . . will be developed. Teachers will begin to reject the obsession with test security (protecting exams as though they were the Academy Awards), time limits ('fifteen minutes remain . . .'), artificial deadlines, and a belief that individual performance is a virtue superior to collaboration" (1998, 61).

Major Speedbump Ahead: The Dreaded Prompts

If we ever doubted the value of students' selecting their own writing topics, large-scale assessment has convinced us (most of us, anyway). It's only a matter of time at any writing assessment scoring session before some rater throws down her pencil in disgust and shouts, "Who *wrote* these prompts?" The prompt writers—who are often present, disguised as normal, everyday teachers—look around, shrug innocently and shake their heads to throw off suspicion, and sensing danger, wisely disavow any knowledge of the prompts' origin. For all anyone knows, these wretched prompts just appeared one day, mysteriously, on *someone's* desk, and through equally mysterious channels, were adopted and printed on the assessment booklets before anyone could put a stop to it. *No one* wrote them—because obviously, no one in his/her right mind would write that badly.

Because the identity of prompt writers is so hard to discover (I think there is a Prompt Writers Protection Program), they often live to write another day. And in all fairness to prompt writers everywhere (I have been one myself and have written my share of losers), let me say at the outset that writing good prompts is *very* hard. On a scale of 1 to 10, measuring difficulty and tendency to promote frustration, writing a dictionary is a 4, while prompt writing is roughly an 8. They look so good on paper when you first think them up, but somehow, the ugliness, banality, and total lack of logic *no one sees during the review process* suddenly scream loudly from the page during scoring.

A FEW GOOD PROMPTS

Yet, contrary to that ugly rumor circulating throughout the U.S. at present, there actually *are* a few reasonably good prompts out there that allow *most* students to show off their writing skills. Don't get too excited; the list, in my experience, is *very* short. Further, no prompt is perfect; no prompt will work for all students—or motivate all students. I don't claim that any prompt on this list will cause students to say, "Hurry—a pen!" But for what it's worth, here are some of my favorites. Don't take this as a definitive list. Rather, use them as models of what workable, functional prompts look like:

1. Think of something you own that was not purchased in a store. Explain why it is important to you OR write a story connected to this object.

2. Can very young and very old people be friends? Use your experience to write a convincing paper that answers this question for your reader.

3. Think of a place so important and special to you that you would like to return to it many times. Describe it so clearly that a reader can see, hear, and feel just what it is like to be there.

4. Think of a story (funny, sad, frightening, or embarrassing) that you might still enjoy telling to friends when you are old. Write your story as if it were going to be published in a magazine.

5. Think of a teacher (friend/family member) you will never forget. Tell one story that comes to mind when you think about what makes this person so unforgettable.

6. Some people feel that video games, television, and other electronic media have decreased our ability as human beings to concentrate and learn new things. Do you agree—or not? Write a convincing paper, based on your experiences and observations, that would make a reader agree with your point of view.

7. Imagine you are a historian living 200 years in the future. You are writing a description of life on planet Earth in the year 2000. Think carefully about what you will say because your writing might be published in a future textbook for fifth graders. It must be clear and interesting.

8. What is it like to be in your place in your family—youngest child, oldest, middle, twin, only child, or whatever? Write a persuasive essay that defends your position as the best, worst, or just OK. Give reasons from your experience.

9. Sometimes it's fun to imagine what the world would be like if *you* were in charge for a day. Perhaps rain would be cancelled—or vegetables would taste like chocolate. Be as crazy or as serious as you want in writing a paper about things you would change if you could be in charge for just one day.

10. What if you won a time travel contest and you could spend one day with any person, real or fictional, from the past or present? Who would you choose? Write a story about your day together.

11. Many people would like to reduce the legal age for driving to 14 (it is now 16 in most states). Do you think this is a good idea—or not? Defend your position with a convincing argument that could be printed in the editorial section of the paper.

12. It is the year 2200. Interplanetary travel is common. You have been asked to write copy for a brochure inviting people to visit Earth on vacation. Your brochure must make Earth sound appealing, and must provide details on what visitors should expect.

Following are a few favorites from my friend and colleague Barry Lane (1993, 56), who often favors a single-word or phrase approach to prompts:

1. Lost
2. A time you ran away

3. A time you came home
4. A time you were confused
5. The day you were no longer a child
6. Funny now—not then
7. You won't believe this, but . . .
8. The other side of the story
9. The way *I* remember it
10. The key

Pictures are excellent, too—you just won't know whether you'll get a description, story, expository essay or persuasive argument—if that matters to you. One of my favorite prompts was a simple picture of an old leather suitcase, circa 1940. Looked like something Humphrey Bogart might have carried into an exotic hotel. Students could create a description, story, mystery, travel brochure, travel essay, or whatever. Good prompts always yield variety in the responses.

For countless additional ideas, I recommend Marjorie Frank's delightful book *If You're Trying to Teach Kids How to Write . . . you've gotta have this book* (2nd edition, 1995). Another excellent source is the new writing journal *r.w.t.,* published by ECS Learning Systems in San Antonio. It regularly includes numerous prompts on a wide range of topics (see the list of sources for more information).

BAD PROMPT ALERT

Of course, there's the dark side. Just because a prompt is on a list is no sign you should use it. Here are some prompts to avoid at all costs:

1. Describe your favorite dinner. Be specific. (We should have said, "Be global, general, and *brief*. Do not use the words 'fluffy' 'crispy,' or 'tender' in your description. Do *not* refer to potatoes in any form.")

2. Should you or should you not eat junk food? Write a letter to a friend explaining your position and convincing your friend to agree with you. (Who needs more lectures on the wonders of broccoli? Breathes there a man with soul so dead who never to himself has said, "Sometimes, you just *gotta* have a doughnut"?)

3. What are the qualities required to be a good president? (It takes *leadership*. It takes *communication skills*. Right. Why didn't we think of these things? At least the papers were short.)

4. Think of a time when weather affected your life. Write a story about what happened. (Think of a time weather *didn't* affect your life. Now *that* might have had possibilities.)

5. Explain how to make a decision. (We should have asked, "Explain how to write a good prompt. All reasonable suggestions will be welcome.")

Writing good prompts is a challenge. Here are a few rules of the road to keep in mind:

1. Consider the grade level and experience of the student writers. The topic should be reasonably familiar (they won't have time or opportunity for research), but also interesting. If you aren't sure, ask students.

2. Do NOT give students any prompt you would not like to write on yourself. The revenge factor is built in (You will have to read the results).

3. Avoid any prompt that is likely to elicit 5,000 responses that sound like clones of one another (e.g., "What does it take to be a good student?"). Be sure your prompt gives students room to individualize.

4. Avoid highly controversial, personal issues that are likely to trigger rater bias (e.g., "Has the women's movement gone too far in the U.S.?").

5. Think about wording. Avoid wording prompts so they can be answered with a simple yes or no: e.g., "Should the driving age in our state be lowered to 14?"

6. Avoid wordy, overwritten prompts that offer too many clues and suggestions about what students might do: e.g., "Write about a time you will always remember. It could be a happy or sad time. It could even be a funny or embarrassing or exciting experience. It could be a time long ago or something that happened recently. Put in as many sensory details as you can—sights, sounds, smells, feelings—to help your reader experience this special time with you. Be sure to read your response to yourself so you can revise and edit." (Oops—time's up and we've only read the prompt! Even from the speedy writers, expect a worksheet-like response in which all your questions are methodically answered as if the student were under hypnosis.)

7. Ask yourself whether you care if students write a narrative, an informational piece or a persuasive essay. If you do, then wording of the prompt is a BIG issue. Key words can help direct students to the form you want:

- *Narrative:* Tell the story, Tell about time when
- *Informational:* Explain, Give directions for, Provide an analysis of
- *Persuasive:* Write an argument, Convince, Give reasons for your position
- *Descriptive:* Describe, Give details that help your reader picture

If large-scale assessment has taught us one most important lesson, it might be this: Next to the quality of writing instruction going on in the classrooms affected, probably no single thing influences students' performance in a writing assessment as much as the prompts. So—choose with care. Don't be wordy. Write clearly. Avoid vague words—like "object." One eighth grader told us his "favorite object" was his baby brother. Hardly what we expected, but by then, we were so tired of lockets and footballs that we were willing to accept a broader definition.

Being a rater is a humbling experience, but enormously educational. It's a whirlwind tour of what can go wrong with writing and what successful writers do. That is why, if we really want to improve students' writing skills, we must let them be raters, too. We just move the rating into the classroom.

Lessons From the Classroom

In the classroom, the world of writing usually looks quite different from what precedes formal assessment. Given a process-based curriculum and a teacher with a strong commitment to writing instruction (someone who writes with students, models prewriting, revision and editing, and reads aloud often), student writers have both time and opportunity on their side. They are not mentally bludgeoned by topics that feel restrictive or hard to decipher, nor are they held to deadlines no writer (even a professional) could hope to meet. If something is unclear about the prompt, the teacher can explain it, or abandon the prompt altogether, or invite students to select their own topics. Students have the opportunity and responsibility to explore personally important subjects, engage in real revision, share writing with peers and often with the teacher as well, and watch their writing skills evolve over time. They can use resources of all kinds—dictionaries, handbooks, spell checker, or whatever—as any real-world writer would do without a thought. Some may keep portfolios that showcase their work, help track their growth as writers, and chart emergence of new skills.

Thus, the message from the classroom to planners of large-scale assessments is this:

- Provide time for students to write
- Provide some mental elbow room in topic selection—through a choice of prompts or the option to use a personally selected prompt
- Provide time for revision—and encourage it through use of checklists or similar written aids
- Test what you have taught, so that students are invited to use the process skills emphasized in the curriculum

Of course, classrooms are not perfect. While opportunities for writing may abound, many student writers do not know how to go about choosing their own topics; someone else has often done this part for them. It's tough for teachers, too—if you don't think so, grab a piece of scratch paper right now and jot down five possible topics you could write on. And if you *can* do this, do it at your very next opportunity *while your students are watching*—on the overhead, perhaps. If you cannot, at least you've gained some appreciation for what students face in finding good topics.

Many students breeze through prewriting and drafting, then hit a brick wall. They do not know what true revision is and often settle for neatening up the piece, making it longer, or using the spell-checker. While ample time may be provided for writing, time is of minimal help to the student who does not know how to narrow and define a topic, craft a good lead, play with phrasing, "hear" the conclusion, or otherwise shape and experiment with his or her own writing.

Further, assessment may be mysterious to both teacher and student. It has to occur somehow, at some point in the process. But how? When?

Students may feel they play little or no role in defining how their work will be assessed, may feel quite unprepared to assess their own work as a first step in revision, and may also wonder what it is teachers are truly looking for. Teachers who have not been taught to assess writing often fall back on what they know, imitating what their own teachers did: e.g., correcting the text, then grading it, but always wondering, "Is this really the best way?"

In many classrooms, students do not have opportunities to engage in the many forms of writing through which they can find their personal voice. Not everyone is a poet or story writer. While one student may find her true voice writing mysteries, technical writing or business writing fits another perfectly. We need to recognize this both for students' development and because twenty-first century writing demands it.

Twenty-First Century Writing: What Will It Look Like?

We used to write to expand our knowledge. Now we write to condense; it's a matter of survival. Imagine for a moment the rate at which new information is being generated; it doubles now every few weeks, and soon no doubt that will shrink to days, then hours.

Anyone who feared that telephones and computers would make writing obsolete ought to revisit today's workplace.

Patrick Sebranek, Verne Meyer, Dave Kemper, and John Van Rys (1996)

With each passing year, we view our solar system and indeed our whole universe differently. It may collapse in on itself, we're told, or stretch on indefinitely. Some argue that we will one day have the capability to go back in time, while others dismiss this as poetic nonsense. As time goes on, new planets appear. We come closer to tracking our genetic destiny through DNA research. We discover life-forms we didn't know existed within the depths of the ocean and the shrinking rain forests. Soon, we're told, we may be able to grow whole new body parts from single cells, making transplants and artificial joints obsolete. We're cloning sheep—perhaps woolly mammoths, too. (What's next? Teachers? Doesn't hurt to hope.)

We now do much of our shopping by computer, and perhaps will one day tour the "ancient" malls as we now do the pyramids, looking up in wonder, trying to imagine what shoppers of the last millennium thought about as they walked the crumbling corridors of commerce.

In their capacity as writers, our students will document these discoveries and events and thousands of others through essays, textbooks, travel brochures, voter pamphlets, maps, greeting cards, cartoons, letters and journals, poems, legal briefs, medical reports, advertisements, bumper stickers, editorials and countless other forms. Someone will probably write a play satirizing over-dependence on e-mail or the fashion industry's reaction to the discovery of the "fat gene." Only a few of our students will compete for the Pulitzer Prize. But like it or not, we will all, through most of our working lives, be writing to inform, to record, to define and explain technical concepts, to condense, summarize, and interpret data, to teach, to persuade, and generally, to make sense of the world.

We can probably anticipate great pressure to make classroom practice reflect what people will be doing on the job—what some people call "real life" writing. It is already happening, as more and more teachers of math, science, P.E., art, music and social sciences make writing a routine part of their curriculum. Other teachers, language arts or otherwise, are discovering alternative forms of that old standby, the research paper: letters, posters, copy that could be used in a museum display, brochures, etc. In addition, we see an ever-increasing focus on informational and business writing in classrooms throughout the country. These forms are showing up in large-scale assessment, too, where the once-prevalent story is now yielding more and more to informational forms of writing.

> Recently there has been a strong movement in the U.S. to include in the curriculum more about work. Unless there is a drastic change in the approach to the curriculum, much of the new information will be presented in the form of lists, identifications, classifications, and the like. What will be missing, we fear, is experience in how to work [as a writer] and how to enjoy it.
>
> Alan C. Purves (1992)

GOODBYE, E. E. CUMMINGS?

We must be careful, as we expand and create curriculum to match changing workplace demands, that we do not slash too much in order to make room for the "practical." True enough, few jobs demand critical analyses of works by Shakespeare or F. Scott Fitzgerald. But does that mean this kind of writing is a waste of time? Definitely not.

As a student drafts a business letter, she learns how to capture the vocabulary and tone that present her as a professional person. As she analyzes *Romeo and Juliet*, she learns how to read thoughtfully, to extract meaning from language that demands concentration, to think through images, dialogue, and metaphor, to understand characterization, and to appreciate that literature teaches us about life.

In Short

The classroom message to large-scale assessment is this: If you want to really test how well students can write, allow them to personalize topics. Assess multiple forms; do not rely solely on imaginative writing to judge proficiency. Assess writing—not the meticulous following of directions. Incorporate imaginative prewriting activities—such as the reading of fine literature—into the assessment process to provoke thought and to set the tone for the writing to follow. Allow time for reflection, planning, and revisiting the writing in order to make changes or add new information. Emphasize revision, for it is the heart of good writing. And prepare students to self-assess by teaching them the criteria that define good writing.

The message of large-scale assessment to the classroom is this: Use clear, detailed, carefully developed criteria in assessing students' work to ensure that assessment is consistent, thorough, and sound, not based on changeable, personal (and highly individual) impressions. Teach criteria to students prior to large-scale, formal assessment so they become self-assessors and members of an interpretive community, capable of meaningful, in-depth revision that goes beyond a facelift.

Research by George Hillocks, Jr. (1986) suggests that of the numerous methods used to teach writing over past decades, provision of good models and well-defined criteria are the most effective, particularly where students are actively engaged in assessing and discussing the samples they assess:

> If we wish our schools and colleges to teach writing effectively, we cannot retreat to the grammar book or rely on the presentation of rules and advice, or expect students to teach themselves how to write effectively simply by writing whatever they wish for varied groups of their peers. We must make systematic use of instructional techniques (e.g., scoring guides) which are demonstrably more effective.
>
> (p. 251)

REFLECTING ON CHAPTER 2

1. Think of assessment as a basis for learning. Think divergently—take yourself outside the academic context. Where else does assessment occur in life? In other words, when or where might you "assess to learn"?
2. Can you think of an everyday situation in which you use criteria to make judgments? Where do those criteria come from? Do they change over time? Why?
3. Do you think of large-scale and classroom assessment as more adversarial or more mutually supportive? How can each best support the other?

ACTIVITIES

1. As a class or study group, practice writing some prompts that might be used in a district writing assessment. Analyze your list. Which ones seem strongest? Why? What problems do you anticipate with others?
2. As a group, write a series of indirect writing assessment questions. Discuss the kinds of information such questions provide in comparison to direct assessment methods. Are their times each would be useful? When?
3. Brainstorm a list of advantages or areas of improvement for large-scale assessment, classroom assessment, or both. Compare the lists. On a scale of 1–10, how would you rate the quality of your own classroom assessment in writing (whether you are experiencing it from a student's or teacher's perspective)? Why?
4. As a group or class, outline a large-scale assessment procedure that you feel would be worthy of a 10. (Include all steps: Writing the prompt, providing directions to teachers and students, collecting and scoring papers, interpreting and reporting results, etc.)

LOOKING AHEAD

In Chapter 3, we will get inside student writing by taking a close-up look at the scoring guide. We will also practice scoring papers from various modes and grade levels.

MEMORABLE MOMENTS FROM STUDENT WRITING

- Joe impels me to be courageous.
- I'd like to travel inter dementionally and outer dementionally.
- Tap dancing is the actors acting loudly, while ballet is the actors being as quiet as possible.
- Being in his mid 30s, fun and laughter weren't too far from his reach.
- He aspired to dry his hair before ascending to the dinner table.
- It took Brad the rest of his school years to wake up and smell the gym bag.

3

GETTING INSIDE STUDENT WRITING

Rubrics can do something grades alone have never accomplished: They can define quality. They give students the criteria and terminology to respond to their own and others' work.

Strickland and Strickland (1998, 77)

The difference between assessment that is busywork and assessment that reflects the essence of our teaching is what we and our students make of what we collect.

Lucy McCormick Calkins (1994)

Weaving revision strategies into the discussions of . . . papers helps reduce test anxiety by giving young writers tools to use in their writing. And by the time . . . students take their writing test, the rubric that will be used to assess their work has already become part of their thinking.

Tommy Thomason and Carol York (2000, 31)

WHO INVENTED THE 6 TRAITS?

No one. They are an inherent part of what makes writing work, and they have been around virtually as long as writing itself. We might think of them as distant planets—always there, awaiting discovery. What teachers and writers *have* invented is a language for *describing* the qualities, or traits, that most other teachers, writers, and readers think are important in good writing. Among the true pioneers in this effort is Paul Diederich (1974), whose early research in identifying and describing the salient traits of quality writing yielded some of the clearest and most precise definitions up to that time.

Diederich's method was ingenious in its simplicity. He asked teachers, writers, editors, business people, and other readers to rank samples of student work—high, medium, and low—then identify those qualities that had caused them to rank the papers as they did. Using this method, Diederich's rater-researchers came up with five key traits (listed here in order of apparent influence):

Ideas

Mechanics (usage, sentence structure, punctuation, and spelling)

Organization and analysis

Wording and phrasing

Flavor (voice, tone and style, and personal qualities)

Ideas and organizational structure were slightly weighted in later ratings, since these were perceived to be the most significant of the traits identified. Mechanics was subdivided into (1) usage and sentence structure, (2) punctuation and use of capitals, abbreviations, and numbers, (3) spelling, and finally, (4) general neatness.

Over the years, Diederich's method of ranking and systematically recording the thinking behind that ranking has been replicated by other researchers, including Alan Purves (1992) in his work on international writing assessment. In the international writing study mentioned in Chapter 2, raters identified as significant the traits of content, organization, style and tone, surface features (essentially conventions, but also including neatness), and personal response of the reader.

In 1982, Donald Murray (66–67) identified these six traits—not too different from those in this book: meaning, authority, voice, development, design, and clarity. "It is my belief," Murray claimed at that time, "that these qualities are the same for poetry and fiction as well as nonfiction."

In 1983 and 1984, a group of 17 teachers from Beaverton, Oregon—known then as the Analytical Assessment Model Committee—set about replicating Diederich's method of analyzing student work to see what traits they might consider most important. They spent weeks reading student papers at every grade level from 3 through 12, rank ordering them high, middle and low, and documenting their reasons for their rank ordering. They read countless papers aloud to one another, discussing them, looking for common ground. It was my privilege to work with them as a writing consultant during this period. What emerged from their notes was a rough draft of what would eventually become the six-trait assessment model.

Shortly thereafter, Portland Public Schools conducted a similar study—in which I also participated. Not surprisingly, perhaps, but much to our mutual delight, the two groups (Beaverton and Portland), without any collaboration whatsoever, came up with virtually identical traits, their lists closely matching that of Deiderich. Since Portland had no knowledge of Beaverton's work, or Deiderich's, this similarity demonstrated to us all that teachers did—and do—share common values about what is important in writing.

Ongoing Validation

Since the early 1980s, I have posed this question to countless teachers across the country: What traits are critical to good writing? The results are remarkably consistent, and the following six traits (originally identified by both Beaverton and Portland) come up repeatedly as the things that influence teachers most:

1. *Ideas.* Clarity, detail, original thinking, and textual interest
2. *Organization.* Internal structure, a captivating lead, logical sequencing, and a sense of resolution
3. *Voice.* Liveliness, passion, energy, awareness of audience, involvement in the topic, and capability to elicit a strong response from the reader
4. *Word choice.* Accuracy, precision, phrasing, originality, a love of words, and sensitivity to the reader's understanding
5. *Sentence fluency.* Rhythm, grace, smooth sentence structure, readability, variety, and logical sentence construction
6. *Conventions and Presentation.* Overall correctness, attention to detail, and an editorial touch—along with effective use of white space (layout and formatting)

Notice how much these six traits resemble the lists generated by Diederich, Murray, and Purves. True enough, the language may be slightly different (voice versus flavor, tone, or style; internal structure versus organization; surface features versus conventions or mechanics). Yet, the similarities suggest that the traits are not random or whimsical. They are real. It would seem there truly are common threads bonding what teachers in New Hampshire and Minnesota, Kansas and Florida, Washington, California, Alaska and New Mexico see as important in student writing—or any writing.

Creating Criteria

Traits are essentially qualities or characteristics. The traits of good ice skating, for instance, might be balance, grace, athletic agility, and so on. The traits of a good restaurant might be ambiance, good food, cleanliness, excellent service, fair prices, and so forth. Criteria are the language we use to define those traits at various levels of performance. Thus, at a beginning level, we might describe ideas this way:

- *Fuzzy*
- *Undeveloped*
- *A list of factlets*

At a proficient or strong level, ideas might look like this:

- *Clear and complete*
- *Detailed and focused on a main question or idea*
- *Capable of creating a mental picture for the reader*

The way in which criteria are worded is critical. Grant Wiggins (1992) reminds us that, to the extent possible, "scoring criteria should rely on descriptive language, not on evaluative and/or comparative language such as 'excellent' or 'fair'" (p. 30). Such words are impossible to define rater to rater and promote inconsistencies in scoring. Wiggins also encourages us to focus on "the most salient characteristics" of performance at each level—those things, in other words, that would truly cause us to score a performance higher or lower—and to link our criteria to "wider-world" expectations, not limiting our view of student performance to what might make students successful within the classroom. We need to ask, Does what we are teaching and emphasizing lead to successful performance in a broader educational sense—"out there" in the competitive real world?

Where to Begin

Any good performance assessment begins with close examination of the performance to be rated. So, if we were planning to rate speaking proficiency, we would want students to give speeches, live or on video, so that we could review and discuss them and decide through that discussion which performances were stronger or weaker and why. With writing, we begin the same way—with samples. If we were actually developing criteria right now (instead of presenting developed criteria to you in this book), we would want to review hundreds of samples, of course. But here, I am simply trying to give you a sense of contrast so you can see how different papers provoke thoughtful discussion.

Here's an exercise you can try with a group of teachers or students (or parents, for that matter) that stimulates their thinking—and talking—about the qualities of good writing. Copy the following two student papers onto transparencies and share them with a group by first reading each aloud and then asking respondents to discuss the paper (with a partner or in small groups), then share their responses with the larger group.

Record what they say, if you wish. Later, when you hand them a scoring guide, they'll be delighted to see their own thoughts reflected in the language of that guide.

Here's the first, an eleventh-grade paper on a memorable place. By the way, I often do *not* share the grade level of this writer until after people have had a chance to respond to the paper because it is fun to guess. This leads to some intriguing discussions about assumptions we often make as we read (including the sex and age of the writer), and why we make them.

REDWOODS

Last year we went on a vacation and we had a wonderful time. The weather was sunny and warm and there was lots to do so we were never bored.

My parents visited friends and took pictures for their friends back home. My brother and I swam and also hiked in the woods. When we got tired of that, we just ate and had a wonderful time.

It was exciting and fun to be together as a family and to do things together. I love my family and this is a time that I will remember for a long time. I hope we will go back again next year for more fun and an even better time than we had this year.

If you ask teachers what they hear and see in this piece of writing, chances are their responses will look something like these:

- Boring—it put me right to sleep.
- Flat, empty
- Safe
- She was writing just to get it done.
- Mechanics are pretty good—but otherwise . . .
- It doesn't *say* anything.
- The organization isn't too bad.
- *What* Redwoods? The title doesn't go with the paper.
- She (he?) seems like a nice kid—I *want* to like it.
- It's not *that* bad for fourth or fifth grade—I assume that's what it is, right?

Lack of involvement by the writer holds this piece back. It communicates, but only on the most general level. There's a moment—just a moment—of voice: "I love my family, and this is a time I will remember for a long time." It's as if the writer wants to move in for a cozy chat, but just can't quite bring herself to do it.

This paper was written by an eleventh grader. Sometimes (once they know the grade level) teachers say, "Well, for *eleventh* grade I expected more, you know? If you'd told me it was third grade, I would have felt different." But would they really? Would *you?* I agree, the conventions would be excellent if this were a third-grade paper. The sentence fluency wouldn't be bad either, for it's controlled and correct, if not musical. But would it *say* more? Or could we say, "Well, for grade three, this is a powerhouse in voice." Hardly. When the voice is missing, it is just missing.

On the bright side, as one teacher pointed out, "Look, she's in eleventh grade and still wants to go vacationing with her family. I'd like to give her a couple points for that." Me, too. There's a likable tone to this piece that makes me want to say, "Come on out of hiding. I know you have more to share."

Here's the second piece, a seventh grader's account of her summer vacation with the family.

> I have taught college students and first graders in the same day. I can see the same qualities emerging in their work. I see detail. I see voice. I see various forms of organization.
>
> Barry Lane (1996)

MOUSE ALERT

As soon as school was out, we left on vacation. Nothing went the way it was supposed to. Dad backed into a tree on the way out of the driveway, pushing the bike rack through the rear window and nearly scaring my sister to death. She was cranky the rest of the trip. We had to take our other car, which is smaller and you can't hook the bike rack up to it. Now my sister and me were crowded together so much she kept complaining about me breathing on her and taking up all her air and foot room. Plus now Dad knew a big bill would be waiting for him when we got home. It put everyone in a lovely trip starting mood.

We were supposed to go to Yellowstone Park. Well, actually, we did, but just barely. I think we hold the world's record for shortest time spent in the park. This was all due to my mother's new attitude toward animals. The night before yellowstone we stayed in a cabin on the edge of the park. It had a lot of mice but most of them had the good sense to stay hidden in the walls. One poor furry guy had a death wish and showed himself. The whole family went into action. My father got a broom, which looked like an oversized weapon for a mouse. My mother hugged her pink flanel night gown around her knees, jumped up on a wood chair and started shreiking "Kill him! Kill him!" Her eyes were as big as her fists. I had never seen her quite so blood thirsty. My sister spent the whole time dancing on the bed crying her eyes out and yelling "Don't kill it Dad! Don't kill it!" It was up to Dad and me to trap it. We got it in a pickle jar and took it down to the lake and let it go. It seemed really happy to get away from us. I thought I knew how it felt.

The next day we raced through Yellowstone and then headed home. My Mother said she had enough of animals. For weeks afterwards, this was the big story she told everyone who asked about our vacation. You'd have thought the whole point of our trip was to go on a mouse hunt. Dad said all the money we saved by not staying at Yellowstone could go to pay for the broken car window, so for him the trip worked out perfect. As for me, I'm still planing to get back to Yellowstone one day. I want to see something bigger than a mouse.

Does this sound more like the real-life vacations you recall? I'm intrigued—and also comforted to know someone else has sibling squabbles and mice in the walls. Also, this writer has learned an important secret: Vacations on which all goes wrong may be miserable to live through, but they can be the stuff of delightful writing. Teachers' comments on "Mouse Alert" typically include these:

- I can just *see* it. I feel like I'm *in* that car. (Actually, I was once.)
- I love the line "Her eyes were as big as her fists."
- He's having a good time [most readers assume the writer is male].
- I know these people.

- Lively!
- I sympathize with Mom—I hate mice, too. "Eyes as big as fists"—*love* that.
- I like the pickle jar. I can see it and I even smell the pickles.
- This writer is a storyteller. Erma Bombeck, move over.
- Great images—love Dad backing into the tree and Mom in the nightgown.
- Lots of voice. Who *is* this kid? Can I get him next year?
- It comes full circle—great organization.
- You get every point of view in this story—even the mouse's!

This writer gets involved and so do we. There are minor problems with conventions, many more than in "Redwoods," but the text is a bit more complex, after all. Moreover, we tend to be much more forgiving of conventional errors when we are having a good time. If the "Redwoods" writer made this many errors, we might not be so forgiving.

The Next Step

At this point, I ask teachers to become just a little more structured in their thinking about writing. Using their comments on "Redwoods" and "Mouse Alert" as a starting point, and looking at additional samples of writing as well, I ask them to list individually those qualities that are most important in good writing, not just students' writing but *all* writing: novels, texts, histories, biographies, manuals, brochures, letters, or whatever. Then, we compare lists. Here are the things teachers mention most often. Notice that they fit, very conveniently, within six umbrella categories (i.e., the six traits).

WHAT TEACHERS VALUE IN WRITING

IDEAS

Clear—makes sense

Topic narrowed to manageable proportions

Plenty of information

A fresh, original perspective

Important, interesting details—not just common knowledge

ORGANIZATION

An inviting lead

Starts somewhere and goes somewhere

Everything's connected

It builds *to* something

A welcome surprise now and then

Doesn't just stop—sense of resolution or completion

Doesn't end with "Then I woke up and it was all a dream"

Doesn't end with a redundant, banal, or preachy summary: "Now you know the three reasons why we must all join in the war on drugs"

VOICE

Sounds like a person wrote it, not a committee

Writer seems involved, not bored

Sounds like *this* particular writer

Brings topic to life

Makes me feel part of it

Makes me feel connected with the writer—maybe even want to *meet* the writer

Makes me respond to the writing

Lots of energy

WORD CHOICE

Memorable moments

Words and phrases I wish I'd thought of myself

Word pictures

Every word or phrase crystal clear—or defined for me

Strong verbs

Simple language used well

Words used precisely

Minimal redundancy

Written to inform or entertain—not to impress

SENTENCE FLUENCY

Easy to read aloud

Inviting, playful rhythms—cadence

Well-built sentences

Varied sentence length and structure

Direct, concise structure in business writing

CONVENTIONS AND LAYOUT

Looks clean, edited, polished

Most things done correctly

Easy to decipher and follow

Free of distracting errors

Design and presentation make reading easy and pleasant

My eye is drawn first to key points

No distracting overload of multiple fonts or hard-to-read graphics

Graphics used, as appropriate, to enhance text

Attention given to spelling, punctuation, grammar and usage, capitalization, indentation

For years, direct writing assessment was criticized by those who said writing teachers would never agree on what should be assessed. As it turns out, not only do teachers of writing agree, but they can articulate their thoughts very well.

Understand, though: A list, however complete, is not yet a set of criteria. It can be a checklist, but it cannot be a scoring guide. Why not? Take a close look at the preceding list of qualities and you will see that it is, in effect, a set of *goals* reflecting only the desirable qualities of writing. Two things are needed to complete the picture.

1. *A sense of growth and change* along a continuum of performance ranging from the earliest exploring levels to strong, capable, controlled performance
2. *Language* that is explicit and rich with detail to flesh out what these traits look like at various points along the performance continuum

SIX-TRAIT ANALYTICAL SCORING GUIDE FOR PERSONAL/CREATIVE WRITING

With this scoring guide, scores of 5, 3, and 1 represent strong, developing, and beginning performance levels, respectively. These levels of performance are defined for you in writing. Scores of 4 and 2 are also possible, representing transitional levels from 3 to 5 and from 1 to 3, respectively. So if you say to yourself, "Well, it's surely stronger than a 1, but it's not quite a 3," that's when you give the score of 2. A score of 4 is assigned the same way. These scores are not defined in writing because too much language makes any scoring guide cumbersome and hard to teach from.

Ideas

Ideas are the heart of the message: the main thesis, impression, or story line of the piece, together with the documented support, elaboration, anecdotes, images, or carefully selected details that build understanding or hold a reader's attention.

Score of 5. The paper is clear, focused, purposeful, and enhanced by significant detail that captures a reader's interest.

- The paper creates a vivid impression, makes a point, or tells a whole story, without bogging down in trivia.
- Thoughts are clearly expressed and directly relevant to a key issue, theme, or story line.
- Information is based on experience or investigation of a topic and goes beyond common knowledge.
- Carefully selected examples, rich details and/or anecdotes bring the topic to life and lend the writing authenticity.
- The reader is NOT left with important unanswered questions.

3. The writer has made a solid beginning in defining a key issue, making a point, creating an impression, or sketching out a story line. More focus and detail will breathe life into this writing.

- It is easy to see where the writer is headed, even if some telling details are needed to complete the picture.
- The reader can grasp the big picture but yearns for elaboration.
- General observations and common knowledge are as plentiful as insights or "close-up" details.
- There *may* be *too* much information; it would help if the writer would trim the deadwood.
- As a whole, the piece hangs together and makes a clear general statement or tells a recountable story.

1. The writing is sketchy or loosely focused. The reader must make many inferences to grasp the writer's main point. The writing reflects more than one of these problems:

- The writer still needs to clarify the topic.
- The writer has assembled a loose collection of factlets that do not, as yet, have any real focus.
- Everything seems as important as everything else.
- It is hard to identify the main theme or story: What is this writer's main point or purpose?

Organization

Organization is the internal structure of the piece—like a skeleton or the framework of a building. Strong organization begins with an engaging lead and wraps up with a thought-provoking close. In between, the writer links each detail or new development to a larger picture, building to a turning point or key revelation and always including strong transitions that form a kind of safety net for the reader, who never feels lost.

5. The order, presentation, or internal structure of the piece is compelling and moves the reader purposefully through the text.

- The organization showcases the central theme or story line.
- Details seem to fit right where they are placed, even when the writer hits the reader with a surprise.
- An inviting lead draws the reader in; a satisfying conclusion helps bring the reader's thinking to closure.
- Pacing feels natural and effective; the writer knows just when to linger over details and when to get moving.
- Organization flows so smoothly the reader does not need to think about it.

3. The organizational structure guides the reader through the text without undue confusion. The route may be circuitous, but the reader can see where this writer is headed.

- Sequencing seems reasonably appropriate.
- Placement of details is workable, though sometimes predictable.
- The introduction and conclusion are recognizable and functional.
- Transitions are present but may sound formulaic: e.g., *My first point . . . My second point . . . .*
- Structure may be *so* dominant that it overshadows both ideas and voice; it's impossible to stop thinking about it!

1. Ideas, details, or events seem loosely connected—or even unrelated. It is very hard to see where this writer is headed. The writing reflects more than one of these problems:

- The writer skips randomly from point to point, leaving the reader scrambling to follow.
- No real lead sets up what follows.
- No real conclusion wraps things up.
- Missing or unclear transitions force the reader to make big leaps.
- It is difficult to see any real pattern or structure in this writing.

Voice

Voice is the presence of the writer on the page. When the writer's passion for the topic and sensitivity to the audience are strong, the text virtually dances with life and energy, and the reader feels a strong connection to both writing and writer.

Strong writing always has some kind of voice to it. It may not be a personal, informal voice, but there is something in the prose which tells you that a person wrote it.

Barry Lane (1996)

5. The writer's energy and passion for the subject drive the writing, making the text lively, expressive, and engaging.

- The tone and flavor of the piece fit the topic, purpose, and audience well.
- Clearly, the writing belongs to this writer and no other.
- The writer "speaks" to the reader in a way that makes him/her feel like an insider.
- Narrative text is open and honest.
- Expository or persuasive text is provocative, lively, and designed to prompt thinking.

3. The writer seems sincere and willing to communicate with the reader on a functional, if somewhat distant, level.

- The writer has not quite found his or her voice but is experimenting— and the result is pleasant and sincere, if not highly individual.
- Moments here and there snag the reader's attention, but the writer holds passion and spontaneity in check.
- The writer often seems reluctant to reveal him- or herself, and is "there" briefly—then gone.
- Though clearly aware of an audience, the writer only occasionally speaks right to that audience.
- The writer often seems right on the verge of sharing something truly interesting—but then pulls back as if thinking better of it.

1. The writer seems distanced from topic, audience, or both; as a result, the text may lack life, spirit, or energy. The writing reflects more than one of these problems:

- The writer does not seem to reach out to the audience or to anticipate their interests and needs.
- Though it may communicate on a functional level, the writing takes no risks and does not involve or move the reader.
- The writer does not yet seem sufficiently at home with the topic to personalize it for the reader.

Word Choice

Word choice is precision in the use of words—wordsmithery. It is the love of language, a passion for words, combined with a skill in choosing words to create just the mood, meaning, impression, or word picture the writer wants to instill in the heart and mind of the reader.

5. Precise, vivid, natural language paints a strong, clear, and complete picture in the reader's mind.

- The writer's message is remarkably clear and easy to interpret.
- Phrasing is original—even memorable—yet the language is never overdone.
- Lively verbs lend the writing power. Precise nouns and modifiers make it easy to picture what the writer is saying.
- Striking words or phrases linger in the writer's memory, often prompting connections, memories, reflective thoughts, or insights.

3. The language communicates in a routine manner; it gets the job done.

- Most words are correct and adequate, even if not striking.
- Energetic verbs or memorable phrases occasionally strike a spark, leaving the reader hungry for more.
- Familiar words and phrases give the text an "old comfortable couch" kind of feel.
- In one or two places, language may be overdone—but at least it isn't flat.
- Attempts at colorful language are full of promise, even when they lack restraint or control.

1. The writer either over-writes, smothering the message, or struggles with a limited vocabulary, searching for words or phrases to convey the intended meaning. The writing reflects more than one of these problems:

- Vague words and phrases (She was *nice. . . . It* was *wonderful. . . .* The new budget *had impact.*) convey only the most general sorts of messages.
- Redundancy is noticeable—even distracting.
- Clichés and tired phrases pop up with disappointing frequency.
- Words are used incorrectly ("The bus *impelled* into the hotel.").
- The writer overloads the text with ponderous, overdone, or jargonistic language that is tough to penetrate.

Sentence Fluency

Sentence fluency is finely crafted construction combined with a sense of rhythm and grace. It is achieved through logic, creative phrasing, parallel construction, alliteration, absence of redundancy, variety in sentence length and structure, and a true effort to create language that literally cries out to be spoken aloud.

5. An easy flow and rhythm combined with sentence sense and clarity make this text a delight to read aloud.

- Sentences are well crafted, with a strong and varied structure that invites expressive oral reading.
- Purposeful sentence beginnings show how each sentence relates to and builds on the one before it.
- The writing has cadence, as if the writer hears the beat in his or her head.
- Sentences vary in both structure and length, making the reading pleasant and natural, never monotonous.
- Fragments, if used, add to the style.

3. The text hums along with a steady beat. It's easy enough to read aloud, though somewhat difficult to read with great expression.

- Sentences are grammatical and fairly easy to get through, given a little rehearsal.
- Graceful, natural phrasing intermingles with more mechanical structure.
- Some variation in length and structure enhances fluency.
- Some purposeful sentence beginnings help the reader make sentence-to-sentence connections.

1. A fair interpretive oral reading of this text takes practice. The writing reflects more than one of these problems:

- Irregular or unusual word patterns make sentences hard to decipher, or make it hard to tell where one sentence ends and the next begins.
- Ideas hooked together by numerous connectives (*and . . . but . . . so then . . . because . . .*) create one gangly, endless "sentence."
- Short, choppy sentences bump the reader through the text.
- Repetitive sentence patterns grow monotonous.
- Transitional phrases are so repetitive they become distracting.
- The reader must often pause and reread to get the meaning.

Conventions

Almost anything a copy editor would attend to falls under the heading of conventions. This includes punctuation, spelling, grammar and usage, capitalization, and paragraphing—the spit-and-polish phase of preparing a document for publication. (For layout and formatting, see the Informational Scoring Guide, Chapter 10.)

5. The writer has excellent control over a wide range of standard writing conventions and uses them with accuracy and (when appropriate) creativity and style to enhance meaning.

- Errors are so few and so minor that a reader can easily overlook them unless searching for them specifically. Highly skilled writers may "play" with conventions for special effect.
- The text appears clean, edited, and polished.
- Older writers (grade 6 and up) create text of sufficient length and complexity to demonstrate control of a range of conventions appropriate for their age and experience.
- The text is easy to mentally process; there is nothing to distract or confuse a reader.
- Only light touch-ups would be required to polish the text for publication.

3. The writer shows reasonable control over the most widely used writing conventions and uses them with fair consistency to create text that is adequately readable.

- There are enough errors to distract an attentive reader *somewhat;* however, errors do not seriously impair readability or obscure meaning.
- It is easy enough for an experienced reader to get through the text without stumbling, but the writing clearly needs polishing. It's definitely not "ready for press."
- Moderate editing would be required to get this text ready for publication.
- The paper reads like an "on its way" rough draft.

1. The writer demonstrates limited control even over widely used writing conventions. The text reflects at least one of the following problems:

- Errors are sufficiently frequent and/or serious as to be distracting; it is hard for the reader to focus on ideas, organization, or voice.
- Errors in spelling, punctuation or grammar cause the reader to pause, decode, or re-read to make sense of the text.
- Extensive editing would be required to prepare this text for publication.

GETTING READY TO SCORE PAPERS

Just to Warm Up

Begin by making yourself a copy of the scoring guide so you can have it handy and make notes on it. Make it your own. Next, to get a general idea of how the guide works, score both "Redwoods" and "Mouse Alert" on all six traits. Compare your scores with those of a partner—or a whole group. We have provided the suggested scores for these two papers, along with those for other practice papers, at the close of this chapter (see pages 78–90).

   Also make copies of the scoring grid master in Figure 3.1 (see page 56). You can use a hard copy or make an overhead. Indicate with check marks or numbers in the appropriate squares how many persons in your discussion group assign each score on each trait.

Things You Should Notice As You Score Papers

Refer to the scoring guide often. Don't try to memorize it. You'll be surprised how quickly it will feel as comfortable and familiar to you as your name and address—but don't press. Let this internalizing come naturally.

   Second, score each trait (ideas, organization, voice, etc.) separately. The resulting six scores provide a kind of profile of student performance on a given piece of writing. Any piece may receive high scores on some traits, lower scores on others. Further, a student may receive very different "profiles" on different pieces of writing, and this can be a good way to show growth over time—in a portfolio, for example.

   Third, notice that the language, even at beginning levels of performance (scores of 1), is fairly positive. It identifies problems clearly but avoids accusatory phrases such as "poorly done" or "weak." This is very important, and sad to say, it is unusual; many scoring guides tend to have fairly negative descriptors at the lower end of the continuum.

> In addition to avoiding unclear language, rubrics should not use negative language.
> Strickland and Strickland
> (1998, 85)

Why a 5-Point Scale?

This scoring guide is based on a five-point scale, rather than a four- or six-point scale. You may be wondering what difference this makes, and curiously enough, it does not make as much as you might think. The reason for this is that nearly all scales are conceptually the same, regardless of the number of points represented. No matter whether there are 4, 5, 6, 9, or 100 points possible, the scale reflects a range of proficiency from beginning (lowest scores) through developing (middle scores) to strong (highest scores) levels along the type of performance continuum discussed in Chapter 2.

   We can put as many numerical points along a performance continuum as we wish, but it does not change this basic concept. For instance, if we want a six-point scale, we simply define the beginning level scores as 1s and 2s, mid-level or developing scores as 3s and 4s, and strong performance scores as 5s and 6s. Similarly, a nine-point scale is really just a series of three 3-point

Title of Paper:_____

TRAITS	Scores					
	6	5	4	3	2	1
Ideas						
Organization						
Voice						
Word Choice						
Sentence Fluency						
Conventions						

FIGURE 3.1. Scoring Grid Master

scales: beginning performances receive a score of 1, 2, or 3; midlevel performances a 4, 5, or 6; and strong performances a 7, 8, or 9—*barely strong, strong,* and *very strong.* You get the idea.

We could even put 100 points along our continuum if we seriously believed we could distinguish between, say, a 72 and a 73. But of course, it is ridiculous to even suggest anything approaching such precision. In fact, you know when you've pushed the limits of precision when you can no longer identify sample performances to represent each point on your scoring scale. That is to say, if you cannot tell a 7 from an 8 (and cannot find a sample 7 or a sample 8 to show what you mean), your points are no longer meaningful.

Are There Advantages to the 6-Point Scale?

Many people think so. They prefer an even-numbered scale in order to avoid the so-called "midpoint dumping ground" associated with scores of 3. However, the notion that expanding the scoring scale will solve this problem is the height of irony. The problem lies with the *writing*—not with the scale. The simple truth is that, especially under the structured, timed conditions of writing assessment, a great percentage of writers of all ages produce samples that are appropriately scored as "midlevel" or "developing." On a 6-point scale, these samples will receive scores of 3 or 4; on a 5-point scale, they will receive 3s; on a 100-point scale, they will receive 49s, 50s, or 51s. We can pretend these scores are different, but in reality, their interpretive meaning is the same. The *only* real way to change the scores is to improve our writing instruction so that our students are stronger writers in the first place.

The "Leaping the River" Model

Of course, a 3–4 split at the midpoint *does* allow us to break out the middle, to distinguish between scores (of 3) that are *almost* within the upper half of the score range—*almost* proficient, that is; and scores that are firmly planted within that upper half of the range (scores of 4), or just on the beginning edge of proficiency. I call this 6-point scale the "Leaping the River" model because it makes me think of children leaping a creek bed. Have you ever done this? Picture one child just making it to the other side—it's close, but her feet land clearly on the far bank; she has done it. This is a score of 4. The other *almost* makes it, but the far slope is slick and though she grabs for a branch or tuft of grass to pull herself up, she slips down into the water and soon her shoes are soaked. *So* close. That's a 3—on a 6-point scale.

SO WHAT'S A 6?

Let me suggest that if you prefer a 6-point scale (and you'll probably choose it for the purpose of breaking out that midpoint), you use the 6 to indicate those papers that have exceeded expectations—that is, gone literally "off the chart." But *do not* make the common error of merely making a 6 a "killer 5" with language that says things like "really, *really* sharp details," or "*remarkably* clear main ideas," "or "*overwhelmingly* strong imagery." This is cheating. Words like "really," "exceptionally," or "very" are by nature subjective, and allow us an out; we do not have to define what we mean by off-the-scale writing. No fair. If we use it, we must define it. So—here are definitions for level 6 writing:

Ideas

6. The paper is not only clear, but compelling. It offers a unique perspective or point of view unlike others. It is marked by insight and indepth understanding of the topic that affects the reader's own thinking and reflects experience, research and/or careful thought.

- The paper makes the reader think of the topic in a whole new way.
- Thoughts are expressed with both clarity and purpose; the writer takes the reader on a journey of understanding.

- Anecdotes, details and examples keep the reader continually informed and/or entertained.
- The reader feels enlightened, satisfied, stretched and enriched by the experience of reading. "I wouldn't have missed it" is the internal response.

Organization

6. The order seems so natural and right that it is difficult to imagine the information presented in any other format. It is easy to discover the writer's pattern upon close investigation, but it is so smoothly embedded within the text that it tends to go unnoticed.

- The organizational pattern fits the topic perfectly; it enhances both the reader's understanding and enjoyment of the text.
- The beginning has a "just right" feel—as if the writer had written many leads before settling on this one. "I can't improve upon it," is the reader's response.
- Transitions within and between paragraphs take the writer by the hand from point to point—but never stand out like road signs.
- Sequencing is never predictable, but it works. The organization leads the reader right to the main points and answers questions the reader didn't even anticipate.
- The conclusion is often the highlight of the piece—unexpected and enlightening, it builds a bridge to the next level of thought.

Voice

6. The voice is so clear, so individual, that the reader feels he/she could recognize another piece by this same writer without difficulty.

- "I *must* read this aloud to someone," is the reader's immediate response.
- The text is passionate without being overdone. Restraint keeps the sense of tension and feeling high; the text never dissolves into sentimentality.
- The reader feels moved enough to pause momentarily and reflect on the writing.
- Voice is used purposefully to enhance meaning..
- It is impossible (for all but the most indifferent of readers) to put this piece down.

Word Choice

6. The language and phrasing are so right for the piece that the reader feels compelled to read the paper—or parts of it—more than once, just to enjoy the way the writer puts things.

- "I wish I'd written that," is the reader's frequent response.
- Every word "tells"—which is to say, carries its own weight. There is no filler whatsoever.
- Numerous words and phrases are quotable.
- The reader wants to s-l-o-w down, savoring each line.
- The writer has his/her own way with words; no clichés, no echoes from others mar the beauty of this original crafting.

Fluency

6. This text is easy to read with maximum expression and inflection that brings out every nuance of meaning. It virtually dances—like a good, lively script from a film or play.

- Nearly *every* sentence begins in a new way, and the whole sounds completely natural—never forced.
- The text begs to be read aloud; it is one you'd choose to illustrate the concept of fluency.
- Prose may seem, at times, to dissolve into poetry; it's that lyrical.
- Variations in sentence length give the text just the right snap and bounce, so fluency supports meaning.
- There is not even ONE point at which the reader says, "This could use some smoothing out."

Conventions

6. Only the pickiest of editors will find errors in this text. It may not be flawless, but it could pass for flawless under the scrutiny of most eyes.

- The text is essentially correct in all ways.
- In addition, the text shows complexity: dialogue, length, complex/compound sentences, wide variety in use of punctuation, and spelling of difficult words. Yet the writer/editor *never* stumbles.
- Conventions are so skillfully handled that they consistently enhance meaning.
- As appropriate, the writer uses special conventions such as dashes, italics, ellipses, quotation marks, colons, etc. to add emphasis or to invite interpretive reading.
- This text is ready to publish.

Again, you need not use the "6" category unless you *wish* to reflect "over the top" performances that exceed the normal requirements of the scoring scale. As I provide scores for the sample papers in the book, I will point out those that teachers have typically felt could earn a 6 on one or more traits, given a scale that allowed for that.

TIPS ON SCORING EACH TRAIT

Ideas

Think quality, not quantity. It isn't *more* ideas that make a paper strong but the writer's effective use of just the right information. Consider Charles Kuralt's (1990) description of the Blackstone Hotel in New York, March 1937. He has just checked in to await a job interview with CBS for $135 per week.

> *The Blackstone was a shabby-genteel old institution somewhere in midtown. My room for the night was on a high floor, the fifteenth or so, a higher floor than I had ever been on in my life. When I stepped over to the window and looked down at the street below, full of tiny pedestrians and toy cars, it made me dizzy. I knew New Yorkers lived at such altitudes, but I couldn't even get to sleep up there.*
>
> *(p. 28)*

"Tiny pedestrians . . . toy cars . . . such altitudes . . ." A good writer will never tell everything but will zero in on just those details, bits, or moments that guide the reader toward the internal meaning. As Grant Wiggins (1992) reminds us, "too many essay scoring systems reward students for including merely more arguments or examples; quantity is not quality, and we teach a bad lesson by such scoring practices" (p. 30).

Organization

If you look deep within, you should find a pattern—a skeletal structure that holds the body (the ideas) together. We don't want to be overly conscious of the skeleton ("*My first point . . . Next I'll explain . . . Now for the third step . . . Having considered all three reasons . . .* "), but we want the comfort of knowing it's there, and that things are not going to fall apart. When the writer has a strong point to make or the need to share a story, the ideas drive the organization.

Look for a powerful lead that truly sets up the piece and tells you this writer knew where he or she was headed. Look for an insightful conclusion that shows the writer made some discoveries and is hoping you did, too. (The lead and conclusion should connect.) In a narrative, look for a turning point, resolution, moment of discovery. In an expository piece, look for a most significant statement or statements. A persuasive essay should contain a primary argument or compelling summary of several arguments. In short, there is a moment of significance in most pieces of writing, and everything else leads up to, supports, or winds down from that moment. As Hemingway said, "Good prose is architecture."

Voice is the quality, more than any other, that allows us to hear exceptional potential in a beginning writer; voice is the quality, more than any other, that allows us to recognize excellent writing.
Donald Murray (1985, 21)

Voice

When a writer has a chance to choose a topic he or she cares about, voice explodes from the page.

How long has it been since you wrote a story where your real love or your real hatred somehow got onto the paper? When was the last time you dared release a cherished prejudice so it slammed the page like a lightning bolt? What are the best things and the worst things in your life, and when are you going to get around to whispering or shouting them?

(Bradbury, 1990, 5)

You will find that the more you read, the easier it is to score the trait of voice, and once you've read text that is alive with voice, you will find it's addictive. It is much harder to tolerate voiceless writing. Pieces that are strong in voice are rewarding to share aloud. Think of the books you like to read to students in the classroom. Here are just a few of *my* favorite read-alouds (add yours to the list):

The Beauty of the Beastly by Natalie Angier
"A Christmas Memory" by Truman Capote
The House on Mango Street by Sandra Cisneros
Alien Invaders by Sneed B. Collard III
Monteverde by Sneed B. Collard III
Iron Man by Chris Crutcher
Boy by Roald Dahl
Danny, the Champion of the World by Roald Dahl
Matilda by Roald Dahl
Out of the Dust by Karen Hesse
A Life on the Road by Charles Kuralt
Lonesome Dove by Larry McMurtry
The Pooh Story Book by A. A. Milne
The Big Box by Toni Morrison
The Bluest Eye by Toni Morrison
Harris and Me by Gary Paulsen
The Winter Room by Gary Paulsen
Puppies, Dogs and Blue Northers by Gary Paulsen
The Best Christmas Pageant Ever by Barbara Robinson
Holes by Louis Sachar
Cosmos by Carl Sagan
Maniac McGee by Jerry Spinelli
Abel's Island by William Steig
Charlotte's Web by E. B. White

These books resound with voice. They make it easy to be expressive be-cause the writer's sheer joy in the writing comes through in every line. Similarly, if a student's writing has voice, you may feel an irresistible need to share it with someone. "Listen to this," you hear yourself saying. You will not feel compelled to share "Redwoods." That's how you'll know the difference.

Word Choice

Adjectives and adverbs are rich and good and fattening. The main thing is not to overindulge.

Ursula K. LeGuin (1998, 61)

Pretend you're holding a yellow marker in your hand, and just imagine that you are going to highlight each word or phrase within a student's paper that strikes you or captures your attention—words and phrases that seem right or noteworthy or commanding in some way. Perhaps you wish you'd written them, or you think, "That's original. I never heard it said quite like that." Your word choice score is just a function of how often the words and phrases grab your attention. *Every* line? That's a 6. Often? That's a 4 or 5. Sometimes? Perhaps a 3. Not sure? Maybe a 2. Not even once? That's a 1.

Sentence Fluency

If you ride, think of a horse's gaits: walk, trot, canter, gallop. If you're musical, use your toe or an imaginary baton to mark the tempo: adagio, andante, allegro, presto. Think of an oncoming train, the waves of the sea, wheels on a cobblestone street.

Patricia T. O'Connor (1999, 79)

Try reading the text aloud. You don't have to read the whole thing (though that's often helpful). Put expression in it. Don't be inhibited, or you'll wind up scoring your own inhibition and not what's in the text. Imagine you are trying out for a highly competitive part in a stage play; you won't get the part unless you summon every bit of emotional fiber within you and project. *Now* read. Does the text help you give a good performance? Is it easy to relay meaning, nuances, flavor, feelings? Can you awaken that sleepy guy in the back row? Do you feel as if you're floating from one sentence to the next almost effortlessly with the text carrying you? The piece gets a 6 or 5 in fluency. Score down a bit if you bump along, need to stop frequently and reread, or find yourself repeating patterns.

Conventions & Presentation

This one should be easy, shouldn't it? Isn't it the most clear-cut? Not really. We do not all agree on what is correct, for one thing. Look carefully at the list of pet peeves that follows this discussion, and identify things that might cause you to score down more than you should. Such things as failing to capitalize the pronoun *i* or writing *alot* as one word might be annoying, but they are not federal offenses and should not cause a drop in a student's score from, say, a 5 to a 1 or 2, but sometimes this is just what happens. That's how strongly many of us react to conventions we perceive as faulty. Here are four keys to scoring conventions well:

1. *Look beyond spelling.* Spelling is important, yes, but it is not the whole of conventions. How is the punctuation? The paragraphing? The grammar?

2. *Look for what is done well,* not just the mistakes. Balance the two.
3. *Do not overreact.* One mistake—or two or three—cannot spoil the whole performance. If we put three skilled editors in a room, it is highly doubtful any one of us could create a text of any length or complexity that would pass the critical eye and pen of all three, nor would they likely agree on which texts were conventionally strongest. We make a mistake when we demand conventional perfection of students, for we cannot teach to such a standard or even meet it ourselves. So ask, *Overall,* how well does the student control and use conventions to make meaning and organizational structure clear?
4. *Do not consider neatness or handwriting in assigning a score.* They may be important, but they are separate issues that we do not address within this scoring guide. Writing beautifully (or even legibly, for that matter) and editing text to make it conventionally correct and communicative are different skills altogether.

CAUSES OF RATER BIAS

Many little things can get in the way of scoring fairly or appropriately. Here are a few pitfalls to watch out for, whether in large-scale assessment or in the classroom.

The positive-negative leniency error. This is a technical-sounding term that means a tendency to be too hard (or too easy) on everyone, just as a matter of principle. We've all known the teacher who cannot bear to give anything but an A or B—or the one who is holding A's in reserve for that special student he/she hopes to meet one day. Good scoring shouldn't be about the rater's attitude or philosophy of life. Remember, the scoring guide is the final authority.

The trait error. As the name implies, this is a tendency to lend too much weight to one trait (e.g., conventions) while ignoring others.

Appearance. This is a biggie. We may find ourselves irritated by messy or tiny handwriting, especially when we're tired. But poor handwriting, while often annoying, is not the same thing as weak voice or unsupported ideas or faulty conventions, and should not influence trait-based scores. Similarly, neat word processed copy, while attractive, should not rescue weak, unsupported ideas.

Length. Is longer better? We might like to think so. This is another one of those traits that is easy to assess because it's easy to see. In fact, though, many students who write well for one or two pages have enormous difficulty sustaining the flow. They just run out of juice. Furthermore, ability to condense is often a virtue; it may give voice just the boot it needs.

Fatigue. This is an occupational hazard for teachers. The trick is to pace yourself so you are not scoring dozens of papers in a row without at least a stretch break, a moment to refresh, an opportunity to talk with a colleague or look out the window or gulp some fresh air. It makes more difference than you might think.

Personality clash. So you love football? Hate cats? Vice versa? These little quirks and preferences can and do get in the way of fair scoring. In large-scale assessment, you can ask another rater to score the paper. In the classroom, you usually do not have that option, but you can occasionally ask for a second opinion—just to be sure you are not overreacting. It's also amazing how much it helps just to list your personal biases so you are aware of them.

Repetition factor. What if all the papers have crashing waves, roaring surf, screeching gulls? This happens when a narrow topic forces writers into predictable responses. An open topic—"A Memorable Place" versus "My Trip to the Beach"—encourages more individuality, making papers easier to score.

Skimming. Some raters think they can tell after the first few lines whether the paper will be strong or not. Rarely is this true. A strong lead may disintegrate into banal generalities; a slow start may explode into a burst of inspiration on page two. To score fairly, read the whole thing.

Self-Scoring. Are you a perceptive reader? If so, be careful that you score the work of the writer and not your own talent in deciphering the hidden message.

Sympathy score. Papers on illness, grandparents, pets, and many other topics can touch our hearts in a way that makes fair scoring difficult. A short or sketchy sample can suggest that the student is struggling with the topic or with writing in general, and you may wish to reward even modest effort with an extra point here and there. What is so wrong with this? Isn't it right to encourage students?

Encouragement is good, but it must not come at the expense of honesty. When we assess effort and performance together, we confuse students. To see how and why, just think of something you would like to do really well but can't. Personally, I would like—no, I would *love dearly*—to dance like Chita Rivera, but I can't, no matter how hard I try. That's the thing. I can earn a 5 in effort, and that's an honest assessment, but the quality of the performance is still a 1, and that's an honest assessment, too.

Vulgar language. How do you respond to vulgar language in student writing? To profanity? To extreme violence? Your school or district may have an official policy for dealing with this sensitive issue, and you may or may not feel at home with this policy. Some people have a very ho-hum attitude; others are readily offended. This is not a question others can really resolve for you; it's too personal, and responses are too variable.

My position has usually been this: If the language works in context and is not used simply to distract or shock the reader, I assess the work as I would any piece of literature. Profanity is part of the landscape in a narrative on Vietnam; it may seem jolting, cumbersome, or self-conscious in a persuasive essay on school locker searches. The question is not really about violence or profanity per se, but about whether the writing works, and whether the language is appropriate for the context and intended audience.

> While conflict, fear, heartache, and humor may be desirable, they are not, by themselves, sufficient to hold the attention of readers or listeners. I have discovered that, through storytelling. The plot may be filled with blood and guts, but it's fine writing that keeps the audience rapt.
>
> Mem Fox (1993)

Pet Peeves

Everyone has a pet peeve. Some of us have many. The trick is to know what they are so they will not trap you into assessing unfairly. Here are a few of the most often mentioned pet peeves. Do you recognize any of your own in this list?

- Big, loopy writing
- Teeny-tiny writing
- Writing that fills the whole page, leaving no margins
- Commas or periods outside quotation marks
- *Hopefully* misused, as in "Hopefully, they will come."
- Shifting tenses without reason, and then going back again!
- Writing in ALL CAPITAL letters
- Mixing *it's* and *its*
- Mixing *their, there,* and *they're,* when we've just finished a unit on it!
- Mixing *are, hour,* and *our*—they don't even *sound* alike, do they?
- Run-on sentences
- Endless connectives: *and, but then, but, because, so now, and so . . .*
- The words *ugh, yuck, awesome, neat, rad, dude, guy, great, too much, bad, humongous, in the zone* or *cool* (I use it myself but still hate it in print)
- Spelling errors that the spell checker obviously missed and the student did not bother to look for
- Writing just to fill the page with no substance, no point, no passion, no heart, and no topic (no reader, either, if I had a choice)
- Empty words used to snow the reader: "She was obliterated by her compassion for nostalgic memories."
- *The end* (as if I would look for more)
- Backhand that tips so far it looks tired
- Writing that is too light (**burn** all No. 3 pencils)
- The phrase "You know what I mean"—I can't tell if it's more annoying when I do know or when I don't
- The cop-out ending "Then I woke up and it was all a dream"
- *Alot*
- Adjectives that are clichés: *fluffy* clouds, *clear, blue* skies, *crashing* waves, *screeching* gulls, *roaring* traffic, etc.
- A jaded tone in someone 14—give me a break!

- A total absence of paragraphs
- Lack of voice, honesty
- Repeating a word or phrase every few lines
- *Different than* instead of *different from*
- The phrase "between you and I"
- Using *very* instead of really showing me how it is
- Burying an idea under mounds of stilted, impenetrable jargon
- Safe, boring papers
- Exclamation points after every breathless line!!!!!!

In the classroom, pet peeves are less likely to influence scores or grades if we simply take time to be aware of them and even admit them honestly to students. Keep a list. It can teach us all a little about the way we respond to writing.

Remember—There is no "Right" Score

All the student papers in this chapter have been scored by many teachers, using the Six-Trait Analytical Scoring Guide. Their suggested scores appear at the end of the chapter, but remember, *they should not be considered the "correct" scores.* There is no such thing. They are only the *suggestions* of other trained teachers. You may have justifiable reasons for scoring differently, and that is fine so long as your scores are based on consistent criteria, not personal bias. The papers have been scored using both 5- and 6-point scales. Both sets of scores will be given.

General Approach

TIME
You should spend about five minutes scoring each paper, and—this is VERY important—you should score *individually* before checking with your partner(s). That's the only way to know whether you truly agree.

GRADE LEVEL
Do consider grade level as you score, but be careful not to overweight it. The traits do not change from grade to grade. Voice is still voice, whether it appears in the work of an eight-year-old or of someone sixteen or forty-two, but some expectations do change slightly. For instance, more knowledge of conventions is expected of a middle or high school student than of an elementary student. Similarly, vocabulary is expected to expand over time. Ideas may become somewhat more sophisticated with experience and with living, but good writing always has detail, voice, internal structure, and fluency.

MODE

Do *not* worry about mode (narrative, expository, etc.). The six-trait scale will work equally well with all samples, and part of our reason for including a variety is to demonstrate that.

The most fundamental criteria don't change very much [with mode]. For example, vivid and explicit detail is as important in a short story as it might be in a business letter or research paper.

Barry Lane (1996)

SAMPLE PAPERS FOR PRACTICE SCORING

PAPER 1. "MAKING DECISIONS"

Grade 8, Expository

Thinking helps you make good decisions. When making a decision, take your time and not rush into a hasty conclusion. Clarify the decision you are making. Be sure you understand all aspects of your decision, without confusion. Reason out the consequences your decision will effect. Question whether the concluding effects will be positive or negative.

Before proceeding ahead with any decision making process, devise other alternatives, if any, noticing who and what may be effected. Be sure to ask others for their opinion on the subject. Keep in mind, however, that their opinion may not be correct or even helpful. Quality decision making depends on facts, not opinions. Eventually, your decision will have impact on other things. These impacts cannot always be foreseen. Take your time in determining which impacts are most effected, and be careful in the end.

PAPER 2. "TELEVISION: HELPFUL OR HARMFUL?"

Grade 10, Persuasive

Is television helpful or harmful? That depends partly on the viewers. Take my Aunt Marva, for example. The minute she enters a room where there's a television, she turns it on. The very minute. Does she know what's on? It doesn't matter. It might be a soap opera or a football game or one of those animal shows on red ants in Africa. She sits there mesmerized. Sometimes she even forgets to take off her coat.

Marva does watch the news. But the interesting part is that she doesn't watch the news for the news. She does this sort of running critique on the newscasters: "Oh, look at Paula's hair tonight. She's gaining a little weight, isn't she? Who picks out Peter Jennings' ties anyway?" In other words, she doesn't listen, so details on what the President said or how the stock market did that day are all lost on her.

It seems to me that if you choose what you watch, pick good shows, and then listen while they are on the air, TV might be pretty helpful and pretty entertaining, too. For instance, let's say you get ready for work or school between 6 a.m. and 8 a.m. You listen to the morning news while you brush your teeth. You would then be able to carry on an intelligent conversation later. If someone asks you about the war in Bosnia, you won't stare blankly and say, "Where's Bosnia?" You'll know if the economic indicators are up or down, how the Celtics (or your favorite team) played in the latest game, and whether to take your umbrella or take off your snow tires. You'll be an informed person.

But to be really well-informed, you also have to watch the shows that are part of our culture. Shows like <u>Roseanne</u> or <u>NYPD Blue</u>. I know these shows get criticized for language and for violence. But a lot of the criticisms come from people who do not ever even watch these shows. If they did, they would see that even though Roseanne yells a lot and fights with her family, she also really cares about them. Police officers on <u>NYPD</u> might go out of their way to help a friend or help a teenager who is part of a gang or on drugs. The values these shows encourage are more important than the words they use. Plus, there is more violence in most Saturday morning cartoons or on the news than there is on <u>NYPD Blue</u>.

All in all, I think television is a good influence in our lives. Without it, we would not have access to lots of important information. We would not have the same window on our world. But as a viewer, you have to be responsible. Switch the channels if you don't like what you see, or turn the television off. Better yet, if there is nothing on worth watching, don't turn it on in the first place.

PAPER 3. "METAMORPHOSIS"

Grade 9, Narrative

Out of all the terrible things that can happen to you on Halloween like getting your candy ripped off, tearing your store bought but precious Halloween costume on your crabby neighbor's deceased rose bushes or being plagued by people with heavier artillery than you (such as shaving cream or Silly String), the absolute worst thing that could ever happen to you on Halloween has got to be someone else choosing a costume for you. Now, I'm not talking about someone making a suggestion to you. I'm talking about them totally choosing an identity for you.

I can remember such a Halloween when I was about eight or nine years old. It was the first year I really had my costume figured out and I was to be a gypsy. I had necklaces, bandannas and the ultimate loop earrings.

It was then the witch entered my life. My Uncle Gus saw the witch face first. Its hue was that of a green olive gone bad. The warts on its grotesque face had little hairs protruding from the midst of the blood red rubber. But not even that was the worst thing about the witch. The dilapidated witch's nose was the most horrid, twisted protrusion I had ever seen in my life. It hung down a good two or three inches total and was covered in those whiskered warts. I hated it. My uncle thought it was too good to pass up. I still hated it. How he could possibly ever like such a detestable vizard I will never know. From the minute he saw that mask, I could see the wheels turning in his head and I saw his thoughts come to words as he mumbled more to himself than to me, "My niece is going to be the best darn witch the world has ever seen."

You know, something very strange happens to adults around the time of Halloween. They get a nostalgic look in their eyes. I was seeing that look in my uncle's eyes and right then I could tell we were not going home without that mask.

I pleaded for him not to get the witch face but he wouldn't listen. I told him that I didn't want to be a witch and I was going to be a gypsy. But when I heard the words, "Here's your receipt, sir," I knew I had lost the battle.

We drove home in silence. I still had a fighting chance to be a gypsy if my mother protested, and I really thought she might . . . boy, was I wrong . . .

"That is the most spectacularly grotesque witch mask I have ever seen!" were her first words. I could feel the walls caving in around me.

Halloween night came. My gypsy costume had been long forgotten, lost in the farthest reaches of my closet. I stood like a mannequin in front of the mirror. Nothing in the mirror reflected my personality at all. "It's so hot in here! Can't I take this thing off for a few minutes??"

"What, honey?" my mother replied. "I can't hear you through the mask."

Ding-dong. "Trick or treat!"

"Gotta go, mom!"

My friends were waiting for me outside. The candy to come would help make up for not being a gypsy. We jogged down the first street, the cold air helping me feel better. Heck, it was Halloween. It couldn't be too bad.

After an hour, though, I was really beginning to sweat. I could feel my face clinging to the inside of the mask. Sweat dribbled down my face, and clung to my eyelashes.

The last house we approached was big and white. We lugged our now enormous bags of candy up to the front door, rang the bell and waited. A woman opened the door. "What a wonderful witch!" she exclaimed, and squeezed my long nose, spraying the salty sweat that had been collecting there all over my face. Right then, no amount of candy could compensate for my discomfort and humiliation. I grabbed my candy, and ran for home.

Once upstairs, I tore my mask off, and crammed it into the darkest hole of my closet where no one but moths would find it again. My mother has searched for it in vain. One time as a witch is enough.

PAPER 4. "EINSTEIN"

Grade 5, Expository

Who lived about 100 years ago? Who made great mathematical theories and ecuations? Albert Einstein, one of the greatest scientists who ever lived! Of course, all scientists are great, but Albert was special. He could look at the smallest thing, study it for hours, and see things others would just miss! He had an eye for detail, and he was never bored. Ever. Even when he was all alone!

What kind of family do you think a genius would have? Not much different from yours or mine, actually. Alberts' parents didn't even know for a long time that he had a great mind. They worried about him because he was alone so much. He liked staring at the stars for hours on end instead of playing with other kids. They didn't think this was normal. They worried that he didn't like to play war games. Instead he would just sit with his blocks and work them into different shapes for hours! What kind of kid was this? finally, when Albert's father realized he was a genius, he felt very proud.

You would think a genius like Albert einstein would love school. Wrong! he hated it! the only classes he liked were math and physics. Albert was so good at math he had to go to a special school to take classes. His math and physics teachers inspired him to become a great scientist.

Albert invented many math theories, but he is most famous for the theory of relativity, which people find fascinating even though they do not understand it. Albert also invented two bombs: the hydragen bomb and the adom bomb.

Einstein made a difference in the world because of his great math theories and his many ecuations. Even though Einstein is dead now, teachers are still teaching his theories. Who knows? People could still be teaching them right on years after you and I are dead, too.

PAPER 5. "THE BASEBALL"

Grade 5, Narrative

I remember the day I got it well. It was an everyday type day until the doorbell rang. I got up to awnser it. But my sister beat me to it, as usual. It was dad's friend Tom. He got back from a New York yankes baseball fantasy camp a couple weeks ago. I said hi to him and he asked me if I knew who Micky Mantel was. I said of corse I do. At that point I was a little confused. Thenhe haded me a baseball. It wasen't the kind of baseball we use in little luege. It was nicer than that. Made of real leather. It even smelled like leather. Like the smell of a new leather jacket. And the seems were hand stitched too. I turned it around in my hand then I saw it. I saw a Micky Mantel aughtograph. I coulden't believe it. I had an aughtograph in ink of one of the greatest baseball players of all time. Wow. I teushered it ever since that everyday type day that changed at the ring of a doorbell.

PAPER 6. "PETS ARE FOREVER: AN INVESTIGATIVE REPORT"

Grade 9, Expository

Many pet owners worry about that difficult day when they must say goodbye for the last time. A new method of preservation could make that day a whole lot easier. It's a sort of mummification of the 90s, minus the fuss of wrapping and the mess of embalming fluid. The new method, believe it or not, involves freeze drying your pet. It's clean, relatively affordable (compared to the cost of a live pet), produces authentic results, and enables you to keep Fluffy beside you on the couch forever, if you wish.

Freeze drying is really a simple procedure. First, highly trained technicians remove all the pet's internal organs. They do leave muscle tissue and bones intact, however, so there will be something to freeze dry. They replace the eyes with lifelike glass marbles in the color of choice. A special procedure temporarily reverses the effects of rigor mortis, allowing the owner to pose the pet as he or she wishes—sitting, lying down, curled by the fire, about to pounce, and so on. It is important to work quickly before the effects of rigor mortis resume. As a finishing touch, the technician uses special blow dryers with a fine nozel to make the pet look more lifelike. One client posed her cat in the litterbox; apparently, that was her most striking memory of "Tiger."

Freeze drying costs from $500 to $1,000, depending on the size of the pet and the complexity of the final pose. "About to strike" is more expensive than, say, "napping by the woodstove." The entire procedure takes about six months, but satisfied clients claim the wait is worth it. After all, once the pet is returned, you have him or her forever-maintenance-free except for occasional re-fluffing of the fur. Technicians report that freeze-dried pets hold up best in a relatively low-humidity, dust-free environment.

Experts also offer one final piece of advice: It is NOT recommended that pet owners try freeze drying their own pets. Proper equipment and experience are essential if you wish your pet to bear a true resemblance to his or her old self.

PAPER 7. "A GREAT BOOK"

Grade 8, Expository

There are many themes in To Kill a Mockingbird. Three of the themes that stand out are fairness, justice and courage. These themes are widely spread throughout the book. Harper Lee helps explain these themes through her characters and the way she writes about them.

Fairness is one of the many interesting themes in this great book. The main character Atticus shows the importance of fairness by the way he tries to treat others. Other characters demonstrate fairness as well.

Respect is another important theme of the book, though not as frequent as some of the other themes. Atticus shows respect for his community and for Tom Robinson, and they respect him as well. This is one of the main themes throughout the book.

Courage is a very important theme in this book. Jem shows courage in several parts of the book. Atticus shows courage by defending Tom in the trial.

These three themes of courage, fairness and justice are important parts of this book just as they are important to our society.

PAPER 8. "HARDER THAN YOU THINK"

Grade 11, Expository

I walk up the hill with my friends, turn into our cul-de-sac, go to the front door, put the key in the lock, turn, and step in. The house breathes a kind of spooky hello as I set my books down and go to the kitchen where the inevitable note is waiting: "Have a snack. Be home soon. I love you." As I'm munching cookies, I think how I'd like to go out and shoot a few hoops if I had someone to do it with. You can play Nintendo by yourself, but it isn't the same. So I forget that for now. I should be doing my Spanish homework anyway. Too bad I don't have an older brother or sister to help conjugate all those dumb verbs. I could call a friend, sure, but if I had a brother or sister, I'd have a built-in friend.

While I'm feeling so sorry for myself, I hear my friends Kelly and Kyle across the street. She's screaming bloody murder because he is throwing leaves in her hair and threatening to put a beetle in her backpack. She has just stepped on his new Nikes. I do not have these squabbles. I guess the big advantage, if you call it that, to being an only child is my room is my own. Nobody "borrows" my CDs or my books or clothes. I also get a bigger allowance than I probably would if I had siblings. My parents take me everywhere, from the mall to the East Coast. Maybe they wouldn't if they had other kids. (On the other hand, it would be more fun going if I had someone my own age.)

All these great advantages are overshadowed by one big disadvantage, though, and it's the main reason I would change things if I could. When you are an only child, your parents depend on you to be the big success all the time. You are their big hope, so you cannot fail. You have to be good at sports, popular, and have good grades. You need a career goal. You have to have neat hair and clothes that look pressed. You have to have good grammar, clean socks, good breath, and table manners. If you've ever felt jealous of somebody who is an only child, don't. It's a lot of pressure. I often wish for a little screw-up brother my parents could worry about for a while.

So—while having a neat room with nothing disturbed is great, I'd take a brother or sister in a minute if I could. The big irony is, if I had that mythical brother or sister, I would probably be wishing myself an only child again the first time my baseball shirt didn't come back or my stereo got broken. Life is like that. What you don't have always seems to be the thing you want.

PAPER 9. "JAPAN"

Grade 3, Expository

An interesting place to visit. That is my idea of Japan. It is my favrite place to visit I have been yet.

japanese people eat a lot of seafood and vegetables. most of their food they eat raw. They do not eat a lot of doughnuts and french fries. They do not have trouble with their weight!

In japan, you might walk or ride a bike. most people do not drive. If you see a whole street blocked off it means do not drive here. Japan also has tranes. They are electric and travel about two times faster than our traines.

If you do drive a car there is alot to remember. like do not drive on the right but on the left. Also a license is hard to get because the test is so, so hard to pass. You might have to take it two or three times and even then you might not pass because they make

you drive in the very worst traffic for hours and if you get mad
you do not pass. If you do not pass you might have to waite two
years to try again and it is not good manners to complain about
this.

The stores are small and even tiny but very crowded. You can
buy every kind of fish you can think of . they have octapus and
squidd and many other things you might not even reckognize. I
didn't! They have baskets too and dishes of all kinds. they have
cloths of all kinds but most of them are small. it is best to be very
skinny!

In your house if you hd a house you would find it crowded. The
whole house might be the size of your living room in America and
your whole family has to fit in no matter how big it is. You do not
have a lot of privecy and you can't make alot of noise because it is
bad manners.

At the end of the day you will fall asleep like anything because
you are just stone tired. I am going back for shure!. Want to come?

PAPER 10. "WRITING IS IMPORTANT"

Grade 11, Expository

Writeing is important. It allows you to express your thoughts but
also your feelings. through writeing you provide entertanement
and information which is useful to others. Writeing is both useful
and enjoyable. it helps you explore ideas and issues you might not
think of otherwise. If you are going to write, you will need plenty
of information.

Writeing well means knowing what you are talking about. This
takes research and information. If you do not know enough about
your topic, your reader will not be convinced. It also means
putting feelings into your paper. no one wants to read something
where the writer sounds bored and like they wish they were
doing something else. it can take courage to say what you really
think and feel but it is worth it. You will get your audiences
attention.

third, keep your writeing simple if you want it to be affective.
Trying to impress people with big long super complicated sentenes
and five dollar words does not work. They might just decide
reading your writing is not worth the time and trouble it takes. So
keep it simple if you want to have an audience.

the most important advice of all is to write about what you
know about the best. If you are a good auto mechanic for
instence maybe you should write about cars or if you have a
summer job at the veteranian's office, you could write stories

about the animals you treat. If you try to write what you do not know it will be obvious to your audience and they will not believe in you. Use what you know and use your experences from everyday life

writeing is important in all occupations. Today, it is more true than ever before. If you do not believe it just ask around. Everyone from doctors and dentists to garage mechanics and salesmen have to write as part of their job. But the most important reason is because writing is a way of sharing the ideas that belong to you. If you work on your writing skills, It just might help you in ways you have not even throught of.

PAPER 11. "THE LIGHT BULB!"

Grade 5, Expository

Inventing electricity led to the television, telephone, blender, pencil sharpener and you name it. But out of these many millions of helpful inventions, nothing is better than the light bulb! Thomas Edison had a wonderful idea when he had of invented the light bulb. it helped america and the entire world.

think if the light bulb had not of been invented. We would still be using torches to light our way. How would we see to sew or do our homework? How would we see to cook and what would we cook it on?? If you used a torch to light your house the torch could fall and catch everything on fire. You can not use a television or video game to light your house. NO!! You need the light bulb.

I think the light bulb is one of our most important inventions. don't you agree?

PAPER 12. "SOME CARTOONS ARE VIOLENT!"

Grade 3, Persuasive

Some cartoons are violent. And sometimes ther not! Some ar just funny like Tinny Tunes but some aren't. Take loony Tunes wich is violent but ther not all violent. They could be both. I wach cartoons alot and some are violent. Thers boms that get thrown down in som cartoons. and blows them up. But me I like cartoons some of the time. never will I stop waching but well more are violent than the loony toons. but if I were to mak a cartoon myself I would have well mabe just 1 mane violent thing and then just keep the rest funny OK?

PAPER 13. "MARCO POLO"

Grade 4, Narrative/Imaginative

Dear Diary,

I'm standing on the deck of our ship, memorizing the beautiful church of San Marco, the pillars and the pink and yellow buildings lining the canals of Venice. Good-bye to the gondoliers! Good-bye to the crowds on the docks, my family, my friends. My Venetian world looks smaller and paler as we sail farther out to the sea.

I'm seventeen years old. Will I be twenty when I return? Who knows? Uncle Maffeo says we might never get home. But papa says of course we will, but to our eyes Venice will never look quite the same. I don't have to say good-bye to our Venetian lion, though. He waves on our flag, red and gold, proud, high up on our masts. A little bit of Venice will always be with all of us.

Without our papa and Uncle Maffeo with me, I might not sound so brave. But, we are the Polo family, and we are strong together. I turn my head to the gray ocean, and don't look back again.

Our journey has begun.

PAPER 14. "A SUNFLOWER SEED"

Grade 5, Expository/Reflective

Now most people I know would think something like a football is most important but this sunflower seed ment a lot to me. It helped me understand the struggles and needs to stay alive in this world. How the seed needed water to live, and that water to me represented the thirst to stay alive. How it needed the sun to grow, and that sun is like our need to be with others.

I thought the sunflower seed died because it had been more than week since I had planted it. The next morning, a clot of dirt was being held midair by the sunflower, so I choped up the dirt to make it softer so the sunflower could grow easyer. In life you have to eas up on other people so they can relax in growing up and don't have to push or force their way up. In life there will be people that will hold you back from what you want (just like the dirt) and you have to break free from them if you want to live your own life.

Just like the seed you must prosper or life will pass you by.

PAPER 15. "ZEENA & THE MARSHMELLOWS"

Grade 5, Persuasive/Narrative

Zeena, I know just how you feel. I love chocolate covered marshmellows too! But let me tell you what happened to me.

My mom came home from the store one day and let me have a chocolate covered marshmellow. It was love at first bite. So lite, fluffy, chewy and slipped down my throat like a small piece of heaven. Just thinking about it makes me want to have another one until I recall what happened when I finished my last bag of those squishy delights.

My mom told me I can help myself to a few and before I knew it the whole bag was gone. My mom called me to dinner, and you know, the last thing I wanted or even cared about was dinner, but you know how mothers are, I had to sit down and take one bite of everything. And after that, I had diaria, diaria, diaria. But I was convinced it wasn't the marshmellows.

Last fall my mom bought me all of these cute clothes for my birthday, shorts, jeans, skirts, so when the weather got warm, and I went to put on my new clothes, they didn't fit to my amazement and not because I had grown too tall, just because I couldn't even zip them up. But it couldn't be the marshmellows, their too lite and fluffy; infact a whole bag of marshmellows doesn't weight as much as one orange.

One day, when I put the tight clothes out of my mind, I grabbed myself some chocolate covered marshmellows, when I was biting down on one, a sharp stabbing pain went up my tooth and the side of my head. And when ever I ate, my teeth hurt. So my mom took me to the dentist, and let me tell you it was not a pretty picture. I had seven expensive, painful cavities.

So Zeena, you can keep popping those marshmellows into your mouth, but before you do, remember not everything about chocolate covered marshmellows is sweet.

PAPER 16. "WHAT CONFUSES ME"

Grade 12, Expository/Reflective

Last night I watched a starving child cry.

I could see the sharp outline of his bones jutting out from beneath his taught skin—his rib cage heaving visibly as the sobs shook his poor, fragile body. I saw his swollen belly and the way his limbs hung limply at his sides, like broken twigs. But what stayed with me were his eyes. Sunken and shadowed in their sockets, his tears seeming to glitter from the depths of some profound emotion that I could not seem to grasp or understand. I watched as they carved shiny, silver traces through the dust on his cheeks, and for a brief moment I wondered whether he could really see me.

Seconds later he was gone—replaced by the image of a dancing Coca-Cola can as the news broadcast switched over to a commercial. And I sat there, mulling over his predicament while wondering whether or not to start my Calculus homework. To me, he was nothing more than a poster child, and I had homework to do.

You ask me what confuses me in life. I'll tell you. I'm confused by the fact that I sleep in a two-story, four-bedroom house while an African family of twelve huddles in a dilapidated old shack made of sticks and mud. I'm confused by the fact that I'm five pounds overweight whereas others haven't seen a bite of food in over a week. I'm confused by the fact that the bracelet I wear around my wrist could support a child for over a month. I'm confused by the fact that I watched that helpless little boy cry—and didn't shed a tear.

I wonder when I changed, when I became so devoid of human emotion that I could look misery in the eye and merely shrug my shoulders. Tough break, kid! Life's rough. When I think about it, I frighten myself. It seems as though there's a side of me that I didn't even know existed—one that has become so numb to the tragedies of this world that it no longer feels the tug of simple human kindness. I can rant and rave about the injustices of this world until I'm blue in the face . . . I can spout out Bible verses about love and charity until my voice turns hoarse . . . But the fact remains the same: I didn't cry. That confuses me.

That night as I lay in bed, the boy's image flashed before me again in my mind. And suddenly it occurred to me: he has a name. In that single, swift instant, something inside of me seemed to give way. He was a real person, flesh and blood—living under the same sky, sleeping under the same moon. It's hard to force yourself to see something you are so willing to ignore. It's easier to spare yourself the pain than embrace the truth. But at that moment I knew that I was helpless to change the reality before me. That boy had gone to bed hungry.

But he no longer cries alone.

SUGGESTED SCORES AND COMMENTS

Redwoods

GRADE 11, NARRATIVE

(5-point scale scores given first, then 6-point)

Ideas: 2, 3 (a 2 on the 5-point scale, 3 on the 6-point)

Organization: 3, 4

Voice: 1–2, 2 (a 1–2 split on the 5-point scale, 2 on the 6-point)

Word Choice: 2–3, 3

Sentence Fluency: 3, 4

Conventions: 4, 4

Comments. This paper is classic in its total restraint. It's safe. It's impersonal. The writer is barely here. It is pleasant in tone but says almost nothing because the language is masterfully vague, and there is a significant lack of involvement in the topic. What about this "wonderful time"? *How* was it wonderful? What is the brother really like? Is he kind? Comical? Pesky? Rude? Clumsy? What happened on this trip to delight, surprise, annoy, thrill, or appall this writer? We never find out. It's a greeting card essay—bright side only, keep it short, make it general. Readers are often surprised to learn that this is a high school student. Both vocabulary and sentence structure suggest a younger writer. Conventions are not faulty, with the exception of some minor problems with commas (which many readers do not even notice). The conventions scores are lowered from a 5 or 6, depending on the scale used, because the text is too simple to show the control or skillful use of conventions we hope to see from a high school junior.

Mouse Alert

GRADE 9, NARRATIVE

Ideas: 5, 6

Organization: 5, 6

Voice: 5, 6

Word Choice: 4–5, 4

Sentence Fluency: 4–5, 5

Conventions: 3, 4

Comments.   This story is deliciously crammed with tiny acts of everyday heroism. Nothing much goes right, but everything from Dad backing into the tree to the mouse hunt, the big release, and the race through Yellowstone is extraordinarily visual (this would *not* be a boring home movie) and a tribute to the pitfalls of planning. These people are extremely human—unlike the people in "Redwoods." They breathe. They argue. They worry over money, mice, and the allocation of air in the car. We can picture Mom in her nightgown and the mouse in the pickle jar. (Smell the pickles?) We are sorry this piece is so short, and that is about the best compliment you can give a writer. Conventions need work, yes, but this writer will find a professional editor one day.

Paper 1. "Making Decisions"

GRADE 8, EXPOSITORY

Ideas: 1–2, 2

Organization: 1–2, 2

Voice: 2, 2

Word Choice: 2, 2

Sentence Fluency: 4, 4

Conventions: 4, 4

Comments. This paper doesn't sound half bad when you skim it, does it? It seems to say *something*. The problem is, it's a compilation of generalizations and platitudes that really add up to nothing much.

No people populate this paper. It is sterile. The strengths of the piece (compare the text of any inflated political speech) are fluency and conventions. While it says virtually nothing, it says it smoothly enough to come across as rather authoritative. The language is sophisticated but imprecise: "Take your time in determining which impacts are most effected." This has no readily discernible meaning, impressive and boardroomish though it sounds. Think how different this paper would be if the writer had chosen one difficult decision (say, leaving home or giving up drugs) and given us possible outcomes; then the writer might have gotten more involved, and so might we.

Paper 2. "Television: Helpful or Harmful?"

GRADE 10, PERSUASIVE

> Ideas: 5, 5
> Organization: 5, 5
> Voice: 5, 5
> Word Choice: 4–5, 5
> Sentence Fluency: 5, 5
> Conventions: 5, 5

Comments. This piece provides a fine contrast to Paper 1 ("Making Decisions"). Again the writer is dealing with an abstract idea—in this case, whether television is helpful or harmful. But what a difference in approach! Can't you picture Aunt Marva, in her coat, watching the red ants or doing her running critique of Peter Jennings? We get personal, specific examples, including names of actual television programs, and a clear thesis: the harm in television lies less in the programming than in our own viewing habits. Notice that the writer does not state his thesis until he is about halfway through the piece; it's unconventional organization, but it works. The combination of wry humor with a strong sense of conviction makes the voice strong, too. Words are well chosen and clear, if not powerful. Fluency? Consider the differences in sentence beginnings and lengths. How much editing would you need to do? Remarkably little. This writer is in control of conventions. It didn't quite have that "over the top" spark and tone to push it to a 6, but basically, it met most of our criteria for fine writing.

Paper 3. "Metamorphosis"

GRADE 9, NARRATIVE

> Ideas: 5, 6
> Organization: 5, 6

Voice: 5, 6
Word Choice: 5, 6
Sentence Fluency: 5, 5
Conventions: 5, 6

Comments. This story deftly blends nostalgia with a warm, loving, but true tension between generations in a way that, though very lighthearted, has an underlying serious message: You must find your own identity. Those created by others do not work. Notice how the adults in this story never listen to the narrator; they are busy fulfilling their own fantasies. This is the heart of the story on one level, and the writer handles it well. The other story, of course, is the Halloween adventure, which culminates in that wonderfully humiliating moment when the writer is drenched in her own sweat by yet another adult who will only see the world through an adult's eyes. By the end of the story, we find ourselves wondering who Halloween is really for. The imagery is strong in this piece, and the word choice is both strong and original: "dilapidated witch's nose . . . horrid, twisted protrusion . . . I saw his thoughts come to words . . . heavier artillery . . . a green olive gone bad . . . I stood like a mannequin." We also like the pacing. The writer spends plenty of time on selection of the mask, which is critical, then speeds the reader through the trick-or-treating, which could have gotten tedious, and ends with the hiding of the mask—just right. Excellent lead and conclusion. Some raters thought it could be more concise; I disagree, but I also thought *Lonesome Dove* was too short.

Paper 4. "Einstein"

GRADE 5, EXPOSITORY

Ideas: 3–4, 4
Organization: 4, 4
Voice: 4–5, 5
Word Choice: 3–4, 4
Sentence Fluency: 3–4, 4
Conventions: 3, 3

Comments. Though this piece is not a powerhouse, it has a kind of quirky appeal. The picture of Einstein as a child offers a fresh, interesting spin on a popular biography. Who knows? Maybe Albert's parents *did* fret over his less than social side. Of course, there must be more to the story, and that is the problem here: what's done is fairly good, but details are a bit sketchy for a life story. The lead and conclusion work reasonably well; this writer needs only a good punch line—a significant moment, turning point, or spectacular surprise—to bring the organizational structure of the piece together. One other problem plagues the piece (as it does many assigned topics), namely, the writer seems to find Einstein mildly interesting but not quite fascinating. One moment of true joyful discovery could have boosted this piece from pleasantly engaging to riveting. All the same, voice is the strength. ("What kind of kid was this?") Given the right topic, this young, curious and enthusiastic writer will fly.

Paper 5. "The Baseball"

GRADE 5, NARRATIVE

> Ideas: 5, 6
> Organization: 5, 6
> Voice: 5, 6
> Word Choice: 4, 4
> Sentence Fluency: 4, 4
> Conventions: 2, 2

Comments. Small moments make the best stories, as this writer shows us so well in his tale of the "everyday type day that changed at the ring of a doorbell." Notice how the story comes full circle, beginning with the doorbell, and returning to it at the end, when it's even more powerful because now we know its significance. You have to respect a writer who, even as a fifth grader, is so careful with his details. There is a reason behind everything. There is a reason for the question about Mickey Mantle; he doesn't know what it is at first, and neither do we, but all becomes clear by the end of the story. It fits. How concise it is, too; in the hands of a less competent writer, this little tale might have gone on for three or four pages, but it's just right. The language is direct and very natural, but this is a writer with enough insight to stretch a bit. Sentences and even fragments are smooth and readable, but many begin with "I." Variation would help. Conventions need work.

Paper 6. "Pets Are Forever: An Investigative Report"

GRADE 8, EXPOSITORY*

> Ideas: 5, 6
> Organization: 5, 6
> Voice: 5, 6
> Word Choice: 5, 5
> Sentence Fluency: 5, 6
> Conventions: 5, 6

---

*This paper was identified in the second edition as a grade 9 paper; it is actually grade 8. Our apologies for the mistake.

Comments. The secret to putting voice into expository writing is to enjoy the topic. Clearly, this writer does. We get the idea that she is mildly horrified by the idea of freeze-drying and stuffing a pet, though the advantages are clear: low maintenance, easy care, and no need to say good-bye—ever. The humor in this piece is ironic, extremely understated, and highly controlled for a writer this age. Who can help but enjoy the image of Tiger posed in the litter box? Art is personal, the writer seems to say. Notice that her language is technically correct, yet totally natural: "mummification of the 90s," "A special procedure temporarily reverses the effects of rigor mortis," "'About to strike' is more expensive than, say, 'Napping by the woodstove.'" Awareness of audience is very strong, adding to voice. The prose is direct, forceful, and crisp, very appropriate for expository writing with flair.

Paper 7. "A Great Book"

GRADE 8, EXPOSITORY

Ideas: 2, 2

Organization: 3, 3

Voice: 2, 2

Word Choice: 2–3, 3

Sentence Fluency: 3–4, 4

Conventions: 4, 4

Comments. Here's a cheery but extremely lightweight analysis of Harper Lee's fine novel *To Kill a Mockingbird*. The paper is fluent, pleasant, noncontroversial. It says virtually nothing except that, apparently, there are some "themes in this great book." A handy approach since this report can now be used for other books, too—*Moby Dick*, *The Great Gatsby*, or, really, any book having themes.

Oddly enough, the organization is stronger than the content, only because the writer presents her points in orderly fashion, skipping right along, never pondering, reflecting, or enlightening us for a moment. The voice is not completely absent ("Fairness is one of the many interesting themes in this great book"), but it's not daring, revealing, or personal. It's almost a dust jacket voice, except that we're tempted to ask (don't say you didn't think of it), "Did you actually *read* the book?" Language is broad, generic, and redundant: "Jem shows courage in several parts of the book." Where? How? Notice, too, that the writer assumes the reader has read the book and knows who Harper Lee, Atticus, Jem, and Tom Robinson are. Lucky for her, she'll often be right, but still. Did you notice that the "great themes" started out as fairness, justice and courage, but shifted to fairness, *respect*, and courage? Doesn't really matter, given the amount of elaboration, but consistency is always good when you can get it.

Paper 8. "Harder Than You Think"

GRADE 11, EXPOSITORY

Ideas: 4–5, 5

Organization: 5, 5

Voice: 5, 5

Word Choice: 4, 5

Sentence Fluency: 4, 5

Conventions: 5, 6

Comments. I like this paper, as do most of the teachers who've scored it. It's convincing. And, it makes a good, strong point without hitting us over the head or smothering us in evidence. The writer uses two contrasting examples—the neighbor children squabbling and his own home life—to make some key points about how peaceful yet rather bleak it can be to go through life as an only child. The examples are realistic, and he seems to have thought through what he has to say. I love the opening for the clear picture it paints of life as an only child; it could probably be condensed. The ending is even stronger, and it makes an important point, too—without being redundant. The voice, a definite presence in paragraphs 1 and 2, springs to life in paragraph 3, the strongest part of the paper. Sentences are reasonably fluent, though many begin with *I*, *You*, or *So*. Similarly, vocabulary is strong, but a few phrases signal a need to stretch: "those dumb verbs . . . screaming bloody murder." Overall, a thoughtful, readable essay. Excellent control of conventions.

Paper 9. "Japan"

GRADE 3, EXPOSITORY

Ideas: 5, 5

Organization: 4, 4

Voice: 5, 5

Word Choice: 4, 4

Sentence Fluency: 5, 5

Conventions: 4, 4

Comments. A more typical paper might have opened by telling us that Japan is far to the east of the United States, that it comprises many islands, or that it boasts a strong, work-oriented culture. It is enormously refreshing to learn instead that the Japanese stay thin by walking and biking everywhere, that they live in relatively small homes where privacy must be respected, or that in Japan a snarly disposition could make a driver's license hard to get. Good writers are adept at selecting the details an audience will find interesting and useful. We think this is a masterful job from a third grader. In fact, a strong sense of audience awareness, combined with obvious involvement in the topic, gives this piece powerful voice. The writer maintains a kind of "Imagine that!" tone, without ever making it sound artificial or forced. Organization is a little random, but easy to follow nonetheless. Many teachers feel this is a strong enough performance in conventions to warrant a higher score; but the fact is, there are numerous errors. This trait is not as strong as others.

Paper 10. "Writing Is Important"

GRADE 11, EXPOSITORY

Ideas: 4, 4

Organization: 2, 3

Voice: 3–4, 4

Word Choice: 3, 4

Sentence Fluency: 3–4, 4

Conventions: 2–3, 3

Comments. This paper is an interesting combination of banal truisms (writing is important; writing is both useful and enjoyable) and thoughtful, useful advice (try to write what you do not know well, and your audience will stop believing in you). The upshot is a fairly high score in ideas, which was the teacher-raters' way of saying, "Give us fewer platitudes and more of yourself—you have some excellent ideas going here."

The organization needs help. The lead does not give us a global introduction to ready us for what's coming; in fact, the lead works against this writer by suggesting that what follows will be rather dull. As it turns out, the writer makes some intriguing points. The three key ideas—write what you know, write with courage, and keep it simple—are not yet completely distinguished from one another, nor are they equally developed. We were a little startled to come to the sentence lead-in word, *third,* at the opening of paragraph 3 (Did we miss points one and two?), then to have the notion of writing what you know repeated in paragraph 4. Meanwhile, the critical idea of saying what you really think and feel is buried in a one-liner at the end of paragraph 2, and the conclusion introduces a whole new topic: writing is important in every job. The points the writer wishes to make are insightful, but they need to be ordered, expanded, and better set up.

Word choice is fairly routine. There's nothing really wrong, but the writer does not snap us to attention either. Many sentences are short and choppy, which breaks the flow and creates the impression that the thinking is overly simplistic, too—which it is not. Some careful reading could correct many small but annoying problems with conventions.

Paper 11. "The Light Bulb!"

GRADE 5, EXPOSITORY

    Ideas: 3, 3

    Organization: 3, 3

    Voice: 2, 3

    Word Choice: 3, 3

    Sentence Fluency: 5, 5

    Conventions: 3, 4

Comments. What a fluent piece this is! "But out of these many millions of helpful inventions, nothing is better than the light bulb!" That is masterful sentence building. This writer has a fine ear for cadence. *"Think if . . . We would still . . . How would we see . . . If you used . . . You can not use . . . NO!! . . . You need . . ."* The rhythm builds to a crescendo. Unfortunately, the ideas themselves do not parallel this cumulative wizardry. In fact, they're somewhat humorous. Are we to seriously imagine ourselves struggling to keep torches upright while we fill our blenders or type away at our computers?

    This is comic stuff. If the writer wants us to take light bulbs seriously, she must tell us about holding down costs, heating with light bulbs, creating atmosphere, boosting technology. Show us light bulbs working their electrical magic in incubators, hatcheries, factories, or tanning salons. If this invention is truly significant, don't toss it off in one glib paragraph on the way to the television room.

Paper 12. "Some Cartoons Are Violent!"

GRADE 3, PERSUASIVE

    Ideas: 2, 2

    Organization: 1, 2

    Voice: 4, 4–5

    Word Choice: 3, 3

    Sentence Fluency: 3–4, 4

    Conventions: 2, 2

Comments. I can almost picture eyebrows going up at this fluency score, but I have to agree with the teachers who scored the paper that it is conversational and more fluent than it looks. In fact, its conversational tone is its strength—and a strong contributor to voice, too.

    The questions of how much violence is too much, or whether violence has redeeming social or aesthetic or artistic value at all, continue to plague television and film executives at all levels, so we should not be too surprised that this question proved challenging to a third grader. Nevertheless, this young writer takes an exuberant stab at the prompt she is dealt. The first problem for us as readers is the same problem faced by the writer: figuring out the main point of the paper. It seems to be something like this: a little violence in cartoons is desirable and entertaining; too much could probably be a bad thing (for reasons not fully explored)—but won't hurt me because I know it's phony! What this piece lacks in persuasive logic—and organization (it's almost humorously random since her key ideas are not clear even to her yet)—it almost makes up for in voice. The writer is clearly speaking to an audience and invites us to share her to and fro thinking.

She also lets us know in no uncertain terms ("never will I stop waching") that she plans to keep right on enjoying cartoons, even if adults think they are harmful. By the end of the essay, she's negotiating for position: how about just one violent episode per cartoon, keep the rest funny, and leave them alone—what do you say?

Paper 13. "Marco Polo"

GRADE 4, NARRATIVE/IMAGINATIVE

Ideas: 5, 5

Organization: 5, 6

Voice: 5, 5

Word Choice: 5, 5

Sentence Fluency: 5, 6

Conventions: 5, 6

Comments. Here's a delightful, deceptively simple paper which creates for us, in a few lines, a vivid and powerful world—not only the visual world of Venice but also the world inside the mind of a seventeen-year-old explorer off to a new land. What does he feel? Pride, anticipation, apprehension, homesickness, love, courage. Notice that the "voice," the persona, is much older than the actual writer. What startles me about this paper is the remarkable amount of information this young writer offers us in so few words: "I turn my head to the gray ocean, and don't look back again./Our journey has begun." Worlds of meaning rest within these two poetic lines. This is powerful writing; everything is understated. Notice the vocabulary: "memorizing the beautiful church . . . world looks smaller and paler . . . to our eyes Venice will never look quite the same." The words are simple, but eloquent; each creates a precise impression. This paper puts us right on the ship, waving goodbye. We watch Venice slip away for what might be the last time. It is not such an easy thing, being part of this Polo family.

Paper 14. "A Sunflower Seed"

GRADE 5, EXPOSITORY/REFLECTIVE

Ideas: 5, 6

Organization: 5, 6

      Voice: 5, 6

      Word Choice: 5, 5

      Sentence Fluency: 5, 5

      Conventions: 4, 4

Comments. The philosophical message and tone of this piece are very strong. The sunflower seed metaphor works well; it is like the hub of a wheel, to which all other ideas connect. Few papers are so well centered; organization (along with voice and the whole insight of the piece) is a real strength here. We picture the writer "[chopping] up the dirt to make it softer" and thinking to himself, *This is how life is for us all.* Here's a writer speaking from experience. The paper makes us think, makes us want to "[ease] up on other people," and encourage them to do the same for us. As in the "Marco Polo" paper, words are simple, yet they carry a lot of weight. This writer uses fragments, but they are smooth and enhance readability. Conventions need a little work.

Paper 15. "Zeena & the Marshmellows"

GRADE 5, PERSUASIVE/NARRATIVE

    Ideas: 5, 6

    Organization: 5, 5

    Voice: 5, 6

    Word Choice: 4–5, 4

    Sentence Fluency: 4, 5

    Conventions: 3–4, 4

Comments. The main thing we want to say to this writer is, "Thank you for helping us understand why diets do not work." It's that dieter's logic: "A whole bag of marshmellows doesn't weigh as much as one orange." Beautiful. This young writer leads us into the world of dieter's temptation and remorse without ever preaching or moralizing. How refreshing. Images: *"slipped down my throat like a small piece of heaven . . . I had to sit down and take one bite. . . . couldn't even zip them up . . . a sharp, stabbing pain went up my tooth."* We love the way this writer pokes fun at herself, along with the dieting world. This is true comedy: convincing—but with just the tiny dose of pain and suffering true comedy needs to work. We feel very persuaded, plus the paper's a knockout in voice. This is a persuasive piece but uses three humorous narrative anecdotes to make the point. We like this technique and agree with the strong scores in organization, too. (A few teachers were troubled by the "abrupt" transition "Last fall," and I see their point, though I don't feel lost here.) The fluency is strong for the most part, though the punctuation does not support it. We're tempted to say, "Hey, throw in a period now and again." Many sentences run too long, but cutting a few words would fix most of this. And oh my—that voice.

Paper 16. "What Confuses Me"

GRADE 12, EXPOSITORY/REFLECTIVE

In the classroom from which this particular paper comes, students assess their *own* work using the six-trait model and defend their numerical scores with a short essay. What a wonderful way for students to become strong self-assessors! Before sharing our scores, then, we will let you take a look at how the writer herself assessed "What Confuses Me," using a 5-point scale. Our scores for 5- and 6-point follow.

Lauren's *Own* Scores (based on a 5-point scale)

Ideas: 4

Organization: 4

Voice: 5

Word Choice: 4

Sentence Fluency: 4

Conventions: 5

Lauren's Comments. I have to admit, this essay was very difficult for me to write. At first, I was tempted to choose another topic and spare myself the grief rather than dredge up emotions I didn't want to face. But because the subject is so personal to me, I felt that I was able to express myself effectively through my voice.

By using the example of the African boy, I sought to draw the reader in and give the essay more impact. It is through this experience that I explain my "confusion" with the world and my apathy towards it. I thought the organization was good—by returning to the boy in the concluding paragraph I tried to leave the reader with something to think about.

The ideas and content may be a little sketchy—when writing on a subject like "confusion," it's hard to convey your ideas without sounding confused yourself. I had a hard time expanding on my central theme; it was as if I got to a certain point and had nothing more to say. I felt that if I wrote any more, I would just be generating a lot of filler to take up more space, so I went ahead and ended it. This may actually have been to my advantage; sometimes, shorter is better.

I admit that my word choice may have been less than exemplary, but I was trying to avoid a "scholarly" tone and keep it on a more personal level. I tried to make up for the basic word choice by constructing powerful imagery when describing the boy. Reading over it, I wonder whether I may have unintentionally used too many cliches. I guess that's for the reader to decide.

As for sentence fluency, I noticed that I like to use a lot of parallel structure. Though that may be good in some cases, there is something called "too much of a good thing." I think that in the future I should experiment a little more with how I construct my sentences. One thing I did like is the way I placed the opening and closing sentences by themselves.

I think that some phrases belong alone, without the distraction of a surrounding paragraph.

Overall, I am satisfied with the essay, because I think I was able to get my point across in a powerful way. Besides just answering a question, it gave me the chance to learn something about myself.

<u>Our</u> Scores

> Ideas: 5, 6
>
> Organization: 5, 6
>
> Voice: 5, 6
>
> Word Choice: 5, 5
>
> Sentence Fluency: 5, 6
>
> Conventions: 5, 6

<u>Our</u> **Comments** This is a remarkable piece of writing. Quietly powerful and extraordinarily focused. The haunting image of the starving child juxtaposed with the dancing soda can jars us with the suggested power of affluence to diminish our feelings. This is a voice that touches something so deep, so fundamental within us that it is almost irreverant to put a number on it.

Like Lauren herself, we liked the stand-alone sentences. It is very satisfying when a young writer is this deliberate in her technique and this aware of her ability to change the tone or impact of the writing with a little editorial flair. As a fan of parallel construction, I see this as a real plus. Too much of a good thing? Maybe. But how many students even know what parallel structure *is*? I had not really noticed the clichés until the writer mentioned them herself. I did notice the plainness of the language and liked it very much: "*sharp outline . . . rib cage heaving visibly . . . like broken twigs . . . Sunken and shadowed in their sockets . . . I frighten myself . . . the tug of simple human kindness . . . something inside of me seemed to give way . . . sleeping under the same moon.*" There is so very much to applaud, what is a cliché or two tucked among the roses?

We were so moved by this essay that looking at the student's scores gave us a moment of much-needed comic relief. 4s? No way. However, it *is* good to know that this student sets such high goals for herself. We want to see her stretch. *Teaching tip:* For an interesting class discussion, compare this essay to "Making Decisions." As a follow-up activity, ask students to revise the "Decisions" piece in teams.

Student's Reflection (One Month Following Composition of the Essay).

When I asked Lauren for permission to use her work in the book, I also asked if she would do a short reflective piece on herself as a writer. Here it is:

> *To me a piece of writing is like a photograph. Be it in color or black and white, it can capture a single moment and hold it forever. In my experiences as a writer, I have often found that I am not content until I have "frozen" such moments on paper, a need which leaves me scribbling notes on everything from gum wrappers to the back of a*

shopping receipt. As can be seen by the pile of wrappers on my desk, most of my writing never reaches an audience. But for some reason, that doesn't seem to matter. Writing is the only outlet through which I can express myself honestly and without inhibitions.

Whether or not my desire to become a novelist will pan out remains to be seen. I may never see my name grace the spine of a New York Times *best seller—in fact, I may never even see my name in print. But that's only the frame on the photograph. I'll never stop taking pictures.*

I think we'll see your name on that best seller, all right, Lauren. I'll be in line to buy a copy.

IF YOUR SCORES DON'T AGREE

Don't be too concerned if your scores don't completely agree with ours, but *do* have good reasons for scoring as you did. Our scores result from several careful readings of each paper and from discussion of the paper with other teachers.

We believe the scores are valid and justifiable, and we have tried to indicate some of the reasons in the comments following each analysis. Nevertheless, these scores are impressions and cannot be more. You may have additional or even conflicting responses to any or all of these student writings. Keep in mind that the truth about any piece of writing is *very big*. Not only do raters disagree with one another sometimes, but you may find your own impressions changing over time. Consider the wise words of Peter Elbow (1986) who reminds us that "one of the most trustworthy evaluations we can produce is a 'mixed bag': an evaluation made up of the verdicts or perceptions of two or more observers who *may not agree*" (p. 223, emphasis in original).

> The teacher . . . may encounter a student whose writing differs dramatically from the teacher's idea of excellent writing. A true mentor will not try to penalize the student or clone a duplicate of himself. Rather, the mentor is forever alive to the possibility of something new and distinctly original.
>
> Ralph Fletcher (1993)

REFLECTING ON CHAPTER 3

1. Have you ever received a much higher—or much lower—grade on a piece of writing than you felt you deserved? What do you think caused this to happen?
2. How can you know when criteria are significant? Fair?
3. In *Embracing Contraries*, Peter Elbow (1986) describes research conducted by Alan Purves, in which Purves "discovered that readers make more accurate and reliable judgments about the features of student writing if, while making them, they're also asked to give a quick account of their subjective responses or feelings" (p. 230). Giving voice to a personal response, Elbow hypothesizes, may allow a reader-rater to be more "objective" in scoring or grading. How do you feel about this, in light of the scoring and discussing of papers you did in this chapter?
4. Did your scores on the papers in this chapter agree with the scores of the teacher-raters who looked at them previously? How do you account for any differences?

ACTIVITIES

1. Expand your scoring skills by assessing writing not generated by students. You might look at a company's annual report, a driver's manual, a textbook, a how-to manual for assembling or using any product, an advertisement, a public relations letter or brochure, a complaint letter, a lease agreement—or any other writing that's part of your life. You don't have to assess every piece for every trait. Assess what you think is most important.

2. Be daring. Create a piece of your own writing to assess with your group—anonymously. (It needs to be word processed, clearly.) You can minimize the threatening feel of this activity by focusing on the two strongest traits for each piece, rather than on the problems. Then, ask the group to share one recommendation for revision. See if the group's assessment matches your own!

LOOKING AHEAD

Now that you know the traits, we can take the scoring guide right inside the classroom, and explore a number of ways to use it—just one of them being the sharing and scoring of written work. If you'd like more practice with more papers—or if you'd just like more papers to share with students—you'll find those in Chapter 4. Otherwise, you can skip Chapter 4, and go right on to 5, where we'll show you how to help students become stronger writers through self-assessment and revision.

MEMORABLE MOMENTS FROM STUDENTS' WRITING

- Mom and I split up into teams.
- We're currently undergoing a globonial growth spurt.
- I'm a believer in youth and Asia.
- We have memories that go clear back to yesterday.
- He wasn't God, but he was very talented.
- A definite attitude makes for a disgusting life.

4

IF YOU JUST HAVE TO HAVE MORE PAPERS . . .

The six-trait model is a wonderful way of assessing your own writing. I wish that I had learned the traits when I was younger. The traits are an excellent way to discuss writing with others because you use and understand the same vocabulary. I think the six traits are a great way for students to improve and understand their writing.

Katie Ehly
11th Grade Student
Lincoln, Nebraska

Nothing frustrates a young writer—or an older writer—more than looking at a finished piece and knowing it isn't very good, but not knowing what to do about it.
Tommy Thomason and Carol York (21)

NEVER ENOUGH

I know. You can *never* have enough student papers. So here are a handful to add to your collection—to practice scoring and to share with students. Remember to form a network with two or three other teachers who will save and exchange papers with you—and occasionally score a paper as a team to keep your skills sharp.

Recommended scores on 5- and 6-point scales appear at the end of the chapter, along with brief rationales for those scores. Please note that Papers 7, 13, and 17 were all scored using the *informational writing rubric* in Chapter 10; that is because these papers were not spontaneous, off the top of the head writing; rather, they resulted from research in which students had time to compile information and make use of resources. Others are all spontaneous pieces, written and revised within approximately 45 to 120 minutes.

PAPER 1. "CHAD"

Grade 3, Descriptive

My friend is great because likes the same things I do. His name is Chad.

If theres nothing to do around the house, we get together and do stuff. I phone him up or he phones me. He's a real neat person. He's fun to do stuff with because we mostly like the same games and TV shows. He comes to my house or I go to his house. He has brown hair and is tall, about five feet! It is cool having a friend who is alot like you and likes the stuff you like. Chad is my friend.

PAPER 2. "GUN CONTROL"

Grade 8, Persuasive

I am writing about guns because they are in the news. They are out of control. We have too many accidents and shootings. Kids do not feel safe in the schools. Parents do not feel safe sending their kids to school, which is ridiculous. School should be one of the safest places.

I know people need guns to hunt, though not as much as in the old days. Not that many people eat moose and elk that I know of, but if you do, it is ok to have a gun. It is not ok to use automatic weapons for hunting though. Give me a major break! What would be left of a moose or deer after you killed it with an automatic weapon. This is not hunting to eat. This is hunting to kill plane and simple.

The other reason is we should have stricter laws governing who gets to buy guns and when. Just a wating period doesn't do that much. Alot of criminals do not have guns registered because they buy them on the black market.

If you do own a gun, you need to take care of it. You should be sure the safety is on when you store it and it is not loaded when it is in the house. Keep it in a locked cabinet when you are not using it for a good purpose. Make sure children cannot get at it. Also, do not forget to clean your gun.

PAPER 3. "THE JOKE"

Grade 7, Narrative/Expository

My grandma is 81. She has had rheumatoid arthritis for twelve years. When it was first diagnosed, her chief problem was constant, relentless pain. Now she can no longer walk, take herself to the bathroom, brush her own teeth, or lift a fork to eat; forks and toothbrushes are too heavy for her to hold. To move from her bed to a chair she has to be lifted; sometimes, just the pressure of lifting under her arms causes her to shriek with pain. Despite her problems, though, she loves to sit up and talk with her family. "I'll start dinner in a minute," she tells us.

Unfortunately, pain and medication have dulled her memory, but they have never gotten the best of her imagination. She has many conversations with old friends and long-gone relatives. Sometimes she "goes shopping," then tells us of the bargains she found or the clerks who gave her a hard time. My grandma is feisty, and tolerates no backtalk, even in her imagined world.

Last month, she had two molars pulled. Although she had dreaded it, she really liked the orthodontist, which made her experience a little better. She liked him so much, she wanted everyone to benefit from his services. She told my brother and me—we're 12 and 14—that we should get our teeth pulled now because it would be so much harder if we waited till we were her age. "Just go now and get it over with," she said.

My brother nearly choked on his chicken. It was funny and sad at the same time. I remember my grandma's face. She was so happy to have made her grandson laugh, it made her laugh with us. It was her way of joining in the joke.

PAPER 4. "A RESCUE"

Grade 4, Narrative

Once a bunch of my frieneds and I went to this old hounted house and I'm not talking about some amusment park thing or something like that but but this was a for real hounted house, but we couldn't go in because we were too scared and my friend Robert kept making these jokes that made us laugh so hard we couldn't walk so we just kept talking about should we do it or not?.

So the next day we went back and this time we followed Robert into the front door and I was right behind him and I could hear him breathing in this kind of panting way and I told him to keep quiet or he would wake up the gosts. So just then I saw something real creepy move in the corner of the kitchen, and robert said Shhhh its only a stray cat but I said ha I don't think so buddy in a million years so I took off like a rocket from the moon and waited outside in the fog that was nice and creepy and then I saw the thing again and this time I knew it was too big for a cat so I ran back into the house to save my freniends. I grabed Robert by his hair and he let out this inormous shreek but I had to get him out of the monster's claws and I pulled and pulled and finally got him out of the house and he said what in the name of holey moley are you doing?? I had yainked some of his hair clean out of his head and he didn't like it much. I gues he didn't apreschiate beging saved from the gost so I took off for home to have dinner. And then had dinner and went to bed and that is the last time we went to that house, but me and Robert still are best friends as long as I don't pull his hair.

PAPER 5. "WHY YOU NEED A JOB"

Grade 9, Persuasive

Young adults in our country need to learn more responsibility, and having a job while you are going to school is one way to get there.

Many times, young kids take their lives and theyre parents for granit. Parents have been around to care for them as long as they can remember. But it doesnt last forever. Sooner or later you will be out on your own without one clue of your life or responsibility. A job teaches kids to care for themselves without help from their parents. To buy things like clothes and insurance. Jobs are not just about money though. A job shows you how to get a long with people out side your family. A job is good for your future. It introduces you to new skills and new people. This paper gives solid reasons for getting a job while you are in school. Do it. You will not be sorry.

PAPER 6. "A STRANGE VISITER"

Grade 5, Narrative

The doors flew open, the wind whipped around the room. The startled men looked up. Standing in the door was a man. His royal purple cloak rippled in the draft. The room was silent. There was a sudden noise as the men put down their wine goblets. Tink, tink, tink. The room grew hot and sweaty. Some men tried to speak but nothing came out. The gleam of the strange visiters eyes had frightened the knights who had slain many dragons, and fought bravley for the King. The errieness was unbearable. The visitor's gray beard sparkled in the candlelight giving it an errie glow. The windows let the dark seap in. The large room decorated with banners seemed to get smaller and smaller. The heavy aroma of wine hung in the air like fog on a dull morning. Their dinner bubbled in their stomachs. Their rough fingers grasped their sowrds stowed under their seats. The round table again fell silent. The slowly the man spoke: "The King has come." The End

PAPER 7. "THE ITALIANS IN AMERICA"

Grade 10, Research

The Italian people have a long history of traveling to the Americas and were in fact the first Europeans to explore America. In 1492, Christopher Columbus, an Italian Navigator, came to North America in his search for a shorter route to the Indies. It was this focus that caused Columbus to name the Native Americans Indians. America, in fact, owes its name to another Italian, Amerigo Vespucci, who explored North America and South America in the late 1400's. Vespucci published an account of his journey to South America which was so popular that in the early 1560's mapmakers used his name, Amerigo, to refer to the continents. The name has changed slightly but remains to this day.

Although the early settlement of North America is often credited to the English, whose language we still speak, the Italians had a strong influence too. Early records of the English colonies in America show a number of museums named after Italians. In addition, there are references to Italian sculptors, glass blowers, wine merchants and teachers.

The greatest immigration of Italians to North America did not begin until the late 1800's. It was triggered by an incredible series of natural disasters that affected both Italy and Sicily. During this period there were extreme droughts, numerous earthquakes, and much volcanic eruption that destroyed many towns and crops. Thousands of people were left homeless and without any way to make a living. To make matters worse, a particular plant parasite devastated Italy's vineyards almost completely. People were desperate.

Since many Italian explorers had already traveled to North America and written about it, Italians didn't feel they were strangers to American culture. They saw America as the land of opportunity where jobs were plentiful and it might even be possible to purchase land on which to grow crops or begin new vineyards. Between 1890 and 1950, 4,700,000 Italians immigrated to the United States. Italians accounted for nearly 10% of all immigrants during that period. Most immigrants paid about 30 dollars for the trip and rode in storage at the bottom of the ship with no ventilation. The conditions were brutal—no room to move, no air to breathe. Many died. Those who survived brought many talents with them. Some were artists, some were tailors, and large numbers of them had agricultural skills.

Most of my Italian ancestors originally lived in Northern Italy. In the early 1800's, some of them migrated to Milazzo, Sicily. This is where my great grandparents, Joseph and Pierina were born. Joseph was a marble polisher, like his father before him. Joseph and Pierina married at a very young age; he was seventeen and she was fifteen. Marrying at a young age was customary among Sicilians. Their first child, Frances, was born in 1905 in Sicily. Shortly after that, sometime in 1906, Joseph and Pierina decided to immigrate to America. They had a new baby and no money and they thought that they would strike it rich in "Wonderland."

Like thousands of other immigrants, they first came to New York, where they soon discovered that life in America was not as easy as they had hoped. Most Sicilians did not speak English; they spoke Italian. This made it much more difficult to find work in an English-dominated world. In New York, as in other large cities, the Italians and Sicilians formed "Little Italy's," which were really run-down slums; they depended on one leader in the group, called a *padrone*, for jobs. They were typically given low-wage jobs that no one else wanted. What held my family together during this difficult time was their love and respect for family. As Luigi Barzini points out, "The first source of power is family. The Italian family is a stronghold in a hostile land . . . no Italian who has a family is ever alone" (190).

Despite this strong sense of family though, my great grandfather was unable to find work because there was no call for marble polishers. The search for work eventually brought the family to the Midwest and the city of Minneapolis. There, my great grandfather was able to use his marble polishing skills in working for the city. During their life in Minneapolis they experienced prejudice for a number of reasons. For one thing, they didn't speak English. Italians were also thought of as gangsters because of the perceived association with the Mafia. "There are Americans who believe that criminal groups in their country belong to the Sicilian Mafia . . . and that they are all directed by orders from Palermo. This myth is shared even by some naïve American criminals of Italian descent, who learned it from reading the news papers" (Barzini, 270).

My grandmother, Rosalie, was born in 1918. It was about this same time that my grandfather began allowing English to be spoken in the home. This was an effort to combat prejudice. My grandmother grew up speaking English, not Italian. Though she knows many Italian words, she does not use them much and never taught them to her own children because for her the Italian language carried a kind of stigma. Unfortunately therefore, her second child, my father, never learned to speak Italian. He was different from his parents and grandparents in another important way: He was the first person in his family ever to graduate from college.

Italians have contributed much to our society, from food to clothes to cars. They have given us Boticelli shoes, Armani suits, and Ferrari automobiles. Many of our famous entertainers that we enjoy today are Italians, such as Al Pacino, Robert DeNiro, Frank Sinatra, Lucciano Poveratti, and Sophia Loren. Other famous Italians are also part of our everyday culture, such as Mayor Mario Cuomo and baseball great Joe DiMaggio. Antonini Scalia became the first Supreme Court justice of Italian Ancestry. From the Italians we have also gotten foods such as broccoli, cauliflower, pizza, spaghetti, and ice cream. Next time you go to the shopping mall notice how many products come from Italy. Think about how it would be to not be able to get a pizza, a favorite for many people, or an ice cream cone. Look up at the stars at night and think about how much of our understanding of the universe we owe to Italian scientist and philosopher Galileo. Visit an art gallery and notice how many paintings have been created by Italian artists. Think where we would be without the Italians. I am proud to be a part of this great heritage.

Bibliography

Barzini, Luigi. <u>The Italians</u>. New York: Athenium Press, 1964.
Foti, Lorenzo. Personal Interview. March 15, 1998.
Hillbrand, Percie V. <u>Italian Living in America</u>. Minneapolis: Lerner
 Publishing Company, 1970.
"Italians Immigration to the United States." ABC News, April 1997.
 Address (URL): http://www.ercomer.abc.k12.com

PAPER 8. "WINTER IN MAINE"

Grade 5, Poetry

Note: Score only *ideas, word choice* and *fluency* for this one.
  See the snow fluttering down like
  white butterflies outside the glass window.
  It piles up on the sill.
  Smell the stew cooking on the iron stove.
  Feel the warmth from the fire
  on my back and hands.
  Hear the happy cries of the baby.
  Listen to my sister joyfully playing
  with her rag doll.
  Watch my mother sewing, the needle

gliding through the fabric.
Feel the cool window pane.
See the trees outside, bare like
skeletons looming before me.
Taste the hot stew. It warms my
stomach and body.
Hear the crash,
as icicles fall and
smash on the snowy ground.
Listen to mother shooing
my sisters upstairs for bed.
The winter goes on and on.

PAPER 9. "THE BIG ROAD"

Grade 7, Narrative

From the moment my sister got her license, I knew there would
be interesting and dangerous adventures ahead. Whenever there
was anywhere to go, Jessica always volunteered for the job. She
went here and there and everywhere. What a pro. She liked to go
to the store and pick up dinner. She would do anything. She went
to the gas station, the Cleaners, the Mall. Naturally, when it was
time to go to my baseball game, Jessica volunteered for the job
without hesitation. Obviously, after being driven everywhere by
my parents my whole life, I was a little apprehensive about being
driven to a big game by some one who was fairly inexperienced. I
told my parents I wouldn't feel safe, but they didn't think
anything of letting Jessica drive with me in the car. Was my life
worth so little?

While I put my baseball uniform on, Jessica gathered all of the
things that she likes to take with her whenever she drives: her
coffee cup from Starbuck's, her sunglasses, and her favorite
Beatles CD's. We both got into the car. I buckled up and pulled the
thing snug, wondering if the airbags worked. Jessica started the
car and jolted back out of the driveway. She seemed to drive well
without speeding. As we pulled out of the neighborhood, Jessica
popped in a CD and we headed toward the field. I began to relax.
After a few minutes I noticed that Jessica had picked up the habit
of yelling at drivers who tailgated or drove too slow. It was pretty
funny to hear her ask the other drivers if that piece of #@#$!! had
a gas peddle. We got to the field safely and I had a great game. I
was a little nervous about the trip home even after being driven
safely to the field. After all, it would be dark by the time the game
was over. "What if she can't see in the dark?" I thought. "But what
can I do? I don't want to walk home with all of my gear." The game

ended and she pulled up to the walk and I hopped in the car. The stars were bright in the cloudless sky. Jessica turned on the signal to pull out of the field parking lot. She made the turn and pulled out. "Oh God!", I yelled. A car was tearing right for us. Jessica hit the gas and we lurched to safety. "That was close!" She said. "It sure was," I said back.

PAPER 10. "FAMILY DAY"

Grade 10, Narrative/Descriptive

The first thing you notice as you enter is the heavily guarded door you just passed through. They have electronic security locks and two stern-looking (but sleepy) guards standing by. A grimy and sometimes slippery linoleum floor is under your feet. You can see that the short corridor leads to a desk with a cop, who is obviously bitter about his job, holding out a sign-in sheet and a government pen.

Welcome to the county jail. It is located in the heart of the city. This is where local felons go before they are transferred to a federal prison. This is where my father is.

The place is filthy. Not even felons deserve to live here. Dirt has been gathering on the walls for some time, and it is hard to tell how much of the gray is the actual wall and how much grew there over the years. The cop tells each person to write their name, inmate's name, etc. on a sign-in sheet and then have a seat and wait. Others breeze through this process, but my mother and aunt and I are first-timers, so there is the obligatory fumbling for ID and stupid questions that make the others impatient. When we finish, the guards point to the waiting room.

The group in this room is, to put it mildly, depressing. The young women look trashy, and the old women just look scared. Some are dragging four or five kids behind them. There are few men. They are the quiet ones, sitting patiently while the children run wild and their mothers try to keep them in line, resorting to slaps when necessary. But watching this crowd is one thing; being one of them is another. It strikes me that I am now one of these people.

The wait to visit your inmate is a half-hour. It is a wait I could do without. Never have I been so bored and nervous at the same time. The thirty minutes gives me time to think. Unfortunately. I realize that our fears have become reality. All the tampered-with evidence, the biased judges, the fair-weather friends, the front page of the local papers, the ridicule from classmates, and this is the result. A rotten, stinking hole of a detention center. There is no turning back. This will be every Tuesday for four years.

At last, we can see him. Another security-reinforced door, another corridor. But this one has glass along the walls. In front of each square of glass is a stool, to the right a black phone. My mother sits on a stool, my aunt and I stand behind her. The lights on the other side of the glass come on, and a line of inmates enters. My father is the last in the line. He is wearing the jail uniform, with the county name stenciled on the back of the shirt. He sits across from my mother, behind two inches of glass, and begins crying. Mom is crying too. So am I. No words are said through the tears. My parents just hold the phones to their ears and weep to each other. After a few minutes, my mother sobs, "Would you like to speak to Jessica?" He nods, and I sit down with the phone in my hand. I cannot look at him. He was my hero, and now look what they've done to him. He is a broken man crying over a grimy prison phone to a daughter that he has disappointed. He used to be such a proud man. No one thought they would ever see him like this. Especially not me. I just look straight down and watch the tears puddle on the floor, and there is nothing else. A pool of salt-water reflecting merciless untraviolet light. And my father can only say two words, and he says them over and over:

"I'm sorry."

When I can stand no more, I give the phone back to mom. She is still crying, but now she has to suck it up; there is legal stuff to be taken care of. Once they finish, our time is up. I beg to be taken home. My aunt does so, while my mom stays to wait another half-hour and then visit him once more.

*   *   *

Time has passed. Dad was moved to a much nicer federal prison. He was later released and has been a free man for a year now, and has a respectable job. No one who looks at him would know he was once a felon. He does not talk about being in prison, and I wonder if he still thinks about it, about the first visit we paid him after his incarceration. I still do.

PAPER 11. "THE CAR BY GARY PAULSEN"

Grade 5, Literary Analysis

The Car was written by Gary Paulsen. The book takes place in the early 90's in Cleveland, Ohio. The book starts off with Terry at home and his mom and dad fighting. They get in a huge argument and they both decide to leave. The mom and dad drive off each thinking that the other has stayed behind. Now Terry is alone. He decides to go to his uncle's place in Portland, Oregon. He then remembers a kit car that was given to his father. Terry decides to assemble the car. It is a huge task, but Terry finds he has a talent for it. Once the car is assembled he begins his physical journey across the country. Along the way he meets two Vietnam vets named Waylon and Wayne with whom he becomes friends. They decide to teach 14 year old Terry about life. In their journey they meet Samuel, a Native American visionary and prophet, some very rough rodeo cowboys, members of a strict religious commune, Annie, an old woman who runs a poker parlor in Deadwood, and many other characters. At each stop that is made, Terry learns more and grows.

Geography is a huge part of this book. It influences how Terry thinks. In the city Terry feels trapped like he can't breathe, but when he gets out into the open prairie he feels free and he can go fast. On the prairie Terry is able to think more clearly. At the end of the book when Terry, Wayne, and Waylon make their last stand against evil rodeo cowboys they head into the Big Horn Mountains just as the Sioux Indians did over a hundred years ago.

PAPER 12. "A BALL'S EYE VIEW"

Grade 10, Expository/Narrative (written for a physics class to show the laws of physics operating in a real-life situation)

"As I sit on this bench waiting for my turn, I wonder about things. Why do I not float away? Why do I move the way I do, and why do I fall to the ground if I am dropped? Maybe it is the force pair between any two bodies that keeps me sitting on this bench. I push down on the bench with a force and the bench pushes back up on me with an equal but opposite force. I think I might be onto something here!"

The box of baseballs is opened.

"Oh please pick me, sir. I am so bored being in this box! Spring passes so slowly when I'm cramped up in here."

The man in the hat reaches into the box and tears off the plastic wrapping covering me.

"Yippee Ki Yi Aye! Thanks man. Oh, that fresh air feels so good. I thought I was going to suffocate in there! Just give me a minute to stretch my seams and I'll be ready to go, coach."

The man throws me to the field, showing that I can stay at rest or maintain motion, which is the concept of inertia. As I leave the man's hand, I arc through the air and hit the ground. Since I hit the ground, this shows that I am made of matter and because I have inertia and matter, I have mass.

"That wet grass is terrible, man. Don't you know what water does to leather? Well, dummy? Just you wait until the 9th inning when your pitcher can't throw a strike to save his life! Ah, no one ever listens to me."

The man in the middle of the field picks me up and the ump yells, "Plaaaayyyy baaaallllll!"

"This is my favorite part. I've always wanted to be a part of a real baseball game. Me and the other balls back at the factory used to dream of this!"

The pitcher takes me in his sweating hands and rubs his fingernails over my stitching looking for just the right grip. I am brought into his mitt.

"There's no place like home."

The pitcher's wind-up begins and I am released through his fingers and hurled toward the catcher. I cut through the air like a hot knife through butter, as the force the pitcher has put on my body is greater than the force of air resistance and the gravity pulling me down. Halfway home I realized that I am in serious danger of being torn to ribbons by that wicked stick if it is unleashed upon me. Luckily, my body is well built for this type of abuse—I hope.

"Please don't hit me. Please don't hit me. Oh my God!"

The word "slugger" is tattooed onto me as the bat collides with my body. The force of the bat on my body causes me to accelerate out of the infield. I go sailing through the air like a bird, if only for a short moment, up and up with a force greater than the—9.8 m/s^2 acceleration of gravity caused by the earth's mass being greater than my own. Even though the earth has a much greater mass than my own, I too exert a force of gravity on it. However, the force is so weak, it is nearly non-existent. I can't wait to tell this story to my friends back in the dug-out.

"You better hurry up, kid—he's going for three."

The right fielder responds by rushing at me and scooping me up into his bare hand and heaving me towards the bag. I am relayed past second base by the short stop and finally tossed the remaining distance to third but the velocity put on my body is not enough to get the out.

"Safe!" The umpire screams.

"Nice try, kid," I comment. "Next time you should use your arm to accelerate me at a greater pace from the back of your head to the point of your release."

The third baseman ignores me and rubs my worn body on his knee, trying to clean my exterior, but soon gives up and chucks me back to the pitcher.

"Hey, ump!" the pitcher yells. "This ball is really torn to ribbons."

"I'm not through yet, kid. I'm as good as new, really I am. Just give me one more at bat," I protest.

Those pitchers are a bunch of real idiots I tell ya. Whenever they can't throw a strike, leave it to the pathetic whining pitchers to blame us hard working balls. I am now useless. My life as a big league player is finished. My once perfectly round shape is now not and my sweet, sweet body is torn to ribbons. I will never fly smoothly through the air as I did back in my tender, youthful years. The air resistance, which used to be my friend, is now my mortal enemy. Now all I am good for is batting practice or maybe a dog's best friend if I'm lucky. The only stories I will be able to tell now are of how I could have been a contender, but I blew out my seams in my early years.

The pitcher retires me to the dug-out; that is to say, he chucks me in the direction of the garbage can. Luckily, I am able to spring to freedom off the rim and hit the concrete floor below. By now my intestinal stringing is flying free, and my seams are beginning to give. I hit the concrete hard, real hard, and happen to roll into a few of the old veteran balls also lying outside the garbage can.

I say, "Hey guys—remember me from the factory? Man, those were the days!" But the balls don't respond.

I scream out, "Hey guys, wake up! Get in the game!" But they say nothing.

The only sounds are the voices of cheering players and the screaming fans.

PAPER 13. "WHEN ARE SEARCHES JUSTIFIED?"

Grade 10, Persuasive

Law enforcement officials routinely conduct searches of suspects or their personal property in order to gather evidence. The question is, should school officials reserve the right to search students or their personal belongings if violation of a school rule or law is suspected? If so, under what circumstances is such a search justified?

An analysis of *Mary J.* (not her real name) *v. New Jersey*, a case argued in 1984, shows that under certain circumstances, such a search is justified, even if it violates (or seems to violate) certain rights to privacy. In fact, courts are generally willing to extend a little more leniency towards schools than they are to police officers. To understand why, it is helpful to first look at the basic facts of the case.

On March 7, 1980, a teacher at North High School in Middlesex County discovered two girls smoking in a lavatory. One of the two girls was the defendant Mary J., who at the time was a 14-year-old high school freshman; the other was her companion. After being caught by the teacher in the lavatory, the two students were taken to the principal's office, where they met with the Assistant Vice Principal, Roger Edgeway (not his real name). In response to Mr. Edgeway's questioning, Mary J.'s companion admitted that she had been smoking in the lavatory; however, Mary J. herself did not admit to smoking at all. After that, Mr. Edgeway asked Mary J. to come into his office and demanded to see her purse. After opening the purse, Mr. Edgeway discovered a pack of cigarettes, which he held to Mary J.'s face and accused her of lying. Mr Edgeway also noticed a pack of cigarette rolling papers, which he associated with the use of marijuana. He concluded that he should—and could—do a more thorough search of Mary J.'s purse. As he continued through her purse, he discovered a number of incriminating items: a small amount of marijuana, a pipe, a number of empty plastic bags, a substantial amount of money, an index card with several names of people who owed Mary J. money, and two letters that showed Mary J. was involved in marijuana dealings.

Was Mr. Edgeway justified in his search of Mary J.'s purse? It is possible to argue either side of the case, but the argument in favor of the search is a stronger one. At issue is the question of whether or not Edgeway violated Mary J.'s Fourth Amendment rights.

The Fourth Amendment states, "The right of the people to be secure in their persons, homes, papers, and effects, against unreasonable searches and seizures, shall not be violated; and no warrants shall issue, but upon probable cause, supported by oath or affirmation, and particularly describing the place to be searched and the persons or things seized."

Although the court concluded that the fourth amendment *did* apply to searches carried out by school officials, it held that a school official could properly conduct a search of a student's person if the official had a *reasonable suspicion* that a crime has been committed. By using this conclusion, the court decided that the search done by Mr. Edgeway was a reasonable one. The difference is this: the court requires that legal officers have *probable cause* before conducting a search. *Probable cause* means reason to believe a crime has been committed. The courts only demand that schools act on something called *reasonable suspicion*. *Reasonable suspicion* is a suspicion based on what a reasonable person would believe given the circumstances. Further, it need not be suspicion of a crime, but only of violation of school rules or of posing a threat to students or other persons present within the school.

Since Mary J.'s friend was caught smoking, the court held that it was reasonable to suspect that Mary J. had been smoking too. They also held that when Mr. Edgeway discovered the rolling papers, it was reasonable for him to think that Mary J. was a marijuana user. The facts are on Mr. Edgeway's side. Not only was Mary J. a user, she was apparently a dealer as well.

Let's look at things from Mary J.'s point of view, though. An opposing argument might be that just possessing cigarettes is not the same as smoking them, and therefore would not be a violation of school rules. After all, the principal never actually saw Mary J. smoking. Furthermore, if that initial search of Mary J.'s purse was *not* justified, the marijuana evidence would not have been uncovered, and could not have been used in court. This is a good argument, but it overlooks an important issue: the safety of North High students.

The bottom line is this: Edgeway is responsible for maintaining a safe learning environment at his school. If any student is taking or selling drugs at school, that severely compromises this environment and potentially endangers others. Mr. Edgeway has to weigh the rights of Mary J.'s privacy against the safety of every innocent person in North High School. Also, the finding of marijuana in Mary J.'s purse indicated that she was most likely involved in dealing drugs. If Mr. Edgeway had not investigated by searching her purse, how many innocent people might have felt the consequences? What example would that set for students or parents? If such searches were *never* allowed, perhaps other items could be brought into schools—items such as guns or explosives. Mary J. was a little embarrassed and lost some privacy, but Edgeway was acting in the interest of the students and the school and did not act until Mary J. had broken a school rule. In short, searches in schools based on *reasonable suspicion* are justified.

PAPER 14. "COMPUTING BATTING AVERAGES"

Grade 6, Informational

Math is all around us in almost everything we do. Math is involved in banking, shopping, the weather, the national economy and just about every thing we do. It is hard to think of even one thing that doesn't use math in one way or another.

You wouldn't think math would be such a big part of sports but it is. Take baseball for example. In baseball people use math for many things. One example is figuring out batting averages. This is important because when players see how well they are doing, they have a way to improve. How would players improve if they didn't know how well they are doing.

A batting average is really like a percentage. To find out your batting average, all you need are two numbers: how many times you are up and how many times you hit safely (meaning that you get at least to first base on a hit). Then you need to divide the number of times you hit safely by the total number of times you are up to bat.

Here is an example of a batting average. Lets say you are up 50 times and hit safely 25 of those times. Your batting average would look like this: 25/50. You would have a batting average of .500, which is pretty good. Suppose you hit safely every time you were up. Your batting average would then be 50/50, or 1.000—which is pronounced "one thousand". This were we get the famous saying "batting a thousand." Of course, nobody could ever bat this well in real life.

With the use of batting averages it is easy to set goals for yourself and see how well you are doing. A good batting average for a pro ball player is somewhere between .300 and .400. The all time record is held by Ted Williams, who batted .410.

My best batting average was in the summer of 1998, when I averaged .370. Maybe it was me, or maybe it was the pitching!

Think about your own life for a minute and you'll be surprised what a big role math plays.

PAPER 15. "STOP MAKING PUBLIC FIGURES INTO HEROES"

Grade 12, Persuasive

This country is out of control with its recent condemnation of public figures. People have forgotten that celebrities don't make millions of dollars for their model ethical conduct; they are paid highly for their scarce abilities. Celebrity status should not include a stigma of perfection.

Every human being has the inherent responsibility to establish his or her own moral code, whether we choose to follow the tenets set forth by a religion or do whatever suits ourselves. A public figure has this choice also as a member of the species. People often overlook this fact and subscribe to the misconception that celebrities must be heroes, a flaw in American mass-stereotyping.

If I were to start a bar brawl, the public would pay very little attention to the fact that I threw the first punch. I'd have little publicity beyond the police reports in the newspaper. But once I've attained celebrity status a few years from now, someone, perhaps with a laminated <u>National Inquirer</u> press pass, could boost his career with dirt like my bar fight. My face would permeate the media from the New York Times to Saturday Night Live, as if I'd signed away my personal privacy with invisible ink.

How have we evolved to this point where celebrity supposedly equals virtue? What section of the constitution contains the "President and Moral Compass" clause? For those people who would rather take a reality raincheck than examine the issues at the root of America's decadence, perhaps it would be more

effective to teach children the truth about humans—we're not
perfect—than to lay blame on celebrities.

The days of Tarzan and the Lone Ranger are long gone. Movie
stars, athletes, and politicians do not strive to achieve hero status,
they are just trying to make money. While public figures should
expect more scrutiny than the drive-thru employee at McDonald's,
it is unreasonable to place them under a microscope of human
eyes. Dennis Rodman and Tim Allen are not ideal heroes and never
will be. Parents need to assume the responsibility of teaching
children how to discern between hero and human.

PAPER 16. "TECHNOLOGY: A FORCE FOR GOOD, OR OUR
DOWNFALL?"

Grade 12, Persuasive

I once read a study proving that the more time people spend in
virtual chat rooms, the greater their chance of depression. Why?
They lacked human contact and relied on machines to replace it.

The technological advances that have infiltrated our society are
not just a reflection of our scientific prowess, but also of our western
culture in general. When did we become so reliant on machines and
popular gizmos to survive our daily lives? It was long before the
invention of the microchip, before the washing machine, television,
or even electricity. Since the beginning of civilization, our people
have tried to find ways to live more efficiently. This was never a bad
thing; in fact, it brought us out of the dark ages of illiteracy and
peasant life. Today, in an age where anything is technologically
possible, the question at hand is where to draw the line. When does
technology overcomplicate, rather than simplify our lives? Bill Gates
would like to believe it never will, while some left-over
transcendentalists may say that it has already mutated our culture.

Rather, I believe that our culture has mutilated itself, and the
technology that so many middle-class, middle-aged businessmen
have embraced is not the twisted backbone of change, but more the
product of it. After World War II, a war fought with the lives of
millions of men and ending with the aftermath of one immensely
destructive device, the Cold War gave birth to technological
necessity. Back then, we imagined that the world would be better if
its inhabitants were primarily machines. Maybe the root of this was
our collective guilt over the war and Hiroshima incident. Maybe we
were in denial that one machine could kill so many people.

In the 1950's, America's dream rested upon the idea of the world
as a technological utopia. Humanity would be free of suffering if
only we could create these miracle machines, if only we could live
on the moon. In the last 40 years, technology has progressed so

much and become so accessible that it's difficult to step back and look at the issue objectively. But some things are obvious: despite our technological advances, the world is not utopia. Even though we have traveled to Mars and back, we are still unable to deal with our own waste. We are still unable to stop countries from fighting like children or to distribute food worldwide.

Technology isn't the burden of man, but its creation, whether one uses and likes technology is a matter of personal choice, but to blame it for the downfall of modern man is absurd. Computers don't truly cause missiles to kill people, just like pagers don't cause drug deals. Technology can't solve the deeply-rooted problems of humanity but hasn't created them either.

PAPER 17. "ELECTRIC EELS"

Grade 6, Informational

Eels are a type of fish. They live in the ocean, and many diferent lakes. They are long and slender. They have fins that help them swim. The coloring of eels is blackish brown and their bodies are covered with slimy coating, which makes them difficult to hold. Eels are usually not shorter than three feet long, and they can be as long as nine feet long, and can weigh up to 22 kg. It can be as thick as 12 to 18 inches.

The electric shock from the eels comes from muscles in their bodies, which have lost their ability to work like normal muscles do. These muscles are mainly in the long tail of the eel. The shock coming from their bodies works somewhat like jumper cables for car batteries. The tail of the eel is negatively charged. When an eel touches its tail and head to different parts of an animal, it sends electric shocks through that animal's body. Electric eels mainly shock other fish of different kinds, to stun them so they can eat them. They also shock other animals to keep the animal away from them. If we are in their living area, we scare them, and then they might shock us. However, their shock is only strong enough to knock us down, not kill us. The Electric Eel puts out as much as 500 volts, and can have up to 650 volts. The electricity can discharge at will. This is enough electricity to knock down a mule or light a small electric sign. The Eel's generating organs have the same structure as those of the electric ray, but the shocking strength of the Eel is much stronger, and greater. The Eel produces low energy pulses that flow outward in all directions. Anything nearby fixed or in motion, affects the flow pattern since it conducts electricity differently from water. The electric organs provide the fish with additional sensory, defensive and offensive mechanisms. The electric eel produces from 1–5 pulses per second when resting, and about 20 impulses per second when excited. The electric discharges surround the fish with an electric field, which is able to detect through highly specialized sensory cells in its skin. If a field is distorted by some object of different electrical conductivity from that of the water, the electrosensory organs of the skin are stimulated and the fish is alerted.

The electric organ is made up of cells known as electroplaques. These cells have lost the elongate form of muscle cells and are flattened plates closely stacked in columns. The are as many as 700,00 electroplaques in the 3 pairs of electric organs of an electric eel.

Despite its name, the fish is not a true Eel but is related to characins in the order Cypriniformes. It is a sluggish creature.

The Electric Eel's scientific name is Electrophorus. It belongs to the family Gynotidae, all though it is often wrongly classified as Electrophoridae. The Electric Eel is related to the minnows and catfishes. It is found in South American fresh waters or the Amazon and Orinoco rivers. The electric organs, which are modified muscles, are columnar structures located on each side of the tail.

Electric eels do not shock each other because they don't want to eat other eels, and they don't usually get attacked by other eels. That is the main reason they shock other animals.

When an Eel swims, its body makes S-shaped curves. The outer edge of each curve presses against the water. The water is relatively less movable than the fish so the fish moves forward more, then the water is pushed backward.

Eels don't see very well, but they have a very good sense of smell. Eels usually eat whole shrimp, clams, and other kinds of fish.

PAPER 18. "FREAKING OUT"

Grade 6, Literary Analysis

Introduction

Readers of middle school age will find many reasons to like and appreciate Rodman Philbrick's excellent book <u>Freak the Mighty</u>. This book has an exciting storyline about two friends who are rejected by society, but who become very strong when they are together.

Three Reasons to Read This Book

One of the important reasons to read this great book is the unique character called Freak. Freak is coping with a disease that causes his internal organs to grow much faster than his body, which has stopped growing. Even though Freak knows that he is going to die from his disease, he doesn't tell his friend Max because he doesn't want to hurt Max. Freak is an extremely intelligent person and a computer whiz. He and his pal Max are best friends because they both are different from other kids. Freak is also compassionate. He is the only person that is nice to Max even when others are not. Together they form a team that is more powerful than either one of them alone.

Second, if you read the book, you can participate in the adventures Max and Freak go on, which they call quests. Some of the quests are imaginary and some of them are very real and often dangerous. One of their first quests begins when Freak and Max are at a carnival and a gang chases after them. Freak then climbs upon Max's shoulders to act as a lookout, they can maneuver through the enormous crowd of people. After a vigorous chase, they end up between the gang and a mucky, mud-filled swamp. Max chooses to wade into shoulder-high mud of the swamp, and after a short wait, the police come and the gang members run off.

Another quest begins later in the book when Freak spots a purse down in a storm drain. Freak tells Max to meet him at dark in the street. Together they retrieve the purse. Although all the money is gone, there is ID, so they are able to take the purse to the owner. The owner, Loretta, and her husband Iggy know Max's father, Killer Kane, and this relationship leads to a whole new series of dangerous adventures.

A third reason not to miss this book is because it is a story of friendship. Freak is the only person that treats Max with respect because he understands Max. Everybody else is afraid of Max because of his size. The reason Freak and Max get along so well is because they are both different from everybody else. Freak is very small and smart, while Max is very large and not so smart. When Freak sits on Max's shoulders they become "Freak the Mighty." They feel invincible. Max and Freak save each other's lives at least once in the book. Freak saves Max by shooting Killer Kane in the eyes with vinegar, and Max saves Freak by carrying him away from the gang.

The Climax

Although there are many exciting points in this book, the climax occurs when Max's father, Killer Kane, is released from prison on parole. Killer Kane comes to where Max sleeps and takes Max out of the basement where he lives with his grandparents. The reason that this was so easily accomplished is that Max lives in the basement away from anyone else in the house. Nobody would have heard Max even if he had put up a struggle. The writer sets this up by suggesting that Max is vulnerable down in the basement and by mentioning how dangerous Max's father is. This creates a lot of tension; the reader can feel real danger coming.

It is easy to identify this incident as the turning point because all things change after this occurs. Max must decide what side he is on. Will he cooperate with his father or will he defy him and risk being killed? After the climax many things are resolved. Killer Kane, who was on parole, is captured by the police and is taken back to jail. Freak unfortunately dies, but leaves Max a note that tells him not to forget the adventures that they had together as Freak the Mighty, and to write them down in a book. Max then becomes a writer, and even though his friend dies, he becomes stronger because of his great memories.

Bibliography

Philbrick, Rodman. *Freak the Mighty*. New York: Scholastic, Inc., 1993.

PAPER 19: "FISHING"

Grade 11: Narrative/Expository

"I'm jumping out," I yelled frantically to my father. It was in response to the flopping northern Pike that was near my feet in our boat. I was six and on my first trip to Canada to fish. It was a totally different fishing experience than I was accustomed to in Pennsylvania. It was not like catching Bluegills in Leaser Lake. Surely I had a right to be scared. The Northern Pike is an extremely mean looking fish with sharp teeth which it uses to kill its prey. Being six, I thought I was on its list of prey. My father responded to my plea by saying, "Go ahead and jump, but there are a hundred more in that water."

Most of my knowledge and love of fishing came from that same man who told me to "Go ahead and jump." Since I can remember, I have always fished. My father probably taught me to fish before I could walk. At first he taught me the basics: tying a swivel to a line, threading the line through the pole, removing hooks from any part of the body that they may enter, how to get a lure out of a tree, why to check the inside of hip boots that have been sitting in the garage all year before putting them on, if the sign says "No Fishing—Violators will be prosecuted," it usually means it, and probably most important, if you have to go to the bathroom while on the boat what to do. Occasionally, he also revealed a hot tip while fishing, such as, "See this lure, son? This one is going to catch the big one. It's only legal in two states and this isn't one of them."

The key to fishing, I was taught, is patience. Obviously, my father has a little of that if he could teach me to fish. There were numerous occasions when I crossed my line with his and caused a "rat's nest," or the several times that I used a lure and forgot to close the tackle box, and when he picked it up, all the lures fell out. One time he really showed his patience when I reached back in the boat to cast, but accidentally hooked onto his hat and threw it into the water. My brother and I laughed hysterically while I reeled it in through the water. Eventually, my father joined in.

Since I was young, there was one aspect of fishing my father heavily emphasized. Fishing is not about the amount of fish you catch, but the amount of fun you have. There were times when we wouldn't catch one fish but would still have a great time. I learned fishing is a time to just be with nature and your thoughts, a time to relax and share good times with friends. Anyone who only cares about catching fish all the time is missing the true meaning. Fishing is like an education. It is a lifelong experience. After high school, you could go to college and get a Bachelor's degree. In fishing, if you graduate from regular fishing, you could go on to ice fishing or maybe deep sea fishing. Then, if you move on to get your Master's degree, maybe you could start fly fishing.

One day, I will be teaching my kids to fish and will probably hear them complain about not catching any fish. I will think for a minute what Pop would say: "The worst day of fishing is better than the best day of work."

PAPER 20. "I WANT TO BE MISS AMERICA"

Grade 12, Expository

I want to be Miss America.

For the last four years of my existence, realistic ideologies have gradually replaced visions of virtuous grandeur I once had. But a suppressed childhood fantasy has suddenly resurfaced. Maybe the resurgence of the beauty queen within results from repeatedly smashing my head against the corn-guilded cage of my ultraconservative rural Pennsylvania home. Or maybe the little girl locked inside of me has raised her voice again and I really would like to parade around a stage, a mortal Venus, angelic blonde hair garnished with a silver tiara. I will have to dye my hair.

I want to stand center stage in Atlantic city and stun the audience with my rendition of Rossini's "Una PoccoVoce" from *Il Barbiere Di Sivilglia* and, if only for a moment, become Rosina, the object of America's adoration. Or perhaps I would become Lady Macbeth (although Ophelia would be more apropos for this occasion), sleepwalking to the stage's proscenium, candle in hand, watching admirers gaze upon me in awe. As long as I flash my vaseline-greased, toothpaste-ad smile and wear a tight-fitting, flashy dress from the most exclusive designer I can afford, no one will notice that my Gs are excessively flat or that the elegance of Shakespeare's Elizabethan tongue has been reduced to base English. Only aesthetic beauty matters anyway.

During the interview segment, I will curb my liberal political views and respond to every superficial question with a strategically planned conservative sentiment. Any feminist-inspired views will be quelled in order to retain an untarnished "feminine" image. My voice will waver with contrived emotion as I enumerate the problems of the world and offer hollow, menial solutions with a fixed, ethereal grin. I will speak about suffering and confict but never mention my interest in Tibetan Buddhism; that would be considered eccentric. Conformity is essential for victory.

I will use my title to change the world, flashing my All-American smile from nation to nation, making guest appearances on "Live With Regis and Kathie Lee." I will sacrifice all of my political and philosophical beliefs to uphold a meaningless platform of neo-conservative morality, concurrent with established societal trends. People will listen to me because I am Miss America.

I can always cling to the hope that a glimmer of myself will survive.

Maybe the world will just have to settle for me without the crown.

SUGGESTED SCORES AND COMMENTS

Following are suggested scores for the papers in Chapter 4. Scores on the 5-point scale are given first, followed by suggested scores on a 6-point scale. Please recall that Papers 7, 13, and 17 were all scored using the informational writing rubric in Chapter 10; these papers resulted from research in which students had time to compile information and make use of resources. Other papers in this chapter were produced spontaneously, without benefit of research, and so are scored using the less formal creative rubric in Chapter 3.

Paper 1. "Chad"
GRADE 3, DESCRIPTIVE

Ideas: 2/3, 3
Organization: 2, 2
Voice: 3, 3
Word Choice: 2, 3
Sentence Fluency: 3, 3
Conventions: 4, 4

Comments

This paper offers pleasant reading, but needs expansion. It has the beginnings of specifics (Chad is five feet tall, has brown hair, and likes the same games and TV shows as the writer), but doesn't yet turn Chad into a unique individual. Voice is present, but not powerful; it isn't a read-aloud piece. Sentences show some variety in length, but many begin with "He." Conventions need *some* work, but then, this is just a third grader, and many things are done well, too. It needs a stronger opening and closing.

Paper 2. "Gun Control"

GRADE 8, PERSUASIVE

    Ideas: 3, 4

    Organization: 3, 3

    Voice: 4, 4

    Word Choice: 3, 4

    Sentence Fluency: 2, 3

    Conventions: 4, 4

Comments

This paper has potential, but it needs both focus and development. The first two sentences are telling: "I am writing about guns because they are in the news"; that does not hold much promise for a personalized paper, rich with voice. Guns are "out of control" and so is the thesis of this paper. It is partly about safety and partly about regulation of the purchase of guns. The issues are connected, granted, but the writer does not connect them for us; we have to do it. The concept of school safety is mentioned, but not developed; same goes for the purchase of guns on the black market. The pop-up ending is unexpected and abrupt to say the least: "Do not forget to clean your gun." This is a big leap from the safety issue. Sentences are choppy and do not always link well one to the other. On the positive side, the writer is impassioned, and states his position strongly, even if it is not as well defended (no pun meant) as we might like. Despite some mildly distracting spelling errors, conventions are fairly strong. In fact, conventions are the strength of the paper.

Paper 3. "The Joke"

GRADE 7, NARRATIVE/EXPOSITORY

    Ideas: 5, 6

    Organization: 5, 5

    Voice: 5, 6

    Word Choice: 4, 5

    Sentence Fluency: 5, 5

    Conventions: 5, 6

Comments
This is a heartfelt, understated piece that makes a good point (love over-comes many traumas of life)—and is an excellent read-aloud for illustrat-ing voice. This student's perception of her grandmother's world is very acute; we especially liked her quick read of her grandmother's face at the end, where she senses both the joy of the moment and the sorrow at her grandmother's loss of memory—and realization of what's happening in the world around her. The writer does a good job building to this mo-ment, with many specific details that let us in; hence the strong scores in organization. The beginning and ending are strong, too. The paper has no real weaknesses; slightly lower scores simply indicate relative strengths.

Paper 4. "A Rescue"

GRADE 4, NARRATIVE
> Ideas: 2, 3
> Organization: 2, 2
> Voice: 4, 4
> Word Choice: 3, 4
> Fluency: 1–2, 2
> Conventions: 2, 3

Comments
Fluency is the big problem here. The writer needs to read this aloud—perhaps more than once—to gain a sense of how breathless a reader can get dealing with unpunctuated text and infinite linked clauses. Also, while the basic idea of visiting the haunted house is clear, it is not clear what happens first and next, whether the cat and monster have different identities (is there really a monster at all?), or what happened to the other friends—who seem to disappear into the fog. The dinner and bed ending is always an option—but no one's favorite. On the bright side, it has mo-ments of voice and effective word choice: some strengths from which to build.

Paper 5. "Why You Need a Job"

GRADE 9, PERSUASIVE
> Ideas 2, 3
> Organization 2, 2
> Voice 3, 4
> Word Choice 3, 4
> Sentence Fluency 3, 4
> Conventions 3, 3

Comments

This paper seems earnest enough, but it needs development through examples or anecdotes. It relies too much on generalities: a job gives you experience, a job teaches you new skills, etc. It is unlikely to convince a high schooler who is not eager to get a job. The student says little to actually disagree with, but instead of crafting an argument, he simply voices an opinion. The beginning is fairly strong, and if the writer focused on the idea of developing responsibility, showing how this could happen, the paper could truly become persuasive. Voice, word choice and fluency are all functional but not powerful. More information is what's needed most.

Paper 6. "A Strange Visiter"

GRADE 5, NARRATIVE

   Ideas: 5, 6
   Organization: 5, 6
   Voice: 5, 5
   Word Choice: 5, 6
   Sentence Fluency: 4/5, 4
   Conventions: 3, 4

Comments

Let's start with the problems because they're minor compared to strengths. The paper needs some work in conventions, though many things are done correctly, and many relatively difficult words are spelled correctly. "The End" is an unfortunate conclusion (picky, picky), but it's a minor annoyance, easily dismissed. The sentences tend toward the short side; a little smoothing would raise this to a 5, 6; notice, too, that many sentences begin with "The." This too is easily fixed once the writer takes notice. On the other hand . . . wow. Extraordinary attention to detail. Mood. Tension. Colors. Sounds. Movement. I feel I'm right there in the castle. Who is this man in royal purple? Why, he's the man I've risked my very life for—the king. Who knew? And they often didn't, you know, in Medieval days, when you couldn't know what the king looked like unless you had met him in person. What a nice touch. "The aroma of wine hung in the air like fog on a dull morning." Mostly one-syllable words. That's why it's strong, not overdone. This writer is *capable* of overdoing it; she shows a lot of restraint. Bravo.

Paper 7. "The Italians in America"

GRADE 10, RESEARCH

   Ideas: 5, 5
   Organization: 4, 5
   Voice: 5, 5
   Word Choice: 5, 6

Sentence Fluency: 5, 6
Conventions: 5, 6

Comments

While the first two paragraphs are nicely done, I think Paragraph 3 is the real beginning of the paper, and much of the up-front material, though important, could be cut. But that's a picky point. This writer covers a very large topic quite concisely and with a large amount of detail. Other strengths are reader-friendly language and strong yet appropriate voice for a research piece. The writer sounds confident, authoritative, knowledgeable and interested in his topic. I don't think we can ask more. We also liked the way the writer shifted gracefully from general information about Italian immigrants to the history of his own family—and without bogging down in *too* much detail, which would have been an easy trap to fall into. Sentences are strong and varied, conventions very strong. I would have liked a snappier beginning and stronger conclusion—though I do agree about the art, ice cream and pizza. A few transitions could use some smoothing out; we go very quickly from the Mafia to Grandma Rosalie to things the Italians have given us. The writer sounds a little rushed at the end, but it holds together. In general, very well done.

Paper 8. "Winter in Maine"

GRADE 5, POETRY
    Ideas: 5/6
    Word Choice: 5/6
    Sentence Fluency: 5/6

Comments

We do not usually score poetry using the 6-trait model since it was designed for prose. But we included this example just to show that poetry has some features to which we can respond, even with this rubric (and perhaps you'll now be inspired to develop your own for poetry!). The high scores in ideas are based on the strong imagery: stew cooking on the stove, the needle gliding, trees looming like skeletons, mom shooing kids up the stairs. Words like *warmth, joyfully, gliding through the fabric, bare skeletons looming, the crash, as icicles fall and smash* and *shooing* contributed to the high scores in word choice. We felt, reading the poem aloud, that it flowed like the stream of events it described. Clearly, conventions are, well, unconventional. And it is organized according to the writer's thoughts, so we did not deal with these traits. I feel the voice is gentle but strong; in poetry, the voice is always very personal—so we did not score this trait, either.

Paper 9. "The Big Road"

GRADE 7, NARRATIVE
    Ideas: 5, 5
    Organization: 4, 5

Voice: 5, 6
Word Choice: 5, 5
Sentence Fluency: 4/5, 5
Conventions: 5, 6

Comments

This is a highly humorous, greatly understated paper—with a fine theme. So many students feel they have nothing to write about; here's a perfect example of an everyday event turned into a delightful personal essay. It is easy to picture every part of this scenario. Great character development through detail: Can't you picture Jessica gathering her necessary paraphernalia for the big trip? Some readers wanted a stronger ending, though personally, I liked it. I read it as veiled sarcasm, and it works for me, but you may agree that the writer's response to the near-miss needs to be clearer. I see him as saying, "I'm calm through it all."

Paper 10. "Family Day"

GRADE 10, NARRATIVE/DESCRIPTIVE

Ideas: 5, 6
Organization: 5, 6
Voice: 5, 6 (7, 8—keep going)
Word Choice: 5, 6
Sentence Fluency: 5, 6
Conventions: 5, 6

Comments

This paper is moving, satisfying, disturbing, provocative, and remarkably rich with detail and voice. It's one of those papers you return to and read more than once. An excellent example of voice without a shred of humor. And it's sustained. This is hard to do—the paper is an achievement. Most remarkable of all the unforgettable details (the bored and bitter guard, the gray and grimy walls, the questions that annoy veteran visitors, the bleak surroundings, the hopeless people waiting) is the scene of mother and father weeping to each other over the grimy prison phone. What thoughtful reader could erase such an image? And the "merciless ultraviolet light." Stunning. We can only hope this writer keeps writing.

Paper 11. "The Car by Gary Paulsen"

GRADE 5, LITERARY ANALYSIS

Ideas: 3, 4
Organization: 3, 3
Voice: 3, 3

Word Choice: 4, 5
Sentence Fluency: 4, 4
Conventions: 5, 6

Comments

This is a paper by a competent writer who sounds pretty bored—or who just doesn't want to take time for true analysis. Mostly, it's a rehash of the book's plot. It's a *good* rehash—but still . . . We do not really find out what it is Terry learns on his journey, and though the idea of being influenced emotionally or mentally by geography is enticing, the writer doesn't carry it far enough to give us an indepth look at this intriguing concept. We have to infer a lot: Does Terry identify with the Native Americans of long ago who once felt free on their land? The ending is a puzzle. Good vocabulary, though. Readable, fluent sentences. Strong conventions.

Paper 12. "A Ball's Eye View"

GRADE 10, EXPOSITORY/NARRATIVE (WRITTEN FOR A PHYSICS CLASS)

Ideas: 5, 6
Organization: 4, 5
Voice: 5, 6
Word Choice: 5, 6
Sentence Fluency: 5, 6
Conventions: 5, 6

Comments

In responding to this piece, it probably helps to know (as we did) that students in a physics class were asked to write a short story in which the laws of physics were demonstrated operating in everyday life. That's how we wind up with a baseball saying things like "I am made of matter and I have inertia." We found the combination of physics and the story of one baseball's brief moment in the sun delightful. The writer explains how force, gravity, and inertia work, all without forcing the story—which is entertaining in its own right. Particular strengths include the use of dialogue, the ball's view of life ("leave it to the pitchers to blame us hard working balls"), and the ending—the old, dead balls who can't respond to their former friend from the factory. It's whimsical, quirky, and different—and we felt it worked well.

Paper 13. "When Are Searches Justified?"

GRADE 10, PERSUASIVE

Ideas: 5/6
Organization: 5/6
Voice: 4/4

Word Choice: 5/5

Sentence Fluency: 5/5

Conventions: 5/6

Comments

This paper is focused, clear, expansive and detailed. It does what we want in good persuasive writing: takes a stand, sticks with it, supports it with evidence and/or examples, and considers the other side to strengthen its own position. All well done. Some readers found it a little dry. I'm not sure that's a fair criticism, given the topic. We wouldn't expect a chipper tone here; it's thoughtful and competent. Personally, I think the voice is appropriate, and would rate it higher than a 4, given purpose and audience. This isn't a murder mystery; it's an examination of a legal issue. The writer handles a fairly technical topic with strong but clear language and explains the difference between probable cause and reasonable suspicion well. Be careful! Your personal views on Mary J. and whether the search *was* justified can prejudice your scores. The question is: Does the writer present the issues clearly and thoroughly?

Paper 14. *"Computing Batting Averages"*

GRADE 6, INFORMATIONAL

Ideas: 4, 4

Organization: 3, 4

Voice: 3, 4

Word Choice: 4, 4

Sentence Fluency: 4, 4

Conventions: 5, 5

Comments

The strength of this paper is clarity. The writer very systematically and carefully explains how to compute batting averages. The explanation is easy to follow and well presented. The beginning and ending rely a bit strongly on generalities: e.g., "Math is all around us" and "You'll be surprised what a big role math plays in your life." A stronger opening and closing would really have put some spark into this little paper. As it is, the voice is pleasant and present. But this is probably not a read-aloud. Excellent conventions.

Paper 15. *"Stop Making Public Figures into Heroes"*

GRADE 12, PERSUASIVE

Ideas: 4/5

Organization: 5/6

Voice: 5/6

Word choice: 5/5

Sentence Fluency: 5/5

Conventions: 5/6

Comments

In our discussion, organization, voice and conventions emerged as the strongest traits, though virtually everything about this paper works. It's concise, crisp and to the point. The writer explains her position very well, though specific examples would have made that position even stronger. Still, I found myself agreeing . . . Voice is *very* strong in this paper; it bites hard and never lets go. No hemming and hawing for this writer: "The days of Tarzan and the Lone Ranger are long gone." This is good and convincing rhetoric. The beginning and ending are very strong—making this argument hard to resist. A future speech writer . . . ?

Paper 16. "Technology: A Force for Good, or Our Downfall?"

GRADE 12, PERSUASIVE

Ideas: 4, 4

Organization: 4, 5

Voice: 4, 5

Word choice: 5, 6

Sentence Fluency: 5, 5

Conventions: 5, 5

Comments

This paper is right on the verge of being superb—but it needs clarification. It is a little difficult yet to sort through the writer's many intriguing ideas and come up with one main thesis. It might be that we are responsible both for our technology and our own morality—and neither can be blamed on the other. Or that technology is neither good nor evil—it's what we do with it that counts. Up through the second paragraph, everything seemed clear; then we got into the "twisted backbone of change" (*very* interesting word choice, but what does it mean?), and the writer lost us. After the Cold War, we're told, we imagined the world would be better if we were machines. I don't recall imagining that. I do identify with the denial part—but the two positions (wishing we were machines and being in denial over what technology can do) seem conflicting. Also, several readers wanted the writer to return to the chat room and explain if or how this *really* causes depression. In short, some portions left us confused, but we loved the topic. A little more thinking, sorting and rewording will transform this very enticing beginning into a powerful paper. In Paragraph 4 this writer *really* finds his/her voice!

Paper 17. "Electric Eels"

GRADE 6, INFORMATIONAL

  Ideas: 3, 4 (only because some points were confusing)
  Organization: 3, 4
  Voice: 3, 4
  Word Choice: 4, 4
  Sentence Fluency: 4, 5
  Conventions: 5, 5

Comments

This is *not* an easy paper to score. There is such an abundance of information here, we tend to get swept away by it. That's both a strength and a problem, really—*too* much to tell. We get overwhelmed. On the other hand, the writer makes some good points: e.g., eels shock us because we frighten them—but they also shock prey. Some information seems out of order; at the end, we go back to general characteristics about eels and how they swim. This might have worked better up front with other descriptive details. Also, some information was a bit encyclopedic and needed amplification: e.g., "Anything nearby fixed or in motion, affects the flow pattern since it conducts electricity differently from water." I can't quite figure out what the writer is telling me here. It's also a little confusing that the writer first tells us about eels in general—then tells us the electric eel is not a true eel. The eel's ability to shock is the most intriguing point in the paper, of course, and we learn some interesting things here; for instance, an eel has enough electricity to knock down a mule or light a small sign—that's good stuff! We need more of that, and less about genus and order. When the writer lets her own voice slip in, the writing improves *instantly*; she's better than the textbook/encyclopedia she's using. If only she knew it.

Paper 18. "Freaking Out"

GRADE 6, LITERARY ANALYSIS

  Ideas: 4, 4
  Organization: 3, 4
  Voice: 4, 4
  Word choice: 5, 5
  Sentence Fluency: 5, 5
  Conventions: 5, 6

Comments

This is a well written paper by a writer who just needed to dig a little deeper. (Compare it to paper #11, "The Car," though, to see how much more literary analysis and less plot summary we get here.) It does a fine job of analyzing the characters of Freak and Max and exploring the nature of their friendship, but never touches on the larger meaning or theme of the book. What is the author's point? The organizational structure seems a little stilted: Introduction, Three Reasons (Why are there always three of everything? It's getting annoying.), and The Climax. This may be the result of the way in which the assignment was set up—but at all events, it lacks a natural flow. Identifying a turning point is a good skill, but it doesn't necessarily make for interesting reading; a more interesting question might be "Why should anyone read this book?" or "Did this book change your opinion/attitude about anything?" Or even, "How did you feel when Freak died? Would you have ended the book differently?" Responding to questions someone else thinks up for us sometimes kills voice, and it seems to have held this student in check a bit. He writes with ease, though—and when allowed to structure his own thoughts, will write with real style.

Paper 19: "Fishing"

GRADE 11: NARRATIVE/EXPOSITORY

Ideas: 5, 6

Organization: 5, 6

Voice: 5, 6 (7, really)

Word Choice: 4, 4

Sentence Fluency: 5, 6

Conventions: 5, 6

Comments

Fly fishing as a Master's degree? Beautiful. That's ingenious. There is so much to love about this paper—where to begin? Images of Dad teaching, coaching—the wonderful tip about the illegal lure that catches the big one. We know all about Dad after that revelation, and it only took a couple of lines! The beginning and ending are trophy winners. Well done. This paper tells *just* enough—not all, but enough to make us feel relaxed, at home, nostalgic, and part of the writer's world. Nothing's really wrong with the word choice, but by comparison, it didn't sparkle quite so much as the other traits.

Paper 20. "I Want to be Miss America"

GRADE 12, EXPOSITORY

Ideas: 5, 6

Organization: 5, 6

Voice: 5, 6

Word Choice: 5, 6

Sentence Fluency: 5, 6

Conventions: 5, 6

Comments

The word choice in this paper is dazzling. It's impressive, but totally natural. The voice is spunky, sophisticated beyond the writer's age, informed, insightful, and cynical. The premise is intriguing; you cannot be yourself and be the embodiment of what America is about. The irony there is delicious. And this writer handles it with such style, going back and forth between the childhood dream and the awakening consciousness of someone who takes a close-up look at society. It's a no-holds-barred indictment of the shallowness of beauty pageants—and if you do *not* subscribe to this view, it may be hard to score the paper objectively. On the other hand, it's also hard to be objective if you *do* agree; you may find yourself saying, Yes! Yes! To clear my own head, I read the paper several times, and yes, it has attitude, but . . . it's darn good. This is truly fine writing.

REFLECTING ON CHAPTER 4

1. Did you agree with the suggested scores? If you did not, do you see any patterns? For example, were you consistently lower in voice—or conventions? If so, you might have another look at the scoring guide(s) to see if it's you, the guide—or our scores!

2. It's pretty clear from our comments that we had favorite papers in this group. Which were your favorites? Why do you think that is?

3. Were you able to judge voice differently in expository/informational pieces? If not, you might look again at the way voice is defined in the informational scoring guide.

ACTIVITIES

1. Consider any "missing pieces" or wording within the scoring guide(s) that did not quite work for you. With the help of colleagues, and using sample papers to guide your thinking, make changes in the scoring guides to help them serve you better.

2. Keep in mind that you do not always need to read or score a whole paper to make a point. Choose one trait—say ideas or word choice—and see if you can come up with two or three short examples (not whole papers) from this collection that you could use with students to illustrate strengths and weaknesses in this trait.

LOOKING AHEAD

In Chapter 5, we will consider other ways—in addition to sharing writing samples—that you can use the 6-trait model to strengthen students' writing in the classroom.

5

WHAT YOU CAN ASSESS YOU CAN REVISE

Assessment is not the private property of teachers. Kids can learn to evaluate their own writing. They must take part in this . . . it is central to the growth of writing. Even before they write, they need to know about what makes writing strong or effective. And they need to know the criteria by which their own writing will be judged.

Marjorie Frank (1995, 175)

All [the] studies show that innovations that include strengthening the practice of formative assessment produce significant and often substantial learning gains.
Paul Black and Dylan Wiliam (1998)

LINKING ASSESSMENT TO INSTRUCTION

Ask any teacher what is the most difficult part of the writing process to teach, and 999 out of 1,000 will say "revision." Without hesitation. This is why assessment is so powerful in the classroom—and why we should bother teaching it to students. *What you can assess, you can revise.*

The reason we so often fail to see the link between assessment and instruction is that we have been conditioned to connect assessment with grading, and to see it as coming at the *end* of the writing process, where it is least powerful. This approach puts all the power in teachers' hands, for power is grade-related. Suppose for a moment, that students were the first and *primary* assessors of their own work, and that they did this assessing early in the writing process, while there was still time for change—before a grade signaled the end of the writing (It's a rare student who will even look at the work again once the final grade is assigned). They would assess their own work *prior* to revision (this is key), not to grade themselves, but to lay a foundation for that revision.

Now we're getting into the spirit of what assessment should be about. Consider this: the word *assessment* comes from a Latin word *assidere*, meaning roughly "to sit beside." The implication is that assessment should be a support piece, a friendly sort of complement to writing, and often it is the thing students fear most. Putting assessment power into their hands can lessen their fear by increasing their control.

CONNECTING TRAITS TO WRITING PROCESS

The writing process approach to instruction has been with us long enough to make some teachers wonder why process alone does not have more impact on students' writing. The chief misconception, I think, is that process writing, rather than a personal path invented by each writer, is a step-by-step automatic recipe for writing. Follow these steps and out come the cookies (i.e., essays). But we cannot just plug students into the writing process (prewrite on Monday, draft on Tuesday, etc.) and hope for dazzling manuscripts by Friday. It's not that simple. It is not enough to just list the steps within the writing process and describe them to students, either. If we do not *model* those steps, students do not really understand what to do.

Further, writing process is not linear. "Well, of course it's not," you're saying, "I've seen the diagrams." I know writing process is usually diagrammed as a circle (see Figure 5.1), but while the concept is *visually* circular, I would suggest that in our minds it's still *conceptually* linear; by which I

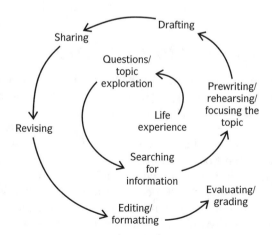

FIGURE 5.1. Generic model of the writing process spiral

mean that we tend to envision the steps as occurring independently, one neatly following the other. Actually, writing doesn't work like that at all, and the more we ourselves write, the more we understand this. I would describe the process—speaking as a writer, not a teacher—as a series of interactive, recursive phases, in which various stages of writing build upon one another. These phases are never exclusive; it is all but impossible to do just one "step" in the writing process (such as prewriting, for instance) while ignoring all others. The phases—prewriting/rehearsing/gathering information, drafting, sharing, revising, editing and publishing (or making your writing public in some way)—are all interdependent and overlapping, more like a scaffold in which you move to a newer, higher step all the while pulling along all the best from all preceding steps (see Figure 5.2).

Author Louis Sachar (*Holes*) says that he rarely revises any piece fewer than five or six times, and that along about draft #3 he can begin to really sense and feel where he wants to take the writing (Florida Reading Association Conference, Orlando, October 16, 1999). This means that he repeats the "drafting/revising" portion of the process several times, and also that even as he "completes" each draft, he is already revising it in his head (maybe on paper, too)—and still prewriting as well, for he is continuing to gather new information. "Sharing," for this author, does not occur until after draft #6; that's the first time, according to Sachar, that his editor, or *anyone* other than himself and his dogs ("who cannot read, anyway"), sees what he has written.

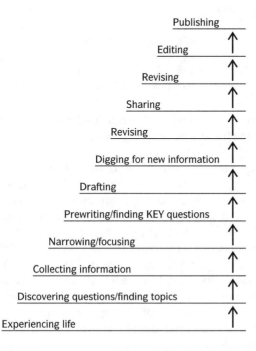

FIGURE 5.2. Writing process scaffold—each step builds on the one before

It's Still New in Our Minds

Many of us learned about the process approach to writing as teachers, not as students; so it's hardly surprising that we're continuing to unravel its mysteries. Initially, the process approach to writing was an attempt to capture more closely in writing instruction the things that writers *do*—as well as to escape the traditional, more structured approach that many of us over 40 grew up with: "For Monday, write five hundred words on an unforgettable experience." What happened between the Friday assignment and the Monday turning in of the papers certainly was not observed or supervised, let alone coached. The most frequent piece of advice to us: "Remember to check your spelling."

Teachers of decades past focused so heavily on the final product (and on the conventions within that product) that they scarcely concerned themselves at all with the "how" of producing it, nor did they teach anything like a step by step writing process, much less model it. How could they? Few were writers themselves, and trying to teach what you do not do is bound to be challenging.

As student writers, we felt stumped and bewildered. Mostly because we did not know exactly what the teacher wanted—nor did we always identify with the topics assigned. In *'Tis*, author Frank McCourt talks about the fear that gripped him when asked to write about a favorite object from his childhood. In McCourt's impoverished experience, treasured objects did not exist. His family had a tiny allotment of space—a little food on the good days:

> *I can't think of anything like the things other students talk about, the family car, Dad's old baseball mitt, the sled they had so much fun with, the old icebox, the kitchen table where they did their homework. All I can think of is the bed I shared with my three brothers and even though I'm ashamed of it, I have to write about it. (172)*

Like McCourt, we often felt on the outside looking in, feeling the stress of "putting on" someone else's topic that seemed to us fit as badly as second-hand shoes.

A few of our papers were labored over from Friday right through Sunday—but many were written against the locker door just before the bell rang. We usually met the requirements of the assignment because over the years we'd learned some writers' survival tricks: make it neat, type it if possible (a process that looks as primitive to today's students as chiseling on stone), use words from the weekly vocab list, repeat the language of the assignment (in several ways, if you can), use words the teacher uses in class (for one of my teachers, ideas were forever "gelling," so they gelled in my essays, too), and insert long quotations. We wrote to get by and to get done. We wrote for grades. Only occasionally did we produce something we cared deeply about, something we would have felt proud to read aloud.

A New Way of Seeing Writing

In the early 1970s, huge shifts occurred. Janet Emig, Donald Murray, Donald Graves, and then Lucy Calkins, Nancie Atwell and many others revolutionized the way we teach writing with their research on writing process. Because these people were writers themselves, they knew firsthand that writing was not so simple as thinking up ideas and then writing them down; they also saw through the phoniness of outlining and ridiculously rigid rules like having precisely 100 note cards for your report on Brazil.

From their own experience and from years of research in which they took time to observe what successful writers actually *do* when they write, they learned (and taught us) that in any strong writing, prewriting (or rehearsing) and revision are key. Writers spend lots of upfront (prewriting) time, defining a topic, collecting information, sorting and discarding, and whittling away at the whole until a main point takes shape first in their minds and then on paper. They also spend reflective (revision) time, rereading what they've written, both to themselves and to others, leaving it alone for awhile and then returning to rework it like a clay sculpture.

Drafting—which had for most of us been the biggest part of writing during our school years—seemed to diminish as we began to recognize the power of gathering information and getting our thoughts together (prewriting), then rewriting (revision). For me, it was like looking at a bookshelf and watching the books themselves shrink as the bookends (prewriting and revision) grew bigger and bigger.

Student writers often do not realize how important good information is to good writing. If you've done your research (whether it's reading or personal experience), drafting is relatively easy; if you have not, it's all but impossible. Further, seeking good information isn't just for research writing; it's also for fiction. Think of a student writing about an interplanetary trek to Mars. How much more interesting her story will be if details about color, temperature, size of the planet, surface features, atmosphere, and gravity are based on accurate data.

In his masterpiece *A Writer Teaches Writing* (1985), Donald Murray also explains that there is no *one* writing process (4), but that it is different for each writer—and can even change with content, since writing a novel is not the same as dashing off a birthday note to a friend or responding to a prompt in a state writing assessment. He adds that "the writer passes through the process once, or many times, emphasizing different stages during each passage." Moreover, once we gain a sort of writing frame of mind, he tells us, we are *always* writing: "The most important writing takes place before there is writing—at least what we usually think of as writing: the production of a running draft. Writers write before they write" (17). Next time you are running through ideas in the shower or in the car while stalled in traffic, realize that you are in fact "writing," and that your thinking is more important than moving pencil over paper or attacking the keyboard.

This cannot be stated bluntly enough: The writer must have something to say. . . . It doesn't matter if a writer begins it cleverly or ends it neatly, organizes it smoothly, writes it dramatically, writes it with voice. The "it" itself has to have merit.

Ralph Fletcher (1993)

Many students have the misconception that writers write with words, language detached from information. They think that words are pretty balloons filled with air. But writing that is read has words that are firmly anchored to meaning.

Donald M. Murray (1984)

LAYING THE FOUNDATION FOR TRAITS

Make Writing Process Foundational

Writing process lays an important foundation for using traits in any program of writing instruction. The traits do *not ever* replace this process, and this point is critical. Writing traits simply provide a language to strengthen the process foundation and give students possibilities for revision.

So when you're thinking, "How do I fit all this into my curriculum? Now I have process *and* traits *and* modes (forms) of writing. Help! It's all so confusing!" remember this: Process comes *first*. Traits enhance process. Traits also help students understand modes or forms of writing, which are mostly about *purpose* (and audience).

The first five traits—idea development, organization, voice, word choice, and sentence fluency—primarily support *revision*. Conventions, of course, primarily support *editing*, though editing also incorporates elements of word choice (e.g., replacing a misused word) and sentence fluency (e.g., ensuring that subject and verb agree).

Process First, then Traits, then Modes

Begin with process. Students need to understand the components of prewriting, drafting, revision and editing before they can make good use of trait language. Remember, the six traits are not an approach to writing in and of themselves. Rather, they are language used to describe good writing, and as such, they *mainly* support revision. So, teach process first, *then* traits. *Then* modes (see Figure 5.3). Modes—or forms—of writing come last because the traits vary across modes. Consider how different the introduction to an Edgar Allan Poe mystery is from the introduction to a business letter. Consider how they differ also in voice, in word choice—even conventions. See how much more sense it makes to talk about these variations once you know the traits? In fact, understanding traits helps students understand how and why forms of writing differ. It also gives them a language to describe such differences.

Now let's consider six ideas for making the writing process foundation as strong as it can be. Each one will help you build a bridge to the traits.

Idea 1: Recognize the Importance of Questions

Though "living" rarely appears as a step in writing process diagrams, life itself is the natural precursor to more formal prewriting. Out of our personal experience come our ideas for writing, our sense of what is important, and our natural impulse to write what we know best. In *Winterdance*, Gary Paulsen writes of the Iditarod, the stillness of the Alaskan northlands, the beauty of the Aurora Borealis, and his near-death experiences from freezing and being attacked by an enraged moose. In *Travels*, Michael Crichton writes of his

1. Process: The Foundation
   - Gathering
   - Focusing
   - Prewriting
   - Drafting
   - Revising
   - Editing/publishing

2. Traits: The Writer's Language
   - Ideas and details
   - Organization
   - Voice
   - Word choice
   - Fluency
   - Conventions

3. Modes: Forms of Writing:
   What is my purpose?
   Who is my audience?
   Notice how traits shift in—
   - Descriptive writing
   - Narrative writing
   - Informational writing
   - Technical writing
   - Business writing
   - Persuasive writing

FIGURE 5.3. Process, Traits, Modes: What to teach first

personal challenges in completing medical school: how he nearly fainted drawing blood and had to hang his head out the window to keep from passing out in front of his patients, and how his hands shook when he dissected his first cadaver.

If we are writers ourselves, we know how important it is for writers to identify the topics that are important in their own lives. "Children who are fed topics, story starters, lead sentences, even opening paragraphs as a steady diet for three or four years," says Donald Graves (1983), "rightfully panic when topics have to come from them. The anxiety is not unlike that of the child whose mother has just turned off the television set. 'Now what do I do?' bellows the child" (p. 21).

On the other hand, identifying writing topics is *very* challenging, and takes practice. We must model this for our students, not just once, but repeatedly, helping them become comfortable with the process. Otherwise, they will remain dependent on us to choose topics for them—topics they find convenient but often uninspiring. Then we get "Redwoods."

Writing often begins with questions, so keep a running list yourself, share them with students, and encourage them to keep a list, too. When I visit classrooms, I frequently share my current list of writing questions with students, questions I can draw upon for essays, stories or poems, and I invite them to ask questions *about* my questions—because this extends my thinking and also lets me know what an audience might find interesting. Here are some of my current writer's questions:

- Why do I still dream about one of my grade school teachers? (More about her in a later chapter.)
- What will happen to Barney?
- How is Suki doing these days?

Students want to know what I think about the teacher, who she was and what she was like; they want to know who Barney is and why I'm concerned for him; and finally, they want to know who Suki is and what role she played in my life. The grade school teacher was a giant of a woman who terrorized me—and all of us; Barney is a scruffy but loveable dog in my neighborhood who has taken up the odd habit of sleeping in the middle of the road; and Suki was my beloved Persian cat, given to another owner because our traveling schedules made it too hard to keep her—I still am haunted by her sudden and sad departure.

Important as these topics are to me, none of them is particularly newsworthy. Diane Sawyer won't be coming to interview me. So what? Students need to know that little topics, personal topics, make the best writing. As Barry Lane (1999) says, "Write small." Don't write about how horrible the holocaust was; describe a mound of children's shoes. Don't write about how annoying your brother is; describe your irritation when you enter the shower and find hair on the soap. Think small. Think *questions*. What is in your mind today? Write down three or four writer's questions *right now*. Share them later with your study group or your students—or both. Write more tomorrow and the next day. Never stop.

Idea 2: *Provide a Range of Prewriting Strategies*

Prewriting techniques are as varied as the writers who use them, so we do well to give our students a wide range of strategies. Many writers like webbing (see Figure 5.4), and though it does not work well for me, I think it's important to teach it and model it because it does work well for many writers. I love lists of potential readers' questions, and will often elicit these from a class of students if given the opportunity (see Figure 5.5). This is my favorite prewriting technique because it inevitably gets me going. I like teaching it because it's a way in for many writers to whom webbing does not come naturally. Some writers find drafting itself a good prewriting technique. "It gets the garbage out," one teacher told me. "You find your paper really begins on page 3, but you had to write through all that junk on pages 1 and 2 to get there."

Other prewriting techniques could include drawing a picture or time line or diagram, talking, interviewing, reading, viewing a film, browsing through the Internet, or just looking out the window. Many writers talk to themselves or role-play the part of a character. Recently I did a sketch of my grandmother, an incredibly feisty woman who scratched her way through the North Dakota drought of the 1930s. My prewriting activity for that piece was poking through old family albums to see what stories her clear gray eyes and deeply lined face would tell me. You'll read about her and her legendary cat Snooky in Chapter 8.

Much of the bad writing we read from inexperienced writers is the direct result of writing before they are ready to write.
Donald M. Murray (1985, 17)

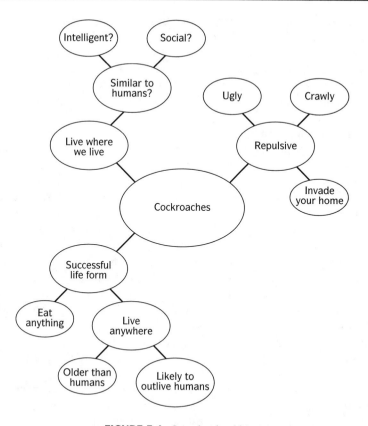

FIGURE 5.4. Sample of webbing

Idea 3: Make Drafting Less Rigid

The key to drafting is to *keep writing.* Writing is generative. The hardest line to write is the first one. I begin with the most startling thing I know about my topic: "It took me years to understand that my grandmother had in her the potential to be a killer—not just of rattlesnakes, but of pesky neighborhood dogs as well" Now the next line is easier: "Living through the Dust Bowl era can do that to a person." And this line makes the next one and the

<u>Cockroaches</u>

1. How long have cockroaches been on earth?
2. Why are cockroaches so successful?
3. Can cockroaches "think"? Are they intelligent?
4. Can anything exterminate the cockroach?
5. How big do cockroaches get?
6. Will cockroaches likely outlive the human species?

FIGURE 5.5. Potential readers' questions

next come to me: "I would never have guessed it looking at her kindly gray eyes or watching her bake the cinnamon rolls that made her famous in a small way throughout her home town. It was listening to her stories. I listened. And then I began to see the hardness that has to emerge when you do not have enough to eat and must feed your children cake for dinner, and when the relentless dust claims what little you have before you can get it into your mouth."

Drafting is more than keeping on keeping on, though. It needs to be free. It is important, for instance, not to get too locked into an outline. Remember how quickly we learned in grade school to write first, *then* outline, so we would seem to follow our outlines precisely, as the teacher had told us we must? Rarely—except perhaps when doing a technical manual, recipe, or other step-by-step sort of writing—does a writer know where the trail will lead when he/she begins. It is important to have the mental freedom to follow an unexpected impulse. A good way to model this is to write on the overhead in front of students. See Figure 5.6 for the opening of a rough draft I composed on the overhead about a night my airline flight was delayed and I was stranded at a motel. I modeled this for a group of teacher/writers, who had chosen the topic for me. We brainstormed a list of potential topics from things they would like me to write about, and from their list I chose "Rough Travels" because the memory of being stranded sans toothbrush, hair dryer, or pajamas was fresh in my mind and the writing came easily.

Another secret to drafting is to find the right balance between quick writing and revising. Nearly all the books on writing process say we should get our ideas down quickly and NOT revise or edit *anything* as we go. But I find this to be just another of those highly restrictive "rules" (almost like the 100 note card rule) that's almost impossible to follow. I don't try to make everything just right, mind you; I know that's not only hopeless in a first draft, but impractical, as well. I *do* write quickly. I *do* push myself. But if I notice something or have a better idea of how to say it, I will write my thoughts down *right then* before they fade away. If I do not, then later, on "revision day," they'll be gone like the morning mist.

Idea 4: Use Sharing to Make Coaches of Your Student Writers

For many writers, sharing is the most difficult part of the whole process. Most of us probably felt this way in middle and high school, when we were writing not for an audience but for a grade. We did not always love what we wrote. We mumbled, looked down at our shoes, spoke too softly to be heard, rushed, and never used any inflection because that might have implied we felt our own writing was worth sharing.

Over time, however, a writer's need for an audience grows. Sharing becomes meaningful then because it's linked to revision. When we no longer write for a grade, our writing begins to seriously improve. Your students

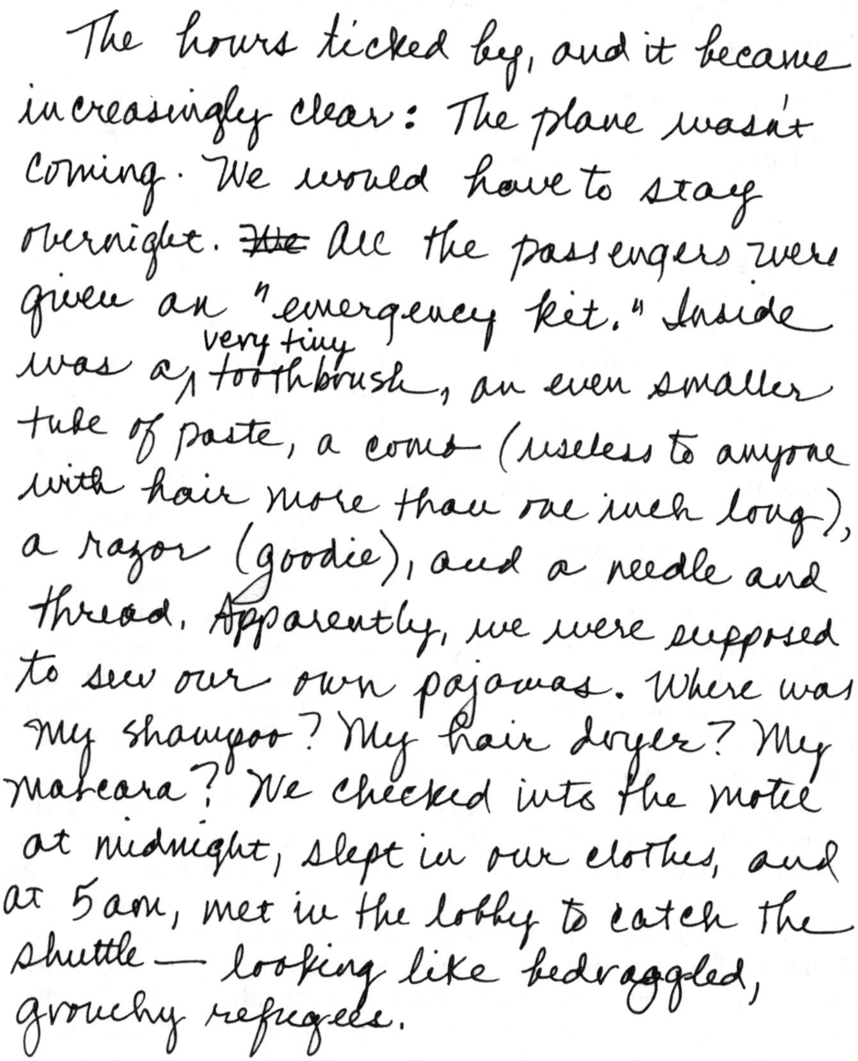

The hours ticked by, and it became increasingly clear: The plane wasn't coming. We would have to stay overnight. ~~The~~ All the passengers were given an "emergency kit." Inside was a very tiny toothbrush, an even smaller tube of paste, a comb (useless to anyone with hair more than one inch long), a razor (goodie), and a needle and thread. Apparently, we were supposed to sew our own pajamas. Where was my shampoo? My hair dryer? My mascara? We checked into the motel at midnight, slept in our clothes, and at 5 am, met in the lobby to catch the shuttle — looking like bedraggled, grouchy refugees.

FIGURE 5.6. Rough draft of "Rough Travels"

will learn to share by watching you model it. Share your writing with them *throughout the process.* Do more than just read drafts. Show them how you pick a topic, how you begin, where you go next. Write in front of them, make mistakes, overwrite, omit details, goof up. Write some junk. When you get stuck, ask for their help. Read your writing aloud, with confidence, but with an open mind. Invite suggestions for revision. Show the next draft so your students can see how or whether you used any of their suggestions. This thinking and coaching is as important to their becoming writers as actual writing practice.

One of the main weaknesses in student writing comes from students' tendency to think of writing only as "performing for a verdict" rather than "trying to communicate with actual readers." For students to find out what their words actually did to readers—even if we think some of those readers have the "wrong reactions"—often leads to a remarkable gain in skill.

Peter Elbow (1986)

Idea 5: Make Sure Students Distinguish Between Revision and Editing

If revising and editing are clearly separated in their minds, students are less likely to kid themselves that they have revised when they have only re-copied or corrected the spelling.

REVISION

Revision is that part of the writing process that truly allows a writer to "see again," to "re-vision" what she has written. Revising involves expanding or clarifying ideas, discovering new connections, deleting trivial or irrelevant information, reordering sections, condensing, ending things in a whole new way, gaining a clearer sense of audience, changing your voice—and more. It is big, bold, and sweeping. It could involve hacking out whole paragraphs or even starting over. Like remodeling a house, it changes the look and feel of the whole. When I teach this to students, I tell them, "Revision is knocking out a wall to make the room bigger, vaulting the ceiling, putting in a new bank of windows and changing the carpeting from dark paisley rose to soft cream plush. Editing is dusting the furniture, putting flowers on the table, dimming the lights, and turning on some music." Editing, in short, is touching up; revision is rethinking the whole project. Students who know and have worked with the six traits can make big changes in their writing; they can say, "My voice is strong, but the organization needs work," or "I have flawless conventions, but this argument isn't very convincing."

It's a mistake, of course, to insist that *everything* be revised. Or published, for that matter. Some classrooms are in a veritable publication frenzy these days. Why? To what end? I doubt the writing assessment gurus *ever* meant for this to happen, but we are inexplicably guilt ridden if we leave a single step out of the process. Stop. Stop right now and think. Would you wish to begin today a regimen of having to publish *everything* you write for the next year? How stressful! I sympathize fully when Mem Fox (1993) declares, "It depresses me utterly to see children being forced to finish a piece of writing when they're sick of it, lacking in inspiration, and getting negative feedback in writing conferences. No one forces me to finish my writing, and I'm a published writer, so why should any writer be ruled in such a manner by someone who doesn't own the writing anyway?" (p. 39). Do not revise everything. Do not publish or assess everything. Toss this burden away like a big rock you just discovered sitting on your left shoulder. Let students' *desire* to publish, plus your own common sense, guide your publication schedule.

EDITING

Compared to revision, editing is small. Editing is trimming, tidying, and polishing. It involves correcting spelling, punctuation, or grammar, deciding issues of formality (contractions or not?), considering usage and idioms,

Few of us express ourselves well in a first draft. When we revise that early confusion into something clearer, we understand our ideas better. And when we understand our ideas better, we express them more clearly, and when we express them more clearly, we understand them better. . . . and so it goes until we run out of energy, interest, or time.

Joseph M. Williams (1994)

You just can't force romance. If an assignment is dying . . . bury it!

Marjorie Frank (1998, 106)

and ensuring that sentences are well built, that parentheses come in pairs, that colons do not follow verbs, and that paragraphs begin where they should.

The main thing to remember in teaching editing is to model it, to clarify procedures, to practice editing strategies frequently (daily, if possible), but NOT to do it *for* students. Allow students to be their own editors. Few teachers would consider writing rough drafts for students—you know, just to get them off to a good start. Yet these same teachers will spend hours editing for students, to be certain all is done correctly. I understand the syndrome. When my teenage son doesn't clean his room to suit me, I eventually do it myself. I'm not proud of this, but it's ingrained, and I recognize the truth: ultimately, I care more about having the room neat than about improving my son's cleaning skills—for now, anyhow. Such out of balance priorities make a poor basis for teaching editing or housekeeping.

As with revision, do not insist that students edit everything they write. There are important—even critical—times to edit, and, realistically, there are times when editing is as unimportant as dusting every piece of furniture in your house every single day. When we insist on compulsive behavior, we get what we ask for: students who, to survive, will keep their text short, simple, and barren of meaning.

In Chapter 7, we will look closely at ideas for teaching editing effectively, for it is becoming a major concern in districts across the country. For now, think about this: Editing is *not* writing. It is a skill onto itself, just as diving is different from swimming. Yet it influences how people look at our writing. And so we as teachers must help our students to put on their best editorial faces.

> Too many of us now approach a blank page not as an occasion for discovery, but as a minefield to be traversed gingerly. We inch our way from word to word, concerned less with clarity and precision than with sheer survival.
>
> Joseph M. Williams (1994)

Idea 6: Make Self-Reflection a Major Priority

Remember the student paper entitled "Writing Is Important" from Chapter 3? In assessing her own writing, what if that student could say to herself, "I have important things to say—dig for information, write what you know, have the courage to say what you truly think—but I need to put things in order. I have to say more about writing with courage. I only wrote one line on that. If I took my own advice, my writing might have more voice. I'm trying too hard to sound academic." Think how powerful her revision would then be.

This is our goal: Students who can not only assess their work, but use that assessment to reflect on their progress as writers, and eventually, manage their whole writing process by setting goals for themselves, building on strengths and tackling problems.

With writing process as our foundation, let's look at specific strategies for teaching traits. In this chapter, I want to focus on five key steps; in Chapter 6, we'll look at the teaching of focused revision, a broader, more advanced way of expanding trait-based instruction.

> Cambridge University undergraduates, who ought to be pretty well qualified, [were asked] to read some poems and tell what they meant and whether they were any good. But [researchers] didn't give them the names of the poets—and without that information, the students had no idea which poems were good and which were bad.
>
> Howard Gardner in Ron Brandt (1993)

SIX KEYS TO TEACHING TRAITS

Teaching traits to students, and teaching them to use this knowledge in the self-assessment part of the writing process, is not complex. It involves six key steps, each of which we will explore in depth. They are to

1. Take time to introduce the concept of traits—and the traits themselves
2. Surround students with writers' language
3. Teach students to be assessors of their own and others' work and to use their self-assessment in revising and setting goals
4. Use written works to illustrate strengths and weaknesses in writing
5. Use focused lessons—including practice revision—to help students develop skills in each trait
6. Teach students to do focused revision

(As noted earlier, we'll begin with the first five on this list; Chapter 6 will deal with focused revision, an advanced step that bridges the gap between assessing writing and actually revising it.)

Relax—You're Already Doing It

If you are teaching writing now, you will likely find you are already teaching traits. This is all but unavoidable because the six traits, as we've pointed out, are not new. They're just the same old characteristics of good writing that have been with us since writing first appeared on Earth. What this means, though, is that you will NOT—oh, happy day—need to make big adjustments to your curriculum or add new components or complicate your life. What you may find yourself doing is *talking* about writing a little differently.

Ask yourself these questions. Do you teach students to

1. Focus on a central idea, theme, argument, or story line? Use detail to add interest or to expand or support main points? You're teaching *ideas*.
2. Write killer leads, put things in a pattern or order that makes sense, use transitional (linking) words or phrases to tie ideas together, or bring things to resolution with a solid conclusion? You're teaching *organization*.
3. Consider the informational needs or interests of an audience, let their enthusiasm for a topic show, project their own individual perspectives through writing, make the tone match both purpose and audience so poems do not sound like complaint letters—or vice versa? You're teaching *voice*.
4. Use strong verbs and precise nouns, avoid jargon and redundancy, and resist the temptation to drown readers in modifiers; write to inform, not to impress; and find new ways to say things? You're teaching *word choice*.

5. Vary sentence beginnings, alternate long and short sentences, get rid of the deadwood in business or informational writing? Read their own writing aloud to make sure it makes sense? You're teaching *fluency*.

6. Edit and proofread, check their spelling, punctuation, capitalization, paragraphing, and grammar? Practice editing on the text of others? Use copy editors' symbols? You're teaching *conventions*.

Each time you answered yes, know that you are *already* making trait-based instruction part of your curriculum.

As one teacher told me, "I never knew what that something was that I was responding to so strongly in students' writing. Now I have a name for it—*voice*. It's so much easier to teach something when you know what to call it."

Here, then, are the five of the six *basic* steps for teaching traits (Step 6 to follow in the next chapter).

Step 1: Introduce the Concept of Traits—and the Traits Themselves

WHAT'S A TRAIT?

It wouldn't make sense to simply come into the classroom one day and say, "OK, so the first trait we'll discuss will be *ideas*." First, students need to know what a trait is. It may help to take the whole thing out of an academic context. Explain that traits are nothing more than features—or characteristics. You could ask students to brainstorm, for instance, the traits of a good sandwich or a good film, just to give them the idea. Then, it's time to move the discussion to writing.

At this point, you *could* just list the traits. Here's trait one, *Ideas* . . . now, here's trait two, *Organization*. . . . pretty boring, no? The idea is to get students themselves to name the traits, to pull it out of their own thinking. One way to do this is by asking what your *students* see as the traits of good writing. You may get some very intriguing answers. Figure 5.7 shows the responses I got from a group of elementary students to whom I posed this question.

Do you see a pattern here? *Very* heavy emphasis on conventions. But perhaps this is what these students felt was important in getting a good grade; perhaps this is what they had been rewarded for. Now, of course, we *do* want our student writers to think that good spelling is important and that punctuation matters. These things are critical, but writing is very big. We want their vision of good writing to be big, too. How do we make it happen?

One way is to share samples of writing and ask for their responses. We might begin with the two papers contrasted in Chapter 3, "Redwoods" and "Mouse Alert." I did this, but over the next three weeks or so, also shared writing from other writers, including Sandra Cisneros, Shel Silverstein, Roald Dahl, Gary Paulsen, Louis Sachar, E.B. White, and others. I also asked

FIGURE 5.7. The important qualities of good writing, Version 1

students to bring in pieces by their favorite writers. And in addition, I shared some writing—some of it my own—that I did not consider to be very good. I wanted them to hear both sides.

As students began to see and hear writing differently, their vision expanded. They began to make the kinds of comments recorded in Figure 5.8. Notice that the students are not simply adding more characteristics to their original list; their whole way of thinking about writing has changed, broadened.

This will happen with your students, too—or perhaps you'll be very lucky and get responses more like those in Figure 5.8 in the first place. Either way, now is a good time to share the six-trait scoring guide—but with an important difference. We want a version that will speak to students in their own language, a real guide that will coach them along when their work needs revision. We call it the *6-Trait Scoring Guide for Students*. This one is based on the teachers' scoring guide introduced in Chapter 3, but is written with students in mind. It features

- simpler language and phrasing;
- a first-person perspective; and
- a positive approach to help students see scores of 1 or 2 as beginning points, not points of failure.

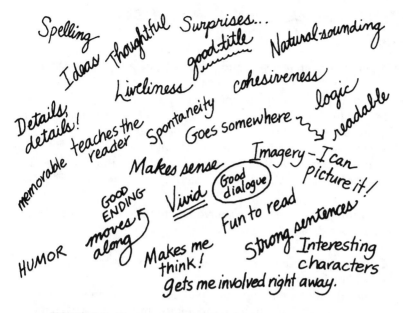

FIGURE 5.8. The important qualities of good writing, Version 2

We recommend that you make a copy for each student, and perhaps for parents, as well.

6-TRAIT SCORING GUIDE FOR STUDENTS

Ideas

5. My paper is clear, focused, and filled with details not everybody knows.

- You can tell I know a lot about this topic.
- My writing is full of interesting tidbits, but it doesn't overwhelm you.
- I can sum up my main point in one clear sentence: _____.
- When you start reading, you *won't* want to stop.
- You can picture what I'm talking about. I *show* things happening (*Fred squinted*); I don't just *tell* about them (*Fred couldn't read the small print*).

3. Even though my writing grabs your attention here and there, it could use some spicy details.

- I know *just* enough to write about this topic—but more information would make it more interesting.
- Some "details" are things most people probably already know.
- My topic is too big. I'm trying to tell too much. Or else it's too skimpy.
- It might be hard to picture what I'm talking about.
- I'm afraid my reader will get bored and go raid the refrigerator.

1. I'm still figuring out what I want to say.

- I need a LOT more information before I'm really ready to write.
- I'm still thinking on paper. What's my main idea? Beats me.
- I'm not sure *anyone* reading this could picture *anything*.
- I wouldn't want to share this aloud. It's not ready.
- Could I sum it up in one clear sentence? No way! It's just a list of stuff.

Organization

5. My paper is as clear as a good road map. It takes readers by the hand and guides them along every step.

- My beginning hints at what's coming, and makes you want to read on.
- Every detail falls in just the right place. Nothing seems out of order.
- You never feel lost; however, there could be a surprise or two.
- Everything connects to my main point or the main story.
- My paper ends at just the right spot, and ties everything together.

3. You can begin to see where I'm headed. If you pay attention, you can follow along pretty well.

- I have a beginning. Will my reader be hooked, though?
- Most things fit where I have put them. I might move *some* things around.
- Usually, you can see how one idea links to another.
- I guess everything should lead up to the most important part. Let's see, *where* would that *be?*
- My paper has an ending. But does it tie things together for the reader?

1. Where are we headed? I'm lost myself.

- A beginning? Well, I might have just repeated the assignment . . . .
- I never knew what to say next, so I wrote the first thing that came to me.
- I'm not really sure which things to include—or what order to put them in.
- Things are just piled together—like in a messy closet!
- An ending? I just stopped when I ran out of things to say.

Voice

5. I have put my personal, recognizable stamp on this paper.

- You can hear my voice *booming* through. It's *me.*
- I care about this topic—and it shows.
- I speak right to my audience, always thinking of questions they might have.
- I wrote to please myself, too.
- My writing rings with confidence.

3. What I truly think and feel shows up sometimes.

- You might not laugh or cry when you read this, but you'll hang in there and finish it.
- I'm right on the edge of finding my own voice—so *close!*
- My personality pokes out here and there. You *might* guess this was my writing.
- I didn't think about my audience *all* the time. Sometimes I just wrote to get *it over with!*

1. I did not put much energy or personality into this writing.

- It could be hard to tell who wrote this. It could be anybody's.
- I kept my feelings in check.
- If I liked this topic better or knew more, I could put more life into it.
- Audience? *What* audience?

Word Choice

5. I picked *just* the right words to express my ideas and feelings.

- The words and phrases I've used seem *exactly* right.
- My phrases are colorful and lively, but not overdone.
- I used some everyday words in new ways. Expect a few surprises.
- Do you have a favorite phrase or two in here? I do.
- Every word is accurate. You won't find yourself wondering what I mean.
- Verbs and nouns carry the meaning. I don't bury my reader in adjectives.

3. It might not tweak your imagination, but hey, it gets the basic meaning across.

- It's functional and it gets the job done, but I can't honestly say I stretched.
- OK, so there are some clichés hiding in the corners.
- I've also got a favorite phrase lurking around here *someplace.*
- Verbs? What's wrong with good old *is, are, was, were* . . . ?
- I might have overutilized the functionality of my thesaurus.
- You can understand it, though, right? Like, nothing's really wrong.

1. My reader might go, "Huh?"

- See, I'm like this victim of vague wording and fuzzy phrasing.
- It's, you know, kind of hard to get what I'm talking about. *I* don't even remember what I meant, and *I wrote this stuff!*
- Maybe I misutilized a word or two.
- Some redundant phrases might be redundant.
- I need verby power.

Sentence Fluency

5. My sentences are clear and varied—you'll WANT to read it out loud.

- Go ahead—read with expression! You won't need to practice.
- Sentence variety is my middle name.
- Hear the rhythm?
- Deadwood has been cut. Every word counts.

3. My sentences are clear and readable.

- My writing is *pretty* smooth—you can get through it all right.
- Some sentences should be joined together. Others might be cut in two.
- There's a little deadwood, sure, but it doesn't bury the good ideas too badly under extra verbiage, even though I must say it wouldn't hurt to cut some unneeded words here and there and shorten things up just a bit now and then.
- I guess I did get into a rut with sentence beginnings. I guess I could use more variety. Sometimes I start a sentence a different way .

1. I have to admit it's a challenge to read aloud (even for me).

- You might have to stop or reread now and then it just feels like one sentence picked up right in the middle of another a new sentence begins and, oh boy, I'm lost . . . Help! Untangle me!
- My sentences all begin the same way. My sentences are all alike. My sentences need variety. My sentences need work. My goodness.
- Some sentences are short. They're too short. They're really short. Way short. Short. S-h-o-r-t. Get it? Right.
- Reading this is like trying to skate on cardboard. Tough going!

Conventions

5. An editor would fall asleep looking for mistakes in this paper.

- Capitals are all in the right places.
- Paragraphs begin at the right spots.
- Great punctuation—grammar, too.
- My spelling (even of difficult words) would knock your socks off.
- I made so few errors, it would be a snap getting this ready to publish.

3. Some bothersome mistakes show up when I read carefully.

- Spelling is correct on simple words.
- Capitals are mostly Ok. maybe i should look again, Though.
- The grammar and usage are OK for everyday writing.
- A few pronouns do not match what IT refers to.
- You might stumble over my innovative! punctuation.
- It reads like a rough draft, all right.
- I'd definitely need to do some editing to get this ready to publish.

1. Better read it once to decode, then once again for meaning.

- Lotsuv errers Mak? the going ruf.
- i've forgotten some CAPS—otherS aren't Needed.
- Look out four speling mysteaks.
- To tell the truth, I didn't spend much time editing.
- I'll really have to roll up my sleeves to get this ready to publish.

Ideas for Using the 6-Trait Scoring Guide

MAKE SURE KIDS "GET IT"

While the 6-Trait Scoring Guide for Students can make teaching ever so much easier, you cannot simply hand it out and forget it. You have to work with it. Explain any words or phrases that do not make sense. Give students numerous opportunities to use the guide in scoring and discussing writing.

BE FLEXIBLE

Second, think of the guide as a living, breathing document. Add to it, if you wish. Change the wording. Expand. Condense. Simplify if you need to. Make it serve *your needs* as a writing community.

TRAIT BY TRAIT

Third, *teach traits one at a time*. You might begin with ideas. I do. That is the foundation of everything: the message, the main theme, the primary story line. Without an idea, there is nothing to plan, write, revise, or edit, so it makes sense to begin here and to spend all the time you need making this first trait clear. You might devote as much as three weeks (or even more) to a single trait, spending the most time on ideas because the first trait is foundational. During the two to three weeks (or so), you can

- read samples of other students' work and score their writing on the trait of ideas (or whatever trait you're working on).
- look through written materials of all kinds for samples that are strong or weak in a given trait and make bulletin board displays of the results. (A good weekend assignment is to look for a paragraph—anywhere—that is strong or weak on a trait of ideas, and bring it in to share with the class.)
- ask students to help you revise your *own* work for a particular trait.
- practice revising any *anonymous* sample that is not their own (and that, in fact, belongs to no one else in the class—more on this in the next chapter).

Once students know the trait of ideas, you can build on what they know by weaving in the traits of organization, voice, word choice, and sentence fluency.

Conventions are part of ongoing instruction in editing, which we like to see students practice each day. Assess what you teach, so that students can be truly responsible for their own writing. See Figure 5.9 for a visual picture of the order in which most teachers like to teach the traits.

Step 2: Surround Students With Writers' Language

In providing student scoring guides, you've already taken an important step, but there's more you can do to bring writers' language into your classroom.

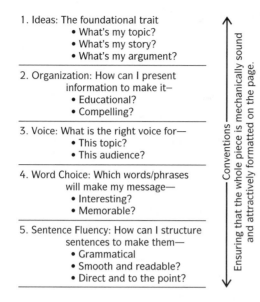

1. Ideas: The foundational trait
    - What's my topic?
    - What's my story?
    - What's my argument?

2. Organization: How can I present
   information to make it—
    - Educational?
    - Compelling?

3. Voice: What is the right voice for—
    - This topic?
    - This audience?

4. Word Choice: Which words/phrases
   will make my message—
    - Interesting?
    - Memorable?

5. Sentence Fluency: How can I structure
   sentences to make them—
    - Grammatical
    - Smooth and readable?
    - Direct and to the point?

Conventions

Ensuring that the whole piece is mechanically sound
and attractively formatted on the page.

FIGURE 5.9. The order in which teachers like to teach traits

KNOW THE TRAITS WELL

If *you* know the traits well, you'll find yourself referring to leads, conclusions, and transitions as easily as a surgeon refers to sutures and tracheotomies. So this is one way to surround your students with trait (i.e., writers') language. You can and should use the language of the traits in the comments you make on students' writing, too: "Your conclusion surprised me," "The paragraphing in this essay was dead on," "This paper rings with voice—I could hear you in every line,"

POSTERS

You can also put up posters highlighting the key components of each trait. Here is a set of posters developed by students to hang on the walls of their classroom. The originals were about two feet by three feet per trait, and the teacher put them up one by one, as she taught the traits—except for conventions, which was up from the beginning.

SOUND IDEAS

A clear message

Plenty of information

Details not everyone would think of

Clear purpose

You can't stop reading!

GOOD ORGANIZATION

A great opening to hook you
Easy to follow
Transitions link idea to idea to idea . . .
Builds to the good parts
A powerhouse ending ties it all up

INDIVIDUAL VOICE

Sounds like the writer
Enthusiastic, energetic, confident
Personal, individual
Makes the reader respond
You want to read it aloud

POWERFUL WORDS

Wow! The *best* way to say it!
You can picture it
A new twist on an old phrase
Powerful verbs!
Words you love

SMOOTH FLUENCY

Easy to read aloud
S-m-o-o-t-h
Different sentence beginnings
Some long sentences, some short

CORRECT CONVENTIONS

As close to error-free as I could make it!
Correct spelling
Correct punctuation
Capitals in the right places
Grammar needs *no* work
Indentations for new paragraphs
Ready to publish
The editor loves me!

You could use these very posters, but my suggestion is that you and your students develop your own. You will think of new twists that have not occurred to the rest of us yet, and the traits will become yours.

Step 3: Teach Students to Be Assessors of Their Own and Others' Work

If you do not do *one other thing* differently in your teaching because of the six traits, just try this: once a week (or more often, if time permits), ask students to assess and discuss a piece of writing by an *anonymous* student writer or work by any writer who is not a member of the class. In doing so, they will think—they *must* think—about what makes writing work, and you will see the influence of that thinking in their own writing and revising.

Use writing samples in pairs so you can offer a contrast. For example, if I were structuring a lesson on ideas, I might begin with "My Bike," a good paper to use because it clearly lacks detail. Many students write in this general, floaty way, but they have a much easier time seeing the problem in someone else's work. Read it aloud when you share it with students. You may even wish to make an overhead transparency of it and share it in that way. Then ask students to score it for ideas, using their 6-Trait Scoring Guides for Students.

MY BIKE

Grade 5, Descriptive/Narrative

The neatest gift I ever got was a bike I got for my birthday. It was really cool. It was red and kind of silver but mostly red. I had been wanting a bike for a long time, and when I finally got one, I just could not believe it was mine. It was the best gift I got for my birthday. It was very shiny with red paint and lots of chrome on the wheels. I was only eight when I got it, so I could not ride it right away. But soon after I got it I could ride it and then I rode it all the time. I had that bike for a long time, and it really meant alot to me.

Give students a few minutes first to make a final assessment, working with a partner. Tally scores with a show of hands, and ask students to share the reasons behind their scores. Prompt them with some key questions: What else would you like to know? Can you picture the bike? What's missing? After brainstorming a few missing details, you might follow this up by reading aloud the description of a boy and his new bike from Chapter 3, pp. 154–157, of *Boy's Life* (Robert R. McCammon, 1991)—one of the best coming of age stories ever written.

You need a contrast to really bring home what a given trait (in this case, ideas) is about. In addition to the McCammon piece, you can give your writers another student sample:

FISHING LESSONS

Grade 7, Narrative

It was a cool, crisp morning, about the time when the dew begins to form on the grassy banks of the stream. I had been anticipating this moment for some time and now it was here. Grandpa and I were going fishing at an ideal spot swarming with fish. We had left at about 4:00, but by the time we got there and unpacked, the sun was just creeping over the horizon.

Grandpa pulled the rod back and let it fly, right down stream, farther than I could see. Then, I lowered my toy fishing line down until it was just under the surface. Right away, Grandpa got a tug on his line, but it wasn't a fish, it was a baby alligator. The alligator was semi-small but it still put up a fight. Grandpa would gently reel it in, give it some line, then reel it some more. Just then, I realized he had gotten the scissors and was trying to cut the jumping line. Before I could blink, he cut the line and the alligator swam into a drain pipe. That had really surprised me because that was his favorite hook.

I pondered over this while I doodled around with my plastic hook in the water. About when the sun got all the way over the horizon, and it slowly was starting to get hot, we headed home with a puny guppy I caught in my plastic net. On the way to the house, I asked Grandpa why he hadn't just caught the alligator or at least reeled it in. He replied with a question—"Why cause the little fella any more pain than what life dishes out?" I learned that day that all things have a right to life and that life has a reason to be had.

Can you picture these two fishermen together, with the sun "just creeping over the horizon"? The detail in this story is striking; and you might begin with just asking students to list images that come to mind—or even connections to personal experiences. Getting them to work in small groups of three or four is very helpful; it encourages more talking. Sensory details are vivid; make a list on the overhead. In addition, the paper has focus; the strong sense of friendship between grandfather and grandson is never stated outright. It's all implied. Get your students to recognize this, too; give them time to discuss in small groups what they see as the main theme or main point of the piece—then contrast this with "My Bike," where the focus is not so strong.

You will also notice—and you can lead your students to this, too—that from strong and vivid detail comes a powerful voice. The story is tightly woven, with not one wasted phrase—no vague generalities for this writer. Word choice is sometimes inspired: "swarming with fish . . . let it fly . . . I doodled around . . . I pondered over this." A great mini lesson on word choice is simply to list the words and phrases you love. Remember that just because you use a paper for one trait (ideas), there is no reason not to use it for other traits, too (voice, word choice). Readers of all ages love this paper and generally give it 5s or 6s in ideas (and high scores in most other traits, too).

In sharing papers with students, select those that clearly make a point; for example, "Detail creates voice." Also, choose papers you enjoy reading aloud and discussing. Here are other suggestions to make your sharing and scoring of papers easier:

1. *Start with papers that are clearly strong or clearly weak.* Midlevel papers are the most difficult to score.
2. *Do not worry about the grade level of the writer.* You can use third-grade papers with high school students and vice versa. I tend to favor papers by younger writers because they're short and almost always make important points as well as longer, more complex papers.
3. *Read the papers aloud.* All writing plays differently to the eye and ear. We are so visual in our response to writing that we automatically form an impression upon first seeing text. If conventions are weak or the piece looks a little sloppy on the page, students may have a hard time getting beyond cosmetics to the heart and soul beneath.
4. *Ask students to provide the reasons behind their scores.* We have a tendency to think that numbers have a kind of super-reality. Test scores, percentages—ah, that's the real thing. Actually, this is an illusion. What is real is the interpretation behind those numbers. Nowhere is this more true than with a numbered scoring scale. Scores are only as valid as the numbers behind them. Don't let students get by with saying, "It's a five," or, "It sounds like a one or a two." Ask them to share the thinking behind their scores.
5. *Do not limit your practice to student papers.* Once you've warmed up a little, you can apply your skills to scoring other types and forms of writing, too: a job application letter, a sample of technical writing, a brochure from the local aquarium. Some years ago, one of our sixth-grade classes scored a social studies textbook for ideas (it came out a 3), voice (a definite 1), and conventions (a 5). We also scored a central office memo teachers had received regarding an upcoming curriculum meeting: ideas, 3 ("clear but boring"); voice, 2; and conventions, 2 (they found six spelling errors—e.g., *Febuary*—and much terminal punctuation was missing).

I believe it is important not only to share a common vision for lifelong learning and literacy, but a common vocabulary for how we talk about such issues.
> Beverly Ann Chin (1996)

Terms like "coherent" and even "specific" are notoriously hard for students to grasp because they do not read stacks of student writing.
> Peter Elbow (1986)

Step 4: Use Written Works to Illustrate Strengths and Weaknesses in Writing

When I began teaching the traits to students, I gathered some of my favorite literature and scanned it for samples. I found that passages from *To Kill a Mockingbird* helped illustrate strong ideas, while *Lonesome Dove* was excellent for voice. The lyrical writing of Dylan Thomas (1954/1962) was truly stunning in its fluency and its creative, unconventional word choice.

I was born in a large Welsh town at the beginning of the Great War—an ugly, lovely town (or so it was and is to me), crawling, sprawling by a long and splendid curving

> *shore where truant boys and sandfield boys . . . watched the dockbound ships or the ships steaming away into wonder and India, magic and China, countries bright with oranges and loud with lions. (5)*

Here are simple words used in new and sometimes startling ways. You don't need a thesaurus to write "bright with oranges" or "loud with lions." You only have to love language.

Please keep in mind that YOU DO NOT NEED TO READ A WHOLE BOOK to illustrate a trait. Short passages work beautifully. I emphasize this because so often teachers tell me, "I don't have time to read three or four books aloud per trait." I realize then how unclear I have been in my writing and in my workshops on this point. So let me clarify: Collect *brief* passages— *moments*, I call them—to illustrate each trait. That way, you'll always have time for a read-aloud, and you'll never feel overwhelmed.

Imagine yourself teaching, say, the trait of voice. Nothing helps make this trait clear like examples. Following are just a few favorite moments guaranteed to get student writers thinking (You only need to use ONE to illustrate the trait, though you could use more, if time permits):

> *I'm a writer. As such I often see myself as a bloodied and wounded soldier staggering around a battlefield in an attempt to conquer the blank page.*
> *(Mem Fox, "Notes from the Battlefield," in* Radical Reflections, *1993, 1)*

> *It's a funny thing about mothers and fathers. Even when their own child is the most disgusting little blister you could ever imagine, they still think that he or she is wonderful.*
> *(Roald Dahl,* Matilda, *1988, 7)*

> *Calves come early in the spring.*
> *It was how we knew the winter would die, would end.*
> *In the dark of the barn night when it was still cold enough outside to make things break, in the warm dark night of the closed barn they came, and when we would open the door in the morning to start chores we could smell them, the new calves.*
> *(Gary Paulsen,* Clabbered Dirt, Sweet Grass, *1992, 3)*

> *In English my name means hope. In Spanish it means too many letters. It means sadness, it means waiting. It is like the number nine. A muddy color. It is the Mexican records my father plays on Sunday mornings when he is shaving, songs like sobbing. . . . At school they say my name funny as if the syllables were made out of tin and hurt the roof of your mouth. But in Spanish my name is made out of a softer something, like silver.*
> *(Sandra Cisneros,* The House on Mango Street, *1989, 11)*

> *Warts are wonderful structures. They can appear overnight on any part of the skin, like mushrooms on a damp lawn, full grown and splendid in the complexity of their architecture.*
> *(Lewis Thomas,* The Medusa and the Snail, *1979, 76)*

In Lake Wobegon, we grew up with bad news. Since I was a little kid I heard it wafting up through the heat duct from the kitchen below. Our relatives came to visit on Saturday evenings and after we kids were packed off to bed, the grownups sat up late until ten-thirty or eleven and talked about sickness, unhappiness, divorce, violence, and all the sorrows they felt obliged to shelter children from, and I lay on the bedroom floor and listened in, soaking up information.

(Garrison Keillor, We Are Still Married, *1989, xix)*

You may notice that the ideas are clear, and the word choice and fluency are striking in these examples, too—so when you choose a piece of well-written text, it's likely you can use it to illustrate several traits. Notice, too, how different these voices are; in teaching this vital trait, variety is key. We are delighted by Mem Fox's battle metaphor because writing *is* that exhausting and demanding, and only those who do it know. Roald Dahl is, of course, a master of satire, but even more than this, we admire the way he never shrinks from stating outright just how he feels. "Disgusting little blister" is not polite phrasing, but it's unflinchingly honest. We want our students to write with that kind of courage because voice can't thrive without it. As Mem Fox (1993) reminds us, "Life isn't all sugar—there's a lot of vinegar as well" (130).

Gary Paulsen's voice is equally powerful, but quiet. In *Clabbered Dirt, Sweet Grass,* his stunningly reverent tribute to farm life, he creates incredibly beautiful images and sensory perceptions: "the dark of the barn night" and "cold enough outside to make things break." With the humblest of phrases, he transports us into the cold of a Minnesota winter.

Few writers go so deeply and daringly inside the human spirit as Sandra Cisneros, whose profound insight captures the way the world looks and feels to a child who is not accepted by all the adults around her. *The House on Mango Street* is an excellent text for teaching both ideas and voice, not only because it is alive with detail but also because it presents so many faces of human experience, from humor, joy, and whimsy to melancholy, jealousy, heartache, reverence, loyalty, and love.

Lewis Thomas can be enthusiastic and eloquent on almost any topic, from cloning to the medical curriculum, the health care program, committees, punctuation, and, yes, warts. Who knew warts had architecture?

Then there's Garrison Keillor, who slips his humor in on you as subtly as a second piece of chocolate cake during a Saturday soiree.

As you select your examples, don't overlook the bad writing. Sure it's fun to share wonderful excerpts, but we need to show students that just because it's published, we should not assume it's well done. Newspaper articles are excellent for illustrating clarity (or the lack thereof). Directions on everything from macaroni boxes to bicycles or computers are fine for illustrating strong or weak organization. When I purchased a computer, I quickly discovered I could use the instructions as a sample of perfectly wretched word choice. Here is the opening line in my *Concise User's Guide,* which runs 400 pages (think if they'd printed the *Not-So-Concise Guide*):

> *Most computers are sold with an operating system pre-installed. However, if your computer doesn't have this version of the MS-DOS operating system installed, you must run the Setup Program. You cannot run the MS-DOS directly from the Setup disks because the files on those disks are compressed.*
>
> *(Microsoft Corporation, 1994, 1)*

Veteran computer buffs will scorn my inability to penetrate and even enjoy this kind of technospeak, but when I read this, not only do I find it strenuous to follow, but (what is worse) I feel as welcome inside this book as surprise in-laws who pop in for the weekend. How about just a line or two saying, "Welcome to the world of computing! You are about to discover unprecedented power in designing documents that reflect your special style." Too folksy? Perhaps. But do we want more students who think that good technical writing means making it sound as technical as you can? If not, we need to show them samples like this and ask them to talk about what they hear and see. Ask them what they might do differently if they were writing computer manuals for a general audience. Here's what some high schoolers said when they looked at the preceding paragraph:

- It's not friendly enough.
- It starts out with a warning—look out, you might have forgotten to preinstall something.
- It doesn't explain anything. Is the reader supposed to know everything when he or she walks out of the store? What's a Setup program? What's a disk, for that matter? I happen to know, actually, but not everyone knows. What's an operating system? What do you mean by "compressed"? It's presumptuous not to think of your audience.
- I feel like this writer is just showing off instead of trying to help me.

Of course, it can be argued that the world of the computer is specialized—technical—but so are many other fields. Listen to the difference when Pulitzer Prize and Lewis Thomas Award winner Natalie Angier (1995) takes the reader inside the world of science to make the point that nothing is as it seems, that the deeper truths in science are very large, and that we add to them each day through our observations.

> *Hyenas sit at the top of the carnivores' pyramid, with all the ferocity that implies. Unlike lions, they consume every last body part of their prey—meat, fur, skull, bones. The moment two sibling hyenas emerge from the womb, they start mauling each other, usually to the death of one. Yet when a hyena is in a good mood—and if it knows and trusts you—it'll plop all two hundred pounds of itself down on your lap like a pet and beg to be scratched behind the ears.*   *(xiii)*

Ask students what they hear in Angier's writing. "Confidence," they'll often say, or, "She makes me want to hear more about hyenas." I do not remember even as I write this what the computer manual was trying to tell me—something about preinstallation and the need to run a Setup program correctly, I think. But I don't have to look back at Angier's text to recall that image of the two-hundred-pound hyena plopping onto my lap.

TIP: BE A COLLECTOR—AND GET COLOR CODED
Start today collecting pieces of writing from everywhere: the dentist's office, veterinarian's clinic, auto repair garage, stores of all types, theaters, the police or fire station, schools, restaurants, the Internet, junk mail, newspapers, etc. Collect annual reports, sports stories, book or film reviews, voters' pamphlet inserts, editorials, advertisements, manuals, menus, brochures, bios (on actors) from theater programs, greeting cards, resumes, song lyrics—any writing at all. Keep 12 folders, two for each trait, one for the good writing, one for the not-so-good. *(Hint: Color code them, to simplify your life, so each trait is a different color: ideas red, organization white, and so on.)* From your collection, you can always pull a read-aloud (perfect for a mini lesson on any trait), and if you like, turn it into an overhead so you and your students can score it or discuss it in detail, or use it as a practice piece for revision.

Step 5: Use Focused Lessons

Many of the best writing activities encourage strengths across all traits. Suppose, for example, you brainstorm the sounds, sights and smells of autumn—following which your students compose poems on impressions of the fall season. Or, you ask them to write a personal essay following your reading of Judith Viorst's poem "If I Were In Charge of the World." Or, ask them to respond to a more probing, philosophical question based on history. One fifth-grade teacher from Bend, Oregon (whose students were studying World War II and the Holocaust), asked his students to respond to this hypothetical situation: Suppose Mr. and Mrs. Hitler had received a notice from the German army stating: "Dear Mr. and Mrs. Hitler: We regret to inform you that your son Adolph has been killed in battle. We hope you will accept our condolences." How might world history have been changed? (This could conceivably have happened, since Adolph Hitler did serve in the German army, and did come close to losing his life.)

As you can see from these examples, a writing project with depth calls for clear ideas, organized thinking, personal voice, the right words—in short, all the components of good writing. And eventually, we must bring them together anyway since writing is a whole, not a six-slice pie. We divide the pie (temporarily) to make the process of revision simpler to teach. So focused lessons deal with small issues—and for students who thrive on a little more direct instruction, they can be just the thing to make it come clear.

FOCUSED LESSONS FOR IDEAS

When you're teaching ideas, picture students looking at the world through a magnifying glass. You're trying to teach them to write with detail, with a

"... in the case of struggling writers, explicit instruction should be added to the largely intuitive development of writing abilities at the heart of workshop methods."

James L. Collins (1998, 7)

sharp eye, with clarity and with focus. You're also trying to teach them to separate the interesting (sharks eat their young alive at birth) from the mundane (sharks live in oceans throughout the world). Here are a few ideas:

1. Dig for the potatoes. Barry Lane (1999) calls the good ideas the "potatoes"—because they're hidden, and you have to dig for them. I love this analogy. I like to compare the potatoes with the snoozers—the information everyone already knows or that everyone will find boring. Make a list of details on any topic—you should have at least 20 in all. Of the 20, about 5 should be "potatoes" (*sharks are revered as ancestors in Hawaii, sharks cannot blink or cry*). The rest, general information (*sharks live in the ocean, sharks can be dangerous*). Ask students, in pairs, to go through the list and pick out the good details. Discuss their findings as a class. Do they agree? If you want to extend the lesson, have them do the same kind of search through a newspaper article, encyclopedia entry or Internet printout. They can highlight "potatoes" in yellow. Now they have a leg up on what to emphasize in their own writing—and how to take notes for a research paper.

2. Highlight the details that strike you. In any given piece of writing, some details catch your eye or imagination. Some you hardly notice. Pull a piece from any literature you and your students are studying; it should be at least a half page long, but no more than two. Ask students to work with a partner to highlight in yellow those details that capture their imagination. Discuss results as a class to see how closely students agree. Talk about what makes some details more important or interesting than others. Do certain details appeal to a certain audience? How much should writers think about this?

3. Brainstorm questions. In writing any paper—whether a story, personal essay, research piece or persuasive essay—it is important to ask, "What will my readers want to know?" Model this first, so students can see how it is done. For example, let's say I'm writing about pet adoption. What would readers want to know? Here's my list of possible questions (I talk through these as I write them on the overhead):

- How much does it cost to adopt a pet from the Humane Society?
- Are the pets in good health?
- What kinds of pets are available?
- What happens to pets that do not get adopted?

This isn't a very long list. Only four questions. But I do not need dozens of questions to write a good, clear essay. In fact, too many will only overwhelm the reader—and me. Notice that my questions provide an organizational structure, too. I simply answer them in order, and I've organized an essay. Perhaps, in finding the answers to these questions (by phoning or visiting the Humane Society), I also form an opinion that adopting pets is a good thing to do; it saves owners money and it saves pets' lives. That might make a great lead or conclusion. I may also learn the story of one pet owner and the pet he/she adopted; this too could make a good lead or closing.

Keep a bulletin board display

Ask students to hunt for written passages bursting with rich, interesting detail, such as this one from William Steig's *Amos and Boris* (1971): "One night, in a phosphorescent sea, he marveled at the sight of some whales spouting luminous water; and later, lying on the deck of his boat gazing at the immense, starry sky, the tiny mouse Amos, a little speck of a living thing in the vast living universe, felt thoroughly akin to it all." Also include some that are flat and dull, such as this one from a technical manual: "In this manual, we have tried as much as possible to describe all the various matters. However, we cannot describe all the matters which must be done, or which cannot be done, because there are so many possibilities. Therefore, matters which are not especially described as possible in this manual should be regarded as 'impossible.'" (from COREComm's Worst Technical Writing Contest, a GE Fanac Automation, Series 15 MA Operator's Manual, copyright 1992 GE Fanac Automation North America, Inc.). Can writing get worse than this? We can only be thankful, as I'm sure the manual readers were, that they did not attempt to describe "*all* the matters which must be done."

FOCUSED LESSONS FOR ORGANIZATION

In teaching organization, you want students to focus on leads, sequencing, transitions, and conclusions. You can structure lessons to meet all these considerations. Here are a few ideas:

1. Focus on leads. Again, model first. If you are writing a brief essay or story, model three or four possible leads you might use, and ask students to help you choose the one that is most effective. Here are a few possibilities for an essay on a teacher who terrorized her class:

- Following will be an essay on a teacher I will never forget.
- We could feel her coming even before we heard her.
- I'll never forget my fourth grade teacher.

Which would you choose? Discuss differences, then ask students to try two, three or four leads for a piece they are working on, and to share them in response groups.

2. Build strong transitions. Find a passage that has fairly strong transitions, and rewrite it, *removing* the transitions. The result might look something like this:

Bill wanted a dog for his birthday. _____, his parents didn't like dogs. Bill was determined, _____. He thought he could convince them to think differently. _____, his plan backfired. Here's what happened . . . .

See how words like *However, though*, and *Unfortunately* would help make connections clear? Students do not have to choose these precise words. They simply need to choose words that show they know how ideas connect. Then they need to look at their own work and identify transitional words and phrases. Have they made connections clear? (Note: You can easily slip into transition mania, so be careful. This is no more than an *awareness* exercise. Students need to understand they do not need a transitional phrase at the beginning of *every* sentence.)

3. Play the merry mix-up game. I love this activity because students enjoy it and it suits all grade levels. Begin with a text that is well organized: good sequencing, clear transitions. It should not be too long—perhaps three lines for younger students, up to eight or nine for older students, but not much more. If the piece has a clear beginning and ending, so much the better. Rewrite it, line by line. Cut the copy into strips, so students can play with it like a puzzle (if you're ambitious and can afford it, you can laminate the strips, so you can use them over and over). Give them to students out of order, and ask them, working in groups of three or four, to order the strips so they make sense. Note: Their final may or may not match the author's original, and that is OK IF they have a good reason for ordering things as they did. Stories work well for beginners because they usually have a clear organizational structure. Expository writing is a little harder; you have to connect each supporting detail to a main idea. Persuasive writing is harder yet. But notice: If you do one of each, you can talk about how organization shifts with mode. How-to pieces, like recipes, are usually organizationally very clear; they're good for beginners and younger students. Want a challenge? Add a line or two that do not belong. A great lesson on eliminating filler from your writing.

4. Work on conclusions. This lesson can follow that for leads (See #1 above), or you can build in a little variety by making a Conclusions Quiz: Give students three possible conclusions for a book you're reading from (any kind, fiction or nonfiction, any grade level), and see if they can tell which is the author's actual conclusion. For example, Pamela Duncan Edwards' brilliant picture book *Barefoot* (1997) tells the story of how slaves escaped using the Underground Railroad. In her authentic yet fanciful tale, sympathetic animals befriend the slaves, aiding their escape. Which do you think is her ending?

- So it all worked out, and the barefoot found refuge in the cabin. Later, other slaves would escape along the same route, and the animals would help them, too. The Underground Railroad made an important contribution to U.S. history.
- The barefoot escaped and that is the end of my story. I hope you liked it.
- Silence fell along the pathway, and the animals slept. But through their dreams the heron's cry once again screamed a warning. Another barefoot was approaching.

You probably have little difficulty determining that the third conclusion is how Edwards ended her story. Students can usually tell, too, but the interesting question is, *How* do you know? *Why* is the third one different?

5. Make bulletin board displays. Leads are naturals to collect for your bulletin board when you're studying organization—and conclusions as well. Remember to make two collections, the successful and the not-so-successful.

6. Teach the concept. Sometimes we have difficulty teaching organization because we focus so much on organization of *writing* and so little on what organization itself is. You might begin by asking students what things we organize in our daily lives: our time, our living rooms (and all rooms), our closets and drawers, our hair, our clothing, our week or month to come, our curriculum, an anniversary party, a trip—the list is endless. Now ask them to organize one thing, such as coins. Put students in groups of three or four and ask each student to contribute four or five coins to a large central pile (they'll need to recall, of course, the amount of their contribution!). Now, as a group, have them organize the coins and write down how they did it: e.g., by year, by value, by size, by color. Now, do it again, and again, and again—until they can no longer come up with a new way to organize (there are dozens, so don't let them quit too soon). Use the experience to talk about how many ways there are to organize information and why a person chooses one way over another. What is organization? Finding a pattern that perhaps was not immediately obvious.

FOCUSED LESSONS FOR VOICE

Voice is arguably the most interesting of the traits, but many people find it elusive, and thus hard to teach. True, it's not quite so simple to get hold of as organization or conventions, but its many guises make it fun to work with, regardless of the kind of writing you teach. Through voice, we reveal our tone, attitude, philosophy and perspective. Voice plays a role in every kind of writing from poetry to textbooks because it is voice, as much as clarity, that creates meaning. As Nancy Slonim Aronie tells us in *Writing from the Heart* (1998), ". . . if your voice has been silenced for too long, let the idea of writing begin to take hold, to gnaw and to push and to build until, like a pressure cooker full of fresh corn, it will start to leak out in sprays of hissing steam."

1. Read aloud. Read from the books you love, and as you do, encourage students to listen for the voice within. Ask them to describe the voice they hear. Is it timid, bold, funny, irreverent, brazen, accusatory—what? Each voice is different, and voices have names, character, personality. Describe each one in precise and colorful terms if you can. (See page 61 for a list of favorite books for teaching voice.)

2. **Compare voices.** I will often read a passage from Carolyn Lesser's *Great Crystal Bear* (1996) and one from an encyclopedia entry on polar bears—then ask students which is which and how they know. You could make the same contrast using a newspaper article on automobile safety, annual report on economic returns, or whatever. You just need one piece that is full of voice, one that is drier. This is not to say that encyclopedias should sound like poems (though personally I can't say I'm fond of how they sound now); different voices for different purposes! By all means. But we can teach the concept of voice best through contrast, and encyclopedia entries, while serving the worthy purpose of presenting concise, accurate information, are rarely stimulating.

3. **Listen to students' voices.** You can also read (with students' permission, of course) their own work aloud to the class and see how many students can identify which work goes with which writer. It's often hard at first. It gets easier as students work at making their voices identifiable, and as students' "ears" for voices sharpen.

Whenever I write, whether I'm writing a picture book, an entry in my journal, a course handbook for students, or notes for the milkman, there's always someone on the other side, if you like, who sits invisibly watching me write, waiting to read what I've written. The watcher is always important.

Mem Fox (1993)

4. **Ask students to identify favorite voices.** Have students identify a favorite passage from any writer whose work they feel has voice. They should bring their passages to class, read them aloud with plenty of feeling, and see if other students can identify the voice, or at least describe it.

5. **Do a quick-write on voice.** Do a quick-write in which you and your students write one-liner definitions of voice. Post them on a bulletin board, along with professional writers' definitions, and perhaps some samples of passages you feel have voice. Do not forget to include appropriate voice for business or technical writing, along with the more passionate voice of narrative. Here are some of my favorite student/teacher definitions:

- Voice is hearing the exclamation point, even when it's not there.
- Music, making harmony between writer and reader.
- A bond that says, "I want to let you in."
- It's the passion that makes words dance.
- It's curiosity, passion, and the need to be heard.
- The choreography of the writing.
- Voice is the writer reaching out to the reader.
- It is deft and careful use of words to create that just right sound.
- Lighting a fire in the reader.
- The spark that makes meaning come alive.

6. **Write letters.** When students write to someone, they tend to put more voice into their writing. One biology teacher tells his students, "Don't just write about photosynthesis. Explain it the way you would explain it to Miss Piggy." What a difference it makes in their writing, not only in voice, but in ideas, organization, word choice—everything!

Students who have worked with the traits for a while may enjoy writing to a favorite author. Consider, for example, this fourth grader's letter to author Roald Dahl:

Roald Dahl
c/o Bantam Books
666 Fifth Avenue
New York, New York 10103

Dear Roald Dahl:

I'm nine years old. My purpose of writing is to tell you I know
all of your books by heart.

I think you should write more books, and make them come out
all around the globe. I'm talking about books with voice, like
Matilda. Maybe even some sequels. Like *Matilda II* or *Twits II* and
III. Maybe more *Revolting Rhymes.*

I've always wondered how you get such creative ideas, and I am
hoping if you send back a letter, you will send some tips for putting
in just the right amount of information.

When you do send your letter, I would like it hand written and
signed in pen. I hope you can come to our school.

I better sign off now. My time is limited.

Your truly grateful, super wonderful fan,
Nikki

Nikki isn't writing here to show off her knowledge of the traits. Her comments on voice and ideas appear naturally because they are part of her thinking now and because she is clearly captivated by Roald Dahl's work. As Mem Fox tells us, "Clarity, voice, power and control are much more easily developed through letter writing [than through writing stories] because, perhaps, the audience is so clearly defined and will, if all goes well, respond" (1993, p. 28).

Responses can be thrilling. I wrote to Larry McMurtry just after reading *Lonesome Dove,* and floated two feet above the ground when I received a response (Figure 5.10), short though it was.

FOCUSED LESSONS FOR WORD CHOICE

When I read the first two lines of Janet Fitch's remarkable *White Oleander* (1999), I knew—*knew* for certain—that it would become one of my all-time favorite books: "The Santa Anas blew in hot from the desert, shriveling the last of the spring grass into whiskers of pale straw. Only the oleanders thrived, their delicate poisonous blooms, their dagger green leaves" (3). In this book, language thrives. And it is wholly original. What do the words "shriveling," "thrived," "poisonous blooms" and "dagger green" make *you* think of? I thought danger, plotting, scheming, death, treachery, struggle—survival. Every word is carefully chosen to create just the right anticipation—a mix of curiosity and anxiety.

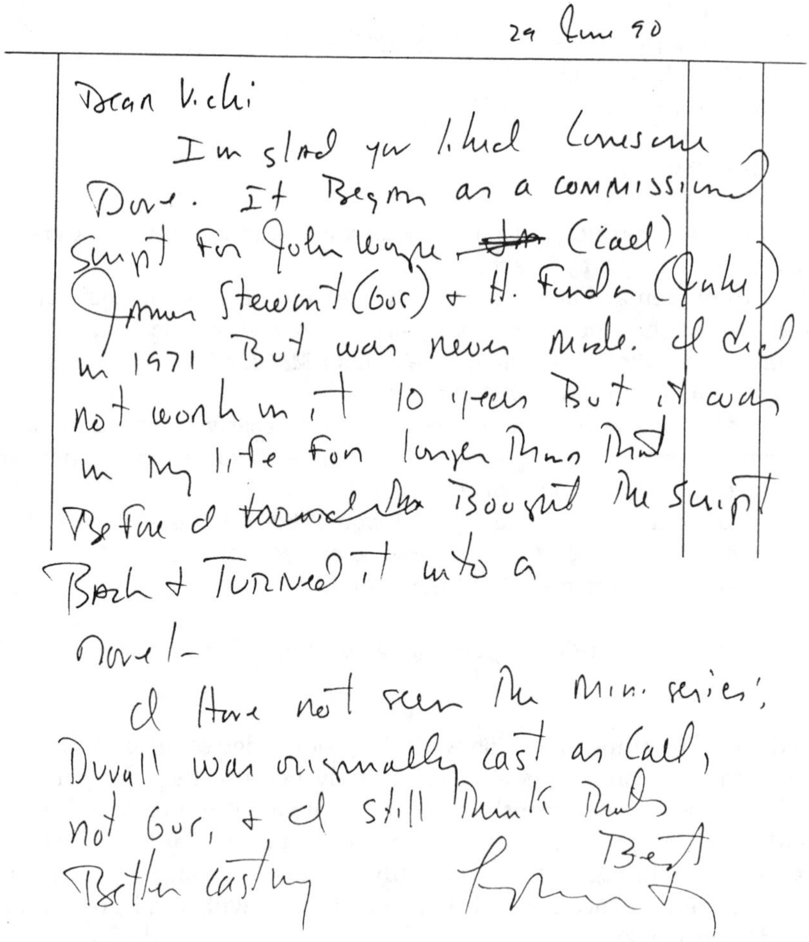

29 Jun 90

> Dear Vicki
>
> I'm glad you liked *Lonesome Dove*. It began as a commissioned script for John Wayne, (Cael) James Stewart (Gus) + H. Fonda (July) in 1971 But was never made. I did not work on it 10 years But it was in my life for longer than that Before I turned the Book into the script Back + turned it into a novel—
>
> I have not seen the Mini-series; Duvall was originally cast as Call, not Gus, + I still think that's Better casting   *Best* [signature]

FIGURE 5.10. Response from Larry McMurtry

1. Read, read, read! The books of William Steig, Gary Paulsen, Roald Dahl and Mem Fox are all renowned for excellent word choice for younger readers/writers—though I would not overlook them for older writers, either. Any high schooler who has not read *Matilda* (which is really more a book for adults than for children, no matter how much kids love it) has missed the best of reading times. Don't forget to check out the nonfiction, either. Try this tidbit from Porter and Prince's travel book (1998), *London:* "The very name, LONDON still sounds heavy, ponderous, like the ringing of Big Ben in one of those low budget, old black-and-white films that the Rank group used to turn out." Not bad for something I expected to be lots drier. Are you a fan of science essays? Perhaps you would be if you read David Quammen's *The Song of the Dodo* (1996) in which he describes how biogeography traces the comings and goings of species: "On the island of Madagascar, for instance, there once lived an ostrichlike creature that stood ten feet tall, weighed half a ton, and thumped across the landscape on a pair of elephantine legs. Yes, it was a bird" (17). Find the best tidbits you can, share them, and save the gems—*thumped, elephantine*—in personal dictionaries for future use. Other excellent choices for older reader/writers include E. Annie Proulx, Nikki Giovanni, Norman Mailer, Toni Morrison, Jeffrey Mousaieff Masson, Carl Sagan, and Wallace Stevens—to name but a few.

2. Encourage students to collect, too. You're not in this alone. Send your students on scavenger hunts for good and not-so-good word usage. Check out any textbooks you're currently using. Are they reader friendly? Verb-infused? Jargonistic? Bland? Could parts be better written? How? Try your hand!

3. Brainstorm alternatives. Here's an idea I learned from my friend Lynne Shapiro, who is a teacher and language arts specialist in Connecticut. I've found it enormously successful with students from primary through adult. Find a passage with lively verbs—Mem Fox's enchanting *Night Noises* is exceptional. Rewrite a short portion (a paragraph will do) replacing the lively verbs with dull cousins—same general meaning, but no pizzazz. Underline your replacements and make an overhead, double spacing your text and making the print large so there's plenty of room for notes. Then, brainstorm alternatives for your dull verbs, jotting down all your class can think of. While the overhead is still up for them to compare, read Fox's original so they can hear her wonderful word power and see how close they came to matching her word choice. Follow up by having them circle one or two words in their own text they'd like to enliven; do a brainstorming in small groups of three or four to come up with alternatives. (Notice by the way that this creative lesson is adaptable to any form of writing; you do not have to use a picture book. It's just that picture books, like short student papers, make the point quickly.)

4. Keep personal dictionaries. Encourage students of all ages to keep personal dictionaries of favorite words and phrases. They should be alphabetized for easy reference. Occasionally, older students can conduct mini lessons based on their dictionary words—read-alouds, simple quizzes, etc.

FOCUSED LESSONS FOR SENTENCE FLUENCY

When you teach fluency, you're teaching more than grammar. You're teaching rhythm and grace. It's the difference between dancing by placing your feet in the appropriate markings on the floor and just letting your body move to the music. Once they're moving to the music, they've got it.

1. As with organization, teach the concept. What is fluency? Rhythm, motion, grace. Where do we see it in real life? Here are some examples students have given me:

- Wheat in the fields
- Grass blowing in the wind
- A flag waving in the breeze
- A mountain creek
- Waves pounding on the shore
- Geese in formation
- Gravy pouring over the potatoes
- A ballet dancer
- A bull fighter
- A waterfall
- Leaves flickering in the wind
- A person hand writing a note
- A bicyclist
- A skier
- An ice skater
- A trapeze artist
- Horses running
- A heart pumping

2. Model fluency through poetry or music. So many wonderful recordings exist now of poets reading their own poetry. From Shel Silverstein to Robert Frost, you know you'll have a winner, and listening will help students both hear and feel the fluency. Younger children can actually march to the rhythms of music, dance, or even beat out the rhythm on a drum.

3. Bring on the poetry. What's more rhythmic than poetry (other than music itself)? So let poetry be a focus of any unit on sentence fluency. You can read it yourself, of course, but encouraging students to be the readers (singly or in pairs or teams) is an excellent idea.

4. Perform it. Whether it's a bit of drama from Shakespeare, a poem by T.S. Eliot, or any text that allows itself to be divided into sections, your students will benefit by presenting it orally. Seek out samples with dialogue and you'll find yourself combining voice and fluency. They can do a choral reading, with multiple voices, echoes, sound effects—the works! Or take turns, playing parts, depending on the text. Either way, get them on their feet, get them reading so that yours is not the only voice in the land.

5. Don't forget good business writing. Good business writing and informational writing in general has a rhythm and style all its own. It's generally clean and crisp, a nice neat box step rather than a tango. So occasionally, it's good to practice this concise approach, for not all writing is poetry or narratives. You can create a marvelous lesson by taking an ordinary business letter and making it grotesquely wordy. See if your students can strip it back to sanity:

Dear Mr. Blanchard:

Thank you with my deepest appreciation for your thoughtfulness and kindness in sending me the information I had requested in my letter of last week. It was a great pleasure for me to receive such a quick response, and I am most grateful for your kind attention. I hope to hear from you again soon and look forward with great anticipation to further communication from your office.

Blah, blah, blah. You get the idea. Junk mail is full of inflated letters like this one, just awaiting your students' slashing red pens. But if you can't find one, make up your own. If you work with older students, let *them* write (in groups) letters to each other for editorial critique. They'll learn from both the writing and the revising.

There's More

More ideas for teaching traits follow in Chapter 7, "Troubleshooting." In addition, that chapter deals extensively with the teaching of editing, which is my reason for omitting conventions from this quick list. As you teach traits, you'll find yourself thinking of many more lessons to add to this list, too.

ANSWERS TO FREQUENTLY ASKED QUESTIONS

Do I need to change the way I am teaching now?

No! That's the beauty of the six-trait analytical model. It's such a natural fit with either the writing process or writers' workshops. Do not change any of the successful things you're already doing.

What if I teach ninth grade, and my students had six-trait instruction in seventh or eighth grade? Won't they be bored going over old ground?

Understanding what makes writing work and learning to write takes a lifetime. Even if your students have already been introduced to the traits, there is always a more complex paper to assess, discuss, or revise. There are always more voices to hear in literature, more fine phrases to discover in the writing we love. Challenge your students with additional (and harder) editing practice. Raise the expectations on voice and fluency. Discuss various forms of writing: technical, business, creative, informational, public relations, reflective, persuasive. How does each trait change as the purpose and audience change?

How long should I spend teaching each trait?

As long as your students need. Do not feel rushed. Some teachers spend three or four class periods per trait. Some spend as much as two to three weeks. The first trait (*ideas*) generally takes the longest. After that, students know how to use a scoring guide and understand the assessment process. You've taught the logistics; now you're just fitting in pieces of the puzzle.

How will I know when my students understand a trait?

Your students understand a trait when you can put on the overhead a paper that is weak in a particular trait and students can score it, telling you what is wrong and precisely what they would do to revise; or when you put up one that is strong and they can score it accurately, telling you precisely what the writer did to succeed. Students who know a trait can also find strong and weak examples of that trait in virtually any form of writing, from a business letter to a technical manual to a mystery story—without your help.

Does there ever come a time when students put all the traits together?

Of course. It's *essential*. Writing isn't just ideas or just internal structure. The problem is, when we've said to students in the past, "You need to revise this paper," the task has been overwhelming. Think of it. In the student's mind, it must sound something like this:

> *Use more examples. Condense. Expand your ideas. Be concise. Be precise. Be clear. Tell me more. Don't tell me* everything. *Put in some voice. Watch your tone. Change the words. Be fluent. Know your topic. Remember your audience. Have a topic sentence. Be definite. Be subtle. Say what you think. Think of time/place/setting/characterization. Say what you feel. Support your opinions. Make it visual. Make it sensory. Don't overload. Don't overdo. Don't overwhelm the reader. Keep it interesting. Make it significant. Use more complex sentences. Keep it simple. Keep it flowing. No fragments. Unless they're stylish. Be witty. Not that witty. Stretch your vocabulary. Hands off the thesaurus. Show restraint. Take a risk. Show control. Use a new word. Sound natural. Be yourself. Adopt a persona. A different persona. Be realistic. Use your imagination. Use what you know. Get more information. Be accurate. Tell me more. Show, don't tell. Be specific. Draw conclusions. Make predictions. Keep it organized. Don't be predictable. Look at your lead. Use transitions—but not every time. Don't end with "the dream." Don't end with a summary. Don't end suddenly. Don't end with "The End." Know when to end! Don't worry about spelling yet. Check your spelling. You need a different ending. Too obvious. Too vague. Redundant. Non sequitur. Try again.*

When we teach revision in chunks, we make it manageable. We show students a range of revision possibilities.

Is it healthy for students to be making judgments on others' writing all the time?

Most assuredly, as long as they learn to do it well. Assessing is not really *judging* in the critical sense. It's taking a close-up look, discovering, gaining perspective.

Remember, assessment in the form of observation occurs everywhere, all around us, all the time. We assess everything from books to wines, from political candidates to the weather, from television programs to potential spouses. So students will assess writing whether we ask it of them or not. Let's teach them—and ourselves—to do it well.

Is it OK to share really strong samples with students? Won't that be intimidating?

Not if you present them thoughtfully. The best examples should not be held up as expectations for all but, rather, as samples of what is possible. When I read Janet Fitch's *White Oleander,* and E. Annie Proulx's *Close Range,* I didn't think, *Well, no use for me to write anything more—I could never match that.* My writing is markedly different from that of either author, but oh, how I love to see what can be done by someone who has the gift. Don't you? Books like Ursula Hegi's *Stones from the River* (1994) or Larry McMurtry's *Lonesome Dove* (1985) thrill us because they remind us what writing can be in the hands of someone who does it well. Aim high.

What about students for whom writing is just very, <u>very</u> hard? They may only write a line or two—and even then sometimes I cannot read it.

There are students—lots of them, at all levels—for whom writing is physically, mentally, or emotionally challenging. Here is an opportunity like none other for analytical scoring, with its sweeping and generous profile of writing qualities, to truly shine—if we let it.

Many students who cannot physically write much are writing in their heads all the time. After all, do we not tell our students that writing is thinking? By that don't we mean that writing is partly the conceptualization, planning, and plotting of ideas? Let these students "write" in whatever way feels comfortable, which might include dictation to another person, oral storytelling, or recording their writing on tape. Some may wish to include illustrations as well. You won't have conventions to score, true. So what? Let the conventions go for a time. These students know, and you know, that they are not yet ready for formal assessment in conventions. Such assessment serves no instructional purpose; it only serves to remind them of what they cannot do.

What they often can do, however, is identify, expand, and enrich an idea, organize information, speak with voice and fluency, and use words that are striking, original, and correct. Why not give them credit for their thinking, planning, organizing, and attention to audience? Every paper has a positive quality; analytical assessment helps us identify what's done well.

Couldn't I teach the traits but still grade with letter grades as I've always done?

My recommendation is that you use scores on individual pieces of writing (because once students know the traits, scores will be more meaningful than grades); and reserve grades for a body of work (more on how to do this in Chapter 12).

Students who know the traits begin to use them as a kind of shorthand, quickly reading more into those numbers than they could ever glean from a letter grade. A student who is receiving 4s, 5s, or 6s on writing performance, and who has a *6-Trait Guide for Student Writers* has no reason to wonder how well she is doing. She knows.

My state is establishing guidelines for the assessment of writing that are similar to the six-trait model but do not seem to match it exactly. How much difference will this make in my students' performance?

Not much at all unless there are serious philosophical gaps between the two models. The traits help prepare students for success on virtually *any* direct writing assessment because they are not a gimmick, but the real foundation of what makes writing work. Chances are that your state standards, if you have them, match the traits very closely, even if there are slight differences in wording. In fact, consider these few examples excerpted from a much longer document written by the State of Virginia (a state with very clearly written standards, by the way). In each case, the traits identified in italics are inserted by me to show connections:

The student will write narratives, descriptions, and explanations. (ALL TRAITS)

- Use a variety of planning strategies to generate and organize ideas. *(IDEAS & ORGANIZATION)*
- Establish central ideas, organization, elaboration, and unity. *(IDEAS & ORGANIZATION)*
- Select vocabulary and information to enhance the central idea, tone, and voice. *(IDEAS, WORD CHOICE, & VOICE)*
- Expand and embed ideas by using modifiers, standard coordination, and subordination in complete sentences. *(IDEAS, WORD CHOICE, & SENTENCE FLUENCY)*
- Revise writing for clarity. *(ALL TRAITS)*
- Edit final copies for correct use of language, subject-verb and pronoun-antecedent agreement, consistent tense inflections, and adverb and adjective usage. *(CONVENTIONS)*
- Edit final copies for writing mechanics: format, capitalization, punctuation, and spelling. *(CONVENTIONS)*

From *English Standards of Learning for Virginia Public Schools, Grade Six Writing Standards, 6.7*

These connections are not difficult to pick out, and they exist for virtually any set of standards that is based on the principles and concepts of good writing. True, the criteria are forever evolving, expanding and redefining themselves, to reflect new thinking, but these are refinements, not major re-conceptualizations.

Further, these qualities of writing are important not only in the classroom but in the real world of writing, that world in which students will write proposals, business reports, technical manuals, evaluations, letters, memos, and the rest. This means that students who learn to research their writing and formulate ideas clearly, who organize information for interest and understanding, who temper voice to suit audience, topic, and writer, who select words with precision, and who write fluently and edit with skill can expect to do well on virtually *any direct writing assessment*. But more important—more important by far, far and away—they will become confident and skilled writers for life.

REFLECTING ON CHAPTER 5

1. What do your students think is important in good writing? Do their perceptions match yours? Where did you, and they, get your ideas about what good writing is?
2. Which works by writers you read or admire come closest to meeting your highest expectations for quality writing? How would you describe the writing?
3. Can you think of specific written examples (from your everyday life and experience) of strong or weak performance in ideas, organization, voice, and the other traits? Think about beginning a collection that you could use in teaching; share some of your findings with colleagues.

ACTIVITIES

1. If you are currently teaching, choose *one* trait and think of all the things you are currently doing to support that trait with your instruction. List them and share lists with your colleagues.
2. Ask each person to bring to the discussion group one book that is a favorite. Then, in small groups, share a favorite passage and ask, "What trait might this illustrate?" Take it a step further and see if you can come up with a writing lesson using the book as a starting point.
3. Choose one of the lessons in this chapter and model it, for students or teachers, putting your own personal spin on it.
4. Look closely at the scoring guide in Chapter 3. Choose *one* trait, and going through the guide for that, take it apart into its components, and see if you can

identify the actual lessons you would need to teach to make that trait clear to students. For example, the trait of organization refers to transitions; they would be a focus for one lesson. But what else would you need to teach?

5. Get a copy of your state's writing standards (or those of any state for that matter) and compare them to the language of the six-trait model. What connections do you see? How similar is the language?

LOOKING AHEAD

This chapter showed how writing process provides a foundation for the traits, and illustrated five basic ways to use traits in teaching writing. In the next chapter, we'll expand that base by looking at focused revision: revision which targets a specific trait. We'll also talk about the advantages of practicing revision by working first on the text of others—then using what you have learned to revise your own work.

MEMORABLE MOMENTS FROM STUDENTS' WRITING

- Memories—you can never forget them.
- The truth is, I was afraid of crashing—not flying.
- Her eyes were different colors, brown and green, so you could always tell if it was her or not.
- Like Hamlet, we had to sifer the boles and arrows of outrage and fortune.
- Her death was not the cause of old age, as many people would have you believe.
- It was the beginning of the new millennium—about 0 A.D. . . . .

6

FOCUSED REVISION:
Building the Bridge to Writing Success

Because the best part of all, the absolutely most delicious part, is finishing it and then doing it over. That's the thrill of a lifetime for me. If I can just get done with that first phrase and then have infinite time to fix it and change it, I rewrite a lot, over and over again, so that it looks like I never did. I try to make it look like I never touched it, and that takes a lot of time and a lot of sweat.

Toni Morrison (Murray 1990, 186)

Revision, the "absolutely most delicious part" for many professional writers, can be a nightmare for students. Why is that? Could it be that professional writers have in their minds a wealth of possible revision strategies from which to choose, while students often have no clue where to begin? Take another quick look at the scoring guide in Chapter 3; and this time, see it not as an assessment tool at all but as a list of possibilities—possibilities for revision—and then imagine yourself teaching it just that way. Now imagine students

1. working with partners, and
2. *practicing* revision first on text that is not their own—before revising their own work for a grade.

   Both elements take some of the threat out of revision, which often feels like a penalty for having written "incorrectly" in the first place. It also feels like a lot of work. It's hard to experience joy when you don't see the vision yet, and you don't know the road to take you there. A chance to practice, especially on someone else's writing, can make revision feel almost like a game—a game in which you are free to try new things, and take new risks.

MAKING THE TASK MANAGEABLE

My father in law could build a house from the ground up, everything from foundation to roof. This is no small accomplishment. You can bet, though, that he didn't learn all the steps in a day, nor did anyone ever teach him a general, overall process called "house building." He learned step by step to lay a foundation, to frame, to plumb, to wire, to mount sheetrock, to install insulation, to paint, build a roof, build a fireplace, lay carpet, tile and linoleum, install appliances and light fixtures—and all were individual steps, each of which contributed to his ability to put the final structure together. Did he have in his mind a clear vision of how the finished house would look? Not the first time he did it, no. He saw the house go together step by step and the final vision did not come together till the end. But years later, when he was an experienced builder who had gone through each of the steps many times, when he built the house in which my husband grew up, he saw the vision of the whole clearly from the first footing, because he knew by then exactly how each part contributed to the bigger picture.

When it was finished, it was not a jumble of house parts, but a home with ambiance and light and the love that shines from handcrafted cabinets and polished hardwood floors laid to fit beautifully together, one board at a time, and doors that swing into place without squeaking or sticking. In Leo's home, the floor joists were sound, the roof did not leak, the plumbing always worked, the wiring posed no dangers and his house remains as solid this day, forty years after its construction, as on the day he poured the first concrete into the first moldings. When you understand precisely how to do each step correctly, the whole tends to hang together better.

Focused revision makes writing more manageable because it focuses on just one step at a time—details, the lead, sentence fluency, the conclusion, and so on. Does this mean we no longer see writing as holistic? Absolutely not. We are simply focusing on individual components to make the revision task less daunting for beginning writers. Eventually, all the pieces come together like Leo's house because students who study the individual components of writing come to know them so well that global assessment (and hence revision) becomes, over time, both natural and comfortable. Look again at Lauren Rothrock's assessment of her paper on the African boy in Chapter 3, and you'll see that she is looking not just at one aspect of her writing, but at many, and also at how each affects the others; but the point is, she learned them one by one, trait by trait.

Focused revision makes the revision process feel not just comfortable, but literally doable, period. It is easy for people to whom writing comes easily and naturally to think that *anyone* can revise. If you're just willing to take the time, put in the effort, you can do it—can't you? Actually, for some young writers, each word must be sweated onto the page. Breaking revision into steps puts it within their reach. It also says, "You don't have to work miracles every time you write. You don't have to bedazzle audiences or bring them to their feet. If you did just *one* thing (added detail or considered voice, re-wrote the lead, made it more fluent, matched the word choice to your audience), that would be a *big* step."

MORE THAN THE SUM OF THE PARTS

I recognize fully the discomfort of those who agree with Edward White (1985) when he states that "writing remains more than the sum of its parts and that the analytic theory that seeks to define and add up the subskills is fundamentally flawed" (123). Writing is indeed more than the sum of its parts. *That is the point precisely.* If we teach it as "writing," we give ourselves the perfect excuse to never explain or understand this complexity. This feels to me like a valid philosophical stance, but a poor base from which to teach. It is like trying to understand—or teach—anatomy without cutting into the body. Of course a body is more than the sum of its organs just as a cake is more than the sum of its ingredients. This is so obvious it is impossible for any thinking person not to agree. But the point is, students will never—not *ever*—truly appreciate the complexity of writing without understanding in depth those components that make it work. A master baker knows how to add a pinch of salt or a splash of vanilla to bring out the flavor of the cake. Sandra Cisneros (1989) brings out the flavor in her writing with a dash of fluency ("When I am a tiny thing against so many bricks . . ."); but that is only *one* path to writing well. Voice is another, precise use of detail another. Through the traits, we give students many paths in.

Both Edward White and R. Lloyd-Jones have also stated (in Wolcott, 1998), "the categories isolated for analytical scoring may be difficult to identify" (102–103). On the contrary. As I have recounted in earlier chapters, the salient features of good writing are remarkably easy for any thoughtful group of writing teachers to identify, and the number of teachers who agree on the basic traits is testament to the validity of those traits. Of course, someone, somewhere, could argue that *verbosity* and *length* are the true keys to excellence in writing, but even if this *did* happen, we must remember that the whole point in defining writing is to engage in *discussion,* to get teachers in an interpretive community talking together and teaching one another.

Peter Elbow (in Wolcott, 1998), argues in favor of analytical scoring precisely for the value of this intercollegial discussion because it requires us not only to look closely at writing, but also to "acknowledge the individuality" (103) of our responses. Voice—to cite one example—is vast in its complexity, and in order to teach it well we must acknowledge this vastness and show students how and why voice varies from narrative to informational to business writing. If we cannot do this—if we cannot define what good writing is and show our students examples of what it looks like and how it changes with audience and purpose—how can we possibly have the audacity to teach writing? Of course, this does not mean we will never change our minds or expand our thinking. As Carl Sagan (1995) reminds us, even "the history of science—by far the most successful claim to knowledge accessible to humans—teaches that the most we can hope for is successive improvement in our understanding, learning from our mistakes . . . with the proviso that absolute certainty will always elude us" (28).

So—let's not wait for "absolute certainty." Our student writers need help right now. We have a very clear vision of good writing, the clearest in history. Let's use it.

BEGIN BY MODELING REVISION

Unlike our students, most of us do not see revising and editing as punishment. We see it as opportunity. We have been building castles out of air; now there is a tangible object, and we can go to work to make it work.

Donald M. Murray
(*Shoptalk,* 1990, 171)

It is enormously helpful for students to see writing not just as a final, polished, published product, but to see it as it grows—from the germ of an idea through the gangly rough draft stage and on into revision. You can make this happen by modeling your own writing and revision in process. So, let me show you one of my papers, a piece I've used with students to show them what revision looks like as it occurs—something I wish my teachers had shown me.

"The Pitcher"

In a high school class we did some brainstorming on the topic of favorite place. I asked students to focus on a place personal and special just to them, and together we came up with some examples, such as a tree in the back yard, a childhood fort, a hammock, the place under the stairs where you could listen in on adult conversations. Disneyland and comparable neon-illuminated, pay-to-enter places were off limits. Too public, we thought, too overdone. Our brainstorming included sensory details for sights, sounds, smells associated with the place. I asked students to close their eyes momentarily and picture themselves right there, then to think of (and list) those sensory details that would put me right there, too. Their list of places was personal and wonderful: the old worn reading chair, the rug by the fire, the pile of leaves after fall raking, grandmother's kitchen table, at the window when the first snowfall begins, in the garden pulling up the first carrots, knee deep in the river, inside any good book, in the kitchen with my hands buried in bread dough, on my bike, "buried" in my car engine, reading a magazine with the cat on my lap.

Then we wrote some short papers. I wrote mine on the overhead, but did not turn the light on till I was finished because I wanted them to focus on their writing, not mine. The place I chose was the local ballpark, but I called my paper "The Pitcher" because he became the focus of my writing; it was a favorite place only because I was there watching him work out. We were working on the trait of ideas, so I deliberately left my first rough draft vague, undeveloped, hoping the students would help me fill in the gaps. So often teachers think they must be excellent writers to effectively share their writing with students. Not true. Weaknesses are an advantage. Really. If your writing starts out being so good your students can't think of *anything* to suggest, your whole lesson is down the drain. Here's draft 1:

THE PITCHER

Draft 1—Ideas

The bleachers aren't too comfortable, but I like sitting here anyway. I like the feel of the wind in my face and the sounds of the ball field. I like watching the kids play ball. I'm glad this coach doesn't yell as much as some do.

The kids are warming up and they head out across the field. I am watching the pitcher walk toward the mound to practice. He walks with a lot of confidence. You can see he's had a lot of practice. There is something about the way he stands that catches my eye. I love watching him throw, as if he can see right where the ball should go.

Reading Aloud

Reading and sharing are important parts of the revision process. So I decided to model this part as well, turning on the light so students could read along with me. I asked students for their immediate reaction, and they said, "Pretty good." Oh, man. I thought of what I had heard Peter Elbow say in an NCTE seminar once—that the phrase "It's pretty good" or "I liked it fine" is the equivalent of saying "Your writing made absolutely no impression on me at all." I shared this with the students, which made them laugh, and also told them their body language (slouching, arms folded, faces blank) was telling me more than their comments. They *hated* it. This was actually pure drama on my part. In truth, they weren't paying enough attention to hate it.

We then scored it on the trait of ideas. Most of them gave it a 3 on a 5-point scale. I think that's generous, but they did say that even though the paper lacked details, the description of the ballpark and the pitcher were fairly clear. Personally, I think it is closer to a 2. Here are their comments:

> When they saw me, the vulnerable, egotistical writer, offering up my work to their questions, it gave them an incentive to do the same.
>
> Roy Peter Clark (1987, 41)

- This really isn't about a place, is it? But I guess that doesn't matter. Your topic can change as you write.
- You have too many I's. It sounds like the paper is about *you*.
- The second paragraph is better. It's more specific. But I still don't see the pitcher. Show him in action.
- You need more colors, smells, details, something.
- Put me right there. I'm not there yet.
- What color were their uniforms? What was the coach saying? How high up did you sit? There's almost nothing specific in here.
- You talk about the sounds of the ballfield, but I don't hear anything. *What* sounds?
- I know this is organization, but your paper just stops. You need a better ending.
- You also need some feeling. I know that's voice, but doesn't voice come partly from the details?

They raise some excellent issues. Is it all right to wander from the original topic? Not always, but in free writing such as this, sometimes it's essential in order to find your real subject, in this case, the pitcher, not the bleachers. Too many *I*'s? Absolutely. The focus of the paper *is* on me, the writer, not the pitcher or the ballpark, and that is all wrong. Comments on organization and voice are not irrelevant. Sure, we're mainly working on ideas, but every trait affects every other trait. As you will see in a minute, revising for one trait influences others.

Recording and Saving Comments

You may wish to record students' comments and make an overhead you can share with the class next time. I did this. It's very useful in showing which of their comments influenced my revision most, and it keeps them engaged. Right now they're teaching not only me but also themselves, about clarity and detail (the heart of ideas).

I revised the paper (twice, actually), and shared both revisions with students (aloud and on the overhead). Revision one was *terrible*—long and clunky; I am not (you'll be happy to know) reprinting it here. You can take my word (the students concurred), it was tedious cubed. This third draft was more concise:

THE PITCHER

Third Draft—Ideas

The bleachers are hard, splintery and unforgiving, as worn and raggedy as much of the district's outdated PE equipment. They shake when you step aboard, and it's part of the fun—looking up to see if the guy at the top notices you're rocking the boat.

The coach isn't a screamer like some, but you can hear his voice above the wind all right. "Jesse! Kevin! Cody! Let's see some hustle . . ." They run for left field, grinning and punching each other's arms, pulling down red cap brims, blue legs pumping. Wind sweeps the grass and fills our faces.

I'm not watching the other kids, though. My eye is on one player. Normally shy, a kid with quiet eyes and a keep out of your way kind of walk, he strides up to the pitcher's mound like he owns it. Like it's his special place. One foot kicks the dirt, nudges and shapes it as if someone has messed it all up in his absence. He turns a bit and stares, but you have to know him to know what he sees. It isn't the catcher, nor the mitt the catcher holds up in anticipation. It isn't the plate. Or the fence.

It's a spot. One spot in all the universe, special for no reason except it's there and it's all his. And when he hits it just right, the rest of the world goes away.

The students agreed this version was stronger and had much more detail. They scored it 4s and 5s on the trait of ideas. They did notice that I had played with the special-place theme, focusing on several kinds of places and ending with that elusive perfect strike zone in the pitcher's head. What I really wanted to share with the students, though, was my writing process.

As I explained to them, I couldn't quite get the ball park right in my head sitting at home staring at the computer—that's why my first revision was so bad. So I took that revision with me to the ballpark, sat on the bleachers, and wrote what I really saw and felt. It made all the difference. You may notice, too, that the second draft is also stronger in organization; it has a much improved ending (The last line is my favorite part of the paper) and, I think, smoother transitions. I'm a more involved writer this time, too, so the voice emerges, and I think it's a little more fluent. Revise one trait and others come along for the ride.

GIVE STUDENTS OPPORTUNITIES TO PRACTICE REVISION

Once students have seen you model focused revision, students are ready to try it themselves. Several things will help you make focused revision lessons successful:

1. Have students **work in pairs** so they will discuss as they write.
2. Begin by scoring and discussing a **VERY weak piece of writing**—one for which students will be able to think of many revision ideas.
3. Make sure students **understand the scoring guide** for a given trait well. If they do not know what to look for, revision is hard.
4. **Score** the piece **prior to revising** it.
5. **Discuss reasons** behind the scores: What is missing? What would have made it stronger?
6. Assure students that **no two revisions must**—or for that matter, should—**look alike**.
7. Give students editorial license to **add detail.** Many pieces that are good candidates for revision practice are so sketchy that unless students add LOTS of detail, nothing much will change. That's fine.
8. Be SURE you **practice on copy that is NOT students' own.** This gives them freedom to make sweeping changes they might feel hesitant about in their own work.

The Advantages of Partnership

As students work, they talk, they plan, and they learn. Together, they think of more ways to revise than either might think of separately. What's more, the whole concept of revision, which seemed so unappealing when they were tackling their own work exclusively, suddenly takes on a whole new allure when students have the chance to mess around with someone else's work. Now the sky's the limit.

Here again is "Redwoods" from Chapter 3, together with a revision by a pair of middle school students. Want to challenge yourself a bit? Write your own revision, with or without a partner, prior to looking at what the middle school students did. Then you can compare. If you don't have time to rewrite the whole thing, do *just the lead*.

REDWOODS

Original—Grade 11

Last year we went on a vacation and we had a wonderful time. The weather was sunny and warm and there was lots to do so we were never bored.

My parents visited friends and took pictures for their friends back home. My brother and I swam and also hiked in the woods. When we got tired of that, we just ate and had a wonderful time.

It was exciting and fun to be together as a family and to do things together. I love my family and this is a time that I will remember for a long time. I hope we will go back again next year for more fun and an even better time than we had this year.

Two middle school students who scored and revised this piece rated the original a 2 on the trait of ideas. Here is the revision that took them two 45-minute class periods:

THE REDWOODS

Revision—Grade 8

Last summer, my family and I went on a vacation to see the California Redwoods. Most of the time was great, though not everything turned out the way we expected. We spent most of our time basking in the sun and hiking. We basked so much I got a sunburn from head to toe, and had to spend the next several days peeling my outer layer of skin.

One day we hiked the Sunrise Trail. The cool morning air was easy to hike in so we ended up doing the whole thing. The giant ferns were like something out of a prehistoric movie. The trees were so huge we could not see the tops. Three of us linking arms could not reach around the trunks. It was amazing to think how old they were and to try imagining what they had lived through. It made us feel tiny and transient.

Like sun bathing, hiking had its drawbacks. The main one being my brother. We saw a gorgeous sunrise and several deer. I had never been close to a deer before and I was very excited, but I knew better than to yell. Not Tom! He came crashing out of the brush yelling, "A deer! A deer! Look you guys!" We just glared at him. That was the last time we took the Sunrise Trail.

My parents aren't big hikers, so they spent their time visiting friends, mostly people I wasn't too fond of, but my parents loved. They took what seemed like thousands of pictures to show the folks back home. Practically every rock was photographed. Every tree was in a picture. It got quite nerve-wracking having a camera pointed in my direction constantly, so I took off for the woods, secretly hoping to get lost.

My family doesn't take many vacations, so it was fun being together. I will never forget those deer or hiking the Sunrise Trail with the people I love. Maybe we'll come back next year, or go someplace different. It doesn't really matter as long as I am with my family. Next time, though, I think our camera may experience an unfortunate accident.

This is a vast improvement, full of telling details about the sunburn, the enormous ferns and trees, the boisterous Tom, and the omnipresent camera. Much of the vague language is gone. I would rate it a very strong 4. It's just a draft away from being wonderful; perhaps a more focused angle—more about Tom or the camera—would take it to that next level.

Here, just to compare, is a second revision by a twelfth grader, who dares to go a step farther from the original and put some real attitude into her revision:

> Becoming a writer is about becoming conscious. When you're conscious and writing from a place of insight and simplicity and real caring about the truth, you have the ability to throw the lights on for your reader.
>
> Lamott (1994, 225)

THE REDWOODS

I'll be the first to admit I've pretty much outgrown the family vacation. So when my father announced that we were going to spend a week down in California seeing a bunch of trees, you can imagine how thrilled I was. Until the day of the trip, I kept hoping for some ailment to afflict and rescue me from this world of family fun. Nothing struck. No compassionate neighbors volunteered to take me in. No desperate local business people called with an urgent job to be filled. I was free, capable of packing, and unemployed. It looked more and more as if I'd have to go.

The day we set out (or as I like to think of it, "Hell: Day One") arrived. I packed in five minutes flat, yanking items at random out of my drawer (Who cares what you wear in the woods? It's dark in there, isn't it?), stuffed my bag in the trunk of the car and plunked onto my side of the backseat (already polluted with my brother's gum wrappers, inane video game magazines, and empty remains of old gummy bears bags). Mom turned and smiled gamely at me, and I tried to respond, but the corners of my mouth seemed frozen as if shot through with novocaine, and would not turn up. Mom gave up, and returned to the safety of the front-seat world of mom and dad.

Dad swung back out of the driveway and headed out with a cheery "Here we go!" Mom's shoulders took on a kind of jaunty look, and knowing better than to sigh out loud, I slumped down low into my backseat prison. One whole day of my life, stuck next to my un-shampooed little brother. Luckily, I had brought a book, and immersed myself in it as soon as we hit the freeway. "Don't touch my book," I hissed at him, knowing his fingers were sticky with gummy bear remnants. I didn't even want to ask what that gunk on his shoes might be. "I don't want your dumb old book," he retorted. "Play a game with me." Dear God, I thought, this is going to be a *long* trip. Cooped up with a non-reading Video-Maniac who's gooey to boot.

Finally, we arrived at the Redwoods. I didn't look up from my book at first, even though my parents were pleading with me to "Look! Oh, look!" At length, I raised my eyes, and for just a moment, I couldn't breathe. I hadn't thought that a sophisticated, worldly high school student like me would be in awe over a few big trees. Yet, I was. They towered over our car like huge pre-historic creatures, breathing gently, allowing us to pass, as they dangled their graceful, swinging arms just over us.

I dropped my book, forgetting about the world of courtroom trials, corrupt judges and the unsolved mysteries of dead wives and lovers. I felt compelled to touch one of those trees, the way you always want to touch amazing things like orchid petals or the inside of an oyster shell. How unimportant novels and gummy bears seemed to me as I embraced that ancient giant.

My reflective thoughts were interrupted as Jimmy the Gooey blurted out in his squeaky eighth grade voice, "Stand in front of the tree, Dodo-Head, so I can take your picture." I stood in front of the tree, looked deep into his camera and smiled—not at Jimmy, of course, but at the whole feeling of being alive. That photo is still in one of our albums at home. I will leave it to you to imagine what the Video-Maniac wrote as a caption, but I'll give you this hint: He didn't come close to capturing what I felt.

The brother in this version comes to life as Jimmy the Gooey, the Video-Maniac; he's no longer a fuzzy entity. What I like most though is the packing scene ("Who cares what you wear in the woods?"), and the clear contrast between disgruntled teenagers and the forcibly cheery Mom and Dad who retreat to their own "front-seat world" to escape the bickering. I have no difficulty giving this revision 5s and 6s.

For a powerful lesson on ideas, have students

1. Revise "Redwoods" themselves, working with a partner
2. Compare their revisions with the eighth or twelfth grade versions in this chapter—or both

What About the Other Traits—and Other Papers?

"Redwoods" is a classic for revision practice in ideas, and as you look through Chapter 3, you'll spot other papers that will work equally well, for ideas or other traits (you can use a paper for more than one trait). In addition, you can save rough drafts from your own students (with their permission) and exchange them with other teachers or hang onto them for a couple years so that the identity of the student is protected, then use them for revision practice. You do not have to use student papers all the time, either. Use excerpts from e-mail, the newspaper, advertisements, textbooks, or manuals and pamphlets, and you'll *never* run out of writing in need of revision.

Following, to get you started, are practice revision papers for each of the other traits (except conventions, which is a special case we'll deal with shortly). First, some how-to's on setting up a practice revision lesson.

PROCEDURES FOR SETTING UP THE LESSON

Note: We're using <u>Organization</u> as an example here; the procedure is the same for any trait.

<u>Time</u>: Two 45-minute class periods, or three 30-minute class periods

<u>You need</u>:

- An overhead of the Scoring Chart (Figure 6.1)
- A blank overhead for making notes
- 6-Trait Scoring Guides (student version) for each writer
- An overhead copy of the paper to be revised
- (Preferably, if possible) hard copies of the paper to be revised, so students can make notes
- Paper on which students can draft their revisions OR access to word processors with printing capabilities

<u>What to do</u>:

1. Divide students into pairs. If it does not come out evenly, you can have one group of three.
2. Ask students to take out their 6-Trait Scoring Guides (the student version).
3. Put the writing sample on the overhead projector and read it aloud. Ask for general comments, then ask students, with their partners, to score the paper for the trait of Organization (or whatever trait you're working on).
4. Tally the scores, using the Scoring Chart. Discuss results—especially if scores vary. Try to bring scores across the class to within a one point difference: e.g., a 1–2 split, or a 2–3 split.
5. Ask for suggestions on what might be done to revise this piece of writing so it would receive a 5 or 6 in the trait at hand. Jot down suggestions on the blank overhead.

Title of Paper:_____

	Scores					
TRAITS	6	5	4	3	2	1
Ideas						
Organization						
Voice						
Word Choice						
Sentence Fluency						
Conventions						

FIGURE 6.1. Scoring grid master

6. Ask students, again working with their partners, to revise the weak piece of writing for the given trait. Allow the remainder of this class period plus another—or whatever time you feel students need. *Don't rush.*

7. Once revisions are completed, invite three or four revision teams to read their revisions aloud. Discuss differences you hear from draft to revision, as well as from team to team. It is usually very interesting to see how much the revisions differ one from another.

8. After practicing revision on someone else's writing, students are ready to work on a piece of their own. This should be the final step. Working **individually** this time, they should go through their own writing folders and choose a draft they'd like to revise for the trait you've just worked on. Allow one or two class periods for this revision, which may include sharing results with a partner or small group. (Note: Once you've done all the traits, you can continue the revision practice—only now you simply let students decide what needs work and what they will revise. You can tell them this is the advanced trait practice; they must not only revise, but make the diagnosis themselves!)

PAPERS YOU CAN USE FOR PRACTICE REVISION

Organization, Grade 8

So the reason why football is my favorite sport is I am good at it. Although I am good at basketball and hockey, too, but football is still my favorite. At football games the fans go wild. They chear there lungs out and it is the best. I love that sound. It keeps me going. When I was in fourth grade I was sure basketball would be my favorite sport because I was pretty good at it and could usually score some baskets during most of the games. One time I scored the winning basket! My dad has a picture of me doing that. It is blurry, but you can tell it's me, and we have it framed and sitting on the mantle in the living room. But when I got into Middle school that's when I started plying football and their was just no turning back. I can't even describe the feeling. Some kids get football scholarships or even scholarships from other sports. That would really make my parents proud. But I think the main reason to play is just because you love the game.

Another way to plan a piece of writing is simply to list the main points that will be made in the piece of writing. I call these points sequences, because I like to move them around until they're in a natural order so each point leads to the next one.
Donald M. Murray (1984, 98)

Organization, Grade 4

I did not want to get my cat declaued but when I told my dad he would not lisen to me. It turned out I was right!! Now our cat is so so so so cranky you cannot come near it. This is what happens when you think abowt your own feelings and do not think of the feelings of your pet. Like when our dog ran away I think my dad was secritly glad because he is mostly the one who takes are of it. But he came home, so now my dad just has to live with it. Our cat and dog get along pretty good but not that good, so if we could only keep one I would pick our dog because he is so friendly. The cat is in a bad mood because after we had her declaued the dog could pick on her and she culdn't do anything abowt it.

Voice, Grade 11

Voice separates writing that is not read from writing that is read.
   Donald M. Murray (1984, 144)

Locker searches should not be legal in my opinion. A locker is private and if you let people look in your locker it could be an invasion of privacy. It is not OK just because lockers belong to kids. Most of the time people who search lockers do not find anything, anyway. Most kids who do drugs do not keep their drugs in their lockers. Only a moron would do that. It isn't like people mind having their lockers searched all that much because they are not hiding anything. They do not usually have guns or stuff in their, so it is not that worthwhile for the authorities to do locker searches in the first place. They even bring in dogs. This could be threatening to students safety. All they find is old lunches and backpacks with kids stuff in them. It is a waste of time. Plus it is humiliating to us as students. It does not contribute to school safety. That is just an excuse. So as you can see it is not really fair to search lockers. Lockers should be private. That is the main reason I am not voting for locker searches.

Voice, Grade 5

This paper is about what it would be like to be a porcupine. I guess it would be kind of cool because nobody much would boss you around. I would go where I want and do what I want and nobody much would try to stop me because they would be afraid of my quills and stuff. But if I were a porcupine, I'm not sure where I would sleep or what I would eat in the winter. Or the summer for that matter. I don't know if it would be that neat because they are kind of ugly once thy are grown up and nobody really likes them all that much. People are afraid of them, and I would not want everyone going around being afraid of me. For instance, people do not feed porcupines. You don't see like a lot of tee shirts with porcupines on them. My dad says they can kill trees by eating the bark. If that is true then porcupines can be harmful to the enviroment.

Word Choice, Grade 10

Adjectives and adverbs are rich and good and fattening. The main thing is not to overindulge.
   Ursula K. LeGuin (1998, 61)

Elephants devour humongous quantities of water each day of their lifetimes. Even baby elephants consume as much as 28 gallons per day, and adult elephants can consume more than triple this prodigious amount. It is no real quandry then that the future prolonged preservation of elephants is in dubious plight. With humanity descending upon these enormous but gracious creatures, we can readily perceive that humans are encroaching upon the natural resources elephants need to retain their survival. We must learn to share to eradicate the endangerment we ourselves have initiated.

Word Choice, Grade 6

Do not spend too much time in the sun. It could be dangerous to be in the sun for too long. If you get a sun burn, it could cause cancer. Cancer can kill you. Do not spend more than ten minutes in the sun. If you are going to be in the sun for more than ten minutes, wear some kind of protection. That could be a big hat or sun lotion. Sun lotion is good but it will not last a real long time. When they say "all-day sun lotion" do not believe it. It does not last all day. It lasts about two hours. At the most. If you are going to be in the sun for many hours, wear a big hat and use a lot of lotion. Put it on more than just once and put it on in a thick layer so you can still see it on your skin. Otherwise, you could burn and get skin cancer. It can even hurt you if the sun burn was a long time ago like when you were a small child. The sun is stronger now. Even on a cloudy day you can still get a sunburn. Even if you have dark colored skin you can get a sun burn. So, do not spend too much time in the sun. And do not forget your sun lotion! Even put it on your feet. I got burnd there and it is no fun.

Sentence Fluency, Grade 9

You might not know this but at any given time somewhere on the face of the earth 10 to 15 volcanoes are erupting so there are volcanoes erupting constantly. A lot of scientists are looking for ways to predict when and where volcanoes will erupt so people can know when the eruptions will occur but the reason why it is so hard is that no two volcanoes are alike. Because no two volcanoes are alike they make different seismic patterns in the surface of the earth, but it is the gases escaping from the cracks volcanoes create in the earth's crust that make the detection by satellite possible, though this is not a wholly accurate predictor of eruptions. Someday we will know when and where volcanic eruptions will occur. We will then be able to predict eruptions on the weather just like the temperature for tomorrow or the rain or snow. Then we will be able to prepare for volcanic eruptions. Until then, we must hope for the best and stay alert.

Sentence Fluency, Grade 4

I love dancing. I take ballet classes twice a week. I have this really neat teacher, Mrs. Graham. She used to be a dancer herself. I get so excited when it is the day for my dance class because I know it will be so fun. I could not keep my balance last year when I first started lessons, but now I can. I could not get all the way up onto my toes or get full extension of my legs, but now I can because I have the strength and flexibility it takes. I have put in the time to practice. I feel proud of myself, but I know it is all because Mrs. Graham is such a great teacher. She will not let me fail! I am going to be a professional ballerina some day and do dance recitals. I may even teach ballet myself. I think I will invite Mrs. Graham to one of my recitals if she still remembers me. I guess when you have as many students as she does, it is hard to remember them all. Mrs. Graham is the best ballet teacher who ever lived. She is graceful, patient, and a true athlete. I hope I can be like her one day.

Just a Beginning Point

Consider these few sample papers just a beginning point. As your students become more proficient, challenge them by giving them stronger papers to revise—and papers of many different kinds, including business letters, informational pieces, advertisements, and narratives. As you do so, ask

- What is the purpose of this piece?
- Who is the intended audience?

These basic questions help keep any revision activity in focus. And of course, don't forget that ultimately you want them to transfer their revision skills to their own work. Notice how Nancy, a 12th grader, goes here from a tiny sketch to lively, expanded story of her night with Tommy the Terrible. Her first assignment was to write a piece no more than 50 words long; it just captures the essentials:

"BABYSITTING"

Little Tommy begged me to go outside and get the dog. Tommy's orders weren't part of my job. Click! The door locked behind me. Tommy was upstairs playing with trucks. I sat on the porch. Finally, his parents came home.
  "How nice of you to bring out the dog. That deserves a bonus!"

Now, here's Nancy's expanded version. Notice the differences not only in detail, but in voice, fluency, organization, and word choice also.

"LITTLE TOMMY"

[Revised, expanded version]

"I never have milk with my dinner," hissed little Tommy, while he picked at the macaroni with his fingers. How was I supposed to know what he drank at dinner? I knew this evening of babysitting would be another night to remember.

The house was located back in the woods, about a mile from the main road. It stood on a large embankment overlooking a lake that I didn't even know existed until I started watching little Tommy. Their house was huge. It was more like a hotel than a home. Tommy's playroom was bigger than my parents' master bedroom. His mom's good taste was reflected in the decorating. Countless pieces of flowered furniture and drapery reminded me of photographs I had seen in *Better Homes and Gardens*.

Tommy threw his spoon across the room just missing the glass Japanese vase that stood on the counter. He scowled at me and began moaning about the hot dog that I cut up for him.

"Mom cuts up only half the hot dog so I can try using the knife on my own!" he yelled, pushing the plate across the table, announcing he was done. Was his mom crazy? How could she even think of putting any sort of knife in front of this child? Tommy shook his head of red curls and wailed at the top of his lungs while trying to undo the belt of his booster seat. I couldn't believe I'd agreed to do this. He squinted at me and started pulling my hair as I tried to calm him down. He had a dried grape juice mustache around his tiny lips and numerous food stains made his solid yellow shirt look more like a print.

I glanced at the clock. It was only 6 pm. One more hour till his bedtime! I decided to let him play for a while because I had obviously failed at the dinner-time task of getting Tommy to eat. All of a sudden, he broke out of his booster and sprinted across the room.

"Come back here!" I called, as I heard his little bare feet smacking across the floor and around the corner. I tried following, but he was gone. First, I tried the basement. I was definitely not in the mood for his hide-and-seek games. At least this situation was not as bad as the last time, when Tommy got himself so tangled up in the tire swing that when his parents came home it looked like I had tied him up. Or the time little Tommy had tried his new fingerpaints out on the livingroom walls and turned the piano keys into an assortment of fluorescent colors.

I ran upstairs and searched closets, under the beds, even the attic—until I found him in his toy chest. I was shocked to see him in there, wondering how he had squeezed his pudgy body into such a tiny space. He burst out with laughter, saying I had taken the longest of any of his babysitters to find him.

Suddenly Ribo, the family's dachshund, was barking and prancing around the room, excited by the commotion Tommy had created. "It's time for Ribo to go out!" Tommy demanded, scooping up the little dog and shoving it into my stomach. His orders weren't part of my babysitting plans, but to keep him quiet, I took Ribo downstairs to the front yard, which looked like a war zone, filled with Tommy's and Ribo's toys. Click. The door locked behind me, and Tommy was upstairs. I sat on the porch to think. There wasn't a spare key, but it sure was nice to have some peace and quiet for once! Two hours later, Tommy's parents returned home.

"How nice of you to bring out the dog!" they exclaimed. "That deserves a bonus!"

SELF-REFLECTION: THE END OF THE RAINBOW

Certainly, we want students who can manage revision on their own—and even teach us how to revise writing effectively. The ultimate goal of all this is to lead students to a point where they can look down from the mountain: reflect on how far they've come as writers and figure out where they'd like to go next. You've seen two memorable examples already: Taylor's piece from Chapter 1, and Lauren's piece from Chapter 3. Here are three more to help you keep in mind that the traits are nothing more than a springboard to good thinking.

Sample 1

See how much this twelfth grader is able to "read" in her own writing when she looks at her portfolio through the eyes of specific written criteria.

My goals in September were to gain more experience in writing and improve my organizational techniques.

I definitely acquired experience, which will be helpful in college and beyond. I became a more seasoned writer by realizing that my writing had tone, a thesis, voice, word choice and many other literary devices. Previous writings show little awareness of these things. Learning this definite structure was very helpful in making advances that are not apparent in this portfolio. I am now able to begin an essay without hesitation. Based on a given topic, I decide on a thesis, supporting details, a method of organization, and appropriate word choice. I no longer make long lists of useless notes, and write essays that are unfocused.

Reading the essays in the textbook enhanced my understanding of word choice and tone. I realize now how important the topic and audience are to this decision, and I am more capable of making the correct choice. I also learned how to vary my sentence length for emphasis. This is an important technique for a persuasive writer.

Sample 2

This high school student has been in classes that emphasize both writing process and the six traits for several years. If you've ever lost a computer file, you'll enjoy her tongue-in-cheek essay—as well as her reflection on what she feels is best about her writing.

Computer Blues

So there I was, my face aglow with the reflection of my computer screen, trying to conclude my essay. Writing it was akin to water torture. It dragged on and on, a never-ending babble about legumes, nutrients, and soil degradation. I was tranquilizing myself with my own writing.

Suddenly, unexpectedly—I felt an ending coming on. Four or five punchy sentences would bring this baby to a close, and I'd be free of this dreadful assignment forever! Yes!

I had not saved yet, and decided I would do so now. I scooted the white mouse over the pad toward the "File" menu—and had almost reached home when it happened. By accident, I clicked the mouse button just to the left of paragraph 66. The screen flashed briefly, and the next thing I knew, I was back to square one. Black. I stared at my blank screen for a moment in disbelief. Where was my essay? My ten-billion-page masterpiece? Gone?! No—that couldn't be! Not after all the work I had done! Would my computer be that unforgiving? That unfeeling? Didn't it care about me at all?

I decided not to give up just yet. The secret was to remain calm. After all, my file had to be *somewhere,* right? That's what all the manuals say—"It's in there somewhere." I went back to the "File" menu, much more carefully this time. First, I tried a friendly sounding category called "Find File." No luck there; I hadn't given my file a name.

Ah, then I had a brainstorm. I could simply go up to *Undo.* Yes, *Undo* would be my savior! A simple click of a button and my problem would be solved. *Undo,* however, looked a bit fuzzy. Not a good sign. "Fuzzy" means there is nothing to undo. *Don't panic . . . don't panic . . .*

I decided to try exiting the program, not really knowing what I would accomplish by this, but now feeling more than a little desperate. Next, I clicked on the icon that would allow me back into word processing. A small sign appeared, telling me that my program was being used by "another user." Another user? What's it talking about? *I'm* the only user, you idiot! Or at least I'm *trying* to be a user! Give my paper back! Right now!

I clicked on the icon again and again—to no avail. Click . . . click . . . clickclickclickclickCLICKCLICKCLICKCLICK!!!!! Without warning, a thin trickle of smoke began emanating from the back of the computer. I didn't know whether to laugh or cry. Sighing, I opened my desk drawer, and pulled out a tablet and pen. This was going to be a long day.

STUDENT'S REFLECTION

In this essay, I tried to capture the feelings of frustration that occur when human and machine do not communicate. The voice in this piece comes, I think, from the feeling that "We've all been there." Everyone who works with computers has had this experience, or something close to it. I also try to give the writer—me— some real personality so the sense of building tension comes through. A tiny writer's problem (not being able to find a good ending) turns into a major problem (losing a whole document). This makes the ideas clear, and also gives this little story some structure. I think the reader can picture this poor, frustrated writer at her computer, wanting, trying to communicate in a human way, but finding that in its own mechanical way, the computer is just as frustrated with her.

Sample 3

Here a fourth grader reflects most thoughtfully and with highly sophisticated language on the total writing process and the overall writing goals she has for herself (Her voice is much stronger than she thinks!):

Writing is good for the heart and soul. It lets you explore places without actually being there. It opens up your mind. It lets you see things the way other people see them. I want to learn more about writing because I want my writing to be clear and to have a compelling sense of direction. I don't think my voice is strong right now. I'm at a 3. For my parents and my teacher, that might be OK, but I think I can do better. I won't be satisfied until it is individual and powerful.

REFLECTING ON CHAPTER 6

1. Have you ever had to learn something complex—a craft, special skill or sport— step by step? Can you recall what it was like? Can you list some of the steps you worked on? How did it feel when you finally put it all together? Can you recall a moment when you knew you "had" it?

2. Some people say writing is too complex to define, so we should not try to identify its salient parts. How do you feel about this argument? What would you say to someone who felt this way?

ACTIVITIES

1. Try focused revision yourself, working with a partner. Choose a short piece— even an excerpt or single paragraph from any source at all; it need not be student writing. (It is fine to use your own writing if you like.) Talk about the process.

How is it different (1) working with a partner; and (2) working on someone else's text? What is easier? What's harder? What did you learn that you can take to your own work?

2. Using a brief rough draft of your own, lead a lesson in revision by asking your discussion group or your class to assess and comment on your writing—then offer suggestions or ask questions to prompt your thinking. Discuss the process. How did you feel sharing your own writing? What parts of revision do you think you modeled successfully for the group? (You might ask them to do a brief critique to see if they agree!)

LOOKING AHEAD

In Chapter 7, we will continue our discussion of using assessment as a basis for writing and revision by talking about problems teachers spot in student writing, and some things you can do as a teacher to help your student writers solve these problems. We will also talk about ways to teach editing effectively without being an editor for your students.

MEMORABLE MOMENTS FROM STUDENTS' WRITING

- Losing my sandals would be like misplacing my smile.
- He was a simple man who died of complications.
- Explaining things to Brad is like trying to build a space shuttle.
- Though it can throw you some hard punches, if you have the right heels, you can kick life back, and it will hurt more.
- Shoes give us individuality and style; without them, we'd be shorter and have cold feet.
- I want to fly to France and have their famous french fries.

7

TROUBLESHOOTING—
From Ideas to Conventions

Writing is about hypnotizing yourself into believing yourself, getting some work done, then unhypnotizing yourself and going over the work coldly. There will be many mistakes, many things to take out, and others that need to be added.

Anne Lamott (1994, 114)

After fifty years of writing, I have pretty much gotten over my fear of writing. Not all, but most of it. I wouldn't want to get over all of it. A little terror is stimulating. Writing is important, and you can say something that is wrong, stupid, silly, clumsy. And you will.

Donald M. Murray (1990, 69)

No matter how are carefully and thoroughly we try to teach anything, including traits, problems arise. In the case of traits, that's not all bad—if we look at writing as problem solving. If you're a writer yourself, then you are continually working on such writers' problems as

- Facing the blank page with ABSOLUTELY NOTHING to say
- Coming up with a title that doesn't sound trite
- Coming up with a lead that isn't formulaic
- Making sentences clear
- Figuring out what to do when you begin in one direction and find yourself going in another altogether
- Turning off the editor in your head who persists in whispering, "This sounds really stupid"
- Finding the courage to write in your own voice, and to say what you truly think

- Reading what you've written in front of other people
- Learning to edit your own text accurately

Being a writer is hard work, and perhaps this is the first thing we should share with students. We do them no favors by suggesting that this nifty strategy or that tested formula will make all the pieces fall into place. I agree with Marjorie Frank when she says, "Students should be told about the energy it takes to write" (1995, 92). In the end, nothing takes the place of writing, writing, writing. Nevertheless, as writing coaches, we can help diagnose various kinds of writing troubles, and provide some direct help.

Here I list a few of teachers' most common concerns about their students' writing and suggest specific things you can do to help your students build strengths trait by trait. At the end of the chapter, I'll cover the teaching of editing in depth, and suggest some things you can do to make writing less intimidating for students who find the whole idea of writing challenging— or who just plain do not *want* to write. In addition, I'll suggest things you can do to make trait writing a little *more* challenging for students who have been through trait-based instruction before.

> I hate to tell ya, but there's no easy answer. If you want discipline you have to keep slowly adding, building, and staying with it until one day, doing it feels better than not doing it. It's like doing sit-ups.
> Nancy Slonim Aronie (1998, 103)

IDEAS

Problem 1: The Information Is Too Skimpy! This Paper Simply Doesn't Say Anything.

TRY THESE STRATEGIES

Encourage student writers to choose their own topics, at least part of the time. There will be those special times, such as when you're studying the Holocaust or the Civil War, that you wish them to focus their writing on a general theme, but even then they can often select topics within prescribed bounds. How to find topics? Keep lists, borrow from one another, read extensively. Remind students to keep topics small and personal. Writers like Erma Bombeck, Jerry Seinfeld and Robert Fulghum know that such things as surviving a stressful family gathering, eating something you cannot identify (!), or losing your luggage are the raw fabric of great writing. Life, not headlines, is what's interesting.

Read *much* more nonfiction aloud. So many students feel writing is about stories. Sometimes, it is. But of equal interest to us should be their reflections on recycling, the rain forest, multi-cultural issues, the economy, video technology, cloning, home schooling, earthquakes, invasion of fire ants, violence in schools, or whatever is on their minds. Reading front page articles, reviews, personal essays, excerpts from well-written nonfiction journals (e.g., *Discover Magazine, Dig, Ranger Rick*), and editorials lends validity to forms of writing that may not be so familiar as the story—forms in which many students find their true voice for the first time. Not everyone is born to be a story teller.

> I can't stand writing stories. Honestly! I never write them from my imagination—only when an idea from life or books jumps into my head, not out of it. I have about four ideas a year, and I'm a proficient, professional, published writer, yet we ask children to write story after story.
> Mem Fox (1993)

You probably think the words research paper and interesting are mutually exclusive. The prevalent belief among my students is that the minute you start having to use facts in your writing, then the prose wilts and dies like an unwatered begonia. . . . But factual writing doesn't have to be dull.

Bruce Ballenger (1998, 12)

Allow much, much more time for prewriting. If your students are exploring a specific topic, fill the room with books and journals on that topic. Make lists of questions an audience would likely have. Assign students or groups to answer each question as thoroughly as possible. Explore other sources of information: films, site visits, interviews, or information via mail or the Internet. The very act of exploring generates new topics. The more a writer knows, the easier the writing.

Practice observation skills. Watch a hamster, turtle, or salamander for a while. Write down what you see. Watch people at the airport. Take a nature hike and record observations. Teach students to look for the less than obvious—not the turtle's shell, but the nicks and scratches on the shell. Not the numbers of people at the airport, but the kinds of shoes they wear or the different ways they walk, talk or manage their luggage.

When I was in school I thought details were just extra words to add in a story to make it better. I thought detail was decoration or wallpaper . . . Details are not wallpaper; they are walls.

Barry Lane (1999, 42)

Start with a sketch. Take a story all students, all ages know well—say "The Three Little Pigs." Tell it in the sketchiest form you can: *Three pigs tried building houses. The first two didn't build very sturdy houses and they got eaten by a wolf. The third pig built a house of brick. He escaped.* Have students fill in the missing details. Write them down. Now have them look at their own writing in this same way. Is it a sketch, too? Or is it rich with detail?

Problem 2: Too Much Trivia Weighs the Text Down. I Don't Care How Much the Dog Weighed or When the Cat Was Born.

TRY THESE STRATEGIES

I try to leave out the parts that people skip.

Elmore Leonard in Charlton (1992)

Figure out who the likely audience is, and then ask, What do they know already? What would they probably like to know? What would bore them? (Don't write about that part).

Pick a topic at random and list, as a class, everything you know about it. Then, ask students to work in pairs to make two lists: one for the critical stuff, the other for the trivial stuff. They must learn to discriminate. No one can write everything, though some writers have surely tried. Who can forget *Moby Dick?*. Listing also helps a writer know what additional information he/she needs.

As you read from textbooks, picture books, novels, short stories, or other sources, stop to ask frequently, **Why is this detail here?** Will it show up again? Students will often begin a story, "This was the day that Fred could not find his special shoes . . ." We say to ourselves, "Ah, the *special shoes—they* must be important to the story." But apparently they're not because they never turn up again. In the hands of a successful writer, *every detail* means something; if the hero wears his special shoes, there's a reason.

Problem 3: There's Too Much Information. Help! It's Huge.

TRY THESE STRATEGIES

Cut the copy in half. Yes, it can be done. Ask wordy writers to imagine they're writing for a newspaper and can only fill four inches on the page—

or whatever. Ask them to cut the copy they have by half, without losing content. That's the trick. No strategy is better for helping writers become concise.

It's hard to make the writing tight when the topic is huge. **Practice narrowing a big topic down** till you can't make it any skinnier. Do this as a class first, then in teams, then individually. For instance, baseball is too big, so narrow it down to Little League ball. Still too big? Then describe how to pitch, how to throw a fastball, how to throw a fastball against the best hitter in the league, how to strike out the best hitter in the league when you're up against a 3-2 count and trying to look cool for your fans—and you have a strained muscle in your back. Small, focused topics are not only easier to write about but more interesting. We experience life in close-ups, one blazing pitch, one pulled muscle at a time. Practice, as a class, on not just one but on five or ten topics in this way. Then have students choose the actual topics they'll write on.

Now go the other way and ask your students **to see how much big information they can glean (as readers, now) from a tiny detail.** If you remember the film *The Big Red One* (1980), you may recall that early on in the film, and then for several scenes afterward, the camera shows the hand of a man lying facedown on the beach at Normandy. You do not see the whole man, just the hand. As the waves wash over him, the water becomes tinted red. You never see the flow of blood directly, just the red of the water, which becomes more intense in every scene. The hands on the face of his watch move slowly, and we study them as if thinking about an appointment instead of the unfolding Normandy invasion. These tiny details suggest the personal tragedy of a man for whom the concept of being late no longer holds significance.

Possessions can be telling. From possessions come character. From character comes an interesting story. Here's a lesson to help build students' inference-drawing power. Ask each student to bring in one artifact—something a person might forget in a hotel room or car or on the kitchen table: car keys, loose change, a note, grocery list, pen, photograph, map, play bill, match book, failed test, set of directions. (Or, if you prefer, you can create a collection yourself.) Break students into small groups of three to five and ask each *group* to make their own collection using the things they have brought. They don't have to use everything; the whole collection should have six to ten items in it. Then, pretend all those possessions belong to ONE person. What conclusions could you draw about that person from this collection? What do the things left behind tell you about what this person was like? How do you know?

Model it. Tell a short story about something that actually happened to you in simple terms, making it complete and engaging, but not overloaded with information. Now, *write* it—on the overhead. Let drivel run rampant. Explode with unnecessary detail; unleash the trivial, the banal, and the thoroughly dull within your mind. Flood the page. Ask students to suggest what to cut.

Write ten-minute stories. Ask students to write stories in which all events must occur within ten minutes—no more. Or, as an alternative, write

> Think small. The best things to write about are often the tiniest things—your brother's junk drawer, something weird your dog once did, your grandma's loose, wiggly neck, changing a dirty diaper, the moment you realized you were too old to take a bath with your older brother.
>
> Ralph Fletcher (1993)

an **informational piece that can make no more than two key points,** each of which must be supported and defended so well that someone who did not believe they were true would accept them.

ORGANIZATION

Problem 1: The Lead Doesn't Work. It Just Restates the Assignment. I'm Bored Already.

TRY THESE STRATEGIES

Brainstorm as many possible leads as you can for a given piece of writing. Do this routinely, sometimes as a class, sometimes with partners, sometimes individually. This gives students invaluable practice in getting started.

Share your own leads. When you write, prepare two to five leads of your own. Ask students to help you select the one that works best.

Write in the lead. Share an article, report or story from which you've removed the lead. Ask students to fill it in, working individually, in pairs, or groups. Read possibilities aloud and compare. (Notice how much you need to figure out about the main idea or main story line before you can do this well.)

Ask each student to write three to five potential leads for a given piece of his or her own writing. Share the leads in writing groups. Ask peers to identify the leads they like best and to say why.

Collect leads from successful pieces of writing: novels, stories, poems, picture books, brochures, news articles, and journal articles. Make a collage. Talk about why some are successful.

Find a lead (newspaper, magazine, whatever) that does *not* work well. Revise it as a group.

Stacking winners and losers. Bring in a stack of books—no fewer than six, no more than ten. Preview them to be sure some have rousing leads, while others are more ho-hum. As you read *just the leads* aloud, invite students to tell you where to stack them—in the successful or less successful pile. When you've finished rating and stacking, re-read the successful leads and ask students what makes them successful. Make a list of lead tips and strategies.

List ways to begin. With your students, list lead possibilities: for example, bold statement, startling fact, humorous anecdote, question to the reader, intriguing quotation, middle of the action, dialogue. Ask students to try each technique at least once.

From ho-hum to catchy. Practice rewriting the lead from your math or social studies or science text.

Go bad on purpose. Write bad leads (e.g., "Hi, there. I'm Vicki and I'm going to write a book on assessment. I hope you'll enjoy it! Well, here goes!")—on purpose. Make a "just for fun" collection, or even have a Bad Lead Contest and see who can write the worst leads. Put them on display.

Starting with what's striking. Here's an idea I borrowed from Barry Lane; it yields striking results. Ask students, in pairs, to *interview* each other

> What's the most boring way you could begin a research report about the human brain? A rattlesnake? The United States Constitution? We all know."In this report I will tell you about . . . "
>
> Barry Lane (1999, 30)

for five minutes each. Then, ask them to pull out the most intriguing detail on which to base a lead. Read results aloud. Compare them to a few biographical leads you track down in your school library.

Problem 2: Details or Events Are Not in Order. Trying to Follow this Writing Is Like Running through a Giant Maze.

TRY THESE STRATEGIES

For an expository piece, make a random list of details, asking students to help, based on what they know. Then, ask students in groups of three to delete what does not matter, write questions for missing information, then put everything in order. Work in groups; compare results.

For a narrative piece, first tell the story orally. Then, list everything that happens, plus some unneeded details; don't worry about putting things in the right order. Ask students to work in pairs to again delete what does not matter, fill in what's missing, and effectively sequence all remaining events. Compare lists across groups.

Make predictions. As you read aloud (students' work or any published writing), pause periodically to ask, "What probably comes next?" It is useful to have students write the sentence they think might logically come next; then compare what the writer actually did. This helps students develop an "ear" for transitions and sequencing.

Map pieces of writing. This is a tough task, but worth the time. Take any article, essay, argument or story and begin with identifying the main point or story line. Then create a visual picture of how the writer develops details. Do they follow in chronological order? Go from big picture to small—or just the opposite? Do bits of information build on one another, each adding something new to the reader's understanding? Is there a sequence of steps? Or a comparison-contrast pattern? Cause and effect? Presentation of two sides, followed by a conclusion? Perhaps a systematic addressing of readers' questions? When you have done several patterns, compare them. How does one mode differ from another? Why is an adventure story organized one way, a travel brochure another, and an argument another? How does organization connect to purpose?

Problem 3: Transitions Are Weak or (Help!) Missing Altogether.

TRY THESE STRATEGIES

Choose a published piece with strong transitions (science and wildlife journals are excellent sources), and rewrite it with all transitional phrases missing. Ask students to **fill in transitional words and phrases that make sense.**

Brainstorm a list of good transitional words and phrases: *However, In a while, Therefore, Next, Because of that, In fact, On the other hand, To tell the truth, For example, Nevertheless,* and so forth. Make a poster from which student writers can "borrow" when they need a way to link ideas. Keep adding to the poster—both you and your students.

Ask students to **search through textbooks, cookbooks, how-to manuals, newspapers, and magazines** for paragraphs with strong and weak transitions. Score samples on the trait of organization. Discuss the differences.

Create a connection. Put any two sentences on the board. They do not have to be related at all:

Frank wanted a new tee shirt. The forecast called for snow.

Ask students, in pairs, to find a way of connecting the sentences, showing how one might relate to the other: *Although the forecast called for snow, Frank had no interest in down jackets; he only wanted a new tee shirt.* This is only one of hundreds of ways to connect these ideas, and that's the point. For example, someone else might write, *The forecast called for snow, and that could mean only one thing: it was time for Frank to buy his traditional "Think snow" tee shirt.*

Ask students to work in groups to **create paragraphs of four to six sentences, in which transitions are deliberately weak or missing.** Exchange the writings to see which group can best fill in another's missing transitions.

Problem 4: Conclusion? What Conclusion? It Just Stops. Wait—No, Not That! Not the Dreaded Dream Ending!

TRY THESE STRATEGIES

Collect successful conclusions from published writers and make a display. Talk about the strategies they use. How do the pro's get out gracefully?

Brainstorm a list of bad endings (make sure students help you identify them): *"Then I woke up and it was all a dream. . . . That's about all I have to say. . . . I hope you liked my paper."* Post the list. Pledge not to use them!

Share a published piece minus the conclusion. **Ask students to invent** one to three possible conclusions. Discuss differences and favorites. Compare their possibilities to the author's original.

Talk about ways to end: insightful observation, challenging question, suggesting another story to come, responding to the situation, summing up how things have changed, pointing out something the reader may have overlooked, suggesting what might happen if significant points in the paper go unheeded, or resolving a question the reader is sure to be asking.

Ask students to **write three to five possible endings** to pieces they are working on and to share these possibilities in writing groups. Join the fun, writing potential conclusions for your own writing.

Ask students to guess how a piece *you* are writing will end. Invite them to play the same guessing game in their response groups.

List kinds of endings. Then, have students experiment with each: a quotation, a prediction of what might happen next, an unexpected action or comment by a character, a new challenge not foreseen, a reflective comment showing the writer's new insight, and so on.

Sidebar quotations:

"Abel! Oh, dear Abel! It's you! It's really, really you!" Amanda came rushing in and flung herself into Abel's arms. They covered each other with kisses.

When he was able to speak, Abel said, "I've brought you back your scarf."

William Steig (1987)

When we came out of the church that night it was cold and clear, with crunchy snow underfoot and bright, bright stars overhead. And I thought about the Angel of the Lord—Gladys, with her skinny legs and her dirty sneakers sticking out from under her robe, yelling at all of us everywhere:

"Hey! Unto you a child is born!"

Barbara Robinson (1972)

In the words of Emerson, with whom we began, "Language is a city, to the building of which every human being brought a stone."

Robert McCrum, William Cran, and Robert MacNeil (1986)

VOICE

Problem 1: There Is No Voice Here. I've Looked.

TRY THESE STRATEGIES

Read aloud lots of pieces that have voice. Search everywhere: novels, picture books, anthologies, greeting cards, brochures, menus, movie reviews, screenplays, letters. Keep reading. Keep asking, What gives this voice? What *is* voice?

Ask students to do some searching of their own. Create a display and label it "Voices We Love." Create another, "Where's the Voice?" for the voiceless pieces. Keep adding to the collection all year; keep changing and expanding.

Define voice. Invite students to come up with definitions for the concept of voice, and to continue adding to the list. Post these definitions—along with those of professional writers.

Reward risk taking. Students must take chances to achieve voice. It does not always work, but then you can say, "Thank you for taking the chance." The irony is that it usually does work because risk taking produces a kind of voice of its own, even when other things in the writing do not come together. But even when it does not, you can say, "I see what you were trying to do here. Keep at it. You're on the right track."

> Writing from the heart is not just about writing from the heart. It's also about writing from and *for* all the senses. Readers want to feel, they want to taste, they want to smell.
>
> Nancy Aronie Slonim (1998, 143)

Ask students to **listen in writing groups for moments of voice**—just moments. These may be a word, a phrase, or a brief line or passage. Voice can come and go; it isn't always sustained throughout the piece. Then tell those moments back to the writer. Once you know the impact of your own voice on an audience, it's hard not to want to do it again.

Encourage students to identify and **write on topics that are personally important** to them, at least some of the time. This demands, of course, that students be willing to ask themselves, What *is* important to me? It also demands that we be ready to accept diverse and unpredictable answers to this question. Are we prepared for student voices that at times are angry, depressed, disillusioned, provocative or even frightening? Voice is not something you pour over your writing like syrup on pancakes. It comes from deep within, from daring to confront your own reality, and for some students, that reality is bleak, forlorn, even alarming.

A few years ago, a high school student who had been physically and emotionally abused by her mother wrote a powerfully descriptive piece in which her text ran parallel to the text of the Lord's Prayer. Following the line "Hallowed be thy name," she wrote, "Hallowed be *her* name, too, and don't you forget it." Her piece was meant to shock, and it did. We sat in stunned silence as her anger, at long last released, sketched a reality we had not dreamed existed for her.

Voice comes in many flavors, but all voices have one thing in common: they spring from courage, from a willingness to look at life both from without and within, and to tell the truth as the writer sees it.

Ask students to rewrite a voiceless piece, putting in as much voice as possible. Here's one to practice on, a letter from a school principal to the parents of the community.

> Dear Parents:
>
> As we begin the endeavor of another year, we shall attempt to pro-
> vide for your son or daughter an educational environment con-
> ducive to learning and growth. We invite you all to participate in
> our decision-making process by providing, from your unique
> parental perspective, any problems, suggestions, or other input
> you may have regarding this process.

This letter is so stiff and formal we doubt many parents will stop by to share
their unique parental input. Perhaps this principal simply wishes to be left
alone to get his personal work done. He'll probably get his wish. When students work on a piece like this, they must think first of the audience (parents), then of the message (let's work together). In putting the two together,
they learn what makes voice work.

Write to your best listener. My friend and colleague Sally Shorr, a veteran teacher, offers this excellent piece of advice—which has worked for me
and for many students with whom I've shared writing ideas. Think of your
VERY best listener, the person in whom you would confide your most important secrets. Write as if you were writing just to that person.

Problem 2: The Voice Is Inappropriate for the Topic or the Audience.

TRY THESE STRATEGIES

Ask students to **write on the same topic (e.g., a problem in our school) for
several different audiences** (e.g., a friend in another state, the principal, a
parent). How do the voices change? Why?

**Write an expository piece (e.g., "How to Use the Internet") for three
groups:** computer buffs, adults purchasing a computer for the first time,
and first graders brand new to computers. How do the voices change?

Write letters to people in the local business community commenting
on an effective or worthy business practice—or a problem. Ask students to
assess the effectiveness of the voice in their own letters and/or to reflect
on how they achieved the right voice for the audience and the purpose.
Share reflections. Save letters and responses and compile them into a class
book titled *Effective Business Voices.* Notice also which letters receive responses and what kinds of responses they get. Assess the responses for
voice, too.

Interview businesspeople to ask what kinds of voice they value and
listen for. (If possible, invite a local business person into your classroom to
talk directly to your students.) How do they want their employees to come
across to the audiences they serve? Don't be surprised to discover that the
quality of voice is more valued than ever by many business executives, who
regard ability to communicate with an audience an essential survival skill in
a competitive world. Notice, for instance, how the Xerox Corporation
(Brown, 1991) ends its welcoming letter to new employees.

If you come to work here, you will sacrifice the security of the safe approach in which you can count on arriving at a predictable goal. But you will have an opportunity to express your personal research "voice" and help create a future that would not have existed without you.   (p. 105)

As you read samples from various written works aloud, ask, **Who is the intended audience?** How do you know? You might ask students to reflect on this in a response journal. Consider this small excerpt from Lewis Thomas's (1979) "Notes on Punctuation" in *The Medusa and the Snail*:

Exclamation points are the most irritating of all. Look! they say, look at what I just said! How amazing is my thought! It is like being forced to watch someone else's small child jumping up and down crazily in the center of the living room shouting to attract attention.   (p. 127)

Who is the audience for this delightful commentary? How do you know?

Play "Whose Voice Is It?" Collect excerpts from favorite or impressive written works, put them on the overhead, and ask students to take turns reading the pieces aloud and then guess, as a class, who each voice might belong to. If they cannot name the person, that's OK. Ask them to guess whether the voice is young or old, male or female, serious or whimsical, philosophical or irreverent, and so on. One of the following voices belongs to Carl Sagan (*Cosmos*, 1980, p. 5), one to Mark Twain (*Huckleberry Finn*, 1965, p. 254). Which is which?

And so there ain't nothing more to write about, and I am rotten glad of it, because if I'd 'a' knowed what a trouble it was to make a book, I wouldn't 'a' tackled it, and ain't a-going to no more.

The Earth is a place. It is by no means the only place. It is not even a typical place. No planet or star or galaxy can be typical, because the Cosmos is mostly empty. The only typical place is within the vast, cold, universal vacuum, the everlasting night of inter-galactic space, a place so strange and desolate that, by comparison, planets and stars and galaxies seem achingly rare and lovely.

Strong voices really are not difficult to recognize, are they?

WORD CHOICE

Problem 1: The Vocabulary Is Too Simple, Too General, Too Vague. It Just Doesn't Say Anything!

TRY THESE STRATEGIES

Read aloud any piece that is richly expressive (e.g., any book by William Steig or Mem Fox, along with selected passages from Pat Conroy, Toni Morrison, Ursula Hegi, Janet Fitch, Wallace Stevens, or any personal favorite of your own). I like this passage from Margaret Atwood's *Alias Grace* (1996, 57) because it makes a movie in my mind: "Dora is stout and pudding-faced, with a small downturned mouth like that of a disappointed baby. Her large black eyebrows meet over her nose, giving her a permanent scowl that expresses a sense of disapproving outrage." I don't fancy having tea with Dora. Ask students to call out or jot down favorite expressions. Talk about why they are favorites. What mental pictures or feelings do they call up? What "movies" do they set in motion?

Brainstorm a list of "tired" words and phrases that need a long (permanent?) rest, such as *fun* (as an adjective), *awesome, great, nice, bad* (meaning good), *way cool, grand, special, super, pushing the envelope,* and so on. For each tired word or expression, also brainstorm as many different "ways to say it" as you can think of. Create word walls or word wheels (which can be mounted on the ceiling for quick reference when students are stuck). Keep adding to the lists.

Create a collection of words or phrases that work. Ask students to hunt with you. Make a giant collage. Word collages make a great resource for poetry.

Treat yourself to a word-a-day calendar. Rather than just peeling off the pages, discuss each word, giving it a critical review. What are the odds we (as writers and students) would ever actually use this word? When would we use it? What audience would appreciate it? Is there a simpler word that works just as well—or is there not? Make a collection of keepers: words that will still be with us in 25 years.

Track word histories. Where do words come from? Why do some words, like *mate, pal, nosh,* and *humbug,* stick around, while others fade away?

Jargon alert! Think about ways we play with or manipulate language for our own purposes: "The White House, referring to the invasion . . . of Grenada, referred to a parachute drop as *a pre-dawn vertical insertion* . . . . The world of euphemistic jargon is the world in which second-hand cars become *experienced,* a hospital death is *a therapeutic misadventure* and an airplane reports a fatal crash to its stockholders as *the involuntary conversion of a 7279*" (McCrum, Cran, and MacNeil, 1986, p. 345). Ask students to look for examples of jargon in the newspaper, journals, their own conversation (!), textbooks, and educational writings. Talk about what makes jargon popular. Is it merely a convenience?

Ask students to rewrite an uninspiring piece. The possibility of life existing somewhere in the Cosmos is a fascinating question that has intrigued countless scientists—and continues to do so. But I think you'll agree that my summary of this speculation (loosely based on Chapter 1 of Carl Sagan's book *Cosmos*) lacks voice, flavor and detail. Here it is:

> *Welcome to the planet Earth! We have skies, oceans, forests and meadows—lots of neat stuff. If you think about how big the whole universe is, Earth is kind of an unusual place. It might even be unique. Some people wonder if other people live on planets out in space. They might. Who knows? Do you ever look up at the sky at night and wonder if there is another planet like ours with people on it? It would be cool to find out. It is fun to live in a time when people are curious enough to wonder about stuff like this.*

After sharing my summary, I ask students to rewrite the piece, breathing some life into it. At first, this was a task I shared only with middle and high schoolers. But I thought it would be interesting to see what younger writers could do. I love Courtney's (a second grader's) free wheeling poetic imagination:

> Welcome to the magnificent earth! We have satisfying skies! Fragrent oceans, Forests and medows with unushwill treeshers! If you think about the fiery mammoth universe, Earth is probly a startaling place! It might evin be a fenominal place. Other people think that the unnown live on far far far far planets! They might. Not even scientists know! Do you ever look at the cristel like stars? Or do you look up into the time zone and hope there's a nother planet to depend on? I do. With human beings like us? Wouldn't it be refreshing to find out? Is it or is it not charming to live on this ever breth tacking earth with lots of daring crechers Always eger to lern new exstordaney things!

Notice the life and voice Courtney weaves into her revision. Is it or is it not charming? I sound bored, half asleep. She doesn't.

Problem 2: The Student Suffers from Thesaurus-Chained-to-the-Desk Syndrome. Reading This Is Like Being Force-Fed Fudge.

TRY THESE STRATEGIES

Give students an overwritten piece to revise. Menus and travel brochures are good candidates—advertisements, too. If they aren't quite overdone enough, you can help them along with some creative revision. Ask students to make their revised copy lean and mean—no clichés and no words longer than two syllables.

Ask students to try writing a good descriptive piece or book review **using words of only one syllable.** Yes, it can be done, but it's a challenge.

Look up a simple word in the thesaurus (e.g., *slow*). Use the word in a sentence: "Jake moved at a *slow* pace." Then try substituting some alternatives offered by the thesaurus.

Jake moved at a *tortoiselike* pace.

Jake moved at a *plodding* pace.

Jake moved at a *shuffling* pace.

Jake moved at a *leisurely* pace.

Jake moved at a *sluggish* pace.

Jake moved at a *methodical* pace.

Jake moved at an *indolent* pace.

How does each substitution change the meaning?

Enter the Bulwer-Lytton Fiction Contest at San Jose State University. You'll need to begin by reading excerpts from *It Was a Dark and Stormy Night,* or *Dark and Stormy Night: the Final Conflict,* or any of the zany, hilarious collections of what is considered to be some of the world's most overwritten writing. Here's just one example:

Daphne ran swiftly across the windswept moor scarcely noticing its heather perfume, down to the rocky cliff where she paused momentarily atop the jagged precipice, looked down at the waves crashing far below, and wished that she had been born anything other than a lemming.

Daniel R. Little in Scott Rice (1996, 83)

Give your thesaurus-happy students a chance to take a crack at this—you try, too. When you've had your fill of laughing at your overbaked results, send the best of them in to the contest:

Bulwer-Lytton Fiction Contest
Department of English
San Jose State University
San Jose, CA 95192-0090

Entries are generally only one sentence long and not more than 50 to 60 words, so this is an exercise in being concise while overdoing it.

Problem 3: The Language Is Not Well Suited to the Topic or the Audience.

TRY THESE STRATEGIES
Give students a passage from some text for which the audience is fairly clearly defined:

1. A cookbook for an adult audience
2. A set of computer game directions for young adults or adults
3. A picture book for young reader-listeners

Ask them to **rewrite the text for a completely different audience.**

1. Adapt the cookbook to suit readers age ten or under.
2. Adapt the computer game directions to suit someone over 50 who is new to the world of computers.
3. Rewrite the picture book to interest an adult audience.

Talk about audience as you read aloud. As you read poetry, technical manuals, song lyrics or greeting cards, ask, "Who is the audience for this writing? How do you know? Which words tell you so?" Who is the likely audience for each of the following pieces? What is the purpose of each?

1. Authors are regularly asked by journalists to summarize a long book in one sentence. For this book, here is such a sentence: "History followed different courses for different peoples because of differences among peoples' environments, not because of biological differences among peoples themselves."
2. Clearly distinguish between those results you believe are fully proven and those that require additional validation.
3. This is the tale of a toad. A muddy toad, a mucky toad, a clammy, sticky, gooey toad . . .

Sample #1 is from Jared Diamond: *Guns, Germs, and Steel: The Fates of Human Societies* (1999, 25). This is written for an adult audience—both to inform and entertain. Sample #2 is from Janice M. King, *Writing High-Tech Copy That Sells* (1995, 93); it's also written for an adult audience—but much more to inform than to entertain. And Sample #3 is from Ruth Brown's delightful *Toad* (1996), a book written mainly to entertain children, though adults love it, too.

SENTENCE FLUENCY

Problem 1: Short, Choppy Sentences Break the Text up into Bite-Sized Pieces.

TRY THESE STRATEGIES

Good old sentence combining still works magic. Try it again and again, asking students to work sometimes alone, sometimes with a partner. Make your own samples, based on creative revisions of famous texts: *Macbeth*, the Constitution, *Winnie the Pooh*, essays by Ralph Waldo Emerson, Edgar Allan Poe's *"The Cask of Amantillado,"* or *Desiderata* (author unknown):

> *Go placidly. Go amidst the noise. Go amidst the haste. Remember things. Remember peace. Peace may exist in silence. Be on good terms with people. Feel this way toward all people. But only feel this way if you can. Do not surrender.*

Alternatively, chop up some text from a cookbook, lawn mower warranty, legal contract, auto show advertisement, or headline news story. Don't forget to compare their revisions to the originals.

Read aloud regularly from text that is strikingly fluent. You never know just where you'll find it, but when you do, the rhythm will beckon you, carrying you right along with it like a good symphony. Consider Gary Paulsen's (1993) lilting prose from the picture book *Dogteam*.

> *Into the night. Away from camp, away from people, away from houses and light and noise and into only the one thing, into only winternight they fly away and away and away.*

Not for the fainthearted, perhaps, is the pulsing, building anticipation of Norman Mailer's (1984) masterfully crafted text, layering meaning on horrific meaning.

I removed the stone and felt into the hole in front of the footlocker, my fingers scraping and searching into this soft loam like field mice at the edge of food, and I felt something—it could be flesh or hair or some moist sponge—I didn't know what, but my hands, fiercer than myself, cleared the debris to pull forward a plastic garbage bag through which I poked and saw enough at once to give one frightful moan, pure as the vertigo of a long fall itself.   (p. 45)

When you find the good moments, take time to read slowly and pump the rhythm into the text so that students can both hear and feel it.

Encourage students to read aloud often to each other so they come to feel that text is to be spoken as much as written. Text can be short. Reading one sentence with all the inflection you can muster is preferable to four pages of monotone.

Ask students to try **bits of drama or choral readings** of poetry. Divide text into four- or five-line chunks (or smaller, for younger students), and divide students into groups, assigning one section to each group. Dialogue is excellent, as well, so do not overlook plays as a source of good read-aloud literature. You'll be teaching both voice and fluency. Give students time to rehearse, and then ask them to do an interpretive reading, using lots of inflection, gestures, movement, echoes, sound effects, or whatever it takes to bring the text to life.

Problem 2: All Sentences Begin the Same Way. I Think I'm Drifting off . . . .

TRY THESE STRATEGIES

Ask students to list their sentence beginnings—just the first three or four words, on a separate sheet of paper. Do they all look alike? There's your problem . . .

Start with one simple sentence, then rework it. Try this one: "You have to be clever to survive school." Ask students to rewrite the sentence as many ways as they can in three minutes (or slightly longer, if you wish). They can change word forms, naturally, but not the general meaning.

Variation: You can give students sample sentence beginnings for the preceding exercise and see whether they can complete the thought in a variety of ways. (This is harder than it looks.)

Being clever . . .
Surviving school . . .
To survive school . . .
If you . . .
In order to . . .
You will survive . . .
Survivors . . .
School . . .
Cleverness . . .

Problem 3: Endless Connectives Turn the Whole Paper into One Monstrous "Sentence" that Chokes to Death Any Sense of Meaning.

TRY THESE STRATEGIES

Ask students to write three paragraphs with **no** *ands* **or** *buts* **at all.**

Give students a piece of writing with all punctuation and capital letters removed. Read aloud, pausing clearly and fully for each comma, semicolon, period, or question mark, and using plenty of inflection to accentuate the punctuation. Ask students to fill in the punctuation they hear as you read. Then, let them try a piece on their own, reading to themselves. (This is an effective way to teach punctuation, too.)

Give students a piece in which you've hooked all independent clauses together with *ands* **or** *buts* **or** *becauses.* Ask them to rewrite the piece, removing some of the *ands*, *buts* or *becauses* as needed, to make it fluent.

TEACHING CONVENTIONS THROUGH EDITING

Because conventions are receiving so much attention these days, both in classrooms and on state exams, I thought it wise to devote a section of this chapter to the teaching of editing—which is the most important step in teaching conventions. *Note that teaching conventions is not the same thing as correcting conventions.*

Though many teachers (and parents) place a high priority on conventional correctness, the teaching of editing is, in reality, often given short shrift in the writing process. No one means to do this. In fact, we are a society that cares *deeply* about conventions and that—for better or worse—often prejudges people on the basis of how well they can spell or punctuate. The problem is, editing is not just a step in the writing process; it's a specialty. Good writers do not always make the best editors, any more than great swimmers make the best divers.

Further, editing falls in an unhappy position—at the end (or nearly the end, except for publishing)—of the writing process. Students are tired, both mentally and physically, by the time they get to editing; plus, they're sometimes bored with the papers they're working on currently, and eager to move on. So editing gets a quick once-over, and we rarely see what students can *really* do. Meanwhile, parents are horrified that yet another paper is getting by without the full red-pen treatment.

The Tradition

We cannot blame parents for their anxiety. They want their children to be employable. Further, many grew up with worksheets, drills, sentence diagramming, and lots of correction. Students were expected to learn by reading through corrections or actually rewriting their text to accommodate the corrections. But—rigorous though that approach might be, is it the best way to *teach* conventions? Hardly. Honestly, short of embroidering the Six-Trait

Teachers and administrators feel pressure from a public that worries about handwriting, spelling and grammar. . . . Yet rarely do parents complain about the inability of their children to formulate and express ideas in a clear and logical fashion.

Donald H. Graves (1994)

Analytical Scoring Guide on tightly woven burlap with a dull needle, I cannot think of a task more arduous, tedious, and unrewarding. The main thing learned through the correct-and-copy approach is unmitigated hatred for grammar and punctuation.

Won't students get the wrong impression, though, if we do not correct all errors? On the contrary, they will get the *right* impression, provided we explain our motives clearly. When we ask students to do their own editing, we are saying in effect, "Your skill as an editor is more important to me than perfect copy."

Further, the fact they have problems with conventions is not news to students. As Frank Smith (1984) tells us, "Correction merely highlights what students almost certainly know they cannot do in the first place. Correction is worthwhile only if the learner would seek it in any case, and to seek correction for what you do, you must regard yourself as a professional" (p. 56). How do you become a professional? Certainly not by having someone else hover over your work constantly.

But if the traditional method isn't the answer, then what is?

Developing a Proofreader's Eye

The secret to student independence and success lies in helping them develop a proofreader's eye: that is, the ability to spot errors. Then, of course, they must also know how to correct those errors. They will need to know copy editor's symbols and what they mean, and they will need to practice editing—every day. *Every* day? You may be thinking that it would just be easier to correct the copy yourself; after all, you know how. You can do it faster, and you won't miss as many mistakes. In your hands, the copy will go from sloppy to near-perfect. It will look better hanging on the wall. All true. Remember though: Once you begin *doing* it instead of teaching it, you will need to do it forever. Do you really want to commit to that? If not, here's an alternative.

The How-To's of Teaching Editing

Begin by teaching copy editors' symbols (see Figure 7.1). Make a poster. Demonstrate use of the symbols, one at a time, on the chalkboard or overhead. Encourage students to use them. Continue modeling, daily, to be sure they understand. Gradually increase the difficulty of your samples, and ALWAYS ask students to try spotting and correcting errors before you show them how it's done.

Give students a simple pretest in editing to see how much they already know, and to know where you need to begin your instruction. The following sample might be suitable for many middle school students; you might want something a little simpler for fourth or fifth graders, something more challenging (perhaps covering the use of quotation marks, parentheses, ellipses, dashes, footnotes, etc.) for high school students. This sample requires students

Symbol	Meaning	Example
ℓ	Delete the material.	There are ~~six~~ six traits.
(sp)	Spell it out.	I LOVE the ⑥ traits. *(sp)*
◯	Close the gap.	Organi zatio n is critical.
⌀	Delete material and close the gap.	Mem Foxx has a wiry sense of humor.
stet.	Return to the original.	Never ~~ever~~ send me a letter that lacks voice. *stet.*
∧	Insert a letter, word, or phrase.	Mem Fox has voice. *a powerful, original*
∧	Change a letter or letters.	She's a slack writer. *i*
⌗	Make a space.	The lead mustbe a grabber. *#*
∩	Transpose letters or words.	Gary Paulsen says, "Read like a wolf eats."
∧	Insert a comma.	Write with voice, spirit detail and editorial precision.
⊙	Add a period.	Write what you think⊙
∧	Insert a semicolon.	Good conventions won't buoy up muddled ideas Good conventions won't rescue voiceless claptrap.
∧	Insert a colon.	Use these marks of punctuation sparingly parentheses, exclamation points and colons.
∧ ⌐/M	Insert an em dash (like two hyphens).	Terry Kay what a fine writer. ⌐/M
⌐?	Add a question mark.	Who stole my scoring guide ?
⌄	Insert an apostrophe.	Garrison Keillors essay on letter writing inspired me.
=	Insert a hyphen.	Novelist poet Maya Angelou can rock a room with her verbal rhythm.
≡	Change lower case to capital.	Roald dahl never shrinks from reality—even if it's ugly.
/	Change capital to lowercase.	The Truth lies in the Details.
¶	Start a new paragraph.	"What can one exclamation point tell us?" queried Watson. ¶ "You'd be surprised," retorted Holmes.
⌒ No ¶	Run lines together. No new paragraph.	*Lonesome Dove* is a long book. No ¶ Of course, *Moby Dick* is long, too— but not everyone finishes *Moby Dick*.
⌄⌄	Add quotation marks.	I try to leave out the parts that people skip, said novelist-screenwriter Elmore Leonard.
ital.	Italicize.	Beach Music left me breathless. *ital.*
‖	Align.	My favorite books are these: ‖*Lonesome Dove* ‖*Crazy in Alabama* ‖⌐*Fried Green Tomatoes* ‖*Beach Music*
] [	Center.	]The Origin of Six-Trait Assessment[

FIGURE 7.1. Copy editor's symbols

to adjust spacing; to insert capitals, missing words or letters, and missing punctuation; to correct misspellings; and to reorder words or letters:

> *sharks canbe dangerous cretures did you no that some sharcks have swalowed itesm as, large a hoarse or the tir of a truck. sharks attack rarly humans however through some spesies are obvious more dangerous than ohters*

Help even very young students to become independent editors by sharing with them those copy editors' symbols that they might be able to use (see Figure 7.2), then gradually adding to the list.

Hold students **responsible only for the editorial skills you have taught.**

Ask students to periodically include samples of their editing practice in a portfolio or writing folder so they have a visual representation of how their editing skills are growing through the year or the semester.

Get a grip on where and when editing is really important. Make a list of all the writing you and your students have done over the last month: lists, letters, reports, memos, notes to self and others, reviews, calendar entries, poems, stories, explanations, journal entries, telephone messages, directions, and so on. Then ask, Which of these would need to be edited and why? When is it crucial, somewhat important, or not important at all? Must *everything* students create in school be edited? Why or why not? Opening this discussion encourages students to think seriously about the real reasons for editing (not just that it is a school requirement).

Do *not* edit students' copy for them. Those teachers I have known to be most successful in teaching editing have demanded that their students do their own work. They have simply refused to be editors for their students. This is a hard stand to take. Colleagues and parents who do not understand that *correcting is not teaching* may look askance. Plus you may feel guilty yourself—all those errors, slipping, slipping away . . . .

When you are editing for students, it feels as if you are doing something. No, really, it feels as if you are doing a *lot*. You are. You are burning yourself up. Never mind that there is no research to indicate that students learn from these corrections. In fact, research overwhelmingly indicates that "Taught in certain ways, grammar and mechanics instruction has a deleterious effect

ℓ	Take it out.	I'm a ~~good~~ good singer.
∧	Put it in.	*good* I'm a∧singer.
#	Put in space.	I'm a#good singer.
⊙	Add a period.	I'm a good singer⊙
≡	Make this letter a capital.	i'm a good singer.

FIGURE 7.2. Copy editor's symbols for primary/early elementary students

on student writing. In some studies, a heavy emphasis on mechanics and usage (e.g., marking every error) resulted in significant losses in overall quality" (Hillocks, 1986, p. 248).

Studies cited by Maxine Hairston (1986) also suggest that students find negative comments and questions offensive, intimidating, and confusing. What does it mean to be "awk"? Or to have mistakes in "punc" or "syn" or "dic"? It is especially useless to speak in this arrogant shorthand to students who are struggling spellers and to whom punctuation is an alien language.

So, when we know better, why do we edit students' writing? Because we run out of time and patience, and we also know that for some students, editing is daunting. In the end, if we do not correct it, who will? *No one.* Some copy is *never* going to get corrected; and effective editing teachers learn early on to live with this. They substitute modeling and practice for correcting.

What about those students, though, who make numerous errors in their text? Shouldn't we point out their mistakes? Yes—but not by doing the correcting for them. Ask yourself this: Will struggling editors be more successful if we send them into the world armed with some corrected copy? We might like to think so, but the truth is no, they will not. Better to put a *few* editing fundamentals into their arsenal (capital at the beginning of a sentence, period at the end); each one makes them less dependent on us—unless of course we plan to accompany them to the state assessments and then on through college and onto the job site.

Give students editing practice on text that is *not their own*. Remember that the hardest editing in the world is editing your own copy. Even professional writers find it a challenge. When we read our own writing, we tend to mentally fill in missing words and correct the punctuation, sailing right over tiny flaws in spelling. Yet, this notoriously difficult task is often precisely what we require of our students.

Students need to edit anonymous copy—such as "Mouse Alert," where there is no vested interest, and where errors are easier to spot because the writing is someone else's. This warm-up leaves them more prepared to work on their own text.

Do it daily. Further, students need to edit *every day*, not just now and then. Practice can be short (five to ten minutes), but it must be frequent if you wish to see results. Some students write extensively only once in two or three weeks. Many do not write even that often. Suppose they are editing only their own work—and only what gets published? How reasonable is it to expect that they will develop any editing proficiency whatever when they are editing only about as often as many of us get a haircut?

Keep it focused and manageable. Too often we ask student editors to look for every kind of error at once: grammatical problems, flaws in spelling and punctuation, faulty paragraphing and missing or misplaced capitals. This is overwhelming for students who have difficulty with conventions; they simply cannot handle it, and many give up.

We know instinctively that this is not the best instructional approach; it's just that we're so eager for them to "get it." In the best journalism classes,

Traditions in the teaching of English hold that compositions must be marked and commented upon—the more thoroughly, the better. But research reported in this review suggests that such feedback has very little effect on enhancing the quality of student writing—regardless of frequency or thoroughness.

George Hillocks, Jr. (1986)

When we re-read our own writing, we usually aren't reading; we're reminding ourselves of what we intended to mean when we wrote it.

Joseph M. Williams (1994)

though, professional editors are taught to spot *one* sort of error before moving on to another, gradually adding more and more to their repertoire until nothing escapes their glance. We should follow their lead.

Work on *one* editorial problem at a time (e.g., failure to capitalize the pronoun "i"), and make sure it is something you have taught directly through demonstration and modeling, putting examples on the board or overhead and showing students precisely what to do. When students become very good at spotting and correcting that one kind of error, move on to another (e.g., periods missing at the end of a sentence). List the errors as you go, building cumulatively, so students know how many things and what kinds of things they're responsible for; you can hand out a list, or better yet, make a poster of "Editing Must's." Start simply. Your list will grow as their skills grow.

Create your own editing lessons. Books with editing lessons are readily available, but for beginners or those who find conventions very challenging, you can create your own practice text from sample student writing. Make the print LARGE, put *plenty* of room between lines and words for corrections, and make sure you keep the practice *simple* at first. Start with three errors. If your students cannot find all three, drop it to two, or one. Make it as simple as you have to. Put your own name on the board and misspell it. Omit the capital. Begin with what they *can* do, and move on from there. The rule is this: *If you have to do it for them, it's too hard.* When it counts, you won't be there.

Figures 7.3, 7.4, and 7.5 consist of sample editing exercises based on the paper "Redwoods" (which in the original is mechanically quite sound). Notice that in Figure 7.3 everything is OK except the spelling. The student editor does not need to look for anything else. Notice that the text is amply spaced to allow plenty of room to make corrections, and the number of errors is given so the editor can know when the job is done.

Redwoods

Last year, we want on a vacaton, and

we had a wonderful time. The waether

was sunny and warm and there was lots

too do, so we where never bored.

My parants visited freinds and took

pictures for their friends back home. My

brother and I swam and also hiked in the

woulds. Wen we got tried of that, we just

eat and had a wondurful time.

FIGURE 7.3. "Redwoods," editing practice 1, spelling (twelve errors)

Figure 7.4 encompasses missing and superfluous commas—always a tricky call because even style manuals do not agree on which commas are essential. Therefore, you may find slightly fewer (or more!) errors in this one than we did. That's OK. You can re-create the lesson to suit your own teaching style and content; this is only an example. Notice that the spelling is correct in this lesson because we want students to focus on commas here.

Figure 7.5 is pretty simple, but it's important editing practice: filling in the missing periods and (necessarily) the missing capitals, too. These really must go together or you give the game away. Paragraphing has also been removed to make this task just a little more challenging. Spelling and commas have been corrected because, again, this is *focused* editing (one error or at most, two to three kinds of errors at a time).

Redwoods

Last year, we went on a vacation and,

we had a wonderful time. The weather,

was sunny and warm and there was lots,

to do so we were never bored.

   My parents visited friends and took

pictures, for their friends back home. My

brother, and I, swam, and also hiked, in

the woods. When we got tired of that we

just ate and had a wonderful time.

FIGURE 7.4. "Redwoods," editing practice 2, commas (eleven errors)

Redwoods

last year, we went on a vacation, and we

had a wonderful time the weather was

sunny and warm and there was lots to do,

so we were never bored my parents

visited friends and took pictures for their

friends back home my brother and I

swam and also hiked in the woods when

we got tired of that, we just ate and had a

wonderful time

FIGURE 7.5. "Redwoods," editing practice 3, capitals and periods (ten errors)

Suggested editing changes for these pieces appear in Figures 7.9, 7.10, and 7.11, respectively, at the end of the chapter.

When assessing, respond to content first. So often students tell me, as seventh grader Jim did one day, "I don't mind corrections. I *want* to know what I'm doing wrong. But I hate it when the teacher looks at spelling first with no comments at all on what I had to say. It makes me want to scream, 'Did you even *read* this?'" Respond to content first; then offer one or two suggestions on how to improve conventions (include an example to show what you mean).

Invite students to tell you what sort of help they'd like. We are so busy looking to see where the problems lie, we often do not think to ask students themselves what would be helpful. They can ask for help with spelling, punctuation, usage, verb tenses—or whatever is most troublesome to them at the time. They know best of all what their own needs are.

Have students edit by hand for a time. Eventually, when editing becomes second nature, they can do most of their editing on a word processor (assuming they are creating text in this way). The pace of computerized writing and editing is faster, however, and it is easy for a novice editor to miss a lot. Moreover, using copy editor's symbols teaches students editing "vocabulary," and awakens them to the possibilities of what can be changed to improve text.

Remember the 72-hour rule. You know how easy it is to spot the misspelled word in that letter your friend wrote, but how hard it is to find the same thing in your *own* work? If you allow students to wait three days—or even more—between writing and editing, they'll spot more errors in their own text. They need this mental distance to make their own writing look a little "foreign," a little more like someone else's.

Ask students to explain orally or in writing why a certain convention is used. For instance, why should a period end a sentence rather than a comma? What difference does it make? Why have periods at all? What is the difference between a colon and a semicolon?

Teach students to score writing analytically for the trait of conventions. Then ask them to justify their scores with a complete discussion of the strengths and weaknesses they find in the writing.

Giv thm some unedted copie lik this thet let's their sea what happens? When, convintions is use incorrect. Porlie riten Koppey helpsthem seee the valeu; of Strong convenshons in Klewing. The reader?

Ask students to become sleuths, hunting for samples of conventional problems in textbooks, memos, letters, advertisements, newspaper articles, and elsewhere (A local grocery marquis recently advertised "brocoli," "onoins," and "pottatoes"—all on the same day. Time for stoo—or soop, perhaps.). Make a display. Reward teams who find the greatest number of

When I examine whole files of papers that have been marked and commented on by teachers, many of them look as though they have been trampled on by cleated boots.

Paul Diederich (1974)

errors or the most egregious errors (i.e., those that cause real misunderstanding of the text).

When a student is formally **publishing,** let the student take the editing as far as he or she can. Then, step in as any professional editor would. If you can confer as you edit to show the student the reasons behind your changes, so much the better. When you finish, ask the student to initial the text to show his/her approval of your corrections. It's only fair. No publishing house would ever edit your work, then publish it without first showing it to you.

Comment on the positive first. In their zeal to make everything right, some teachers offer so many corrections and suggestions that all but the most energetic writers feel buried alive. Many teachers find it more useful to mark two or three conventions handled *well,* along with, perhaps, *one* suggestion for improvement.

Yes, some mistakes will go untouched, but the kinds of errors you *do* focus on are likely to receive more attention next time around. Compare Figure 7.6 with Figure 7.7. Which response would make *you* pay more attention to conventions?

As writer and teacher Donald Murray (1985) assures us, "We learn to write primarily by building on our strengths, and it is important for the teacher to encourage the student to see what has potential, what has strength, and what can be developed" (p. 157).

Share writers' "secrets." My friend and colleague Lois Burdett holds frequent conferences with her second and third graders, and often focuses on just one conventional problem at a time. She does not present them as problems, though; instead, she cleverly slips things around so she is **sharing a "writer's secret":** e.g., "Kirsten, would you like me to share a writer's secret with you? Did you know that when you leave spaces between your words, your text is *so* much easier to read? Would you like to try that on your next paper? Let me make a note of that in my conference book, and it will be our writer's secret, OK?"

Reduce the size of the task, especially for students who find conventions difficult. Ask students to make corrections only in the first paragraph of their text, or only to make one or two kinds of corrections. The size of the task can, of course, expand as students gain skill. But if students are challenged conventionally and if they feel too overwhelmed at first, they'll quickly learn to write only a line or two so there'll be less to correct.

Model. I recall my friend Ronda telling me about her first day sharing her own writing with students by writing in front of them on the chalkboard. "My hand shook so much I dropped the chalk twice, and then a wonderful thing happened. I spelled a word wrong. I didn't mean to do it, and I had thought it would be the end of the world if I made mistakes. I thought kids would say, 'How come you're teaching writing if you can't even spell?' But that isn't what happened at all. They just calmly told me how to spell the word, and that was when I realized how valuable mistakes are. *That's* how you teach kids to be editors."

Haircut from Hell

Grade 7

I failed to tell the new worker at "Haircroppers" how I wanted my hair cut. He swung my chair

away from the mirror. The noises that fallowed [*o* above "fallowed"] sounded like chainswas [*saws* above], hedge trimmers, and

helocopters [*i* above]. Then he swung my chair back to face the mirror . . . .   *helicopters*

 Cap!
 from the time he swung my chair around, I knew that would be my last visit to "Haircroppers."

                              Don't forget your commas!
My hair, or what was left of it, was tinted a brown, olive green color. I felt my hair. A slimey,

                                   smirk
sticky residue came off on my hand. I gave a quick smurk and vigorously rubbed the slime onto my

pants.

                                                    spelling!
    Unbelievably enough, the quick smile I had given the (nin-cum-poop) barber was taken to be

                                                Watch your apostrophes
genuine and he quickly responded, "Glad you like it sir, That's my best one yet!"

    Disgusted, I turned back to my hair. Maybe a wig was the way to go. I felt some of the olive

             dribble
green goop dribbel down my neck.   *Don't get careless.*

        commas!!
    I felt my hair again, and was immediately stopped by a blur of barber's hands. With rage in his

voice he yelled "What are you trying to do, ruin my masterpiece?!"

    "Your masterpiece??!! More like your mess. What is this junk anyway? Some kind of axel

greese?" *grease*

    His voice was wavery, but refused to crack. "It's my own creation . . . face mud, hair spray,

avacado dip . . ."   *This is a brand name.*

    I let him get as far as turtle wax when I roared "Hold it!!"

                                                    spelling!
    My face was beginning to twist, my scalp to burn. "Hose this junk off, you (incompitent) moron.
                 spelling
If my head doesn't just (role) to the floor, I'll have your hide!" I couldn't wait a moment longer. I
 spelling
(grabed) the hose and turned it on myself. Whew. The solution came out into a brown puddle on

the floor, along with great chunks of my hair.

              e
    Fortunatly, I didn't have to pay for what I call today my hair's "mass suicide."

            Too many spelling errors! Did you
            edit this?

FIGURE 7.6. "Haircut from Hell," heavily corrected

Haircut from Hell   Ideas: 5   *Take one more*
                              Org: 5   *look at conventions—*
Grade 7   Voice: 5

I failed to tell the new worker at "Haircroppers" how I wanted my hair cut. He swung my chair

away from the mirror. The noises that fallowed sounded like chainswas, hedge trimmers, and

helocopters. Then he swung my chair back to face the mirror . . . . *Do you*
                                                          know my hairdresser?

from the time he swung my chair around, I knew that would be my last visit to "Haircroppers."
                                                    —yuck!
My hair, or what was left of it was tinted a brown olive green color. I felt my hair. A slimey

sticky residue came off on my hand. I gave a quick smurk and vigorously rubbed the slime onto my

pants.

Unbelievably enough, the quick smile I had given the nin-cum-poop barber was taken to be

genuine and he quickly responded, "Glad you like it sir. Thats my best one yet!"
                                      great voice!
Disgusted, I turned back to my hair. Maybe a wig was the way to go. I felt some of the olive

green goop dribbel down my neck.

I felt my hair again and was immediately stopped by a blur of barbers hands. With rage in his

voice he yelled "What are you trying to do, ruin my masterpiece?!"

"Your masterpiece??!! More like your mess. What is this junk anyway? Some kind of axel

greese?"
          Great word choice!
His voice was wavery, but refused to crack. "Its my own creation . . . face mud, hair spray,

avacado dip . . ."

I let him get as far as turtle wax when I roared "Hold it!!"
                                      Very fluent writing.
My face was beginning to twist, my scalp to burn. "Hose this junk off, you incompitent moron.

If my head doesn't just role to the floor, I'll have your hide!" I couldn't wait a moment longer. I

grabed the hose and turned it on myself. Whew. The solution came out into a brown puddle on

the floor, along with great chunks of my hair.

Fortunatly, I didn't have to pay for what I call today my hair's "mass suicide."

Great pacing and wonderful humor. It's lively
and has just the right amount of exaggeration.
Hey—did you know nincompoop is one word?
(Useful, too.) I like your use of ellipses. You
HAVE VOICE.

FIGURE 7.7. "Haircut from Hell," edited from a positive perspective

WHAT ABOUT PEER EDITING?

Peer editing works wonderfully well when the stakes are low. For instance, when students are practicing on a piece, such as "Redwoods," that belongs to no one in the peer editing group. Further, no grade hangs in the balance. Teaming for *practice* is an excellent instructional strategy because partners teach each other by talking about editing.

When the editing is for real, though (the result is going to be graded), peer editing should be used with great caution. No one wants to edit herself into a lower grade than she would have received had she left the text alone! This can and does happen. Figure 7.8 is a sample of peer editing done by a well-intentioned seventh-grade editor, "helping" her friend.

Notice this student editor has inserted an unneeded comma after the word *accidents;* incorrectly changed *is* to *are* (*cause* is the subject, though some rewording could get the writer out of this awkward single-plural decision pickle); for some reason, removed the word *Yet* from the last line, thereby deleting the transition; and substituted an *s* for a *c* in *licenses,* making the spelling incorrect. She did insert a helpful comma between the two independent clauses of the third sentence, but most of her editing caused this writer's conventions score to fall. We have to hope the writer knew enough to ignore some of these "corrections," but in real life the writer probably (a) never looked, or (b) did not know for sure whether the peer editor was right.

When a lot is at stake (this student was preparing his final draft for a grade), be sure peer editors are up to the job.

What About Peer Review?

Let's be clear, though. While peer editing is often risky and frequently more frustrating than the benefits warrant, peer *review* (quite different) is enormously rewarding and worthwhile. Peer review does not call for students to

Driving Tests

Should Be Harder!

If drivers' test were more rigorous, every one on the road would be safer. About 50,000 people die in traffic accidents every year, and thousands more are injured. The most common cause of accidents is drunk drivers but the second most common cause is incompetent driving. Yet we grant driver's licenses on the basis of a very simple test.

FIGURE 7.8. Sample of peer editing gone awry

suggest corrections, but rather to listen and respond to ideas, voice, phrasing, sentence rhythm, effectiveness of a lead or conclusion, and so on. What's more, students can often do this better by just listening to the text, never looking at it or marking on it at all.

WHAT TO TELL PARENTS

Even parents who do not spell or punctuate well themselves often have high (sometimes unreasonable) expectations for the speed with which their children will develop conventional proficiency. They look to you to make it happen. You can assure them that it *will* happen, but—(1) it will take time and patience because editing takes a lot of practice, and (2) they (parents, that is) can help.

First, let parents know that their children will be taught to think and to work like editors, that they will practice first on text that is not their own, and that eventually, as their knowledge and skill level improves, they will be responsible for editing their *own* text. It may not come home corrected at first though, because you will not be editing *for* students, and they may not (unless they're skilled high school editors) be up to editing every line they write—*yet*. They'll get there.

Invite parents in to observe and to coach students in small groups or one-on-one (assuming they're good editors themselves—*ask*).

A note like this one may help:

Dear Parents:
We will be working hard on conventions this year. We will practice editing *daily* and your student will work on the copy editor's symbols that I have enclosed with this note. You need to know that while I will teach editing by *demonstrating use of these symbols and providing time for guided practice*, I will *not correct your student's work for him or her*. It is very important that each student do this in order to gain the skills necessary to become a fine editor.

I will occasionally let students know that they have missed things in their editing and that they need to give their text another look. But I will not do the editing for them since this will only improve *my* skills—not *theirs*.

Periodically, your student will bring unedited copy home to review. He/she may be asked, for instance, to count the errors to see how many he or she can find. I am asking for your help in this. Whenever possible, I would like you to discuss conventions with your student writer, and having some faulty text you can both critique is a good way to get that discussion going! We will then correct the text in class, discussing any changes we make and talking about the reasons for them.

By the end of the year, you can expect your child to
- Know many copy editor's symbols (see the enclosed copy)
- Gain skills in using those symbols to correct faulty text
- Learn how to spot errors in spelling, punctuation, paragraphing, and grammar
- Know how to assess a text for use of conventions (see the enclosed Scoring Guide for Conventions)
- *Take responsibility for editing his/her own text*

By the way, if you are a skilled editor, and could help us with peer coaching on our publications, please let me know. We would welcome your help.

Sincerely,

We wouldn't do it in math. Here's an analogy that may help parents who persist in thinking that correcting is beneficial to anyone but the corrector. Suppose you were teaching long division, and you assigned students twenty practice problems. Some might get all twenty right. Some might get only one or two right. Would you painstakingly redo all the incorrect problems for students who had difficulty so they could then copy the correct versions into their notebooks? Most of us would view this as doing students' thinking *for* them; most parents would probably see it the same way. Yet this is precisely what we do when we edit for students. We think for them—and then assign them the mindless busywork task of copying our results.

Make it clear what you've worked on. Get a rubber stamp marked "Conventions corrected to this point" and one marked "Rough draft" so that parents do not expect every line of every paper to be corrected.

Share the conventions scoring guide with parents—along with scoring guides for the other traits. Share copy editor's symbols with parents, too, and post those symbols on the wall of your classroom for easy reference. Explain how conventions fit into a larger vision of writing that embraces multiple goals.

Keep resources handy—and model ways to use them. It may be easier at upper grade levels to refer parents to a good resource book or manual of style that will be the final authority on correctness for your classroom. Here are some possibilities for any well-stocked serious editor's book shelf:

Ballenger, Bruce. *The Curious Researcher: A Guide to Writing Research Papers.* Needham Heights, Massachusetts, 1998.

Among the most detailed, thorough, and genuinely entertaining books ever written on the how-to's of sound research. Middle school and high school.

Blake, Gary and Robert Bly. *The Elements of Technical Writing.* New York: Macmillan, 1993.

A concise, superb guide to the basic elements of technical, informational and business writing. Excellent examples. Middle school and high school.

Cappon, Rene J. *The Associated Press Guide to News Writing*. New York: Prentice-Hall, 1991.

An outstanding, witty, and appropriately concise summary of how to present information clearly, achieve the right tone in a factual piece. High school and up.

The Chicago Manual of Style, 15th ed. Ed. John Grossman. Chicago: University of Chicago Press, 1995.

Complete and authoritative, this is *the* place to look it up when in doubt. High school through adult.

Gerson, Sharon J. and Steven M. Gerson. *Technical Writing: Process and Product*. Upper Saddle River, NJ: Simon and Schuster, 1997.

Perhaps the most complete book around on technical and informational writing. Excellent examples geared to today's work environment. Secondary, but adaptable to any level.

Gibaldi, Joseph. *MLA Handbook for Writers of Research Papers*, 5th ed. New York: Modern Language Association, 1999.

An invaluable guide for older students (high school and beyond) on the use and documentation of information from electronic catalogs, CD-ROM, and on-line databases.

Johnson, Eric. *You Are the Editor*. Carthage, IL: Fearon Teacher Aids, 1981.

Sixty-one thoughtfully designed lessons that build upon one another to teach students editing skills systematically. Grade 5 and up.

Lederer, Richard and Richard Dowis. *The Write Way*. New York: Simon and Schuster, 1995.

Light, easy reading on the 5 C's of fine informational writing: *concise, clear, correct, complete, considerate*. Middle school and high school.

O'Conner, Patricia T. *Woe Is I*. New York: Grossett/Putnam, 1996.

Lessons on modern grammar taught with wit and knowledge—plus predictions on where we're headed. Upper elementary through high school.

Sebranek, Patrick, Dave Kemper and Verne Meyer. *The Write Source Handbooks for Students*. Burlington, Wisconsin: Write Source, a part of Great Source Education Group. (Dated individually.)

Simply the finest handbooks published for students of all ages. Easy to follow, complete, and highly student friendly:

- Kindergarten—*The Writing Spot*
- Grade 1—*Write ONE*
- Grade 2—*Write Away*
- Grade 3—*Write on Track*
- Grade 4 & 5—*Writer's Express*
- Grades 5 and Up (Challenged writers)—*All Write*
- Grades 6–8—*Write Source 2000*
- High School—*Writers INC*
- High School (link to work place)—*School to Work*
- High School/College—*Write for College*

Strunk, William Jr. and E. B. White. *The Elements of Style*, 4th edition. Needham Heights, MA: Allyn & Bacon, 2000.

> Still practical. Still wonderful. The essence of good writing in fewer than 100 pages. Secondary—portions adaptable for all ages. Legendary.

UPI Stylebook, 3d ed. Lincolnwood, IL: National Textbook Company, 1993.

> Can *Xerox* ever be a verb? (No.) Is *X-mas* ever an acceptable abbreviation? (No.) Are you sure about the difference between *uninterested* and *disinterested*? *Great Britain* and *United Kingdom?* Which is the correct pronoun when referring to a ship, *her* or *its?* (Its.) Answers to these and hundreds of similar questions that perplex the curious or serious editor are found in this excellent, easy-to-use resource. Entries are boldfaced and arranged alphabetically. For middle school and up.

Conventions Are Not the Whole Picture

Parents—and all of us—need to remember that strong conventions, while important, are not sufficient in and of themselves to ensure overall writing proficiency. Picture a man in a beautiful $200 silk tie and polished shoes; no matter how snappy they might be, he's not fully dressed—yet.

We want fully dressed writing. We want students to express ideas clearly and completely with a strong sense of purpose; organize information to explain, persuade, or entertain the reader; identify and address a specific audience; choose words that are precise and captivating; and write fluently and concisely—*and* edit with skill. These are lofty goals. They require students to think, to work with ideas, and to make a link from writer to reader. Conventions can help, but they cannot, single-handedly, rescue weak writing.

> Research suggests that the finer points of writing, such as punctuation and subject-verb agreement, are learned best while students are engaged in extended writing that has the purpose of communicating a message to an audience.
> Richard C. Anderson, Elfrieda H. Hiebert, Judith A. Scott, and Ian A. G. Wilkinson (1985)

IDEAS FOR HELPING CHALLENGED/BEGINNING WRITERS

Many students dread writing. It may be difficult for them or they think—right or wrong—they are not very good at it. A lifetime of negative comments does little to build enthusiasm for writing. The writing process approach promises help to challenged writers by offering them more time for writing than many of us used to be given.

But time is only useful if you know what to do with it. Students who have no idea how to revise could have years to redo an assignment and it wouldn't help. Traits can help writers understand what revision looks like, and even if they do only *one* thing to revise a given paper, it's a step, one for which they should receive credit.

Here's another reason I like using traits with writers who struggle; almost always there's at last *one* place they shine—if only for a moment. When you put letter grades on papers, it can be difficult to show what is

> Many students (and adults) consider writing to be "but a line that moves haltingly across the page, exposing as it goes all that the writer doesn't know."
> Mina P. Shaughnessy in Lucy McCormick Calkins (1994, 13)

done well versus what needs work. Analytical scoring provides six opportunities for success, so a student who doesn't have clever ideas may have impressive conventions—or vice versa.

Here are some additional ways to make traits work for writers who find writing difficult, or just unappealing:

1. **Keep writing short.** If you're not much of a runner, you probably would rather not sign up for the 26-mile marathon. Fifty yards is plenty. So let students write a little at a time (a paragraph, say), and write often.

2. **Do lots of group writing.** Bring reluctant or challenged writers together in a group and let them write a story together. Brainstorming leads or conclusions or best phrasing lets everyone in on the thinking part of writing.

3. **As a class, critique and analyze anonymous writing.** Even people who do not like to write themselves or who fear writing enjoy judging the writing of others, and they will learn more from being assessors than you think.

4. **Invite them to challenge you**—to give *you* a writing topic or list of topics to choose from, for example. Then, let them help you work your way through the drafting process. Write, revise, and edit in front of them so they can see you do it, see you get stuck, and watch you work your way out.

5. **When students are floundering for details, interview them—let them dictate to you.** Make notes on what they say so you can let them know they had more ideas than they thought; they can then use your notes in their writing. "Here you told me your hamster died but then you went right into your shopping trip at K-Mart. How did you feel when your hamster died? Who buried it? Where did you bury it?" These probing questions from teacher Lois Burdett turned a brief sketch of a hamster's last moments into a touching story of loss, in which we see the second-grade writer gently touch the body of her now-dead hamster, hoping for a sign of a heartbeat but finding none, then trying to hold back the tears as Dad descends the stairs to the basement and she breaks the news. Later we see Dad digging a small grave, and watch her softly place the body inside and say goodbye, then after pulling up a soft earth blanket, mark the grave with the hamster's name and e-mail address. (A reminder of our times.)

We should see our students as smart and capable. We should assume that they can learn what we teach—*all* of them. We should look through their mistakes or ignorance to the intelligence that lies behind.

Peter Elbow (1987, emphasis in original)

6. **Allow a freebie.** Everyone needs a mental health day occasionally, writers included. Struggling students appreciate the notion that they can disregard one assignment of their choice. Most will do this anyway, so why not make a tradition of it?

7. **Look for what is done well.** Whenever you assess students' work, look first for the positive. Sometimes it's hard. It may be buried, tough to spot. Look harder. Just one moment of voice or convention used correctly is cause for small celebration. Let the student feel the success. Build confidence before you find fault. And when you comment, don't be gushy, but don't hold back, either. No one wants to hear, "Well, your voice is starting

to emerge." What is that? A compliment or a complaint? Be enthusiastic: "Your voice grabbed me by the lapels right at this point. I got the chills." The more voice you put in your comments, the more voice you're likely to see in the next paper.

GET PARENTS INVOLVED

It is important to provide ways for parents to feel they can be involved, too. Not all will, but at least you will be providing some options for those who are motivated and who can/will make time. You can provide a list of possibilities something like this:

Ways to Encourage Your Student Writer

1. **Keep a copy of the *Student Writers' Scoring Guide* handy,** and use the language in that guide (*ideas, organization, voice,* etc.)when you talk about writing with your child.
2. **Encourage your child to read his or her writing (or portions of it) aloud** to you. Praise what the writer *does well*, making comments like these:

- "I could really picture _____." (ideas)
- "I liked the way you decided to begin (or end) your paper." (organization)
- "I could really hear your voice in this part: _____." (voice)
- "I loved the word _____." (word choice)
- "How did you happen to use the word _____?" (word choice)
- "I noticed your sentences did not all begin the same way." (fluency)

3. **Read with your child aloud and often,** and encourage him or her to read to you as well—not just books, but poems, newspaper or journal articles, letters, recipes, the grocery list, phone messages, word problems from a math book, whatever.
4. **Be on the lookout for the not-so-good samples of writing, too.** Browse through junk mail. Notice travel brochures, ads, menus, directions, manuals. When you find something that could use revision, talk about what you would do if *you* were the editor.
5. **Let your child see you write,** even if it's only a short note on a post-it. There is no stronger way to say, "Writing is important."
6. **Write to your child.** A small note will do: e.g., *Have a good day.* OR, *I hope you like your lunch today!* OR *Good luck on that spelling test.*
7. **Ask for your student writer's help when you write.** Even the youngest writers can help make decisions: how to begin a thank-you note, how to achieve the right tone in a complaint letter, how to choose the words that are right for a business letter or birthday greeting. When you ask your child to

help you make decisions about writing, you teach the *thinking* part of writing, which is the hardest (and most important) part.

8. **Ask your child to help you edit, too.** If you can't remember how to spell a word, ask your child to look it up for you. If you aren't sure whether to use a comma or a semicolon, figure it out together. Ask for help on capitalization, paragraphing ("Should I begin a new paragraph here?"), grammar, and spelling. When you write or type a short document, ask your young writer/editor to proofread it for you. This is how a beginning editor develops a proofreader's eye.

9. **Find opportunities to write.** Ask your child to help make a grocery list or list of things to do, to write reminders or thank-you notes, letters of request, invitations—anything! *All practice helps.*

ADVANCED TRAIT ACTIVITIES

Maybe your students have worked with the six traits previously and know them well. The last thing you want to hear is, "Oh, no, not 'Redwoods' again!" Often, I'm asked if there isn't something called "Advanced Traits," a term I always find amusing since it sounds as though once we master these basic, simple traits we can move on to the more sophisticated traits—wit, innuendo, subtlety, profundity, etc.

Actually, working with the traits is like anything else; it can be as simple or difficult as you make it. If you wanted to get better at bike riding, you'd go up steeper, rougher terrain or ride faster for longer periods or strap weights to your back. You get better at the traits pretty much the same way—by challenging yourself:

1. **Ask students to score and comment on *your* writing.** Ask them to write essays defending their scores.

2. **Ask them to self-assess their own work** and again, to write an essay defending that self-assessment (See Lauren Rothrock's example in Chapter 3).

3. **Create your own rubrics.** Why not? Rubric development is a terrific way to build thinking skills; it's harder than it looks, and will make you come face to face with what you think good writing is, regardless of what the six-trait model says. You can specialize: a rubric for persuasive writing, business or tech writing, drama, poetry. Here's how to begin:

- Ask students to examine samples of student writing and to rank order them: high, middle, and low.
- Then, ask them to document their reasons for ranking them as they did. Out of this documentation, identify the traits—qualities—you find most significant. Do not be surprised to see a close resemblance to the original six traits!
- For each trait, create a continuum of performance, from low (beginning) through middle (developing) to high (proficient).

- For a 5-point scale, define performance with vivid descriptors for the 5-point, 3-point, and 1-point levels.
- For a 6-point scale, define performance at the 1-, 3-, 4-, and 6-point levels (you need to split the 3 and 4 on a 6-point since the 4 is a "made it" kind of score, while the 3 is a "not quite—but almost").
- Test each rating scale on an actual piece of student writing. See how close your scores come!
- Use differences in scoring to help you decide how to adjust/revise the scale.

4. **Ask students to design their own lessons for teaching traits.** You may wish to assign one trait to each of several groups in your class. Let them use student writing samples, other writing samples, pieces from literature, or activities to enrich the lesson. They should feel free to be inventive! Once they've designed lessons for their own classmates (this is just the warm-up), have them do lessons for

- Younger children
- Parents
- Members of the business community
- Content area teachers

5. **Compare traits across modes of writing.** Talk about how voice changes with purpose (informational to descriptive to narrative) or how even conventions differ in creative versus business or technical writing. You'll find each trait is different, and when you bring modes (forms, purposes) of writing into the picture, you open up a whole new world of ways to apply and think about traits. They change, chameleon-like, as the purpose of the writing shifts.

6. **Ask students to keep portfolios.** Within those portfolios, they can show samples of writing that reflect quality performance on each of the six traits— plus growing editing skill to demonstrate proficiency in conventions.

7. **Reshape the traits to fit your own lessons.** Here are two examples.

Example 1

This lesson was designed by Barbara Galler of Issaquah (Washington) Middle School, based on the Wallace Stegner essay "Thoughts in a Dry Land" (1992).[1] In this lesson, notice how Barbara invites students to connect each activity to one of the traits. The students are not assessing per se, but rather, responding to the text and learning about the concepts of word choice, organization, etc., at the same time. Also notice how this lesson integrates reading and writing. (See Figure 7.9)

[1]Stegner, Wallace. "Thoughts in a Dry Land," from *Where the Bluebird Sings to the Lemonade Springs*. New York: Random House, 1992.

Part I: Vocabulary

Make a "best guess" at the meaning of each word. Work with a partner. Find the work in Stegner's essay and see whether your "best guess" changes, based on how Stegner uses the word. Look up any word you are still not very, very sure of. Was your definition close?

salina	flora	chlorophyll
sinkhole	fauna	sentinels
saguaro	littoral	rapacity
travertine	boosterism	

Part II: Reading for the Scoring Guide

Word Choice   Ideas   Sentence Fluency
Organization   Voice   Conventions

1. *Ideas*
   Briefly state four essential ideas you gleaned (look up) from this essay:
   a.
   b.
   c.
   d.

2. *Sentence Fluency*
   Find three examples of fluent, easy-to-read sentences:

   a. ____ page number. Write a sentence:

   b. ____ page number. Write a sentence:

   c. ____ page number. Write a sentence:

3. *Voice*
   Find an example of superior or striking word choice, one you respond to personally. (The right words make the most vivid picture in your brain.) Page number _____. Write the excerpt:

5. *Organization*
   Based on the four main ideas you identified within this essay (see number 1 above), sketch or outline an organizational plan or pattern which shows how Stegner organized his essay. Use an outline, a drawing, or any other illustration which will help you show how Stegner organized his ideas.

FIGURE 7.9. Reflective response to the Wallace Stegner essay "Thoughts in a Dry Land"*

Example 2

As high school instructor Ellen Tatalias of Allentown, Pennsylvania shows us, you can create a revision checklist based on the six-trait scoring guide, but specific to one assignment. In this case, the theme for the assignment is *doublespeak*.

ASSIGNMENT

Language has a profound impact on our lives. Politicians, advertisers, and business executives shape our world by influencing our perception of people, as well as our position on controversial social and political issues. It's not bombing; it's "air support." It's not acid rain but "poorly buffered precipitation." By using several well-chosen and well-organized examples from your own reading and experience, show how language has been used to conceal or prevent thought, or to intentionally mislead. First, explain why your examples illustrate "doublespeak." Then, explain the possible danger resulting from the use of such language.

Revision Checklist for Doublespeak Assignment

IDEAS

_____ Do your examples show how doublespeak has been used to control or prevent thought?

_____ Do you fully explain the outcome or danger resulting from their use?

_____ Have you avoided stating the obvious?

ORGANIZATION

_____ Are examples presented in a logical way, building to a climax?

_____ Is your introduction compelling and direct?

_____ Have you avoided putting supporting details in your introduction?

_____ Does your conclusion bring closure to your essay and leave your audience thinking about the dangers of doublespeak?

VOICE

_____ Does your writing reflect commitment? Involvement?

_____ Have you made an effort to connect with your audience? Who is that audience?

WORD CHOICE

_____ Have you avoided passive voice?

_____ Have you avoided state of being verbs? Participles?

_____ Have you trimmed unnecessary words?

_____ Is your language clear? Are examples of doublespeak vivid?

SENTENCE FLUENCY

_____ Have you used parallel structure, climax, antithesis, rhetorical questions?

____ Have you begun sentences with the topic, avoiding beginnings like *There is, There are, It seems,* etc.?

____ Have you read the piece aloud to see if it really flows?

CONVENTIONS

____ Have you proofread your essay for misspelled or deleted words?

____ Have you read it aloud and silently to check for correct grammar, usage, use of capitals, and punctuation?

____ Do paragraphs begin in the right places?

____ Do your layout and format enhance readability?

Checklists like Ellen's help students focus in on what is critical in a specific assignment, while still making the traits the foundation of strong writing. In addition, it gives Ellen an opportunity to weave in such writing features as parallel structure or rhetorical questions, which are integral to her current classroom instruction. For an example of how one student responded to the Doublespeak assignment, see paper 9, "Challenger," in Chapter 10.

8. **Score more challenging material:** Look at conventions or word choice in a legal document or résumé or job application letter; voice or organization in a play, recipe, board game instructions, letter of resignation, or set of directions on a box of pancake mix; word choice in a travel brochure or weather forecast or college manual; fluency in a film review or set of song lyrics by Stephen Sondheim; ideas in a political speech or doctoral dissertation. Assess pieces from Edgar Allan Poe, Chaucer, Shakespeare, Melville, Norman Mailer, Virginia Woolf, Emily Dickinson, Tim O'Brien, Maya Angelou, Pablo Piccasso—or Thomas Jefferson, Nelson Mandela, Abe Lincoln, or Franklin Roosevelt. Hold a contest: Who can think up the most challenging assessment? The most unusual? The most riveting? Stretch. Grow. There is always a more difficult assessment task ahead.

9. **Finally, personify the traits and portray them theatrically.** How does Voice dress and speak? Is Conventions really the stuffed shirt everyone says he is? What if Fluency crashed the party? Would she be attracted to the debonair Word Choice—or find him hopelessly dull? You can ask students to select a part and act out a short play—or just a dialogue. Be prepared to let your real attitudes about the traits show!

In the end, it isn't the traits that become advanced, you see, but our understanding of them.

Suggested Corrections for "Redwoods" Editing Activities

Here and on the following page, you will find Figures 7.10, 7.11, and 7.12, containing suggested corrections for the editing practice lessons based on "Redwoods" that were presented on pages 216–217.

Redwoods

Last year, we want on a vacation, and

we had a wonderful time. The waether

was sunny and warm and there was lots

too do, so we where never bored.

My parants visited freinds and took

pictures for their friends back home. My

brother and I swam and also hiked in the

woulds. Wen we got tiled of that, we just

eat and had a wondurful time.

FIGURE 7.10. Suggested corrections for spelling errors in Figure 7.3

Redwoods

Last year, we went on a vacation, and,

we had a wonderful time. The weather,

was sunny and warm and there was lots,

to do, so we were never bored.

My parents visited friends and took

pictures, for their friends back home. My

brother, and I, swam, and also hiked, in

the woods. When we got tired of that, we

just ate and had a wonderful time.

FIGURE 7.11. Suggested corrections for comma errors in Figure 7.4

REFLECTING ON CHAPTER 7

1. What traits are strongest (or weakest) in your students' writing? What about your own?
2. What's the best editorial advice you ever received? What was the least helpful?
3. Have you ever been judged on the basis of your conventions? When? Did it feel fair? Do you judge other people this way? Why or why not?

ACTIVITIES

1. Find an unusual piece to assess—something others might not think of in connec-

Redwoods

last year, we went on a vacation, and we

had a wonderful time the weather was

sunny and warm and there was lots to do,

so we were never bored my parents

visited friends and took pictures for their

friends back home my brother and I

swam and also hiked in the woods when

we got tired of that, we just ate and had a

wonderful time

FIGURE 7.12. Suggested corrections for errors in capitals and periods in Figure 7.5

tion with writing assessment (e.g., song lyrics). Bring it in for your study group or class to assess. Talk about the traits that are most important.

2. Look at any single trait—ideas, organization, voice, whatever—across several modes of writing: say, business writing, narrative writing, and persuasive writing. How do the traits shape-shift to meet the needs of each mode? Do certain elements remain constant?

3. Make copies of "Haircut From Hell" without the corrections. Share it with your writing group or your class. Invite them to respond in any way they feel is appropriate before you share any actual teacher responses. Then compare.

4. Discuss this chapter's recommendations for coping with parental demands for a traditionalist approach to the teaching of conventions. Do you agree or disagree? What are the advantages/disadvantages of each method?

5. In your class or group, personify and create a dramatic encounter among the six traits. What do you learn from this experience about your attitude toward the various traits? Do you like some more than others? Find some more important than others?

LOOKING AHEAD

In Chapter 8, we'll consider the importance of writing with your students. We'll also look at the writing process through the eyes of experience.

MEMORABLE MOMENTS FROM STUDENTS' WRITING

- You'll probably live a little past 40; nevertheless, you can prevent it.
- We had to do the ninedickmanover to see if the person was still breathing.
- I'm too sexy for this test.
- I don't think me liking him had anything to do with his incredibly good looks.
- She couldn't even spell "culdn't" Her spelling was abyzmall.
- And now for a change of paste.
- It was Monday mourning and I was headed to school.

8

BEING A WRITER

Young writers learn best from teachers who write, just as children learning to swim learn best from teachers who actually get into the water with them. Empathy makes a sensitive teacher.

Tom Romano (1987, 43)

If you had asked me, when I was a child, to give a generic description of a teacher, I would have said someone who wears nice clothes, stands in front of the room next to the chalkboard, and knows everything.

Nancy Slonim Aronie (1998, 171)

When teachers share both their writing processes and their writing products with their students, they do the one thing non-writers need most: They demystify writing.

Tommy Thomason and Carol York (2000, 5)

DO YOU WRITE?

When you first thought about being a writing teacher, did you picture yourself writing? I didn't. I pictured myself handing out assignments, being the one with the power (and the red pen) for a change. At last, I would be the one to decide how long the papers must be, how many days students would have to write, whether rough drafts would have to be turned in with the final copy, whether spelling would count. During my "power" period, I certainly handed out my share of inane assignments with meaningless parameters: 500 words on how it feels to take a bath. (I actually liked this assignment so much I repeated it three times). I did not write on this topic myself (or else I would have known to stop after the first time). I had not learned yet to *teach* writing, only to *assign* writing.

ENLIGHTENMENT

One day a student asked me where I got *my* ideas for writing, how I knew how long to make assignments, and how many drafts *I* usually wrote. How many? Why, none. I was not *writing* drafts, for heaven's sake, I was *assigning* them.

After all, writing was not what my teachers had modeled. I do not remember seeing a single one of them with pen in hand except to write marginal comments: "Be specific! Watch your tenses! Comma splice! You've changed person midstream! [A maneuver seeming to demand stunning flexibility.] This is a *new clause!* What do you mean? You lost me." Did they know how to write? To this day I couldn't say. They certainly knew how to whip up a mean critique. Because they were the evaluators of our writing, we trusted them to know what they were about. For the most part, they probably did know; they certainly knew the conventional rules of writing. I now realize, however, how much more they could have taught us had they been writers themselves as well as critics, and had they shown us what writing looks like as it's unfolding.

Teachers of writing, if they wish to be effective, must themselves write (Graves, 1983; Murray, 1985; Atwell, 1987). Almost everyone now accepts this. It's only logical. Yet, many teachers continue to resist writing with or in front of students—for a variety of reasons.

Dare

When I first began writing with my students (responding to a suggestion—almost a dare—from one class), I did not think that I wrote very well. The students were extremely encouraging and complimentary; I thought they were just being polite—but I now know that what they liked was not so much my writing as the fact that I did it. After all, wouldn't it be dishonest to question students about *1984, The Catcher in the Rye,* or *The Merchant of Venice* without first reading those works? Teachers of literature, we think, should be readers. People who teach swimming should know more than how to watch from the edge of the pool as others do laps. For the very same reasons, teachers of writing must write.

In writing I also discovered something wonderful that I had missed from every single one of my teachers. From that day forward, I always had a story to tell about writing. It is satisfying to be able to say to students, "Here's how I revised this piece," or "Here's where this idea came from," or "This way of coming up with a lead worked for me. It might work for you." I was beginning to understand what Regie Routman (1996) means when she says, "When our students see how we struggle, organize, think, reread, revise, edit, and get ideas with and through our writing, they are supported in their writing" (183).

The schoolroom writing rules are so wrong, but they sound so right: Gather your thoughts before you begin to write. Write a thesis sentence that expresses the main thought you plan to convey. Make an outline. Then write, following that outline. That makes perfect sense—to everyone but writers.

Tommy Thomason (1993, 34)

IT CAN MAKE YOU UNCOMFORTABLE

Teachers are very nearly as creative as students in coming up with reasons not to write. I've used some of these in the past. You could, too—or you could come up with a new one of your own.

Excuse 1: I already know how to write. Sometimes people have the notion that learning to write is like learning to ride a bike. Once you've got it, it's yours forever. In truth, learning to write is a lifelong endeavor.

Excuse 2: I'll have to be wonderful. It isn't imperative to be Walter Dean Myers, Nikki Giovanni, or Toni Morrison. There is a lot to be learned and shared this side of genius. Maybe there is Pulitzer Prize material in you and maybe not. If there is not, you can console yourself with the fact that the most gifted writers are not always the best teachers. Teaching is an art in itself. Besides, as writer/author Barry Lane so often remarks, "The best thing to share with your student writers is your own insecurity." That way, they know they're not alone.

Remember this bit of wisdom from Donald Murray (1985): "We don't learn to write from finished, polished, completed, published writing. We learn from the constructive failures of early drafts" (p. 8). Maybe we would learn more often from "constructive failures" if we created within our classrooms a place of safety, where "failure" was looked on as courageous experimentation, and students were challenged to try new things, even if the writing went badly. By insisting on immediate success, we hobble our student writers and ensure that when they do write, they will be cautious—and the results will be boring.

Excuse 3: I'll be *too* good. Conversation was halted one day during a workshop when a teacher remarked, "Won't my students just feel like giving up when I write so much better than they do?" There's self-confidence for you. Actually, it's hard to predict what students will really feel wowed by. Sometimes the pieces you secretly view as your very finest moments can float right by them like dust particles. Students are not necessarily easy to impress, especially once they become skilled assessors. What *does* impress them, though, almost without exception, is your willingness to share your work. And someday, if you teach long enough, you'll encounter a student who will write you right into the ground, no matter how good you are or think you are. Be proud. Not everyone gets to coach a genius. Enjoy it.

Excuse 4: I don't have time to write. Guess what? *Nobody* does. Professional writers are among the most frenzied people on earth. The notion of the writer who takes long walks on sandy beaches, waiting for sea spray and inspiration to strike, is mostly a myth. Donald Murray tells of the need to be anchored to one spot now that he writes on computer; but before, he claims, "some of my favorite places [to write] were diners and lunchrooms or a parked car in a busy neighborhood" (1990, 46). Besides, you don't have to compose a novel each time you sit down. Make time for small writing in your classroom this way. Write when students are writ-

---

The only job I do, the only promise I make, the sole objective that I have is to guarantee safety.

Nancy Slonim Aronie (1998, 122)

I think it might safely be said that in general people don't expect to write much after they've left school, except when it's absolutely necessary—as a tool, in letter writing for instance, or when it's part of their work. In short, it's seen as a chore. The view that writing might be fun, or amusing, or relaxing is not, I imagine, widely held, and we teachers must be to blame for that.

Mem Fox (1993)

I have long since decided that if you wait for the perfect time to write, you'll never write. There is no time that isn't flawed somehow.

Margaret Atwood in Murray (1990, 47)

ing. Write one lead and ask students where the paper might go. That takes a minute. You can take one minute.

The next time you hear yourself say, "I would write with my students, but I just don't have time," ask yourself how you would react to a student who told you that.

Excuse 5: I just have nothing to write about. Oh, but you do. As my teacher friend Lois Burdett is forever telling her students, "Your problem is not that you have nothing to write about. Your problem is that you have *too much* to write about, so you will have to choose your topic very carefully." We just have to learn, along with our students, to identify what is significant in our lives.

REASONS TO WRITE

So many good things come from writing on your own or with students that it is not possible to list them all. You have to experience them. Here are a few.

Benefit 1: You'll learn to dig. In real life, writers sometimes write on assigned topics—often, though, there is no one to hand them a topic on a plate; they must figure out for themselves where the good topics lie. As you do this, you'll discover how difficult it can be, and you'll learn little tricks, like keeping lists of writer's questions, jotting down promising thoughts right when they first come to you (even in the middle of the night), using conversations, reading from favorite writers when you get stuck, being an observer of life—all of which you can share with your students. Donald Murray teaches us that we can *only* learn about writing process from within—not from seminars or lectures or books: "The best preparation for the writing class, workshop, or conference is at least a few minutes at the writing desk, saying what you did not expect to say" (1985, 74).

Benefit 2: You'll teach by example. How wonderful for your students to have a model of a real writer at work! Students mostly see finished pieces of writing. Rarely do they have a chance to see a writer drafting, pausing, crossing out, rewriting, stopping to think, or asking for help—right there at the overhead or chalkboard. Further, you'll come to understand how writing process changes to fit who each writer is and the individual way he/she thinks. Tom Romano (1987) suggests that "The best writing processes are flexible and organic. They bend and grow to meet a writer's needs" (59).

Benefit 3: You'll learn why writing often turns out different from how it began. Sometimes people who do not write do not recognize the value of exploration. They tend to view it as "straying from the topic." This incredibly misguided attitude misses the whole point. Exploratory writing is not straying *from* but rather searching *for* the topic.

It makes me want to stand and cheer when the irrepressible Mem Fox (1993) writes, "I don't know, before I start, quite how an article or a chapter will develop, or how a book will blossom. I never make an outline. For me an outline is like a straitjacket that prevents me from being creative, divergent."

[Successful T]eachers write and share their writing, processes and products, with their students. They personally experience what they ask of student writers, from finding a topic through going public. [They] do not require student writers to do anything they don't do themselves as writers.
Nancie Atwell (1987)

A writer is "someone who is enormously taken by things anyone else would walk by."
James Dickey in Calkins (1994, 3)

Every one of you is a storyteller. Your ancestors sat around a campfire or a sweat lodge or a table and recorded their histories by telling their stories. . . . Now you tell them.
Nancy Slonim Aronie (1998, 129)

I cannot overemphasize how important it is for teachers of writing to write themselves. Albert Einstein once said regarding science that "the years of anxious searching in the dark, with their intense longing, their alterations of confidence and exhaustion and the final emergence into the light—only those who have experienced it can understand it."

Alan Ziegler (1981)

You should write too, under the same conditions—on the board or in your notebook—and share your writing first. It's a matter of ethics. You are going to be seeing their work; it's only fair that they see yours.

Donald Murray (1985)

Writing is risky because we're seeking—consciously or unconsciously—acceptance for our stories and our opinions. . . . When we express an opinion, we can argue for its acceptance. But when we put something on paper, it stands there on its own.

Tommy Thomason (1993, 15)

Sometimes there is a reason to stay right on topic: e.g., "Define the concept of ratio." Other times, we must allow our student writers to find their own path.

Benefit 4: You'll get in touch with the process of revision. Many teachers prewrite with their students. Prewriting is fun, energizing, and fast (too fast, sometimes). Valuable as prewriting is, however, if it stops short of drafting, it is still a little on the fringes of real writing. Student writers need to know how to go from that beautiful cluster, that great list, to the very first line or word. How do you *begin?* Where do you go next? And once your draft is together, How do you decide what to keep? What do you toss out? How do you rework a weak ending? How do you know whether an audience will understand, or whether the writing has voice and what to do if it doesn't?

Prewriting offers hints of where we're going. Drafting and revising actually take us there.

Benefit 5: You'll become more sensitive about assessment. Writing makes for a dangerous spectator sport because it breeds intolerance. When you write with and for your students, encouraging them to review and comment on what *you've* written, you become sensitized to how it feels being the one under the microscope. We need to learn more than just how nervous sharing writing can make us, though. We need to know—and then teach our students—what kinds of comments are helpful. "Good job, Brenda" says next to nothing. "I could picture your mother's trembling hands, and I felt how frightened you were leaving her at the hospital" is a comment on another level.

Benefit 6: You'll learn not to take yourself too seriously. Some of your writing will be really fine. It will give you deep satisfaction, like sharing with friends a good bottle of wine you've made yourself. At other times, the very keyboard will seem to turn on you and everything the printer spits out will sound stupid or false.

If you read aloud what you've written during these times, it may embarrass or just depress you. Take heart. During the dry spells, new ideas are fermenting. I love it when Barry Lane reminds us, "We often do our best writing when we've run out of gas." Those words have kept me going on many a late night. Often, you emerge on the other side a stronger writer, understanding both the process and your topic better. The experience also gives you courage to tell students occasionally, "If it just isn't working, get rid of it." It's not a sin to throw whole pages away.

When Should I Begin?

Begin now, right now. This minute, if you can. Or, write something tonight at home. Write tomorrow in class—and as often as you can after that. Write every day, if possible. Make writing part of who you are. While you're at it, don't write for your mother, your principal, or that teacher who used to stand over you with the red pen. Write for you. Write from the heart, and you'll want to read it tomorrow, next week, and a year from now. Your students will want to read it, too.

TWO STORIES

On the following few pages, I share with you two stories I have shared with students and with adult teacher/writers. In each case, my purpose is to give you a sense of how the stories evolved through my personal writing process, and the value of both writing with students and sharing writing with an audience.

Story 1: "Terror in Fourth Grade"

This story began as an experiment to model the value of questions in prewriting and drafting. When listeners ask a writer questions, they help the writer do two things: (1) focus and narrow the topic; and (2) identify what is interesting to that audience. Figure these two things out and the odds of writing something with both detail and voice increase ten-fold.

I began with a simple statement about one of my grade school teachers, a woman who terrorized us all—with the exception of one student, who became a folk hero in his own time. She is/was a real person, and this story is essentially true, though I have changed all the names—plus other factual information. Her story unfolded in two parts, with two sets of questions, both of which caused me to think deeply about my writing, resulting in a far better story than I could have created had I just sat down to write about her one evening. In fact, it is no exaggeration to say that the questions pushed me to first remember many buried details and then to write; and questions can push you and your students to write, too.

If you follow my model, use a story of your own, something that happened to you and is vivid in your mind. Then, invite your students to use questions as a tool for helping you dig deep into the recesses of your memories.

THE STATEMENT—AND THE QUESTIONS IT PROVOKED

Every time I use this approach to modeling, I begin with a simple statement related to a topic I'd like to explore:

A woman walks into the room.

Then I invite the group to ask me questions that will fill in details and help me create a perspective and voice. Here are the original questions (all of which I saved on an overhead):

- What is she wearing?
- How does she move?

> We need to stay with the low moments. They feed the high ones. They add depth to your writing. They add depth to your soul. We are not wind-up toys with smiley faces. We are real beings with hard days and moments.
> Nancy Slonim Aronie (1998, 89)

> There is no one right way. Each of us finds a way that works for him. But there is a wrong way. The wrong way is to finish your writing day with no more words on paper than when you began. Writers write.
> Robert B. Parker in Murray (1990, 60)

> Anyone who says he wants to be a writer and isn't writing, doesn't.
> Ernest Hemingway in Murray (1990, 54)

- Does she look at you?
- Where is the room?
- Why is she there?
- Does she speak? What does she say?
- What sort of expression is on her face?
- Does she like children?
- What is your reaction to her?
- You seem afraid of her. Is everyone afraid?
- How old is she?

These very basic questions stimulated my first draft, and as you will see, I do not answer them all. This isn't a fill-in-the-blank kind of exercise. But I did keep the list in front of me and paid attention to it because I was writing not only for myself, but for this very real audience.

"TERROR IN FOURTH GRADE"

Draft 1

We felt her coming before we heard her. The hundred year old floors of Oak Valley School quaked beneath her forceful stride. Gradually— so gradually we might have imagined it at first—the sturdy chunk chunk of her thick brown heels on the linoleum told us she was coming . . . coming . . . we couldn't run, so we shrank deep into ourselves, and then she was upon us, moving through us with long, unyielding strides, arms swinging, a ruler in one hand, a dictionary in the other. Her body was a six-foot grenade. She smelled of lava soap. Her nostrils flared like a dragon's and it occurred to me she could smell our fear. She wore no makeup, and no smile. Fourth grade was serious business, as we were about to find out. "Sit down. Be quiet," she commanded. We scrambled to obey. All except Eugene. Eugene had tattoos on both arms and was said to have smoked his first cigarette at age nine. I had not seen him smoke, but I had seen him ride his brother's motorcycle across the school grounds once. Eugene eased slowly into his seat, landing in an insolent slump, legs wide apart, feet well into both aisles where everyone knew feet did not belong. Her steely eyes bore into him, and Eugene's long-lashed innocent brown eyes smiled back. She could not make him look away, and she didn't like that much, we could tell. She had 25 years and a good 80 pounds on Eugene—and yet, I knew in that moment, he thought he could take her. I had never liked Eugene much. But just then, for reasons I couldn't yet understand, I found myself rooting for him.

MORE QUESTIONS

As you can see, my draft turned from a simple description into a story—one that promises an upcoming conflict. All good stories have tension, but without Eugene, the tension in this story would be like a simmering teakettle—there, but not yet menacing. Eugene provides the catalyst that will bring out the character of this teacher, and of the other students, including me. Drafts provoke further questions, and this is where the real writing—revision—begins. Here's what my listeners/responders wanted to know:

- Does anything good come out of this?
- Do Eugene and this teacher have *any* redeeming qualities?
- Why do we see this teacher as a villain? That bothers me. She hasn't really done anything, yet your picture of her is so menacing. Why? Are you being fair?
- I think we need to hear her speak more.
- What will happen when Eugene and the teacher confront each other?
- Will there be more than one confrontation?
- Will they learn from each other? I'd like this to end with everyone learning something.
- Will you be a figure in this story—or is it all about Eugene and the teacher now?
- I'm wondering—is there maybe a dark side to *you* in this story?

These questions really—*really*—made me think. Yes, I thought, there *is* a dark side to me in this tale. I was a "model student," one of those kids too intimidated by the teacher to get into trouble—most of the time. But they can't intimidate the imagination out of you, and in writing about this, it occurred to me how I had looked forward to this showdown between the two—Eugene and Miss Sader (not their real names). It was the OK Corral, and I loved it; we all did. Did Eugene and Miss Sader have redeeming qualities? Absolutely. But I'm not ready to write about those yet; first, I want to show them fighting for their turf:

"TERROR IN FOURTH GRADE"

Draft 2

We felt her coming before we heard her. The hundred year old floors of Oak Valley School quaked beneath her forceful stride. Gradually—so gradually we might have imagined it at first—the sturdy chunk chunk of her thick brown heels on the linoleum told us she was coming . . . coming . . . "She hits kids, you know," someone near me whispered. "And locks them in the closet," came another voice. "I heard she will step on your feet if you put them in the aisle," said a third, just behind me, and I shuddered, even as I felt a jolt of anger at my friend Joyce, who had gotten the good teacher, Mrs. Morgan, the tiny teacher with the tiny voice.

The chunk chunk grew louder, the door swung open, and then she was upon us, moving through us with long, unyielding strides, arms swinging, a ruler in one hand, a dictionary in the other. Her body was a six-foot grenade. She smelled of lava soap. Her nostrils flared like a dragon's and it occurred to me she could smell our fear. She wore no makeup, and no smile. Short, brown, no-nonsense hair stopped just shy of her ears.

"You"—she pointed her ruler at Gary—"Even up those window shades. And you"—pointing now at little Mary, who shook visibly—"line those erasers up on the left. The *rest* of you"—she pivoted to take us all in—"sit down. Be quiet."

We scrambled to obey. All except Eugene. Eugene had tattoos on both arms and was said to have smoked his first cigarette at age nine. I had not seen him smoke, but I had seen him ride his brother's motorcycle across the school grounds once. Eugene eased slowly into his seat, landing in an insolent slump, legs wide apart, feet well into both aisles where everyone knew feet did not belong. Her steely eyes bore into him, and Eugene's long-lashed innocent brown eyes smiled back. She could not make him look away, and she didn't like that much, we could tell. She had 25 years and a good 80 pounds on Eugene—and yet, I knew in that moment, he thought he could take her.

Had we been a little older, we might have laid down bets on the outcome that day. After a morning of flunking surprise quizzes in spelling and math, and watching two boisterous members of our troop dragged flamboyantly to the hall (from which they returned meek and silent, unwilling to share details), the odds definitely seemed to favor Miss Sader. Just the same, I would have put my money on Eugene. He had been unusually quiet, even smiling at her a time or two. She did not smile back. She would show him she was not about to be won over. I had seen Eugene in action before, though, and knew something Miss Sader did not. He wasn't trying to win her over. He was biding his time. Not that she didn't try to provoke him. "Eugene, sit up straight," or "Eugene, take your eyes off your neighbor's paper." That one struck me—struck all of us—as hilarious. Eugene *never* cheated; he didn't care enough to cheat.

The first big skirmish occurred when Eugene, who sat in the front, dropped a whole stack of mimeographed worksheets on the floor. The window was open, and they floated instantly to the far corners of the room, where they were imprinted with muddy feet or torn in the rescue process. Eugene shrugged as if they'd been autumn leaves beyond his control, and that shrug lit her fuse. She was certain Eugene had done it on purpose; and she might have been right.

Her face, naturally rosy anyway, took on a deep umber hue, and her breathing increased noticeably, her ample bosom rising and falling in a hypnotic rhythm. "All right, Eugene," she said, speaking on a low voice that was somehow more menacing than her usual high shriek, "*into* the hall."

Eugene, calm as stone, replied simply, "No."

For a moment, I thought her eyes would squirt clean out of her head and fire at us. We all shrank back instinctively, even as she began to move forward. "Eugene, I said into the hall—*now,*" she repeated, hands on her hips, her mouth stretched tight like a rubber band about to fly, her cheeks aflame. A narrow shank of hair hung down in her face.

Eugene leaned back nonchalantly, as if he was about to light up, or offer a cigarette to Miss Sader. But he only folded his arms and said softly, looking right at her, "And I said *no.*"

What happened next was such a blur that if it had been on video, we would have replayed it just to make sure of what we'd seen. I suppose she strode to his desk, but it looked more like a leap, and then she was behind him, the full six feet and 180 pounds of her strength hoisting him under the arms, prying him up. Fast as she was, though, Eugene was faster. He grasped the seat of the heavy metal desk in a grip that was nothing short of dazzling. So, when she lifted him, the desk came, too, and heavy as they must have been together, she hauled them both to the front of the room. "Eugene, let go of that desk!" she cried, over and over, beginning to swing the Eugene-desk combination in a wide arc, side to side.

"Eugene, hang on!" we prayed silently, no one daring to say it aloud, but all of us willing strength into Eugene's arms—for if he let go, we knew, the desk would fly right for us. He did not let go, though, and in the end, she had to carry them both to the hall.

We knew what to do. We picked up the scattered worksheets and started in. Geography. Not my best subject. In the hall we heard loud voices, scuffles, scrapings, some banging—but no words we could make out. I filled in Minnesota first, grateful for its distinctive shape. I hauled Nebraska over to Ohio, and put New York in Pennsylvania. Rhode Island was very tiny, I knew, so I wrote its name in the Atlantic, and drew an arrow to a little smudge where I thought it might be. I was working on the other easy ones—Florida, California, Texas, Idaho—when Miss Sader returned with Eugene's desk. Her hair was badly mussed and her perspiration soaked blouse clung tightly to her chest.

She told us to finish up our worksheets so we could begin the next one, which she slapped onto the top of her desk.

I did not see Eugene again for two more days. It was geography time once again, and I was just finishing labeling the only river I was ever to know for sure—the Mississippi—when I sneaked a forbidden peek out the window, and there was Eugene, bold as sunshine, doing wheelies on the school grounds. He wasn't dead.

He wasn't even in a cast. So, I thought, *this* is the consequence of defiance—freedom. Then I saw the principal madly waving her arms, and Eugene took off in a blaze of spattered sod, amply coating the principal's shoes. Eugene one, Miss Sader zip. But of course . . . it was only October.

MORE TO COME

Clearly, it is possible to write, much, much more of this story, and indeed these two irascible characters changed each other, along with most of the rest of us, for all time. But I rather like the sketch the way it is since it allows readers to use their imaginations to envision possible outcomes. But someday, someone will ask the right questions, and I will feel compelled to finish it.

We hold on to hopes for next year every year in western Dakota: hoping that droughts will end; hoping that our crops won't be hailed out in the few rainstorms that come; hoping that it won't be too windy on the day we harvest, blowing away five bushels an acre; hoping (usually against hope) that if we get a fair crop, we'll be able to get a fair price for it. Sometimes survival is the only blessing that the terrifying angel of the Plains bestows.

Kathleen Norris (1993, 6)

Story 2:
"Snooky": Coffee and Prewriting

When I first met Susanna, my grandmother, she was in her mid sixties and I was eight. Her hair was snow-white, as it had been from her youth, and was wound tight and clipped in place at the back of her head. Her body had aged past her sixty-some years, but then, she had worked very hard, slept little, and had neither faith nor interest in cosmetics. Her spirit was young, though, and her will like steel.

She was a superb baker, and her kitchen smelled of cinnamon, lemon, caramel, and chocolate. By the time I was eleven, she had introduced me to the wonders of steaming black coffee and what it could do for a home made cinnamon roll and good conversation. It was a gift that would last me a lifetime.

When I asked her one day about the scars on the backs of her legs, she sighed a bit, adjusted her glasses, and smiled at me. "I had this cat once," she said. "Are you sure you want to hear about her?" That was the beginning of my "prewriting" for this story. Conversation. No lists, no word webs. A shared secret, and a deep-down belief that I knew my grandmother better than anyone.

To this day, I feel a chill on the back of my neck when I remember the old stories of Snooky, a scruffy feral cat destined to become a legend. Though no one could tell the stories quite like Susanna herself, it wasn't until I wrote about Snooky myself that I learned—or rather, uncovered—the reason I'd always found these stories so disturbing. I had always known the reason really. I just didn't *know* I knew. I had not been willing to face the harder, more brutal side of my gentle, smiling bread-baking grandmother. That's why it took me thirty years to put her story in writing.

MY VERSION OF DRAFTING

When the need to write is strong, almost nothing can get in its way. That is how I felt about this story, which had been building inside me like a volcano for years. The whole thing came to a head one summer when my family took a trip across the North Dakota prairie, and I felt the incredible tug of a landscape that still called to me from old memories I had thought were gone.

As I wrote, I tried to put myself inside my grandmother's tiny white house on Second Avenue, with six children and not enough to feed them, looking out one small window to the world beyond, hating the dust and the ever-present wind. I tried very hard to become, for a short while, that person trapped on the other side of the window and to write from her head and heart.

THE HORROR OF SHARING

Finishing the first draft always brings for me a sense of relief—for now revision (which I love) can begin. I had looked forward to sharing this draft with someone who did not know the story, but when I first did so, I experienced something every author dreads: indifference.

I first read my draft to a group of a hundred teachers, and as the reading inched along, I found myself wondering what had happened. Gone was my clear, moving, virtually ready-to-publish story of the legendary cat and the feisty hoe-wielding pioneer woman who had loved her. In its place was a pathetically ponderous, lumbering document, which, in addition to being unforgivably dull, seemed long enough to rival anything by James Michener. On it droned, for hours, dallying in the kitchen, falling asleep on the front porch. Though I edited mercilessly, chopping off whole paragraphs as I read aloud, I couldn't slog my way to the end. My glasses were slipping down my nose, and my hair hurt.

When I asked the audience for suggestions, I fully expected someone to say, "Head for the shredder." But once the worst part for them—listening to a too-long tale—was over, they quickly warmed to the task of coaching. The ending needed work, they said, and the whole piece must be shortened. They liked the beginning, and wanted more of that moody feeling. More about Snooky, too. They couldn't picture her. I asked them very specifically what they thought happened to the dog (Rudy) in the story; most did not know. My heart sank, for on this critical piece of information my whole story rested—to say nothing of the reputation of the infamous Snooky.

The purpose of revision is not to correct but to discover.
Lucy McCormick Calkins (1986)

TIME FOR REVISION

First, I had to make the whole thing shorter. It was sprawly and overdone. Second, I had to make it clear what happened to Rudy, but I did not want to come right out and say it. The thing was, you see, my grandmother knew— she *had to know* what would happen when she opened the screen door that night. But she never really saw it. So she could play it both ways, admiring Snooky for what she had done, but putting it out of her mind as well. I had to make all this clear without saying it outright.

My approach was to read the story aloud multiple times—and to cut everything that did not matter. I hacked off whole pages, trimming the text

grief between them.

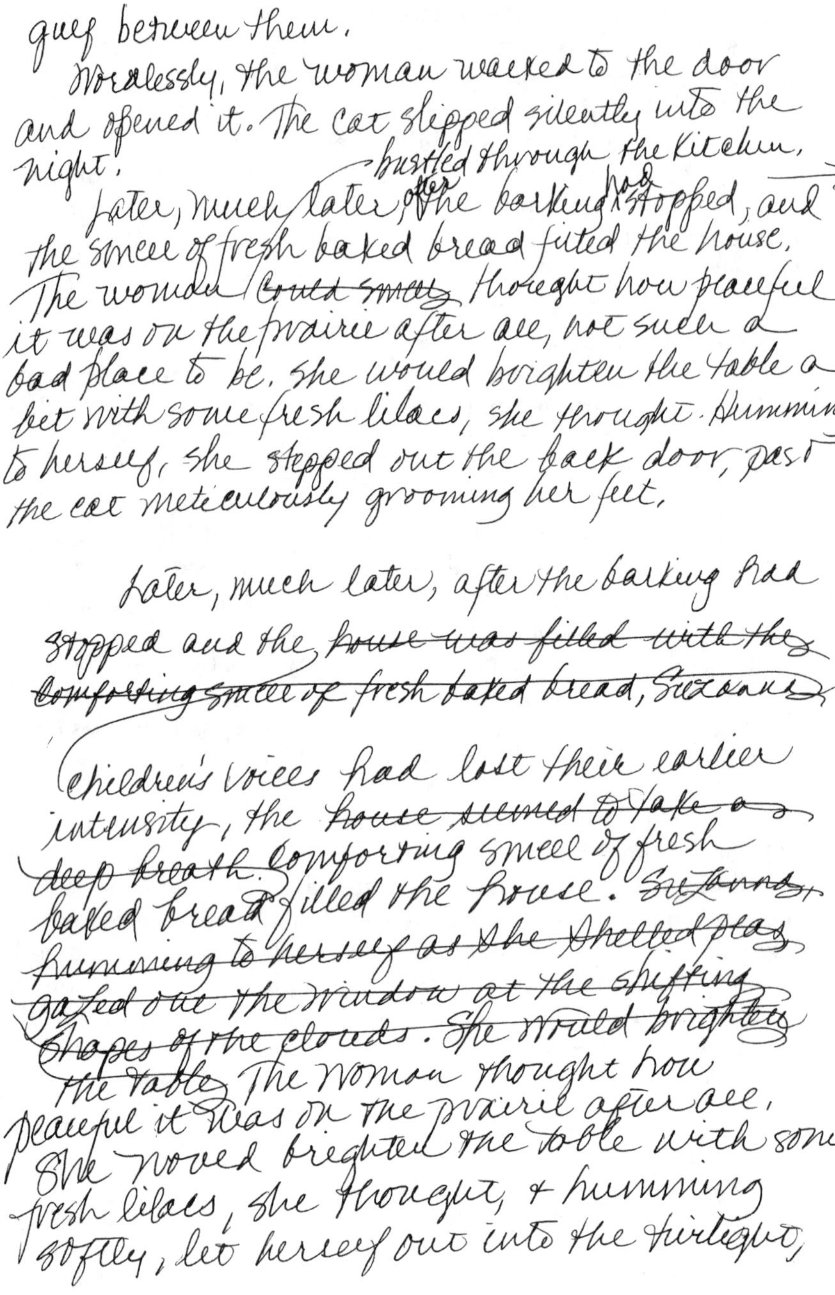

Noiselessly, the woman walked to the door and opened it. The cat slipped silently into the night. ~~hustled through the kitchen,~~

Later, much later, the barking had stopped, and the smell of fresh baked bread filled the house. The woman ~~could smell~~ thought how peaceful it was on the prairie after all, not such a bad place to be. She would brighten the table a bit with some fresh lilacs, she thought. Humming to herself, she stepped out the back door, past the cat meticulously grooming her feet.

Later, much later, after the barking had stopped and the ~~house was filled with the comforting smell of fresh baked bread, Suzanne~~

children's voices had lost their earlier intensity, the ~~house seemed to take a deep breath.~~ comforting smell of fresh baked bread filled the house. ~~Suzanne, humming to herself as she shelled peas, gazed out the window at the shifting shapes of the clouds. She would brighten the table.~~ The woman thought how peaceful it was on the prairie after all. She ~~moved~~ brightened the table with some fresh lilacs, she thought, & humming softly, let herself out into the twilight,

FIGURE 8.1. "Snooky," first draft

to literally one-third its original length, each time reading it aloud as I worked. Figure 8.1 shows a short section of the first draft, Figure 8.2 (see page 249) a section of the second.

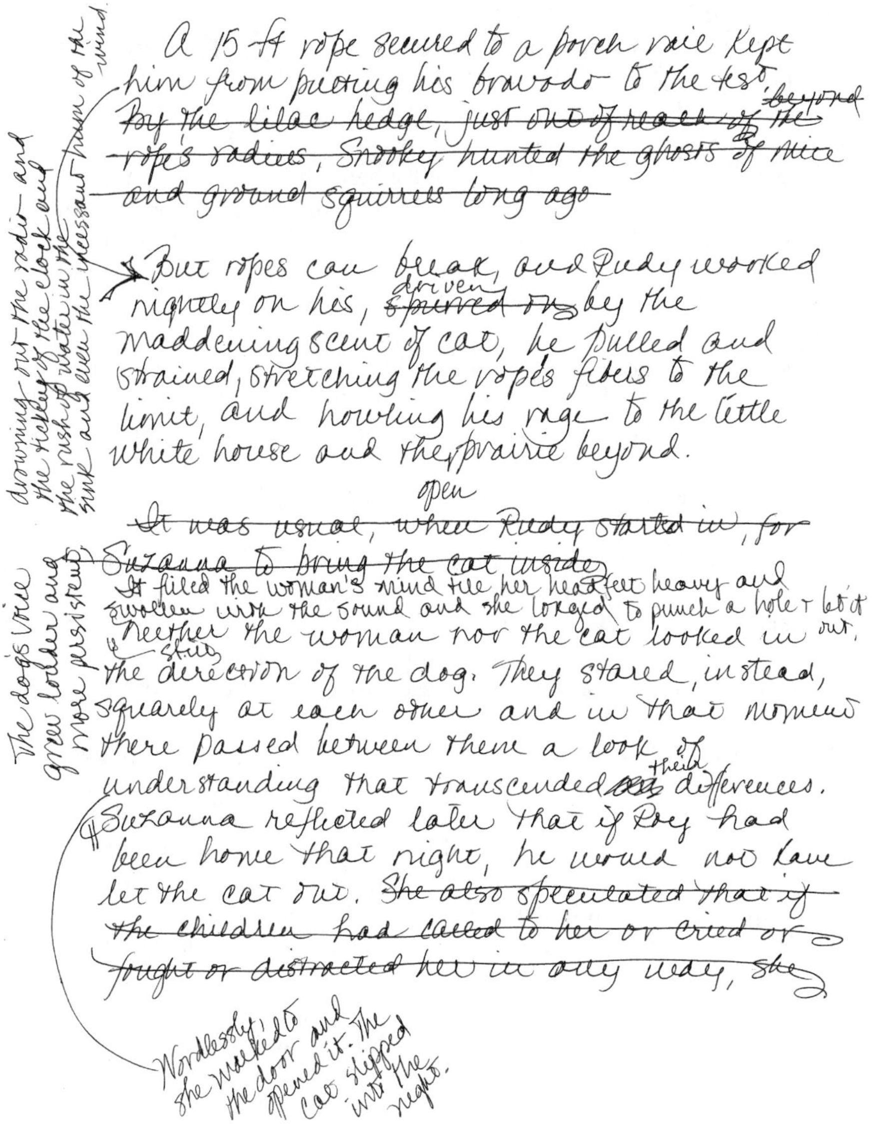
A 15 ft rope secured to a porch rail kept him from putting his bravado to the test. ~~By the lilac hedge, just out of reach of the rope's radius,~~ beyond ~~Snooky hunted the ghosts of mice and ground squirrels long ago~~

drowning out the radio — and the ticking of the clock and the rush of water in the sink and even the incessant moan of the wind

But ropes can break, and Rudy worked nightly on his, ~~spurred on~~ driven by the maddening scent of cat, he pulled and strained, stretching the rope's fibers to the limit, and howling his rage to the little white house and the prairie beyond.

~~It was usual, when Rudy started in, for Suzanna to bring the cat inside~~ open

It filled the woman's mind till her head felt heavy and swollen with the sound and she longed to punch a hole & let it out.

The dog's voice grew louder and more persistent,

Neither the woman nor the cat looked in the direction of the dog. They stared, instead, squarely at each other and in that moment there passed between them a look of understanding that transcended their differences.

Suzanna reflected later that if Roy had been home that night, he would not have let the cat out. ~~She also speculated that if the children had called to her or cried or fought or distracted her in any way, she~~

Wordlessly, she walked to the door and opened it. The cat slipped into the night.

FIGURE 8.2. "Snooky," second draft

When the refreshing ideas of Donald Graves swept through our writing classes in the early eighties, I believed that the ultimate purpose in writing was to be published. Since then, I have become a published writer myself, and I realize how wrong I was. It's what happens beyond publishing that's important; it's the response to my work that matters.

Mem Fox (1993)

I also kept thinking of those bored people who had listened to my first draft. One teacher in particular sat in the back row with his arms folded and his head angled, looking at me as if I had a lot of nerve to read anything so poorly crafted. He became my audience as I revised. When I heard him sigh, I cut. In my mind, I also wrote directly to my grandmother—who is long gone now. And when I heard her say, "That isn't how it was," I rewrote.

NEW AUDIENCE—NEW THINGS TO LEARN

You can sometimes learn more from body language than from what people say. When the text grows long and dreary, people lean away from you and ponder the ceiling. When it's working, you can feel them lean forward, resting their elbows on their knees.

When this draft was almost to a point where I felt happy with it, I decided to risk another reading. This time, with two high school classes. The fifty or so students who served as a writing group for me leaned in for this story (so I knew I'd improved it); they also told me a number of things about my writing that were absolutely true, but many of which I had not seen at all:

- Do not change the beginning, whatever you do. I lived in North Dakota, and you have captured how it feels to be there.
- Don't make it *too* obvious what happens to the dog. I kind of like it just the way it is. All the clues are there.
- You use a lot of flashbacks. I like them, but it's hard to follow the time sequence sometimes. Be careful!
- You need even more about the cat—before she goes out the door. You're trying to suggest something, but it isn't totally clear. Also, isn't it true that Susanna really loves Snooky, even though she claims to hate her?
- The part about the bread dough is very sexual. There is tension between Susanna and Roy, but there is a great love, a great attraction as well.
- I like the part about the bread dough oozing through her fingers. You can feel her anger, her frustration. Her bread baking is a kind of therapy.
- I love the way you go back and forth between the bread dough and the actual story. I love how she thinks as she is doing these daily, routine tasks. Her mind lifts her out of the trap of her life.
- I don't think Miranda will ever really "fly" the way she wants to.
- Susanna is jealous of Miranda because flying is precisely what Susanna wants to do.

These questions and comments were *the single most useful part of the entire writing process* in shaping this story. They were more helpful by far than the comments I'd gotten from my earlier adult audience. They had felt so bad for me sharing my wretched writing that mostly, they tried to cheer me up. Somehow, this made me feel worse. The student responders focused on my writing, and thus helped me make my draft better.

CLASSROOM PROCESS VS. WORKPLACE WRITING

"Snooky" is now eight drafts into the process, and took several years to complete. In the world of work, writers can't usually put a draft aside for a year or two while they think, reflect, and ponder. Employers want reports, letters, reviews, or summaries finished by tomorrow, this afternoon, in half an hour. I would argue, though, that we teach revision not so much to produce outstanding *drafts* as to produce thinkers—people who understand

Meaning is not thought up and then written down. The act of writing is an act of thought. This is the principal reason writing should be taught . . . yet, ironically, it is this concept that is most often misunderstood.

Donald Murray (1985)

The writer sits down intending to say one thing and hears the writing saying something more, or less, or completely different. The writing surprises, instructs, receives, questions, tells its own story, and the writer becomes the reader wondering what will happen next.

Donald Murray (1985)

Responses that encourage revision are those that offer support to the student writers as people, help them find their strengths as writers, set high standards for writing, and do all the preceding while encouraging them to become independent revisers.

Marian M. Mohr (1984)

how to revise writing till it fits both audience and purpose well, and who will forever after do the best they can within the time allowed.

SNOOKY

In Williston, North Dakota in 1924, the land was already tired. Already preparing to sleep through a drought that would shrivel crops to a dry powder, then set them adrift toward an unknown future on a tireless wind.

But for now, in the tiny blue-gray kitchen of the small white house on Second Avenue, what Susanna mostly thought as she kneaded the cool, slick bread dough on the worn, blue linoleum table, was that entertainment was pitifully hard come by these days. Roy, her husband, had stalked off into the dawn to hunt pheasants, and would be gone till Lord knows when. She envied men the easy way they could pick up and walk out on half finished conversations, leaving someone else to deal with the insects and heat and the squealing demands of damp, restless children.

She pictured Roy tramping along the wheat fields near the Little Muddy, and her knuckles thumped the dough in rhythm to his footsteps.

Out the window, she saw Kittridge, the next door neighbor, smoking a cigar in the dimming prairie light, surveying his yard as if it were some prized piece of bottomland instead of this pathetic patch of dust unfit for thistles. She pictured him in the torn coveralls and straw hat he'd worn that Saturday he'd moved in, that obnoxious half-shepherd of his held at bay by a length of hemp. "Don't worry—I'll keep him tied," he'd promised, watching Susanna eye the dog. "I won't let him bother yer garden."

Susanna's gaze had shifted then to the small patch of wilting carrot tops and crisp potato leaves bleaching in the sun and recalled wondering first what made an unimaginative plodder like Kittridge, who had only just met her that morning, presume to read her mind. Then, as she surveyed the sorry mix of weeds and struggling vegetables, she had tried to envision what sort of outrage Rudy could commit to trouble her garden further.

"At least he won't be able to hurt that little cat of yours," Kittridge had added, eyeing Snooky, who lay dozing on the back step. Susanna recalled studying the man's face then with some curiosity, as if this were the first interesting thing he had said. "Rudy here is something of a cat killer, you know," Kittridge had whispered then with a slow, deliberate kind of grin. Susanna smiled back, making no response, for what was there to say really? Kittridge could even be right about the dog. He wasn't big, but he was young, and full of spit. Still, too much trust in your own savvy could be dangerous.

The clock struck and jolted Susanna to the present. Brett and Jack were much too quiet for children of five and six. She ought to go check, she knew. But nothing really serious had happened since that day they'd pushed four-year-old Miranda out of the hayloft in a cardboard box.

"What were you trying to do, see if she could *fly?*" Susanna had shrieked in exasperation, and was struck dumb by the frank calmness of Jack's reply: "Why would anyone think a person in a cardboard box could fly?"

As she gathered the dough close, careful not to tear it, tenderly patting the sides, drawing it into herself, she recalled her hands reaching into the box, trembling with fear and anticipation, exploring the fragile, miraculously unbroken body of the flying Miranda. "I want to fly again," Miranda had whispered, and Susanna could feel herself spitting the words right at Miranda's docile eyes: "For God's sake, don't do *everything* they tell you. Do you want to *die?! Do* you?"

"I only want to fly," Miranda had repeated dumbly, smiling that annoying, accepting smile as the thick bread dough oozed between Susanna's strong fingers.

Susanna brushed the hair from her damp face. "Hair like a black horse tail." That's what Roy had said. God, how she hated that comment. He meant it as a compliment, but still. What good was it to be loved for all the wrong reasons? Loved not for your grace nor for the music of your voice as you recited poems you'd written yourself. Loved because you could work until your hands cracked open and not complain, because you could kill a rattler with a garden hoe and go right on planting potatoes with the next stroke, because you could endure the wind without going insane.

Susanna slipped the bread dough into the pan, turned to wipe her hands, and felt something brush against her legs. She shuddered and looked down without speaking.

Snooky returned the woman's gaze with unblinking yellow eyes. She was not a beautiful cat. Her nose was large, leonine really, her eyes too close together, and her lean gray body was perched atop powerful legs that seemed too long and muscular for a common housecat. She was bigger than most, as if she'd come from something wild that didn't like to shelter with humans. Her speed was legendary, and Susanna boasted a meshwork of slender scars across the backs of her calves to prove it. She kept the cat, though, for Snooky held the rats and gophers at bay. Once she'd dragged home a weasel. Hard to believe—but perhaps, Susanna reasoned, it had been wounded. No cat could get the best of a weasel. Surely not.

Lost in thought, she jumped when she heard the first yelps of the dog. The cat never flinched. In fact, she made no motion at all, but continued staring into the face of the woman, waiting. Susanna felt the heat close in upon her, shrinking and wilting everything within its reach. Deep inside her brain, it seemed, she could hear the desperate buzz of dinnertime flies.

The howling persisted, as it always did, building to a mournful crescendo, then fading to a guttural, strangled sound as Rudy hit the end of the rope full force, responding once again to the hated scent of cat. The relentless rhythm of his nightly complaint drowned out the ticking of the clock, the muffled voices of children on the stairs, even the wind. It destroyed everything but the pounding in Susanna's head.

She reflected that if Roy were home, he might not let the cat out. But then, he wasn't home, was he? It's a hard land, she thought; what will be will be. Wordlessly, she walked to the screen door and opened it. Just as silently, Snooky slipped into the night.

Later, when she thought about it, Susanna could not recall just when the barking had stopped. She did recall standing at the sink, and hearing the sound of her own humming. The clock was ticking again, and the smell of fresh baked bread filled the house. Her shoulders relaxed and her skin felt cooler. She turned and opened the screen, lowered herself onto the porch step, and watched the fireflies dart about. The wind was temporarily at rest. Absentmindedly, Susanna noticed that Rudy, for once, was not visible. Nor could she hear him. She could see a bit of the rope, lying limp across the dirt. Perhaps Rudy was there and only sleeping. Or inside. Perhaps he had somehow broken free. Perhaps.

Beyond the perimeter of the garden, just beyond the rope, Snooky sat meticulously grooming her feet. Something about the way she took her time made a little thought form in Susanna's mind, only it was not a thought just yet, not yet, and she pushed it back and away till it felt distant and shadowy, no longer real.

Things looked a little greener in the twilight. Encouraged by the cool night air, the bunch grass and yellow clover seemed almost lush. Through the bare soles of her feet Susanna imagined, just for a moment, that she could feel the earth breathe. And at the moment it seemed quite possible that this year's potatoes would grow. She might put in carrots too, maybe even some peas. A lilac bush—just there, between her house and Kittridge's. She smiled. It is hard to be the strong one, she thought, but it is not the worst thing.

REFLECTING ON "SNOOKY"

Though this story is primarily based on real characters and real events (e.g., my father, Jack in the story, really did push his sister out of the hayloft), it is still a collage of many stories told by many voices, so I have had to invent and patch. Kittridge is a fabrication, though there was a next-door neighbor whose dog was mysteriously killed one night, and through the years Snooky was given credit for this—though no one could ever prove it. It is a rare cat that can take on a dog, but then, Snooky was a rare cat, and I have no doubt Susanna herself believed her guilty, as do I. It doesn't really matter, though, in my mind, since the interesting part of the story is what Susanna *thought*; and she thought when she let Snooky out that night that her half-wild cat would kill the dog they both detested—or die trying.

Through the eight drafts of this story, Susanna grew ever more determined to escape the land that threatened to engulf her. As I let her real character come out and stopped trying to make her gentle and grandmotherly, her passionate protectiveness of her children became more fierce, even dangerous, and her bond with Snooky more direct and deliberate.

As I wrote, I awoke to a startling truth: My quiet grandmother, who caressed her biscuit dough as tenderly as she hugged her beloved children, could drown unwanted kittens with those same gentle hands, kill rattlers without a thought and fling their limp bodies into the brush. She could also send her killer cat into the night, knowing full well what the likely outcome of that trip would be. I believe that, deep within her, she admired and even loved Snooky for taking on more than she should have and surviving it. For that is precisely how she saw herself. It is *not* easy to be the strong one, and dear God, how I miss her.

REFLECTING ON CHAPTER 8

1. What kinds of writing do you do? For what audiences? How does your own writing process fit with the process approach you teach or plan to teach? How are the processes alike? How are they different?

2. Is the process much the same each time you write, or does it differ? What implications does this have for teaching?

3. If you do not write much right now, can you think what it is—really—that is stopping you? What might be gained if you did write? What will you do to prompt yourself to begin?

4. If you do write, do you find story writing or informational writing more challenging? Why do you think that might be? Can you relate your own experience and background to the kinds of writing you find most comfortable and natural?

5. Have you ever read a piece of your writing to an audience and gotten a response totally different from what you expected? Can you describe how it felt?

ACTIVITIES

1. List the things you actually do when you prewrite and revise. Don't think about what you've read in books or what you've done in other classes. Try to analyze your own *personal* writing process and come up with your own individual answers. Compare your strategies with those of your classmates or students. (Do a series of pictures showing yourself going through the writing process; don't try

for great art—just capture the steps.)

2. Write a short biographical or autobiographical piece, focusing on yourself or someone in your family that you know or knew fairly well. Try to think: What might other people not know about this person? How is the person *inside* different from what people saw on the surface? See if you can make that surprise come out in your writing. Share the results in a writing group or with students.

3. Model the questioning process shown in "Terror in the Fourth Grade." Begin with a statement, and invite listeners (people in a response group or class) to ask you questions. Use their questions and the conversation they provoke to guide your draft. You do NOT need to write a story. The questioning technique will work equally well with informational writing; there, the questions send you searching!

4. What are the important topics in your life right now? Make a list. Even if you do not write on any of them right away, share the list with students (or colleagues). Ask which topic they would like to know more about.

LOOKING AHEAD

In Chapter 9 we will take a peek inside several classrooms to see how teachers are weaving traits into their everyday writing instruction. You will see that there are many options, and that you can make the traits fit *you*.

MEMORABLE MOMENTS FROM STUDENTS

- Have you ever had a teacher you despised more than a lawyer?
- I was only 4'12"—and the kid I had to face was 5'1" so I was a little worried.
- If Einstein had watched Bart Simpson instead of creating the theory of relativity, where would we be now?
- He was poor in riches, but rich in wisdom.
- No matter what anyone tells you, you'll be all right if you have a good heart, a good head, and a good pair of shoes.
- Sometimes I don't even realize I'm in motion—which might explain why I keep running into things.

9

TEACHER TALK: Learning from Other Teachers

What happens in your classroom with writing has everything to do with you and the kids. When instruction focuses on the skills . . . the goals . . . the plans . . . the systems—it often becomes mechanical, detached from kids, lifeless. When it focuses on the persons—the writers, it's just the opposite—it has life!

Marjorie Frank (1995, 21)

The very first thing I tell my new students on the first day of a workshop is that good writing is about telling the truth. We are a species that needs and wants to understand who we are. Sheep lice do not seem to share this longing, which is one reason they write so very little.

Anne Lamott (1995, 3)

In this chapter, we'll visit the classrooms of several teachers, to see how they incorporate the 6-trait model into their instruction. As you'll see, they have very different ways of dealing with the traits and teaching them to students. There is no right way, and you should take what is most useful from their examples and experience, finding an approach that suits your own classroom environment, curriculum, students, and teaching style.

IN ELAINE'S SELF-CONTAINED 6TH GRADE CLASSROOM

Elaine is a veteran classroom teacher of nearly twenty years. She has taught mostly fourth and sixth grades. This is her third year of working with the traits, and she is an unabashed advocate.

Her secret is linking what she already does to the traits, rather than inventing new lessons. "It's so much easier for me to think about writing this way, I sometimes wonder why I didn't think of it before. But the funny part is, my *teaching* isn't any different. For instance, we've always done vocab, right? Well, now I just call that word choice. We do a lot of letter writing—now I just put that under voice. I've always emphasized good transitions. What trait is that? Organization. Details—ideas. This is not new stuff. My way of organizing it is just a little different. We *do* score a lot of papers. That *is* new, for me at least—making kids critics. I can tell you they love it, and they learn it *faster* than we do. They don't come to it with all that baggage we have from years of evaluating student work. They're these fresh little slates, and they pick up on it right away."

Elaine writes with her students, reads aloud to them daily, and sometimes allows students to come up with a creative writing assignment for her to follow. "I like writing to be spontaneous, fun. Kids always seem to be interested in the things that really happen to me, so I base a lot of my writing on that. One day, I got my head stuck in the chimney—I know it sounds insane, but this really happened to me. While I was busy getting myself unstuck, I thought, well, you know, I can *use* this in my writing. (Only writers or writing teachers think like this.) So the next day, we worked on details. I told my kids, 'I got my head stuck in the chimney. What do you want to know?' *Well*—they had a million questions! I wrote for half an hour and they kept asking more and more questions (Did it hurt? Did anyone help you? Could you see anything? Did you get soot in your hair?) so I could fill in the details. They *loved* it. And the next day, they were asking questions of each other."

Elaine also connects literature to the traits very naturally. As she reads, she pauses occasionally to ask, "What kind of voice did you hear in this part?" or, "What do you think will happen next?" or, "What are you picturing in your mind as you listen to this passage?"

She shares copies of the *6-Trait Scoring Guide for Students* with all her students and with parents, too. "The parents need to know what's going on, so I share just the level 5 descriptors with them, not the whole scoring guide. This way, it's more like our 'goals for writing.'" Her students also make their own trait posters.

She teaches the traits one at a time, beginning with ideas, then organization (her favorite), fluency, voice, and word choice. She spends one to two weeks on each trait, then continues to reinforce all traits throughout the remainder of the year with a variety of targeted lessons. Elaine teaches conventions as she goes, with *lots* of practice in editing. "My favorite editing lessons are the ones where students watch me write on the board and tell me when they spot a mistake. They watch like eagles! Right after this, I have them look at their own writing, sometimes with a partner.

"My goal is three hours of writing a week. We don't always make that, but we come close because my kids write in every subject area—social studies, science, math, art, music, and PE. It isn't all stories. We do reports. We do posters, letters, invitations to parents to visit our classroom, travel brochures on our community, recipes, directions, maps, and so forth. We write lots of poems—and news stories. We write to people in the community sometimes. Kids love to write letters that get answered. It's like magic. Suddenly, there's a reason for the writing."

Once a week (or so), the class as a whole will score and discuss an anonymous sample student paper. Since the paper belongs to no one in the class, they can be very frank in their comments. Most of the time, students agree on the scores—but not always.

"The discussions are the best part," Elaine claims. "When they disagree, that's when they teach each other the most."

Elaine uses writers' language in her comments. "I use the vocabulary of the scoring guide when I respond to students' work. I try not to just say, 'Good work, Kyle.' Instead, I'll say, 'I could picture you coming down that ladder with your cat. Great imagery.'"

She also likes to know how much progress she and her students make during the year. "Every class is different, so I use pre-assessment to tell me where to focus my instruction. One year a class will be strong on conventions, another time it will be ideas or voice. The post assessment tells me how far my kids have come in *my* class, just this year, during their time with me. I need to know that, and I think parents like seeing it, too. It gives me more information about my personal teaching than I can get from any district or state assessment."

Elaine does her preassessment during late September or early October. She assesses students' writing on all six traits to get baseline data that tells her where her new students are *right then*, both individually and as a class.

"My post assessment usually comes in April. By that time, I know I'll see most of the growth for that year, and I'll know how far my students have come, and how well I've taught certain things. They look at those two samples—October and April—and they can see big differences. Well, when I say *big* . . . see, for some kids that will mean learning to use a title and maybe writing more than two lines. For others it will mean learning to develop a character through dialogue or defending an argument with more than just your opinion. But we celebrate the small victories right along with the bigger ones. You'll hear kids go 'Wow! Is that *my writing?*' when they see the October piece, and the parents go 'Wow!' too. Their eyes light up. Nothing speaks as loudly as real samples."

Here is one student's April reflection:

SPRING REFLECTION

Grade 6

Writing was easier for me this year because I knew what I was doing! Having the traits and the Student Writers' Guide really helped. In the beginning of the year, my writing had no organization at all. It just bounced around from there to here to there and back. I did not know how to write an introduction. Now I know about six different things to try. I did not know how to write a conclusion and now I do. I did not even know about the trait called voice. I thought textbook writing was boring because it had too many facts. Now I know it is just the voice. It doesn't have any! I am trying to write like a writer and not a textbook.

Parents are brought into the process, too. "On back-to-school nights, I ask parents to write—just for three, four minutes, you know. That's all the time we have. But you should see the fear on their faces. They're terrified! They even ask me if I'm going to collect the writing or if I'm going to read it. I tell them no, it's just for them. But I do ask them to think about how writing was assessed when they were kids. They remember this sea of red marks—so that's what a lot of them expect from me. I also ask them if they know what they're really good at as writers. A lot of them don't have a clue. Then I pass out copies of the *6-Trait Scoring Guide for Students*—and it's like a whole world opens up. One dad asked me, 'Where was *this* when I was going to school?'"

Elaine explains to parents that she will teach students to be editors, but she will not edit *for* them. In her class, they work on editing daily, though some lessons are only four to five minutes long. She also assesses their work for conventional correctness. "I don't hold them responsible for things they have not been taught, though. We do a pre-test in editing the first of the year so I can see what their skills are, and then we build from there. I think we often ask kids to focus on too many conventions at one time. It reminds me of going to a formal dinner with twenty pieces of flatware—which fork do you pick up first?"

Parents who are interested can attend a short two-hour training session on the six traits that Elaine does twice a year. Then they're encouraged to volunteer as "writing coaches," which means they can participate in student writing groups, confer with students who are revising their work or getting ready to publish, help students with editing, or—if they write—share samples of their own work. Elaine gives them the following checklist—reminding them to focus on one or two concerns at a time—not the whole list!

Writing Coach Checklist

INTRODUCTION

1. Do you have a topic?
2. [If not] Could we talk a little about your interests or brainstorm some questions that might help you come up with a topic?
3. How are you planning to begin? Could we make some notes together?
4. [If there is a draft] What would you like me to listen for as you share your writing?[1]

---

[1]*NOTE TO THE COACH:* Choose one or (at most) two traits that will best support the writer's plan for revision. Don't try to discuss *everything,* or you'll both wind up exhausted! Keep it focused.

IDEAS AND DEVELOPMENT

1. What do you see as your *main* idea?
2. What *one thing* do you want your reader to learn from your writing?
3. Would you like to know what I picture in my mind when I hear your writing?
4. Do you have some details you think might be new to your readers?
5. Do you have enough information to keep writing? If not, do you know how to get the information you need?
6. As a reader (listener), this is the main thing I learned from your paper: _____. [*Explain.*] I am still wondering _____. [*Explain.*]

ORGANIZATION

1. Why did you begin where you did? Did you write more than one lead, or were you happy with the first one?
2. [*For expository/persuasive writing*]: What is the *most important point* you make in this paper?
3. [*For narrative writing*]: Does your story have a *turning point* or most important moment?
4. Read *just your conclusion* out loud to me and talk to me about it. Tell me why you ended the paper the way you did.
5. [*Only if needed*] As a reader, I felt lost when _____. [*Explain.*].

VOICE

1. How would *you* describe your voice in this piece?
2. Who do you see as your main audience? Who did you picture when you were writing?
3. What would you like a reader or listener to feel?
4. Here's where your voice seemed strongest to me: _____. Do you agree? Or do you think the voice is stronger in other parts?
5. Here's how I feel when I listen to your paper. [*Explain.*]

WORD CHOICE

1. Do you have favorite words or expressions in this piece? Show me.
2. Are there any words you used for the first time? Which ones?
3. Are there any words you weren't sure of? Shall we look them up?
4. Did you use a thesaurus or dictionary? Did you have any trouble doing that?
5. Are there any words or phrases you're *not* happy with? Shall we brainstorm some other ways to say it?
6. These are the words or expressions that *really* caught my attention: _____.

SENTENCE FLUENCY

1. You seemed to have an easy (not so easy) time reading your paper aloud. Am I right about that? Why do you think that might be?

2. My impression was that your sentences did (did not) tend to begin the same way. Do you agree?
3. Would you like me to read all or a piece of your work so you could be the listener? [*If yes, then*]: Tell me what you hear as I read.

CONVENTIONS/EDITING
1. Have you edited your paper yet? Show me how much of the paper you are editing (e.g., first line, first paragraph, two paragraphs).
2. Do you have any editing questions you'd like to ask me about spelling, punctuation, grammar or *anything?*
3. Is there a handbook you feel comfortable using? Show me.
4. Which copy editors' symbols do you feel comfortable using? [*Refer to chart.*]
5. Do you feel comfortable using a dictionary (spell-checker)? Would you like some help with that?
6. Tell me about this mark of punctuation. [*Choose one from the student's paper.*] Why did you use it here? What does it tell your reader?
7. What do you usually do when you edit your work? Do you read it over? Read aloud? Talk to a friend? Use a dictionary? What works best?

CLOSURE
1. Are there any questions you'd like to ask me about your writing?
2. Do you know where to get the help or information you need?
3. Does this piece feel finished to you? If not, what would you like to do next? Can I help?

Elaine's is a classroom in which the love of writing and reading shines from both teacher and students—and where parents feel welcome to join in as part of the process.

IN JIM'S HIGH SCHOOL CLASSROOM

Jim has been teaching high school for eleven years. He has taught all levels, ninth through twelfth grades, and unlike some of his colleagues, prefers teaching writing to teaching literature.

"Writing is my first love. I had thought about being a writer myself, but it isn't that easy to make a living at it! I do write with my students, though, and I have written some things that were published, mostly poems, and a whole lot that were rejected. Like everyone in America, I'm working on a novel, and I share parts of it with my students and ask for their response and advice. Even if I never publish it, it sure makes for some great lessons."

Jim begins with a one-page scoring guide; then, as students learn the language, he invites them to make their own. "The language of the scoring guide is a little hard for some at first, but we work through it. As we start learning the traits, I have them make their own scoring guides on butcher paper. We simplify the original—trim it down. I like them to come up with their own language. It personalizes the whole thing, and it also helps them remember.

"We read and score anything that doesn't get up and walk away. When we're working on ideas, we'll score some student writing and pieces out of Steinbeck and Hemingway, and then I'll bring in a paragraph from a legal contract. 'Man, this makes no sense at all!' they'll say, but that's a perfect opportunity for a discussion about how it probably *does* make sense if you're a lawyer; you just have to think about audience. What about the person *signing* the contract, though? Does *he* know what he's signing? When we work on word choice, I always use Wallace Stegner. Maya Angelou is great, too. But then, to see the other side, we'll look at some junk mail—ads, for instance, or those letters soliciting donations. Some of those have atrocious word choice and no fluency at all. We score everything for conventions because I want them to have plenty of editing practice."

Jim admits that many of his students come to him already knowing the traits. "So we're not starting from scratch. I take advantage of that by letting them teach lessons themselves. They can work with a partner or in a group and set the lesson up any way they want. One student had us all write for 10 minutes then stop mid sentence to identify our strongest and weakest trait. Then we traded with a partner to see if they agreed. I became a student. I loved it. I said my weakest trait was fluency—and my partner agreed, so it must have been true.

"I try not to get too obsessed with assessment—or publishing. I don't publish everything I write, and I don't think they should either. So we just mess around with writing for a while, creating drafts. Some of those will get revised and some will get published. Some will never see the light of day."

Jim is also selective about which traits he assesses. "When I think about assessment, I always find myself saying, 'OK, so what's really important here?' I do not assess every assignment on every trait because I think that's overkill. That's where a lot of teachers get hung up on this trait thing. If we're doing informational writing, and I have a student writing on say, the rain forest, I might think ideas are especially important and organization because you have to follow it, and word choice because the writer might use some terminology that needs to make sense. I always score conventions because they get so much emphasis these days, but I'm not one of those sticklers where every word has to be spelled right or you can't get a 5 or 6 or whatever. Perfection isn't a realistic goal. It makes students resentful, and rightly so; *no writer* is perfect—including the *New York Times* best-seller authors. I do point out problems that I know an employer would notice in a business letter. Things like misspelled words or semicolons after introductory clauses. I don't freak out when a student starts a sentence with 'And.' To me that's more style than correctness. But I'll tell you this: My kids score every single piece of writing

I write and share with them for conventions, and by the end of the year, they're editing machines."

Like many teachers, Jim no longer has his students keep portfolios. "I think it's a great concept," Jim admits, "but logistically, I couldn't make it work—for me. It might work for others and I think anyone who *can* make it work *should* because students learn so much by charting their growth over time. I had little problems, like students losing papers, or just not putting anything into the portfolio. Some didn't get the whole idea of self-reflection, that it's not introspection but more an analysis of how you've grown as a writer. They had trouble with that, and I had trouble teaching it, to be honest. But I still think that comparing pieces of work over a period of time and analyzing how that work has changed or what you have learned is the most powerful piece of the portfolio process. We still do that."

Here's one sample reflection from Jim's class:

Correctness is of little importance to readers when they are reading flawlessly edited copy. Let them spot one editing error, however, and suddenly correctness is all-important.

Tom Romano (1987, 74)

SELF-REFLECTION

The way I've grown most as a writer is not being afraid to say what I think, so I guess you would call that voice. Maybe ideas, too. Over the last year, I've had a lot of conflicts with my family, especially my father. The thing is, we do not always see the world in the same way, so when I was writing it was like I could never write things he wouldn't approve of. I thought you should only say nice things in your writing, not say what you really thought, so my writing was pretty much on the boring side, even to me. I used to count out the words to see when I had enough. Now I know that length doesn't count for anything. Good writing is honest and it's like looking through new glasses, seeing things you missed when you were half blind. Last week I did a poem on my friend's car. He has an old Thunderbird and he never cleans it out. My father says Kevin never throws anything away and he (my father) is very pissed off about this. This shows how much my father really thinks about things. Kevin throws things away; he just throws them away *into his car*; it's a garbage dump on wheels. Inside you can find old Polaroid pictures of him with his first girlfriend, Popsicle sticks, cat droppings, a dead hamster (it stopped rotting now—it's all dried out), actual slices of pizza so old they're hard as plastic, CDs that won't play anymore because they've been stepped on so much, somebody's loose tooth that finally fell out, about a dozen shoes, none of which go together, some loose change you could have for the taking if you didn't mind touching it, old *TV Guides* all curly and Ketchup stained, menus from every fast food dive in the city, cigar wrappers, and *used* Band-Aids—how gross is that? This car is the stuff of poetry, man.

IN LYNNE'S WORKSHOPS AND CLASSES

Lynne is a former teacher and presently a language arts consultant who conducts workshops on six-trait instruction and assessment for teachers in her school and district—and continues to work with students extensively, modeling lessons in six-trait writing.

"I often begin with something simple—and focused. I might interview the teacher, then show students my notes and have them interview each other. I read them my draft, too, and they see my revisions. With a lesson like that, you're really touching on a lot of traits, but the main thing I'm going for with interviews is detail. I also do a lot of mini-lessons, and right now my focus is on organization. I'm working with second graders, and much of their writing is not organized—they just want to *list* everything. I show them what happens when you put it in a pattern and it all comes together for the reader."

The greatest value of six-trait training, in Lynne's eyes, is that it provides a framework for teaching. "For novice teachers, it's something to hang onto, so you have a starting place and somewhere to go next and next. Many of them have not gotten something this solid, this clear, from their college training. For experienced teachers, it is very affirming—they feel they are doing something right, and now they have names and language to go with what they are trying to teach. With one group I started with six empty boxes. I kept asking them what was important in writing, and as they would come up with things, I'd write them down and put them in the appropriate box. At the end, I flipped all the boxes around so they could see the labels of the traits—and they had fun picking through their notes to see which comments I had put into which boxes."

For students, Lynne maintains, scoring papers is key. "The light comes on when they assess. That's when they *get* it—when they learn to identify strong and weak writing. I use a lot of contrasting pieces, and we make a list of the strengths and weaknesses they hear in the writing.

"I also model comments—and I teach them, very specifically, how to talk to me about my writing. 'I liked your word choice,' they will tell me, and my response is, 'That isn't going to help me when I get home. You need to tell me *which* detail, *which* word.'"

The next "big lightbulb," Lynne says, is revision. "Teachers need strategies for teaching, so we look really closely at the scoring guide and break each trait down into its component parts, see what translates into a lesson. Organization, for example, breaks down into leads, transitions, sequencing, conclusions.

"You can tell when the kids are getting it. You're going along talking about organization and someone says, 'Boy, this has a lot of voice.' Those interruptive sidebars tell you they're getting it.

"I'm very sensitive to what teachers need because I was originally trained in *reading,* not writing. So teaching writing felt, to me, uncomfortable at first. I think that's made me a better writing consultant in the long run, though, because I do not take things for granted or assume people know things that could be new to them; I am always asking, 'Does this make sense?' But the traits are so clear—they gave me what I needed to teach writing, and to show other teachers how to do it."

IN ELLEN'S AP ENGLISH CLASS

Ellen has been teaching AP high school students for many years, and though the traits are an important focus for her curriculum, she is also a firm believer in teaching to the *writer*, and in knowing who your students are before you begin advising them on matters of syntax and conventions.

"My first step is to help my students envision the world they want to live in, and to imagine how their personal, individual voices will contribute to that world. So, I begin with the writers, not the writing; then I shape the writing tasks to what they say and what they see. I like to think I allow my writers to find meaning in contemporary culture—to recognize what's shallow, and even perhaps shoot a few holes in the hypocrisy they see in our society.

"When I teach ideas, I emphasize the importance of a writer opening up people's minds. Your ideas are what you teach your readers, I tell my students. I don't always expect closure, but I do expect them to think: to raise the right questions. Who are you? I ask them. Where do you stand on this issue or that? What is your philosophical approach to the world? I use the traits to build thinking skills."

Ellen shares numerous samples of writing from many sources. "I always read everything aloud. It makes such a difference when the ear is trained. I'm afraid of how little they get to hear. Listen to television for even a short time and see how we are becoming conditioned to sound bites of language. It isn't just the meaning that's lost. So much of our modern language has no real rhythm. I want them to hear language at its best. I want them to slow down long enough to read good poetry, not just process it, to hear the rhythm of the lines rising and falling like the tides.

"To me all the traits are important, but in the end, the final question is, How does each trait bring out the writer's *voice?* It's voice, to my mind, that most influences meaning. We start with an idea, but if our writing is good, we end up speaking person to person. 'When you sign a paper,' I tell my students, 'and you expect me to read it, you've made a commitment to me. I want to hear *your* ideas, *your* voice.' So much of this is missing from today's research writing. There's no passion for the topic, no concern for the audience. That's why it winds up piled in a corner somewhere. Many of our students do not have the patience it takes to sift through volumes of information—our world is so information-laden; we need to show them how. Otherwise, we get informational writing that's just plagiarism, a shortcut. Their eyes glaze over at the thought of doing research, and I think a lot of this is because they wind up writing in someone else's voice, a phony voice, an encyclopedia voice.

"I think it's a breakthrough moment when students are relieved of the burden of having to be someone else. I expect honesty and straightforwardness. I tell them, 'I don't want writing to impress. Write from deep inside you.'"

Ellen also sees writing as potentially therapeutic and empowering for many students. "When I first began teaching twenty-some years ago, students did every assignment. They didn't question anything. For kids today, it's different. So many are emotionally unsure. So many come from broken families and are struggling just to find themselves; school is an additional burden. But it *can* be a place of safety and emotional support, too, if we let it. I don't want this to sound presumptuous; I know my class is one small part of their lives. But I feel strongly that my job as a teacher is to tell students when they write, 'Your writing moved me. You have the power to change the world with these ideas.' Without that, we—and they—have no real reason to write."

IN ARLENE'S K–1 CLASSROOM

You don't teach writing. You teach WRITERS. And believe me, there IS a world of difference between the two.

Marjorie Frank (1995, 18)

Arlene teaches a K–1 split that includes numerous children with late birthdays and others for whom the "school" experience is still too new, or just plain bewildering. As Arlene cheerily puts it, "My job is to grow them up." It's a combination of providing strategies for learning and providing success that builds confidence. In Arlene's classroom, children find a world crafted specially for them, filled with colors, plants, mobiles and light, with real or paper cut-out frogs, fish, beetles, snowmen, bats, cats, and rabbits, hundreds of words, and dozens of books—not to mention cozy corners to sit, ponder, think, read, and write.

"'Kid writing is magic.' That's the very first thing I tell my students. Most of them believe they *can* write—though it doesn't look like traditional writing yet—but a few will say, 'Oh, I can't write yet.' So I tell them, you can do *this*, can't you, like a bird flying? (See Figure 9.1). And I model it on the board for them. Sure, they tell me, they can do that. So that's our first writing venture. Then I ask, 'Do you know *any* letters at all? Put them down, and when I come around, you can read your writing to me—and you can also do a picture to go with your writing.' This is where we begin—with the belief that all children can write. The secret, at this young age, is to accept *all forms* of writing as writing. When we accept where children are, they accept where they are—and feel good about themselves.

We want to avoid dismissing the art of children as mere cuteness and learn to appreciate its authentic content and form. All else aside, the drawings are there to be enjoyed as aesthetic objects.

Bob Steele (1998, 11)

"The traits give me a structure for teaching; they help keep me organized and focused. I like to start with details—that's the word I use for what the scoring guide calls ideas. We start with pictures. I'm no artist, but I'll draw the outline of a face on the board. 'Now help me with details,' I tell the students. 'Does he need eyes? How do they look? A nose? How big? A mouth? What shape?' And so on. Then, when we're reading, we take time to look at

FIGURE 9.1. Writing like a "bird flying"

the pictures, and I ask them to point out details to me. We also play the mind movies game, where every sentence adds a detail. I'll tell them, 'Today I saw *something*. I saw a *dog*. It was a *big dog*. It was *big and black with white paws and a curly tail*. I saw a big, black dog with white paws and a curly tail leap right onto the school bus—and eat someone's cheese sandwich!' I just keep adding detail, and they love it, and often they help me. If I don't go fast enough, they start asking me questions. We're writing in our minds; we're not always putting it on paper, but we *are* writing.

"Organization, I think, should be taught as a concept. I start with one child's desk. I pull everything out—with the child's permission, of course!—and lay it on a table. Then the kids help me organize it. Then they organize their own desks. When we line up for the bus, I point out to them that we're getting 'organized.' When they come in from recess, I ask them to line up alphabetically—that's organization, too. It soon becomes a very familiar word to them.

"Of course, voice is my favorite trait. I use the word a lot, and not just about writing. When someone comes in with bright colors on, I'll say, 'Wow! That outfit has *voice!*' Soon they're saying it to me. I tell them voice is piz-zazz, personality, being *you*. We talk about different voices—how sometimes you talk in a whisper, sometimes you shout or sigh or cry or laugh or scream. And of course, we also listen for voice in all the books we share. One of the moms told me they were driving down the street one day when her daughter said, 'None of those houses have voice, Mom—they're all the same color.' I love it when they teach traits to their parents!

"With word choice, I use my own writing a lot. I ask the children to help me find a better way to say it. 'Cute,' I'll say, 'boy—I'm tired of that word, aren't you? You hear it *so* much.' I haul the trash can over and rip the word up in front of them and toss it into the can. Then I ask them to help me think of some alternatives and we list them in BIG letters. I use them in my writing and let me tell you, they listen for their words—the ones they suggested.

"For fluency, I read lots of poetry and of course we play songs. I en-courage the children to snap their fingers or clap to the rhythm—or get up and move. When you feel the rhythm, then you know it's fluent. Of course, many of my children are not yet writing sentences, but they can dictate sentences—then hear them back. That's a kind of writing, too. And we do family journaling, where the parents write, if they're willing. They take down the child's thoughts and send it back to me. I tell them, 'Tonight your parents have homework.' The kids love that. Then I'll ask the parents to write with the child about 'My Most Unusual Gift'—or whatever.

"At this age, you need to keep conventions simple. I teach it mainly through modeling. Every day we do a newsletter, which I write in front of them, and I ask lots of questions. The kids decide what's 'news' and they make up all the content—I don't do that part—but I'll say, 'OK, this is the beginning of a new sentence, so what kind of letter do we need? Here's the

And in our haste to tell young writers how to do things, we for-get that merely telling of new concepts doesn't usually lead to learning, and that students best learn what they're ready to learn, itching to learn.

Tom Romano (1987, 100)

end of a sentence—should we put a period or exclamation point? That was a question—how do we show that? You use the moment to make a point instead of announcing, 'Today, children, we'll have a lesson on exclamation points.' Yuck. I wouldn't be able to stay awake myself."

Arlene has had her share of nonwriters and reluctant writers. "I had a little girl just last year who announced on the first day, 'I don't write.' I got down on her level, looked her in the eye, and said very simply, 'You know, in this class, we *all* write.' She looked right back at me and said, 'OK, then.' And from that day on, she wrote—every single day. And as she could see for herself, we were all writers—me, too. A lot of it is expectations. We're afraid to expect too much, and when children sense our fear, it robs them of confidence. If we don't believe they can do brave and wonderful things, why should they believe it?"

Aim for the stars, not the mud.
Mem Fox (1993)

IN SAMMIE'S "TIGER LEARNING CENTER"—THE READING & WRITING ENRICHMENT ROOM

Sammie works in an enrichment room: a special learning center devoted half to technology (with a computer lab) and half to personalized instruction in reading and writing. The center is well-named. Sammie's students *are* tigers—ready to leap on new ideas and devour everything she has to give. Her main problem is time; she has but half an hour with each group (they spend the other half of their hour in the computer lab); and with a K–5 rotation, she sees each child only once every six days. Therefore, continuity is difficult, and extended lessons do not work well. Everything has to be tied up, package and bow, within 30 minutes. Sammie has found ways to make it work—and to make the six traits flourish. Her children do numerous poems and books, often class books, to which each child can contribute a page. They write paragraphs (they're short), and they tend to focus on known topics (no research required): themselves, their families, their experiences. Sammie regularly uses brief books or portions of books as models.

Pattern books (e.g., Margery Cuyler's *That's Good, That's Bad* and John Burningham's *Mr. Gumpy's Outing*) have been her mainstay. "When it's a pattern the children can see, they can mimic it, and it helps them feel they're *doing* it. They're writing. Many times they feel they do a better job than the original author, and sometimes, I agree! We do a *lot* of sharing. The atmosphere is very celebrational. When an author has finished a piece, that's reason to celebrate, to gather around and hear another person's work. We all take pride in what any one of us does.

"I also do a lot of reading. For many of my students it's a totally new experience—being read to. No one has done this with them before. We have a high mobility rate in our area. Many of our students do not regularly converse with their parents—or with *anyone* outside of school. Just talking is hard at first. They haven't had much practice at it. I have many fifth graders—kids practically shaving—who have not heard nursery rhymes before, and *love* them. They love the rhythm and the humor. If we don't attach grade levels to things, we give students the freedom to make choices, and why not? Wouldn't it annoy you if someone pulled a book out of your hands and said to you, 'Oh, you won't like *that*—it's only for 35 and under'?

"I talk traits all the time, right from day one. Fluency is a big trait for us because we use lots of pattern books and lots of poetry—*There Was An Old Woman Who Swallowed a Fly*—that's a favorite with students of all ages. We talk about word choice, too, and keep personal dictionaries. I put lots of words on the walls. And we talk about ideas—what do you picture in your mind? And voice—how does this piece make you feel? I comment on the voice, word choice, and so on in *their* work, too. At first it's just me. But by about the end of the second quarter or the start of the third, they're talking traits, too. This is very exciting because at this point they have some built-in, personal way to measure how their writing is changing.

"We do no skill and drill, no worksheets. We write and we read. I want them to love it, and they do. They *want* to come here, that's my goal, and it shows in the work we do together. We're moving all the time. We're moving to the rhythm of what we write. We yell, we beat on the tables. One of the teachers said to me, 'Sammie, I would swear I saw that portable move right up off its block.' Well, that's what teachers are *for*, isn't it? To rock the walls? The most important thing to me is how the kids feel when they leave here. In this room, I want every child to experience success."

REFLECTING ON CHAPTER 9

1. Reading and scoring writing samples seems to have a positive effect on students' writing performance even when they do not do anything else directly related to the traits. Why do you think that might be?

2. How do you see yourself adapting the traits to your own classroom? Would your approach be like that of one of the teachers in this chapter—or something quite different?

3. Several of the teachers in this chapter seem to focus as much on the student *writer* as on writing skills or strategies per se. How do you feel about this? Is it a good thing? Why?

ACTIVITIES

1. Imagine that you are an observer doing a teacher evaluation for any one of the teachers who speaks in this chapter. Write a short paragraph summarizing what you notice and what you feel that teacher does well. (Offer recommendations, too, if you wish.)

2. List three ways that you could weave the traits into your curriculum given your style and preferred teaching strategies. Compare your ideas with those of your classmates/colleagues.

3. Do a written analysis of your own teaching style. Who are you as a teacher? What is it like to be in your classroom? What are your teaching strengths? [If you do not yet have a classroom of your own, that's OK. Imagine! Predict!]

LOOKING AHEAD

In Chapter 10 we will explore some ideas for adapting the scoring guide to fit various circumstances. You will discover that the guide can be used in a variety of classroom settings to assess different types of writing.

MEMORABLE MOMENTS FROM STUDENTS

- When I hugged my grandma I would not squeeze hard for fear she might crumble.
- Though he was a knight, he never went on adventures. He had only one of himself and didn't want to waste it.
- I felt like the third wheel on a two-wheel bike.
- His death made an impact on my life, and an even greater one on his.
- Irma has taught me quite a few stuff.
- The ride I hated most at Disneyland was 20,000 Leaks Under the Sea.
- I could run like the seed of light.

10

ADAPTING THE 6-TRAIT GUIDE TO FIT YOU

We do not teach writing effectively if we try to make all students and all writing the same. We must seek, nurture, develop and reward difference. The rich diversity of our students is to our advantage. There is no single kind of person to teach, no one reason to write, no one message to deliver, no one way to write, no single standard of good writing.

Donald Murray (1985, 5)

THE SIMPLEST ADAPTATION: BEING SELECTIVE

What if the scoring guide does not quite cover all the things you wish to emphasize in teaching writing? Say you are a primary teacher or a biology or history teacher, or you wish to focus primarily on literary analysis. Can you adapt the scoring guide to meet those needs? Absolutely. Countless adaptations are possible, and you should modify this or any scoring guide so that it will serve you and your students well. Lucy McCormick Calkins (1994), in fact, suggests that "published rubrics" are often most useful as "starting points from which we make our own rubrics" (325).

From biology . . . Just because there are six traits in the model, that does *not* mean you have to give every paper six scores every time. Certain traits may be more critical to a given assignment than others. Let's say you teach biology. For a particular writing assignment on how species adapt to environmental factors, you might wish to emphasize clear ideas, good organization, appropriate use of correct scientific terminology—and, perhaps, conventional correctness. For this assignment, you might elect not to score your students' writing on the traits of fluency and voice (though you could).

And of course, as Calkins suggests, you can adapt and refine the language of the guide to match your own thinking.

To algebra . . . Suppose you teach algebra. Let's say that you are asking your students to determine how many different ways rectangular shapes can be combined to create a design for a one-story building, and you wish them to write an explanation of each step in their thinking process. For this assignment, you might choose to focus primarily on ideas (you want clarity), organization (you want steps to be in order), and word choice (you want students to use correct mathematical terminology).

Or global studies. Suppose you are asking students to write an editorial piece reflecting conditions in South Africa from the 1990s through the early 21st century. You might wish to emphasize ideas (understanding of the context and important issues) and voice (ability to reach and influence an audience).

Weighting

Certainly there are situations in which voice or precise wording is critical, for understanding of the topic (ideas) counts more than anything else. Let your assessment reflect that emphasis. If you do not feel comfortable letting go of any trait altogether, try what many teachers have done: weight the traits according to emphasis. For instance, suppose students are writing a persuasive essay on whether to drain a wetlands and build a shopping center in order to boost the economy of a given area. The traits might be weighted for this assignment as follows:

Ideas: 30
Organization: 20
Voice: 20
Word Choice: 20
Sentence Fluency: 10
Conventions: 10

A SCORING GUIDE FOR INFORMATIONAL & RESEARCH-BASED WRITING

In the bad old days, the secret to good research was getting our hands on *The Book* (there was always one main book that held all the critical information, remember?). Because they only seemed to order one copy per library (whose sadistic idea was that?), someone else nearly always got to it first. Then an annoyingly patient librarian would explain that *The Book* was checked out for two weeks—or some period of time that always matched *exactly* the time available to complete the research.

These days, *finding* information is not the problem. We are drowning in infoglut. The key to success in informational writing, therefore, no longer lies in *finding* information, but in sorting through the informational flotsam and jetsam to sift out what is significant, and then synthesizing, condensing, and presenting information in a way that will engage and educate a targeted audience.

Teachers who want their students to develop these skills need an analytical scoring guide to match what they'd like to see in good informational writing. Here it is: the counterpoint to the more creative scoring guide presented in Chapter 3. This guide will work well with *any* research-based, informational, technical or business writing (again, with any tweaking you feel is necessary).

Scoring Guide for Informational Writing[1]

IDEAS AND DEVELOPMENT

5. The paper is clear, focused, and purposeful. It makes a point or answers a well-defined key question in understandable, convincing, and expansive terms, and may raise new questions for the reader.

- The main idea, thesis, or research question is clearly defined. There may be more than one key point, but the paper is not simply a list.
- The writer seems well informed, and as appropriate, draws from a variety of resources, e.g., personal experience, reading, investigation, interviews, and observations.
- The writer continuously anticipates readers' informational needs.
- Supporting details (examples, facts, anecdotes, quotations) are accurate, relevant, and helpful.

3. The paper addresses an identifiable key question by offering the reader general, basic information.

- The reader can identify or infer at least one main assertion or thesis.
- Some support seems grounded in solid research or experience. Some seems based on common knowledge or best guesses.
- The writer sometimes responds to the reader's informational needs; at other times, important questions are left hanging.
- More investigation, stronger support, and greater attention to detail would strengthen this paper.

1. The writer has not yet clarified an important question or issue that this paper will address. One or more of these problems may be evident:

- The writer does not yet have enough information on this topic.
- The writer has not yet focused in on a main research question or thesis.
- The paper wanders or lists random information.
- Support is missing or questionable.
- The reader is left with numerous questions.
- This paper would not be helpful to someone who did not already know the topic well.

---

[1]This scoring guide includes reference to titles, subtitles, tables of contents, footnotes, and bibliographies, all of which may be important in some of the writing your students do but not necessarily all. You need to be flexible, therefore, in considering these items in scoring. For instance, if a table of contents is not important in a given paper, pay no attention to that portion of the criteria. You can base the conventions score strictly on spelling, punctuation, grammar, capitalization, and so on. Add other considerations (e.g., footnotes) only as needed.

ORGANIZATION

5. A strong internal structure highlights the main ideas and leads readers right to the key points or conclusions.

- The introduction engages readers and provides a clear purpose and direction for the writing.
- Details, anecdotes, facts, and examples are closely linked to the main point or key question.
- Purposeful transitions make links between ideas clear.
- The reader's understanding of the topic grows throughout the paper.
- The closing effectively resolves questions and/or reinforces important conclusions or assertions.

3. A mix of key points and generalities forces readers to make inferences about what is most important.

- The introduction is present, but may not give the reader a strong sense of where the writer is headed.
- Details, examples, facts, and anecdotes are loosely linked to main ideas or to one another.
- Transitions are attempted, but the reader may have difficulty linking some ideas to one another—or to any main idea.
- Despite some questions, the reader can follow what is being said.
- The conclusion wraps up the discussion—but may or may not strengthen the writer's position.

1. A lack of organizational structure leaves the reader confused about what to focus on or what conclusions to draw. One or more of the following problems may be evident:

- There is no real lead to give the paper direction; it just starts in.
- Ideas and supporting details seem randomly ordered; the writing meanders from point to point.
- Transitions must be inferred; the writer does not link ideas to one another—or to any key point.
- The conclusion does not help the reader make greater sense of what has been said.

Following a recipe never works. Words become brittle, won't pour into the mold we try so hard to fit them into. That's why writing from an outline usually produces something flat and formulaic.
Georgia Heard (1995, 43)

VOICE AND TONE

5. As appropriate, the writer addresses the audience in a voice that is lively, engaging, and wholly appropriate for the topic and audience. In highly technical pieces, the writer keeps the voice controlled so that it does not overwhelm the message.

- The writer's enthusiasm and/or knowledge of the topic are evident and lend the writing a strong ring of confidence.
- The writer seems considerate of the audience, drawing them into the discussion and showing concern for their understanding.
- From opening to close, the writer sustains an energy that makes the writing readable.
- The reader finds himself or herself engaged, regardless of previous knowledge or interest.
- In business or highly technical pieces (e.g., a lab report, police report), the voice is wholly appropriate and never overwhelming.

3. The writer projects a tone and voice that seem sincere, pleasant, and generally appropriate for the topic and audience.

- The writer's enthusiasm for the topic seems modest and controlled.
- Moments of spontaneity intermingle with a more prosaic, encyclopedic voice.
- The reader must often work at remaining engaged; he/she feels "fact-fed," but not really "invited in."
- In technical or business writing, the voice may be too formal and aloof or overly personal—even distracting.

1. The writer seems indifferent to both topic and audience, and as a result, the tone may be distant, flat, jargonistic, stilted, or just inappropriate. One or more of the following problems may be evident:

- The writer does not seem to think how the voice and tone might affect the message or the response of the readers.
- The writer seems bored, distracted, or just anxious to be done with it; it is hard for the reader not to feel the same.
- The writer may be writing more to show off specialized knowledge than to inform or engage the reader.
- The voice and tone are noticeably inappropriate for the purpose, topic, and/or audience.

WORD CHOICE

5. Well-chosen words convey the writer's message in a clear, precise, and highly readable way, taking readers to a new level of understanding.

- The writer consistently chooses explicit, vivid words and phrases to make the message clear and memorable.
- The vocabulary suits the subject and audience.
- The writer uses the language of the content area with skill and ease, always working to make meaning clear.
- Technical or little-known words are defined or clarified as appropriate.
- Jargon and overly technical language are avoided.

3. Words are reasonably accurate and make the message clear on a general level.

- Though most language in the paper is both correct and functional, the vocabulary is sometimes inappropriate (too difficult, technical, or informal) for the topic, audience, or both.
- The writer does not seem completely at home with the terminology of the content area.
- Broad concepts are clearly stated; however, the writing lacks that "just right" vocabulary (not too vague, not too technical) that would help the reader explore the topic in depth.
- Technical or special terms may sometimes be used without sufficient explanation, leaving the reader on the outside looking in.

1. The writer struggles with a limited vocabulary that does not allow him/her to explore the topic with confidence; OR the writing is so technical and hard to penetrate that most readers feel shut out. One or more of the following problems may be evident:

- Vocabulary is inaccurate or too general or informal for the topic or audience.
- The writing is impenetrable; it speaks only to insiders, and has little meaning to a general audience.
- Technical language or specialized vocabulary may be overused; OR technical terms are missing where they would be really helpful in making meaning clear.
- The language impairs clarity—rather than enhancing it.

A wishy-washy writer uses weak nouns (like *destruction*) instead of strong verbs (like *destroy*). The wimp writes, The storm resulted in the *destruction* of the building, instead of The storm *destroyed* the building.

Patricia T. O'Connor
(1999, 151–2)

I haunt used-book stores, searching for books that contain unusual words. *Elementary Seamanship* has a glossary of sea terms: *scupper, bulwark, winch, windlass, scuttles*. The book is a cup of possibility for those days when I'm thirsty for words.

Georgia Heard (1995, 47)

SENTENCE FLUENCY

5. Sentences are strong, grammatical, clear, and direct. Text can be read quickly and without any confusion.

- Meaningful sentence beginnings (*Then, Therefore, In contrast, To summarize*) lend variety and clarity—but are not overdone.
- Sentences vary in length, but most are compact.
- No words are wasted.
- Sentences are straightforward, clear, grammatical, and complete.

I'll always take a plain sentence that's clear over a pretty one that's unintelligible.
    Patricia T. O'Connor (1999, 40)

3. Sentences are clear and usually grammatical.

- Some meaningful sentence beginnings (*First . . . Second . . . Finally . . . In conclusion*) lend clarity and variety; additional transitions would be helpful.
- Some sentences may be too long and gangly—or too short and choppy.
- Wordiness may be a problem.
- The writing as a whole is mechanical rather than fluent, but the meaning is not obscure.

Put statements in positive form. Make definite assertions. Avoid tame, colorless, hesitating, non-committal language.
    William Strunk, Jr. and E. B. White (2000, 19)

1. Numerous sentences are unclear or ungrammatical. The reader is likely to notice more than one of these problems:

- The writer rarely uses linking phrases (*At this time . . . For this reason . . . In response to your inquiry*). Ideas are hard to connect.
- Some sentences are so long the reader loses the thought—or so short the text feels bumpy and jarring.
- Wordiness is a problem; the writer needs to come to the point.
- It is often necessary to re-read for meaning.
- Grammatical errors are distracting.

CONVENTIONS & PRESENTATION

5. The writer demonstrates a good grasp of standard writing conventions (grammar, capitalization, spelling, punctuation) and also uses specialized conventions (titles and subtitles, footnotes, bullets, sidebars and other graphic devices) to enhance layout and readability. The format/presentation fits the purpose perfectly.

- Conventions (grammar, punctuation, capitalization, spelling) are essentially correct; errors are so few and so minor the reader could skip right over them unless searching for them specifically.
- The layout of the text is designed to catch a reader's eye and direct his/her attention to key points.
- The format is wholly suited to the purpose: e.g., business letter, newsletter, memo, advertisement, report.
- Titles, subtitles, bullets and similar devices enhance organizational structure; a reader can scan through the text and quickly find what he/she is looking for.
- Graphic devices such as charts, graphs or illustrations (if used) are clear, visually appealing, and directly supportive of the text.
- Any informational sources cited are correctly, thoroughly documented.

3. The writer demonstrates a basic understanding of many writing conventions and uses some specialized conventions to enhance layout and readability. The format/presentation is adequate for the purpose.

- Basic conventions are *mostly* correct; errors do not impair meaning.
- At the same time, minor errors are noticeable enough that the text is not yet ready to share with the public.
- The basic layout of the text is visually pleasing; key points can be located with little effort.
- The format is appropriate, if not striking.
- Greater use of titles, subtitles, subheads and similar devices would help visually organize information.
- Graphics, if used, are connected to the text.
- Sources are cited as necessary; not all citations are correct or complete.

1. Numerous errors in writing conventions consistently distract the reader and make the text difficult to read. The format/presentation needs work. One or more of the following problems may be evident:

- Errors in conventions are common and impair readability. This text cannot be shared publicly without extensive editing.
- The basic layout/presentation is visually ineffective or confusing; it is hard to locate key points.
- The format is not suited to the purpose.

- Titles, subtitles, bullets or similar devices would make "text dense" copy more clear and visually appealing.
- Graphic devices are not used (though needed), or their connection to the text is unclear.
- Citations are missing or incorrect.

SIMPLICITY ITSELF: THE CHECKLIST

Clearly, the preceding scoring guide is written for teachers to use in assessing students' work. You could create a student version by simplifying the language. I thought I would show you an even easier way to put this information in students' hands without needing quite so much copy. It simply calls for transforming our very thorough informational scoring guide into a checklist that hits most important points without burying students in language. If you think I've cropped too much, you can always make it longer (personally, I find I like short better and better):

Student Informational Checklist

IDEAS

___ My paper is clear, focused, & purposeful.

___ I have plenty of information from experience and research.

___ I chose information I knew would answer readers' questions.

___ I use evidence and examples to support every single point I make—no gaps.

ORGANIZATION

___ My lead gets your attention and lets you know where I'm headed.

___ My main idea jumps right out at you.

___ The whole thing is organized to help you go from point to point without *ever* feeling lost.

___ Every statement I make relates in some way to my main point.

___ My conclusion reinforces and supports my main point.

> Expect your organization plan to stretch and change as you go along. It's supposed to. If it doesn't, there's something wrong . . . If you have to stand on your head to follow a blueprint, maybe the blueprint is upside down.
> Patricia T. O'Connor (1999, 25)

VOICE

___ I have energy, enthusiasm, and the confidence that comes from knowing a topic well.

___ You can tell I like this topic.

___ You'll want to know more about this topic, too, once you read my paper.

___ I thought of my audience the whole time I was writing—and tried to answer their questions.

___ My voice is strong—but under control (not too funny, sarcastic, etc.).

> We all rehearse what we are going to say—and how we are going to say it . . . . The how is voice.
> Donald M. Murray (1985, 22)

WORD CHOICE

___ I know the territory. The language of this topic is NOT foreign to me.

___ I make the meaning of *every word* clear. I define confusing or new words, or give examples.

___ I avoid jargon. But I do use technical terms if they are needed.

_____ I avoid vague language, too: *stuff that's like, you know, too vague and stuff.*

_____ The words I chose are right for my audience—first graders, high school students, scientists, the general public, or whoever.

SENTENCE FLUENCY

_____ Every sentence in my paper is grammatically correct. I checked.

_____ Sentences begin in different ways.

_____ I use linking words (*My second point . . . On the other hand . . .*) to show how ideas connect.

_____ My sentences are concise, not wordy.

_____ You will find my writing very easy to follow.

CONVENTIONS AND PRESENTATION

_____ My mechanics (spelling, punctuation, grammar) are correct. I *edited* this paper.

_____ The presentation is a *Wow!* It will catch your eye and make key points a snap to find.

_____ The format goes with the purpose: business letter, report, etc.

_____ For reports, I used a title and subtitles, bullets, numbers, etc. to help break up the text and make it easy to find information.

_____ If I used pictures or other graphics you'll see right away how they link to my writing.

_____ If I quoted any sources, or used information from others, I cited my sources correctly and thoroughly.

SIMPLIFIED RUBRICS

Here's another way to simplify. In Figures 10.1 to 10.4, you'll see greatly simplified scoring scales for both creative and technical writing, one of each using a 5-point scale, and one of each using a 6-point scale. Not every point on the scale is defined because the purpose here is to keep things *simple.* It's the low-fat version, if you will. But if you feel compelled to fill in the blanks, this makes a good exercise to do with your students. I used the baseball metaphor with the 6-point scale because it fits so nicely, but if you don't like baseball, you can think of a different metaphor, or even leave the middle numbers blank. You'll find the simple scales work amazingly well even when we do not define all numbers.

SAMPLE EXPOSITORY & RESEARCH PAPERS

No scoring guide is worth its salt unless raters can agree on the scores. Let's put our informational scoring guide to the test with some student samples, just to see whether your scores match those of our teacher-raters. These papers were selected to represent a variety of topics, grade levels, writing approaches,

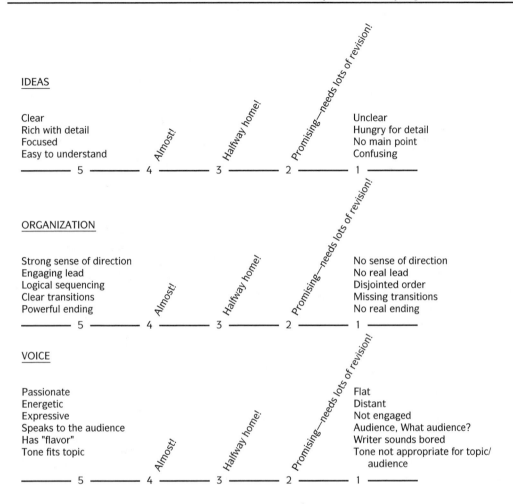

FIGURE 10.1. 5-Point Creative "Shortie"

and skills. As in Chapter 3, suggested scores and rationales are given at the end of the chapter.

1. "BEARS IN THE WILD"

Grade 4, Expository

Have you ever watched a black bear before? Once when we were driving I saw a black bear across the river. she was ambling along the river bank, with her two cubs.

Black bears are usualy black but they can be brown or white. A black bear has four legs and five claws on each paw. The weight of a grown black bear is about 300 pounds or about 136 kilograms.

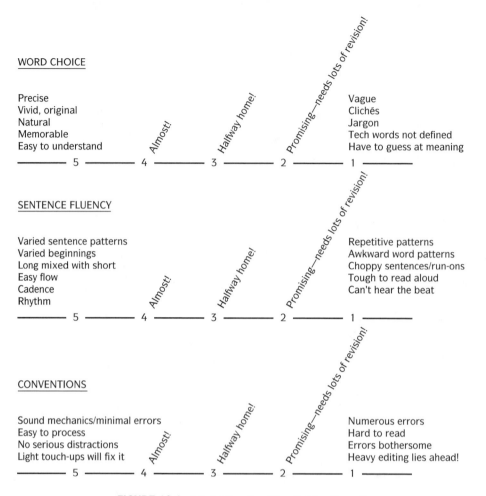

FIGURE 10.1. 5-Point Creative "Shortie" (continued)

Black bears are less than five feet long. the black bear has lots of thick fur and it has big teeth, long, sharp claws, and a huge head.

Some bears live in a hole under a tree or in a dug out cave. Bears eat different kinds of berries and some kinds of inseckts they dig out of rotton logs. They normally live in the woods where they are safe from people there main enemy. Bears also eat honey from bee hives. there thick fur protects them from the bees they also eat many kinds of fish espeshially salmon. when you think about it, they like alot of the same foods we humans like eccept for the inseckts.

Most bears hibernate in the winter, but before they do they need to collect lots of food and stuff themselves to get fat and store food for the winter.

Lots of people think bears will attack you. But the truth is they wont. Bears are mostly gentle. They usually mind there own

IDEAS

Clear, compelling
Shows in-depth understanding
Unique perspective
Unforgettable, original detail
Entertaining, makes you think

Unclear
No main point
No personal point of view
Detail deprived
Prewriting, a list/collection

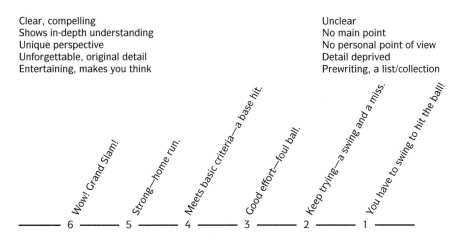

ORGANIZATION

Order natural and right
Structure embedded in text
Compelling lead
Smooth, helpful transitions
Leads reader right to main points
Never predictable/always enjoyable
Knockout conclusion

No sense of purpose/direction
Hard to see any pattern.
No real lead.
Transitions missing/unclear
Seems to wander
Predictable—or confusing
No real conclusion

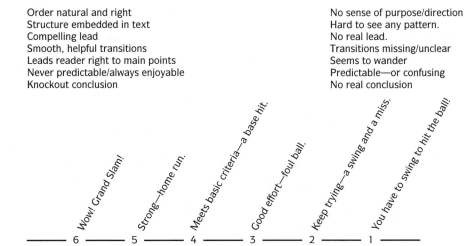

FIGURE 10.2. 6-Point Creative "Shortie"

busness unless you pester them. In the woods in Canada once we got to track a bear but he never would let us get too close because he was just too shy. Its easy to find where bears have been from their tracks and droppings. They rub themselves on tree trunks and leave big tufts of there fur behind.

People are bears only enemies but we could be there freinds if we understood them. we should not kill bears just for bear rugs. there are not enough bears left and if we just keep building houses and shopping malls we will distroy their homes.

<u>VOICE</u>

Easy to tell who this is
Unique in style and tone
A "must read aloud"
Passionate—but controlled
Impossible to put down
Voice enhances meaning
Perfect for topic/audience

The "anybody" paper
Flat, distant
Audience? What audience?
Writer sounds bored
Hard to stay engaged
Voice isn't there
Not right for topic/audience

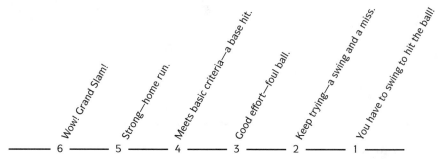

<u>WORD CHOICE</u>

You wish you'd written it
Memorable, quotable
Unique phrasing
Absolute clarity
No "echoes" from other texts

Vague words (nice, good)
Cliches, jargon
No memorable moments
Have to guess at meaning
Making a few words stretch

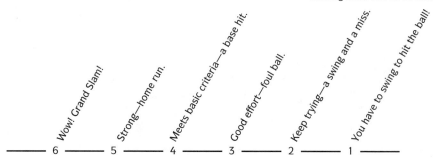

FIGURE 10.2. 6-Point Creative "Shortie" (continued)

2. "DRIVING TESTS SHOULD BE HARDER!"

Grade 7, Expository/Persuasive

If driver's tests were more rigorous, everyone on the road would
be safer. About 50,000 people die in traffic accidents each year,
and thousands more are injured. Most of these fatal accidents
involve 16-year-old drivers. Although one of the problems is
driving under the influence of liquor, an even bigger problem is

SENTENCE FLUENCY

Reads like a lively script   Tough to read aloud
Invites interpretive reading   Better rehearse!
Lyrical—almost poetic   Choppy/awkward
                                             phrasing/run-ons
Each sentence new, fresh   Repetitive patterns

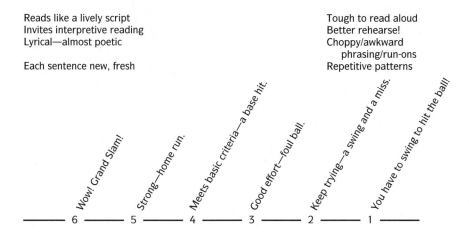

CONVENTIONS

Only picky editors will complain   Numerous errors
Control over complex text   Minimal control over conventions
                                          Errors get in the way of meaning
Conventions consistently enhance meaning

Dashes, italics, ellipses, etc. aid interpretive reading   Conventions do not help
                                             reader understand text
                                          Sharpen the red pencil.
Ready to publish

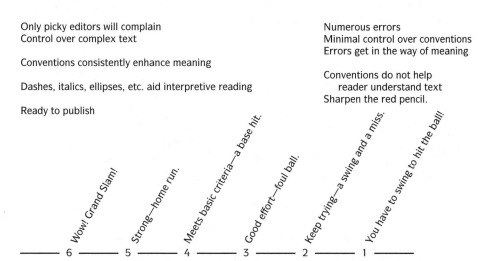

FIGURE 10.2. 6-Point Creative "Shortie" (continued)

incompetent driving. We could do something about this, but we grant driver's licenses on the basis of a very simple test.

Did you know that the part of the test in which you actually get out in a car and drive is only about 20 minutes long? What's more, the test givers are not demanding at all. They only ask drivers to perform a few tasks, such as turning left, turning right, parking and stopping. It has only been in the last few years that they have added entering a freeway to the test

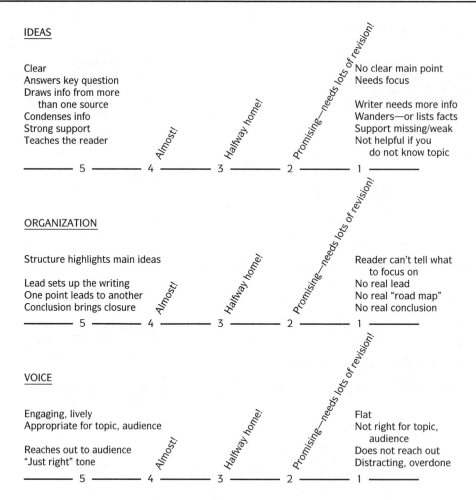

FIGURE 10.3. 5-Point Tech "Shortie"

requirements. How often does anyone have to parallel park compared to entering a freeway? Yet it took all this time to update this test.

Tests are not conducted on the busiest streets or during heavy traffic hours. Anyone can pass this simple test in light traffic on a quiet street. It does not mean that driver is competent.

The true test is real-life driving. I mean things like driving in bad weather, such as on icy streets or in fog. Or coping with bad drivers, such as people who tailgate or honk for no good reason. Or learning to handle mechanical problems such as getting a flat tire. The current driver's test does not measure whether a person can handle any of these difficult but common situations.

Of course, a driver's test that had to cover all of these situations would be difficult to set up. It isn't easy to arrange for people to drive on icy roads, for instance. Plus it could be

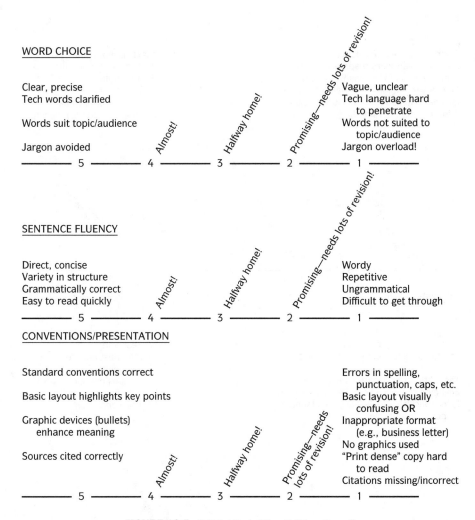

FIGURE 10.3. 5-Point Tech "Shortie" (continued)

dangerous. Imagine if people got killed while taking their driver's test! Besides, a complicated test might cost more and there could be a long waiting line. Imagine if you were 16 and needed to drive to work and you could not get a license because the wait was so long. There is one solution. They could do part of the test as a computer simulation. That way, you would still need the skills, but you would not need to risk your life to show you were a competent driver.

There are several ways to make the current test better. First, make it longer, so people need to drive more. Second, use computer simulation to test skills under dangerous conditions. Third, make sure people really have to do the things they will do in everyday driving, like changing lanes on the freeway. Then, require a score

IDEAS

Clear, complete, informative
Anticipates/answers reader's questions
Synthesizes info from many sources
Condenses info into "just right" package
Includes extensive, convincing support
A journey of understanding

No clear main point
Writer needs more info
First thoughts
Rambles, lists
Support missing/weak
A struggle to make meaning

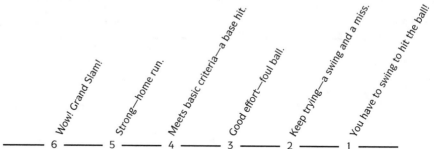

ORGANIZATION

Designed to educate/inform
Lead sets up text perfectly
Structure guides reader to key points

Thoughtful transitions connect ideas
Engaging sequence keeps reader reading
Killer conclusion makes arguments/main
    points irrefutable

No structure yet
No real lead
Reader must hunt for
    key points
Transitions missing
Hard to follow
No real conclusion

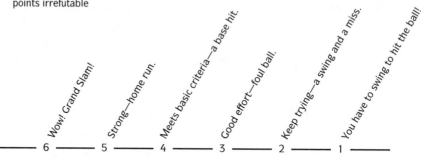

FIGURE 10.4. 6-Point Tech "Shortie"

of 90 to pass, not 70, which is too low. Right now, you can do a lot
of things wrong and still pass.

Sure, it will cost a little to make the tests more rigorous. But
lives are more important than keeping tests cheap. When was the
last time you felt in danger because of an incompetent driver?
Remember, almost every person in this country will have a
driver's license at some time in his or her life. If even half of these
people are not qualified, we are risking our lives every time we go
out on the road. We need better driver's tests now!

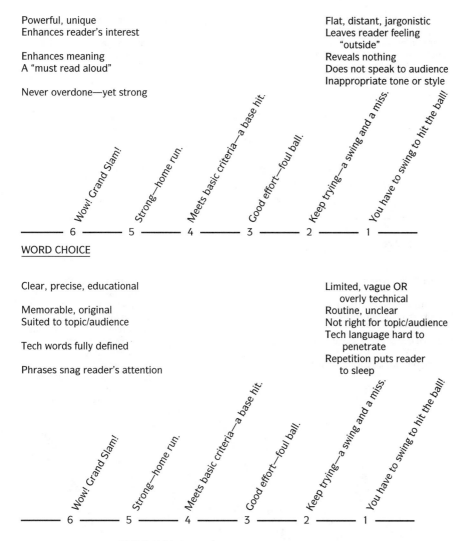

VOICE

Powerful, unique	Flat, distant, jargonistic
Enhances reader's interest	Leaves reader feeling "outside"
Enhances meaning	Reveals nothing
A "must read aloud"	Does not speak to audience
	Inappropriate tone or style
Never overdone—yet strong	

Wow! Grand Slam!   Strong—home run.   Meets basic criteria—a base hit.   Good effort—foul ball.   Keep trying—a swing and a miss.   You have to swing to hit the ball!

—— 6 —— 5 —— 4 —— 3 —— 2 —— 1 ——

WORD CHOICE

Clear, precise, educational	Limited, vague OR overly technical
Memorable, original	Routine, unclear
Suited to topic/audience	Not right for topic/audience
	Tech language hard to penetrate
Tech words fully defined	Repetition puts reader to sleep
Phrases snag reader's attention	

Wow! Grand Slam!   Strong—home run.   Meets basic criteria—a base hit.   Good effort—foul ball.   Keep trying—a swing and a miss.   You have to swing to hit the ball!

—— 6 —— 5 —— 4 —— 3 —— 2 —— 1 ——

FIGURE 10.4. 6-Point Tech "Shortie" (continued)

Source of information: Department of Motor Vehicles

3. "INTERESTING FACTS ABOUT SMOKING"

Grade 10, Expository

Many teen-agers from 12 to 18 smoke every week if not every day. In 1987 along, lung cancer surpassed breast cancer as the leading cancer killer of women.

SENTENCE FLUENCY

Direct, right to the point	Unclear, fuzzy
Every word counts—*no* filler	Wordy
No grammatical errors	Ungrammatical
Noticeable variety in beginnings	Repetitive beginnings
Designed for quick scanning	Hard to read

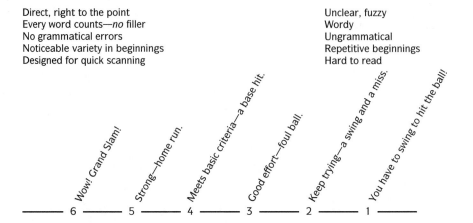

CONVENTIONS

No significant errors	Numerous conventional errors
Conventions enhance readability	Errors block meaning
Layout leads reader to key points	Layout visually confusing OR No attention paid to layout
Effective use of white space	Font overload/"print dense" text
Informative, impressive graphics	No graphics Graphics not coordinated with text
Thorough, accurate citations	Citations missing/incorrect

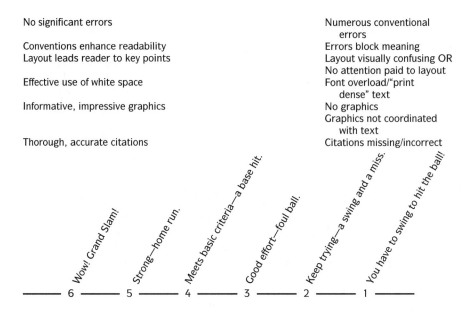

FIGURE 10.4. 6-Point Tech "Shortie" (continued)

Cigarettes are one of the most dangerous drugs that is legal in the U.S. Almost 3 million packs of cigarettes are sold illegally to minors every year. People who began smoking as minors have a really hard time stopping.

Numerous cancers, heart disease and alot of other ailments are blamed on smoking. Infact, 90 percent of all lung cancer is atributed to smoking. if people know all this why don't they stop?

Though many wish they could but it is not that simple. Cigarettes are very addictive, though. You can become adicted in about four to five weeks even if you only smoke two or three cigarettes per day.

People usually start smoking because they think it is cool and it is just a temporary thing. But, studies show that, almost everybody who starts cannot stop Most of the people who start are young women. Although more young women are smoking some studies show the number of blacks who smoke is declining. Who smokes depends alot on who the advertisers are appealing to in their ads. If you smoke, just remember you may not be able to stop.

4. "HUMBOLDT PENGUINS"

Grade 9, Expository

Probably the most startling fact about the gentle Humboldt Penguin is that it is the most endangered penguin in the world. They have been hunted for years. Moreover, their main staple food, krill, are dwindling in numbers with the warming of the oceans, and the range of the Humboldt Penguin is not very big—and is not getting any bigger. Their habitat is unique, and they do not seem able to adapt. The only place it can be duplicated is in the zoo. Odds are, we have only a few decades left—maybe less—to enjoy these remarkable and friendly animals.

Environment

Humboldt Penguins live along the rocky coastline of South America, from Peru to Northern Chile. The warm currents of El Niño bring in plenty of fish and krill—for now—so the penguins do not migrate. They nest right in the rocks, making themselves comfortable along hard, unforgiving rock walls that most creatures would find less than inviting. The rocks and ocean are all they know their whole lives. Because they do not migrate, they know nothing of forests or sandy beaches or even pebbled coves.

Physical Description

Male and female Humboldts are similar in appearance. Both are about 26 inches tall and weigh about ten pounds. They have a black mask with touches of pink around a sharp, heavy beak, well suited to fishing. A black stripe runs like an inverted "U" up and around their sides and down their back. Their belly is mostly white, with scattered black speckles. Penguins have very short legs, perhaps only two inches long, but can nevertheless jump amazingly high, for the leg muscles are very powerful. Their webbed feet are black with pink spots, and they have three toes, with sharp, scaly claws at the end. A penguin's feet work like paddles, propelling the penguin through the water, and are very powerful.

Penguins are normally fairly clumsy on land, and waddle along at a slow pace—though they have been known to "launch" themselves at an enemy if attacked or provoked. They are built for underwater speed, however, and move like tiny torpedoes in the water. Their smooth, oval shape is reminiscent of a dolphin or trout, and they swim with the same ease.

Everyone knows that penguins do not fly. However, scientists believe that once they did. They are almost certainly descended from a flying bird, but so far, nobody has located the "missing link" that would prove this theory.

Food

The diet of the penguin is healthy, if a little monotonous. They dine primarily on fish and crustaceans, plus an occasional squid. They are especially fond of fish like anchovies which swim in large schools. Penguins have a lot of body fat to maintain in order to insulate themselves from the cold water, so they must eat a great deal and eat often to maintain their oval shapes.

The bill of the penguin is equipped with small spines which help hook and hold a fish. Once a penguin gets a grip on its meal, the fish rarely escapes.

Predators

Penguins are hunted by seals, killer whales and sharks. For this reason, they like to hunt close to shore and near the surface. If a penguin ventures too far out to sea, it may not have the endurance to outrun a hungry seal.

Land predators include gulls, jaegers, skuas and other large birds. These birds will not take on an adult penguin, which is a fierce fighter, but will prey on young chicks and eggs.

Behavior

A surprising fact about penguins is that they are quite territorial. They will attack others that come too close to their nesting site. Like humans, they sometimes resent neighbors who invade their privacy or become too nosy. If a penguin must walk through a crowded area, he will keep his head high and feathers sleeked down, as if trying to look invisible. Generally, though, penguins are very social. They swim together and hunt in groups for protection. They watch out for one another and are very affectionate with their young. Humboldts have not learned to fear humans, and will often allow people to come quite close.

Conclusion

The Humboldt Penguin is among the most intriguing of all penguin species. It is more social than most penguins, and remarkably like ourselves. With luck, it may survive long enough for us to study its curious ways further.

Bibliography

Johnson, Russell. "Humboldt penguins: An Endangered Species." In Penguin World. Vol. 4. No 6. Spring 1992.
Seattle Public Zoo. Site visit. May 20, 1994.
Striker, Madeline. *Intriguing Facts About Penguins.* 1994. Philadelphia: Jonathan Weber & Associates.

5. "THE MIDDLE AGES"

Grade 8, Expository

In the times of the Middle Ages, many children drempt of becoming a knight. first they had to be a page. Next you would become a squire. hard training and patience was necessary. A brave young squire could not wait to receive the acolade.

During the period of being a squire, you had to learn chivalry, which consists of loyalty, devotion, politness, and courtesy. Courtessy to women was the biggest part of being a knight. It was also important to be brave, good with horses and weapons and protect the defensless.

Not many people know this, but a knight had to be very wealthy to pay for the equiptment. the equiptment consisted of a suit of armour, shild, sword, and of course a horse which needs special training. the armour consists of many parts we won't name them all because it would take forever. However we could name the helmet which is the most important piece of armour anyone could have. The helmet protects the head from injury which could be fatal or even deadly.

Tournaments took up what little free time a knight might have. Most other time not on the battlefield he would be jowsting or sword fighting another knight. the purpose of a tournament is to test your strength. the object is not to kill a knight, but to capture him. What would become of a knight once captured. This is one of the many questions history never makes clear.

Maners were the main ways of life during the middle ages, which had farms, hunting grounds, people, and of course castles, not to mention vegetable gardens plus kennels for the dogs and barns for domestic animals. Castles were the main point of life during the Middle ages. they were built for defence and were not all that comfortable being cold and rainy in the winter plus uncomfortable for sleeping. They were good for defence however, being stone they would not burn in case of attack.

After all that there isn't much more to discuss. So, Orevwa.

Bibliography

Caselli, Giovanni. *The middle Ages.* New york, 1988, Peter Bedrick Books, pages 12–17.

6. "EXPLORING THE THEME OF PROGRESS IN *A CONNECTICUT YANKEE AT KING ARTHUR'S COURT*"

Grade 10, Expository

In the novel *A Connecticut Yankee at King Arthur's Court,* Mark Twain shows that knowledge can be both powerful and seductive. He also shows that codes or religions can be mentally restrictive and can influence the way people see the whole world. Twain explains these themes by transporting a practical nineteenth century mechanic and factory supervisor named Hank Morgan into the innocence of the sixth century court of King Arthur. The result is a story bordering on science fiction but also full of social criticisms.

The main character, Hank Morgan, really has two sides to his nature. First, he is a practical Yankee, the symbol of American progress in a time of new technology. But also, he is a rather vain, self-centered person, capable of manipulating others to gain their admiration. He views himself as truly superior to the people of Camelot: "Here I was—a giant among pygmies, a man among children, a master intelligence among intellectual moles; by all rational measurements the only really great man in the whole British world" (pg. 90).

The legend of Camelot continues to be one of our favorite "fairy tales." We still celebrate it in the form of plays and musicals. Our view is very different from the one Twain has in the book. We tend to think of Camelot as an almost perfect time with gorgeous princesses, morally upright kings and flashy knights in shining armor. Part of the reason we feel nostalgic is that over time the legend has grown until we see Camelot better than it really was. Twain's description of sixth century England shows a more realistic view. In his world, people can be unscrupulous. For instance, the people of Camelot were threatening to burn Hank alive because he was a stranger whose ways, habits, and clothing were different. The knights in this world ride off to rescue maidens that do not even exist. And the maidens themselves tell tall tales to get the knights to do it: "There was never such a country for wandering liars; and they were of both sexes . . . Now you would think that the first thing the king would do after listening to such a novelette from an entire stranger would be to ask for credentials— yes, and a pointer or two as to locality of castle, best route to it, and so on. But nobody ever thought of so simple and common sense a thing as that. No, everybody swallowed these people's lies whole, and never asked a question of any sort about anything" (pg. 109). Overall, the people are superstitious and closed-minded. Perhaps this is Twain's way of reminding us that fairy tails are only fairy tails in the end. People of all times and places have character flaws.

Twain reveals his true perspective through four major themes. All of them show that things are not always what they appear to be on the surface. As we have seen, Camelot is not really a time and place of purity and innocence. Moreover, Hank Morgan is not really a great man.

One theme in this book is that knowledge is very powerful. Special knowledge can cause people to see a person differently and even fear that person. Throughout this book, Hank uses his mechanical know-how to impress his public: ". . . the populace uncovered and fell back reverently to make a wide way for me, as if I had been some kind of superior being—and I was" (pg. 214). Hank figured that since his technological knowledge was higher, he was some kind of super human. Although he was clever and innovative, he fell victim to his own cleverness in the end when practically all of England revolted against him. "Ye were conquerors, ye are conquered!" (pg. 403).

A second theme is that power is seductive. By the end of the book, Hank never wants to go back to the time in which he belongs. The populace thinks highly of him and he comes to love that. He wants the admiration of the people. Unfortunately, they admire him for the wrong reasons—because he performs clever tricks, not because he is a noble or good person.

The third theme shows how codes and religious rules can be mentally restricting. The people of Camelot have been brought up to believe that the Church is always right, and any representative of the Church, like a priest or the Pope, is equally enlightened. They know nothing else. The Church guides their every thought. They do not think for themselves, or have their own opinions about anything. Hank tries to give them an opportunity to break free of dominance by Church doctrine, but he is unsuccessful.

Finally, Twain explores the theme of progress and whether it is good for mankind. In the novel, Hank brings "progress" to Camelot in the form of technology. This does not differ too much from how people see progress today. Many people think of progress as faster computers, VCRs and new microwave ovens. But is this real progress? As Twain shows us, new technology often just brings with it a new set of superstitions. Progress should be measured at a deeper level by social justice, enlightenment, and free thinking. Twain gives Hank an opportunity to bring true progress to the people of Camelot, but instead of concentrating on ways to help the people, Hank only tries to bring glory to himself.

As writer Margaret Atwood says, "The answers you get from literature depend upon the questions you pose." One question we might ask about *A Connecticut Yankee* is "Why does Twain send Hank Morgan back in time?" Perhaps it is because it is hard for a society to see itself the way it truly is. Nineteenth Century New England probably saw itself much as we see ourselves today, as being very technologically advanced. But by sending Hank back in time, Twain allows us to see Nineteenth Century values and lifestyle through Sixth Century eyes—and vice versa. As a result, we learn more about each period of time, and more about ourselves and human values.

Bibliography

Twain, Mark. 1986. A Connecticut Yankee at King Arthur's Court. New York: Penguin Books.

7. "RA, THE SUN GOD"

Grade 12, Expository

Ra, the sun god, fascinated ancient Egyptians as the chief of cosmic deities. Five thousand years later, people still worship his flaming chariot in the sky. As sunny days tempt flocks of people to the beach, and teenagers wearing summer fashions sport gleaming tans, the sun continues to carry a heavy influence on the American society. Why should the lives on earth not revolve around this solar beauty? It is the star around which the earth revolves. What happens if one day this heavenly body makes life on earth a living hell? What if a day in the sun leads to a lifetime of health complications? This situation just might become the case with the rate of destruction occurring in the ozone layer. What possible effect could this layer of triatomic oxygen molecules located 15 to 20 miles above earth's surface have to do with life on earth? The effect is tremendous because life depends on this ozone layer to filter out the dangerous ultraviolet rays of the sun. When it weakens, there are serious consequences that affect many life forms.

So what could have caused this problem? Studies prove man-made products are the culprits. Dangerous man-made chemicals emitted into the atmosphere attack and destroy the protective screen of the ozone layer. Two of the most common of these chemical compounds are chloroflurocarbons (CFCs) and bromoflurocarbons (halogens) These compounds take five to ten years to reach the stratosphere where the UV radiation breaks down the molecules and releases the chlorine and bromine atoms. Each of these atoms is able to destroy up to 100,000 ozone molecules (Miller). Scientists discovered that in 1991 the ozone began to thin 3.5% in the summer months in addition to the reported 5.5% in the winter months (Miller). Although the ozone constantly creates and destroys itself, the released chemicals have altered the delicate balance. The ozone layer will eventually repair itself once the chemical emission ceases; however, even if all CFC emissions ended today, depletion would continue for 15 to 20 years before repair could begin (Miller). In other words, every second counts.

What does all this information mean? It means living in a world where it may one day be unsafe to go outside. Remember basking in the warm golden rays of the sun on beautiful summer days? Forget it. Without the ozone layer to filter the dangerous UVB radiation from the sun, that golden bright star is just a health hazard. Spending a sunny day outdoors means the risk of sunburn, premature skin wrinkles, cancer, cataracts, and a weakened immune system. The shade of a tree is not enough protection to filter out even half of the harmful rays. Ironically, studies proved that excessive air pollution considerably shelters large industrialized cities like Boston from UV light (Lehman). Could things get any worse? Scientists predict that an ozone loss of ten percent would result in a 26 percent rise of non-melanoma skin cancer which means an excess of 300,000 cases per year worldwide (Lehman). How about these numbers: if the ozone depletion reaches 20 percent, merely two hours in the sun will result in a blistering sunburn (Miller). Anyone care to go to the beach?

Although these facts are both startling and frightening, they are only the beginning. What about other life forms? Humans can slap on some sunscreen or avoid the sun's most intense hours between 10 a.m. and 2 p.m., but what about plants and marine life? Because plants cannot protect themselves, plant damage is a serious concern. The UV radiation reduces crop yields and stuns vegetation growth. These consequences can greatly affect people who depend on plants for a living or for food. In addition to plant damage, the ozone hole also disrupts the marine food chain because the increased exposure to UV radiation harms fish larvae and other marine life near the ocean surface. The base of the marine food chain consists of these organisms which are essential in the production of oxygen.

With the knowledge of these disastrous effects, why have no reforms occurred? Why were there no warnings about the dangerous effects to the ozone layer? Actually, there were many predictions of the potential dangers; however, not many people heard or listened to them. As early as 1974, an atmospheric chemist, Dr. Sherwood Rowland, first suggested the destruction of the ozone from CFCs (Miller). His prediction caused an initial concern that resulted in the ban of the use of aerosols in the United States. By the late 1980's,

America was back to her industrial lifestyle with little concern for the environment. Despite the known dangers, companies widely produced CFCs due to new discoveries of their usefulness in other areas. However, in 1987, most nations signed the Montreal protocol, an agreement to reduce the use of CFCs (Recer). Even so, a newspaper article in the *Morning Call* on March 10, 1992, 18 years after Rowland's original hypothesis, printed startling news concerning a predicted ozone hole developing in the spring. The press directed people "to heed the advice you've been hearing for years about protecting yourself from the sun" (Lehman).

Did people really believe the seriousness of the warnings? In December, 1994, the headline "Study proves man causing ozone hole "blazed across a page of *The Morning Call* (Recer). Was it really a new revelation or a confession to a long standing accusation? Despite all of these "discoveries," the United States is the largest producer and consumer of the very chemicals that destroy the ozone layer. In spite of the known threat that these chemicals impose on the environment, leaking refrigerators and car air conditioners continue to pollute the air, yellow-canister halon fire extinguishers still hang in kitchens, and foam containers and "peanuts" persistently package products (Miller). All of these examples are factors that poke larger holes in the ozone layer every day. What kind of world willingly destroys the natural with man-made, unnatural invaders?

A hole the size of the north American continent penetrates the ozone layer (Recer). It hovers above like an ominous reminder of man's drastic and deadly impact on his environment. At this point, a little sunscreen and common sense can offer some protection, but how much worse must conditions become before people take action? It is time to end the detrimental misconduct towards the environment which is ultimately taking away the freedom to enjoy the outdoors safely. Will children of the 21st century never bask in the beaming rays of the sun, or will tragic outcomes force future generations to live with drapes drawn in houses filled with artificial light? What would the world be like without sunshine? In the words of Henry Beston from his book *The Outermost House,* "When all has been said, the adventure of the sun is the great natural drama by which we live, and not to have joy in it and awe of it, not to share in it, is to close a dull door on nature's sustaining and poetic spirit" (Reader's Digest, 752).

8. "CHALLENGER (DOUBLESPEAK)"

Grade 12, Expository/Narrative

"Five . . . four . . . three . . . two . . . one . . . We have lift off." Millions of people watched the space shuttle Challenger leave the launch pad on January 28, 1986. None of the TV viewers could imagine the tragedy that would occur only 58 seconds into the mission. During the time it takes to read this page, all seven astronauts were propelled towards the endless sky, then killed, plummeting into the Atlantic Ocean at 200 miles per hour.

The last successful Challenger mission took place on January 12, 1986, after four cancelled launches caused by equipment problems and threatening weather. Although NASA had promised to create a shuttle fleet that would fly twenty-four times a year, the program completed only nine flights in 1985. Minutes before the January tragedy, congressional investigators notified NASA they were looking into the slow progress of the program. These pressures to launch shuttles on schedule were most likely the main influence which caused top NASA officials to ignore several warning signals and equipment repair.

Rubbery O-rings lined the joints of the solid rocket booster on the Challenger. On previous flights, rocket exhaust had leaked around these seals, with the worst problems occurring when the temperature fell nearly fifty-three degrees. On the morning of January 28, the temperature was read at twenty-three degrees, and an engineer at Morton Thiokol, the company which manufactured the rockets, "urged" a delay.

"I made the comment that lower temperatures are in the direction of badness for both O-rings, because it slows the timing function," said the engineer. In the thoughts of many observers this statement was meant as a suggestion, not a warning.

Rocket exhaust leaked through one joint immediately upon launch. As the initial shock and vibration from the ignition died down, burned insulation and rocket fuel built up around the leak and gradually plugged. With luck, the challenger could have reached orbit, but soon into the flight, the spacecraft passed through heavy air turbulence. The heavy shaking ruptured the joint again and a flame shot out of the booster into the external fuel tank. It exploded, spilling liquid hydrogen, which caught on fire instantly. At seventy-three seconds, pilot Mike Smith said "Uh-oh" and contact between ground and air was severed.

Could this horrible event have been avoided? Was the extreme cold a definite danger or simply "in the direction of badness"? Whose life could have been saved? Perhaps Christa McAuliffe, the first "teacher in space." Or the pilot, 41-year-old Michael J. Smith. For two and a half years, a presidential commission investigated the greatest disaster of the United States space program to answer this question. Headed by former secretary of state William Rogers and former astronaut Neil Armstrong, the group determined NASA's administrative system was to blame. Specifically responsible was Morton Thiokol's use of doublespeak.

Doublespeak is defined as language which pretends to communicate but really does not. In this situation, doublespeak can be defined as death. This tragic event exemplifies the kind of doublespeak which "avoids or shifts responsibility." When people are faced with difficult decisions accompanied by stiff penalties for a mistake, no one wants to assume control or responsibility.

In this instance, the engineer needed to warn NASA officials of the potential danger. Feeling the time constraints to launch without delay, he expressed this judgment rather timidly, without authority or certainty, despite the extreme danger. NASA decided to go ahead with the launch, an action dictated by this incredibly indecisive, casual comment. The engineer did not want to be held responsible for such a large decision so he simply avoided it.

Later, NASA maintained this sequence of faulty language by calling the shuttle explosion "an anomaly," and the bodies of the astronauts "recovered components." The coffins were named "crew transfer containers." It became evident that the U.S. government is familiar with doublespeak.

If the engineer had simply stated the problem with the O-rings, to convey his message more clearly, perhaps those seven people would be alive today. As a society, a collective decision must be made to end the language which ends so many precious lives.

9. "DECISION"

Grade 12, Expository/Narrative

Exactly three hundred and forty-nine days before I was born, an event occurred that would profoundly affect my future. No one knew it then, of course, not even my parents. They didn't know the full significance of the United States bicentennial celebration, and when they watched the festivities in New York on television, they saw what everyone else did: the spectacles of fireworks and parades, the tall ships sailing into New York harbor, the stream of people converging on the city.

No one saw anything but the glitter, the patriotism and the camaraderie. No one knew at the time that the parties and the convivial gatherings would be the spark that would ignite the long fuse of a different sort of firework, a bomb that would later threaten the health and even the survival of the human race.

That bomb was the AIDS virus, and epidemiologists pinpointed 4 July 1976 as the date when it came to the United States and began to slowly ravage the American populace.

I didn't really understand the impact of AIDS until I was fifteen years old. I knew about it long before, of course. I understood all about its clinical aspects, about how this microscopic virus could enter the human body and eventually turn its immune system against itself. I knew that it facilitated fatal bouts of pneumonia and other "curable" illnesses, how it induced delirium and dehydration, how it could wither away the human body like a blade of grass in the scorching sun.

Still, even though I could intellectually comprehend the significance of the disease and the agony it caused, I could not truly relate to it. I did not know anyone who was HIV positive, and in the small, isolated farming community in which I live, AIDS was not a reality. AIDS patients were simply not something that happened in New Tripoli, and as myopic as it may sound, I suppose that that small town feeling of security infected me as well.

Then, one night, my perception changed. I had a debate meeting at my coach's house with my team, who were three of my closest friends. We enjoyed being with each other, and meetings were something which we all looked forward to, but when we came in from the cold February evening, her warm house belied sadness. We found our coach at her kitchen table poring over a Newsweek magazine with Rudolf Nureyev on its cover and tears streaming down her face.

"Have you read this?" she asked, as she began to tell us about how that virus that seemed so far away was claiming, one at a time, performers and artists in its cruel, systematic consumption. It was taking away our artistic community, something that even isolated rural dwellers like ourselves could appreciate. Slowly, it was robbing our society of the people who recorded its culture, its emotion. "One of you has to stop this," she said. "One of you has to become a doctor and find an end to this."

I didn't know it then. I didn't know that, of the four of us, those few words she said in her warm, inviting kitchen that night would have such a profound impact on me. I didn't know that in just two short years, I would be applying to MIT in the hopes of learning the skills to find some end to this plague, this AIDS. In hindsight, perhaps it was because, at the time, I lacked the confidence to believe I was smart enough or capable enough to dare consider such a thing. When she spoke those words, I didn't fathom I might be the one who would try to make them a reality.

But since that night, much has changed. I learned more, listened a great deal, and even cried over the AIDS quilt. I began to feel, not just know, about the disease. I realized that AIDS did affect me, that the next person to die could be my best friend, not just some sterile statistic. More important, though, I have come to believe that I have the potential to do more than just stand idly by. It has taken me a long time to come to the realization that AIDS research is something to which I wish to dedicate my life, but perhaps my chance to make a difference is only just beginning.

SUGGESTED SCORES AND COMMENTS FOR INFORMATIONAL AND RESEARCH PAPERS

Note: As with the papers in Chapter 3, you should feel free to disagree with these scores if you have a good reason. In addition, in cases where we felt papers went beyond the demands of the level 5 criteria, we assigned them a score of 6, even though using a 5-point scale. The 6 really is the "Wow" of the 5-point scale.

Paper 1. "Bears in the Wild"

GRADE 4, EXPOSITORY

> Ideas: 5
> Organization: 3
> Voice: 4
> Word Choice: 4
> Fluency: 4
> Conventions: 3

Comments: This paper contains some excellent information: bears are shy, they are threatened by people encroaching on their territory, they eat a variety of food, and they won't really hurt you unless provoked—despite what many people think. Its big problem is organization. Details are presented in fairly random, as-things-occur-to-me fashion, which gives the piece a pleasant conversational tone, but does not make it particularly simple to follow. Two personal stories—seeing the mother bear and cubs by the river and tracking the bear through the woods—are begun, but the writer (frustratingly) never follows through. On the positive side, however, this writer seems to like the topic, and his enthusiasm brings to the piece quite a lot of voice. Fluency is by turns awkward and very strong, making some parts highly readable; a few sentences are long. Conventions need a little work, and we have no idea where this information came from. A bibliography would be helpful.

Paper 2. "Driving Tests Should Be Harder!"

GRADE 7, EXPOSITORY/PERSUASIVE

> Ideas: 4
> Organization: 4
> Voice: 4–5
> Word Choice: 4
> Fluency: 5
> Conventions: 5

Comments: Here's a case where you may find your response to the topic affecting your scores. If you agree with the writer, you may have scored it slightly higher; if you disagreed, perhaps your scores went down a notch. The pluses are many: the voice is strong and sustained, the writer is very aware of his audience, the language is clear and crisp and appropriate for the topic, sentences are varied and readable, and the main idea is clear and supported fairly strongly. Had the writer further explored that intriguing idea of computerized driving tests, the ideas score would have gone up; the problem of how to make the test more rigorous without increasing costs remains only partially resolved. Still, the writer does a fine job of raising many important issues in a short space. This was a self-selected topic. Could you tell?

Paper 3. "Interesting Facts About Smoking"

GRADE 10, EXPOSITORY
>   Ideas: 2
>   Organization: 2
>   Voice: 3
>   Word Choice: 3–4
>   Fluency: 3–4
>   Conventions: 2

Comments: This writer has a lot of information to work with but has not focused or organized it to create a centered paper with an important point. Platitudes (smoking is dangerous; smoking is addictive) are allowed to usurp attention that could be given to more interesting issues (advertising is primarily aimed at young people; tobacco is one of the few drugs that remains legal—why is that?). There is no clear introduction; we have the feeling of having turned on the TV in the middle of the news report. Further, the paper meanders mercilessly, barraging us with facts and forcing us to make our own sense of it. The potential is all here. The writer only needs a strong theme; for example, smoking changes a person's life, or people who begin smoking as teenagers cannot stop. The conclusion suggests—perhaps—what she wanted to say most. Despite the lack of focus, this writer speaks with some conviction, and this forcefulness gives the piece more voice than it otherwise might have. It's also more fluent than it looks; if you do some mental editing and fix the punctuation (her real problem), most sentences are sharp and to the point. Some transitions are awkward (*Though many wish they could but it is not all that simple. Cigarettes are very addictive though.*) Conventions need quite a lot of work, especially considering that the text is so short and simple, and a bibliography would help.

Paper 4. "Humboldt Penguins"

GRADE 9, EXPOSITORY

    Ideas: 5–6

    Organization: 5–6

    Voice: 5–6

    Word Choice: 5–6

    Fluency 5–6

    Conventions: 5–6

Comments: This paper is a fine sample of expository writing at its best: informative, readable, well paced, and organized to help a reader understand and appreciate the subject. It does not attempt to tell all there is to know about penguins but selects some of the most significant and intriguing information. This writer has ably focused on many of the questions we would have had—had we only known enough to ask them. It's interesting to learn, for instance, that penguins do not mind nesting in rocks, that they are affectionate with their young, that they bristle (like humans) when nosy neighbors come too close, that they can launch themselves ferociously at a rude intruder (who knew?), or that they turn into feathered torpedoes in the water. At the end we want to say, "Thanks for sharing so many intriguing tidbits—I learned a lot!" That's the sign of a successful paper. It has fine conventions and a bibliography, too.

Paper 5. "The Middle Ages"

GRADE 8, EXPOSITORY

    Ideas: 3

    Organization: 2

    Voice: 3–4

    Word Choice: 3

    Fluency: 3

    Conventions: 3

Comments: If you already know a lot about the Middle Ages, you might sail right on through this essay, but if you are coming to the topic for the first time, you are likely to find the information skimpy at best: "Next you would become a squire." So? Tell us more. "A brave young squire could not wait to receive the acolade." Meaning? What's an "acolade"? Why could he not wait? "The armour consists of many parts we won't name them all because it would take forever." Name a few—we'll wait.

    There are many unanswered questions: Why did children dream of becoming knights? What was so terrific about it? How old were knights? Did many survive? Could anyone become a knight? Why did they have so little free time? Were the knights always at war? The writer seems to assume that the audience is right there in her social studies class and can therefore fill in the blanks. Moreover, the paper is dominated by knights and chivalry. Is that about all there was to the Middle Ages then—or should the title be changed? We need a setting of time and place, a better balance of details to give us a sense of history, and some little-known information to spark the imagination. The bibliography is short, but at least there is one.

Paper 6. *"Exploring the Theme of Progress in* A Connecticut Yankee at King Arthur's Court*"*

GRADE 10, EXPOSITORY

> Ideas: 5–6
>
> Organization: 4
>
> Voice: 4
>
> Word Choice: 5–6
>
> Sentence Fluency: 5–6
>
> Conventions: 5–6

Comments: This piece makes several interesting points—notably about the seductive nature of power and the fact that, in Twain's world, things are often not what they seem. Twain's Camelot is not the fairy-tale world of legend, nor is Hank Morgan a morally upstanding person. We enjoyed this analysis in particular because it is not essential to have read the book to make sense of what the writer is saying. (Compare the analysis of *To Kill a Mockingbird* in Chapter 3.)

The lead is especially strong, and the writer follows up well on the theme of knowledge being powerful and seductive. The organization becomes a little too mechanical halfway through: "One theme . . . A second theme . . . The third theme . . ." However, the points are clear and well ordered, and the ending is especially strong. The quotation by Atwood allows the writer to raise the question about why Twain plays with time, and though she does not explore the question at length (nor does she cite a source), it is an intriguing way to wrap things up.

The tone is mostly academic, so that the power of the piece comes more from good information than from personal voice. But now and again the writer looks us right in the eye: "The knights in this world ride off to rescue maidens that do not even exist." There's the writer having a bit of fun.

The vocabulary is strong, clear, and to the point. Religions can be "mentally restricting"; Hank is a "vain, self-centered person, capable of manipulating others"; and the people of Camelot are "unscrupulous." This writer chooses words well. The only trait stronger is fluency—which, in our view, is the true strength of the piece. Read through just the sentence beginnings (first four to five words) to see how varied they are. The writer is a little stingy with her quotations, but those she has used, she chose well. The length is good. When she was through, she stopped writing. Well done.

Paper 7. "Ra, The Sun God"

GRADE 12, EXPOSITORY

Ideas: 10 (double-weighted score, with two scores of 5)

Organization: 3–4

Voice: 4–5

Word Choice: 5–6

Sentence Fluency: 4–5

Conventions: 5–6

Comments: This paper has many strengths. First, the writer is dealing with a difficult and technical topic and doing an excellent job of making it understandable and engaging. Her approach is refreshing, unstilted, and energetic.

The information seems sound; at any event, it is presented in a convincing manner. The writer seems to have done her homework. She uses terms like *ozone, triatomic oxygen molecules, ultraviolet rays, chlorofluorocarbons, melanoma,* and so on with knowledge and skill, and makes them understandable in context.

The beginning is especially strong and could have been further exploited had the writer kept the theme of true sun worship right in front of us. It is implied in the dangers of skin cancer and the need for sunscreen, but not directly addressed after that powerful opening. The ending is compelling and made us wish that the plausible realities of living in artificial light or never wandering into the sun might have been explored further.

Our criticisms are petty, but here they are. First, the text is too long. The purpose of the paper is to startle readers into action. The main point (that the hole in the ozone is huge, growing, and will not begin healing for fifteen years even if we stop polluting our atmosphere *right now*) could be made more forcefully if it were made more concisely. Second, though we appreciate the occasional welcome relief from statistical information, we would like to get all the facts and figures out of the way right up front, then settle in to a more expanded discussion of how all this affects us personally. Will we really age faster? Can *any* sunscreen protect us or our children? Should we just stay off the beach right now? Move to the rain forest? How come trees don't help (we thought we were safe in the shade)?

To the writer's credit, though, she piqued our curiosity. She would have frightened us, too, had we not already been frightened earlier by other warnings about the sun. (A bibliography was included with the original but was not available at the time of this printing. We have not scored down for that.)

Paper 8. "Challenger (Doublespeak)"

GRADE 12, ANALYTICAL/EXPOSITORY

    Ideas: 5–6

    Organization: 5

    Voice: 5–6

    Word Choice: 5

    Sentence Fluency: 6

    Conventions: 5

Comments: This well-researched piece has the ring of authenticity combined with a good definition (and examples) of doublespeak. The voice is particularly strong (though compare the writer's own analysis of her voice at the end of this section). It has conviction; that is often the source of voice in informational writing. It's a no-nonsense, brook-no-doublespeak sort of voice, with just enough attitude to keep the paper focused and forceful. The language reflects an inside-out understanding of the topic that comes from good research and thoughtful analysis, yet it's never overly technical. This writer knows her stuff, and so does not need to snow us with forced language; her knowledge is enough to impress. The writing is strong, stylish, and free of filler. It goes right to the heart of things: "When people are faced with difficult decisions accompanied by stiff penalties for a mistake, no one wants to assume control." Direct, outspoken, clear, and compelling—it's all this and edited well, too. Fluency is powerful; notice the wide range of sentence beginnings and lengths—smooth as a running river.

9. "Decision"

GRADE 12, EXPOSITORY/NARRATIVE

    Ideas: 5–6

    Organization: 5

    Voice: 5–6

    Word Choice: 5–6

    Sentence Fluency: 5

    Conventions: 5–6

Comments: This is an extraordinary piece of writing. We were particularly struck by the powerful opening, in which the writer uses the metaphor of the fireworks and "long fuse" to introduce the topic of AIDS and her delayed but strong connection. The organization is masterful. From the images of the tall ships, to an "intellectual awareness," emotional connection, and, finally, commitment. It doesn't get much better than this. The ideas are clearly strong, the voice remarkable. But word choice is where this piece really shines. We read it three or four times to appreciate how excellent it truly is: "the tall ships sailing into New York harbor, the stream of people converging on the city . . . the spark that would ignite the long fuse . . . facilitated fatal bouts . . . as myopic as it may sound . . . small town feeling of security . . . cruel, systematic consumption . . . robbing our society of the people who recorded its culture . . . not just some sterile statistic." It's graceful and highly individual. Fluency is strong, though could be improved with repositioning of a few "I's." The paper is a fine piece also for demonstrating what all writers know instinctively: The best writing combines many modes and forms. It's part narrative, part expository or persuasive, part reflective or descriptive. This piece gains much of its force from combining so many forms so well.

ADAPTING THE GUIDE FOR NATIVE SPANISH SPEAKERS

We hope eventually to have the six-trait scoring guide translated into several languages. As a first step, with the help of several colleagues, we can make available a version in Spanish. We hope it will be useful to Spanish-speaking students who write in English but would like a Spanish translation of the English criteria to guide their writing and revision.

We ask that in using this guide you recognize that even though it is translated into Spanish, it continues to reflect many of the nuances of idea development, organization, expression of voice, choice of words, fluent speech, and conventions particular to American culture. We fully recognize that what is valued by native speakers of other languages or by other cultures is likely to look a little different. For instance, Americans tend to favor economical organization and direct, systematic presentation of ideas. In another culture, a less direct presentation might be considered more appropriate—perhaps more entertaining, or even more sensitive or polite. In short, this translation serves only as an example. You may wish to revise the wording or emphasis for students who write in Spanish. Perhaps having this example will motivate some of you to begin translations into other languages, too!

GUÍA DE CALIFICACIÓN PARA LOS ESTUDIANTES ESCRITORES

Ideas y contenido

5. Mi trabajo está claro, con enfoque y abunda en detalles importantes.

- Puedes ver que sé mucho sobre este tema.
- El texto está lleno de detalles interesantes que llaman la atención.
- Puedo resumir el tema de mi trabajo en una oración clara y simple:___.
- Cuando empieces a leer no querrás parar.
- Puedes imaginarte sobre lo que estoy hablando. No cuento las cosas que suceden, las muestro.

3. Aunque mi texto atrae tu atención, aquí y allá podría utilizar algunos detalles picantes.

- Sé lo suficiente para escribir sobre este tema, pero más información me ayudaría a hacerlo más interesante.
- Algunos "detalles" son cosas que la mayoría de la gente probablemente ya sabe.
- Mi tema es demasiado amplio. Quiero decir demasiado. O quizás sea superficial.
- En algunas partes podría resultar difícil imaginar de lo que estoy hablando.
- Me temo que mis lectores puedan aburrirse e irse a invadir la nevera.

1. Simplemente estoy pensando en lo que quiero decir.

- Necesito mucha más información antes de que esté realmente listo para escribir.
- Todavía estoy pensando en el trabajo, buscando una idea.
- No estoy seguro de que alguien que lea esto pueda imaginarse algo.
- ¡No estoy siquiera seguro de que esté listo para que lo lea alguien más!
- ¿Podría resumirlo en una oración clara? ¡De ninguna manera! Aún no estoy listo para eso.

Organización

5. Mi trabajo es tan claro como un buen mapa de carreteras. Toma a los lectores de la mano y los guía en todo momento.

- El inicio da una pista de lo que sigue y hace que se quiera seguir leyendo.
- Cada detalle está justo en el lugar donde le corresponde.
- Nada parece estar fuera de lugar.
- Nunca te sientes perdido o confuso; sin embargo, podría haber una o dos sorpresas.
- Todo conduce a mi idea más importante o al suceso principal de mi historia.
- Mi trabajo termina en el punto justo y te deja pensando.

3. Puedes empezar a ver hacia dónde voy. Si prestas atención, no tendrás ningún problema en seguir.

- Ya tengo un inicio. Pero, ¿atraerá por completo a mi lector?
- La mayoría de las cosas están bien donde las he puesto. Aunque tal vez podría cambiar de lugar algunas.
- Por lo general puedes ver que una idea se enlaza con otra.
- Supongo que todo debería llevar a la parte más importante. Veamos dónde sería eso.
- Mi trabajo tiene un final. ¿Pero, resulta coherente para el lector?

1. ¿A dónde vamos? Yo mismo estoy perdido.

- ¿Un principio? Bueno, podría simplemente haber repetido la tarea.
- Nunca supe qué decir luego, por eso escribi lo primero que me vino a la mente.
- No estoy realmente seguro qué incluir, o en qué orden ponerlo.
- Todo está apilado—¡casi como si se fuera un viejo ropero!
- ¿Un final? Simplemente terminé cuando no tenía más qué decir.

Voz

5. He puesto en este trabajo mi sello personal e inconfundible.

- Puedes oír retumbar mi voz por todas partes. Se sabe que éste soy yo.
- Me interesa el tema—y lo muestro.
- Me dirijo directamente a mi audiencia, siempre pensando en las preguntas que pudieran tener.
- La confianza reluce en el texto.
- Escribí para satisfacerme a mí mismo.

3. Lo que realmente pienso y siento a veces aparece.

- Tal vez no rías ni llores cuando leas esto, pero tampoco dejarás de leer.
- Estoy a punto de encontrar mi propia voz.
- Mi personalidad asoma aquí y allá. Podrías adivinar que éste es mi escrito.
- No pensé en mi audiencia todo el tiempo. ¡A veces escribía para teminar como fuera!

1. No puse demasiada energía o personalidad en este escrito.

- Podría resultar difícil saber quién escribió esto. No creo que mucha gente reconozca que es mío.
- Controlé mis sentimientos.
- Sí, este tema me gustara o si supiera más sobre él, podría darle mayor vida.
- ¿La audiencia? ¿Qué audiencia?

Elegir las palabras

5. Elegí las palabras correctas para expresar mis ideas y sentimientos.

- Las palabras y frases que he usado parecen estar correctas.
- Mis frases son vivas y alegres, sin exagerar.
- Usé de manera orginal algunas de las palabras mas usuales. Espera algunas sorpresas.
- ¿Tienes una o dos frases favoritas aquí? Yo sí.
- Cada palabra es precisa. No tendrás que preguntarte qué quiero decir.
- Los verbos llevan el significado. No cargo a mi lector con demasiados adjetivos.

3. Puede que no encienda la chispa de tu imaginación, pero mira, ¡transmite el significado básico!

- Es funcional y logra el objetivo, pero sinceramente no puedo decir que fui lejos.
- OK, así que hay algunos clichés escondidos en los rincones.
- Tengo una frase favorita que aparece por aquí en alguna parte.
- ¿Verbos? ¿Qué tienen de malo los viejos y buenos *es, son, era, eran . . .* ?
- Tal vez he utilizado demasiado la funcionalidad de mi *thesaurus*.
- Pero, ¿puedes entenderlo, verdad? En realidad no hay nada *incorrecto*.

1. Es probable que mi lector pregunte, "¿cómo?"

- ¡Ve! Soy víctima de un vocabulario impreciso y de frases poco claras.
- Es muy difícil entender de lo que estoy hablando. Ni yo mismo sé qué quise decir, y yo mismo lo escribí.
- Tal vez usé mal una o dos palabras.
- Algunas frases redundantes podrían ser redundantes.
- Necesito la fuerza del verbo.

La Fluidez de las oraciones

5. Mis oraciones son claras y variadas—es un placer leerlas en voz alta.

- ¡Vamos!, léelo con sentimiento. No necesitarás ensayar.
- Por el uso de oraciones variadas me distinga.
- ¿Oyes el ritmo?
- Se ha quitado todo lo que no era necesario. Cada palabra cuenta.

3. Mis oraciones son claras y legibles.

- Mi escrito fluye de forma natural, puedes leerlo sin problema.
- Algunas oraciones deberían unirse. Otras deberían separarse en dos.
- Hay algunas cosas que sobran, seguro, pero no cubren con verborrea las buenas ideas . . . , aunque debo admitir que no vendría mal suprimir algunas palabras innecesarias aquí y allá y recortar algunas cosas.
- Creo que en el inicio de las oraciones incurrí en una rutina. Supongo que podría usar más variedad. Algunas veces inicio las oraciones de forma diferente.

1. Debo admitir que leer en voz alta es un reto (incluso para mí).

- Tal vez tengas que detenerte de vez en cuando y releer; da la sensación de que una oración está correcta y en el medio de otra empieza una oración nueva y, caramba, estoy perdido . . . No puedo sacarle el sentido a esto.
- ¡Ojalá hubiera suprimido algunas partes por completo!
- Tantas oraciones que empiezan de la misma forma. Mis oraciones son similares. Necesitan variedad y más pulido.
- Algunas oraciones están cortas. Demasiado cortas. Realmente están muy cortas. Cortas. C-o-r-t-a-s. ¿Entiendes? Muy bien.
- Es como intentar patinar sobre cartón. ¡Que difícil!

Convenciones

5. Cometí tan pocos errores, que un editor se aburriría buscándoles.

- Todas las mayúsculas están en el lugar que les corresponde.
- Los párrafos empiezan en los lugares adecuados.
- La puntuación es genial—la gramática también.
- Mi ortografía le asombrará (incluso la de palabras complicadas y abstrusas).
- Un editor no tendrá mucho que hacer en este trabajo.

3. Algunos errores molestos aparecen cuando leo con cuidado.

- La ortografía de las palabras sencillas está correcta.
- La mayoría de las mayúsculas están correctas. aunque tal vez debería volverlo a revisor.
- Puede ser que la gramática sea un poco informal, pero es válida para lo mas cotidiano de cada dia.
- Algunos pronombres no coinciden con el nombre al que sustituyen.
- Podrías tropezar con mi puntuación! innovadora.
- Se lee como si realmente fuera el primer borrador.
- Definitivamente necesito editarlo un poco antes de tenerlo listo para publicar.

1. Es mejor leerlo primero para descifrarlo y luego otra vez para entenderlo.

- Muchos errares acen difici! la letura.
- he olvidado poner algunas MAYÚSCULAS—otraS no son Necesarias.
- Buscar con cuydado los herrores de otografia.
- A decir verdad, no pasé mucho tiempo editándolo.
- Creo que tendré que apurarme si quiero que esté listo para publicarlo.

REFLECTING ON CHAPTER 10

1. How many of the model papers in this section seem to combine more than one mode or form of writing? Do you think combining modes strengthens writing? How should a multimode paper be scored in a district or state assessment?

2. In this chapter, you have had an opportunity to examine several forms of criteria: a simple checklist, simplified scoring scales, and a very detailed scoring scale for informational writing. What are the particular advantages or disadvantages of each? Which do you think students would prefer? Which would you be more likely to use in your classroom?

3. If we use a simplified scoring scale, do we lose some valuable information? Why or why not?

4. What are your thoughts at this point regarding a 5-point scale versus a 6-point scale? What advantages might each offer? Can a scale become too small—say a 4-point, 3-point or 2-point scale? Would these work? Why or why not?

ACTIVITIES

1. With your colleagues or your students, develop a scoring guide for a particular mode of writing: persuasive, expository, technical, business.

2. Test your scoring guide by trying it out on at least three samples. What did you learn from your trial? What modifications does your scoring guide need to be truly useful? Did you construct a 4-, 5- or 6-point scale? Why?

LOOKING AHEAD

In Chapter 11 we examine the world of primary writing—and provide some simplified scoring scales you can use with very young writers.

MEMORABLE MOMENTS FROM STUDENTS' WRITING

- My mother tries to execute my curiosity.
- I got stuck in narrative and couldn't write. I'm pushing on to imaginary.
- I'm just an 8-year-old kid. I'm no James Joyce. Give me a break.
- I was 7, wild, and pizza-crazed.
- Fear raced up my spine and when it reached my throat, I screamed.
- We didn't like girls back then. We were more into GI Joe, Tonka trucks, and frogs.

11

THE WORLD OF BEGINNING WRITERS

Children can write sooner than we ever dreamed possible. Most children come to school knowing a handful of letters, and with these they can write labels and calendars, letters and stories, poem and songs. They will learn to write by writing and by living with a sense of "I am one who writes."

Lucy McCormick Calkins (1994, 83)

If you don't have clear expectations, how can your children know what to aim for? If you don't have the highest expectations, how do you know you're not underestimating what your students can do?

Mem Fox (1993)

At primary level, writing is wondrous and magical. It comes in many forms: sketches, scribbles, dictated stories, recordings, word play, "tadpole people" (mostly head, tiny arms and legs), pictographs—and conventional text. Sometimes text goes left to right on the page as we have been conditioned to expect, but primary writers, not yet bound by convention, find their own inventive ways to fill the page: right to left, bottom to top, around in a spiral—or clean off the page and on to adventure.

The writing of the very young reflects both their creative individuality and an uncanny ability to observe, recall, and use the conventions from the print that fills their world. At this age, there are no "errors" in the true sense, any more than beginning walkers make errors in foot placement. Rather, there are hundreds, thousands, of experiments by beginning writers finding their own paths to learning.

Many times children don't realize they can write. An effective writing teacher leads kids to an understanding of the four structures needed for early-childhood writing . . . . Are dictation, scribbling, drawing, and temporary spelling necessary to early writing development? Yes.

Bea Johnson (1999, 42)

TEACHING OURSELVES WHAT TO LOOK FOR

We know that primary writing looks very different from that of older writers. But like impatient parents, we watch for paragraphs to emerge, for the first use of quotation marks, for complete sentences and correct spelling. These things excite us and make us feel successful as teachers. We forget sometimes that there is much to celebrate long before these milestones of sophisticated writing ever appear.

Consider the very early piece of writing shown in Figure 11.1, in picture form, by four-year-old Nikki. What we see here may not be conventional writing, but it is remarkably expressive. Notice the expression on the face of the bat: humorous, mischievous—that's voice. How many writer-artists of this age have noticed that spiders have eight legs and multiple eyes? Notice the toes of the bat, too, and the hollow ears. This is a young writer-artist who takes more than a passing glance at the world around her. As a result, her work is brimming with detail—that's ideas. This picture also has a great sense of balance, not only in the proportions between spider and bat but in the placement on the page as well. This sense of format and layout is one early form of organization.

Another sample of writing—by a slightly older writer, Hannah, at the beginning of her first-grade year—is shown in Figure 11.2. It seems a simple enough idea—"I like my mom." But in fact it has quite a bit of complexity, which would be a good thing to point out to Hannah: "You told me just why you love your mom so much. She reads to you and she's funny. Those are great details."

Notice the line: "She means a lot to me." Her words and the tone say, "I really mean it. This is important to me." Now we can say, "I hear your feelings

FIGURE 11.1. "Bat and Spider"

FIGURE 11.2. "I Like My Mom"

coming through in this line. You made me feel it, too. There's a word for that. We call it voice. I think your writing has voice."

Consider conventions in this piece, too. Remember for a moment that all conventions, even the simplest and most taken-for-granted things, must be learned. What do you see? Left-to-right orientation on the page, top-to-bottom orientation as well, spaces between words. It seems so basic, but it is not automatic, nor is it necessarily simple to learn. This writer is also beginning to distinguish between capital and lowercase letters—and even uses them correctly in most places. But what if she did not? Remember, just *discovering* the difference is a step. Correct placement is a more sophisticated skill.

The same goes for punctuation. Look at the size of that period! It is important to this writer, without question. What does a period signify in her mind? Perhaps "Stop. I have just said something important. Please think about it." The spelling is highly readable—a realistic and worthy goal for primary writers. Conventionally correct spelling usually comes with more observation—though this young writer's spelling is remarkably accurate.

HELPING WRITERS SEE THEIR STRENGTHS

How do we help our young writers see what is strong within their work so they can build on those strengths? First, we must teach *ourselves* to see what each writer is doing correctly across all dimensions of writing—not the gaps, not what's missing, not what she is not doing yet, but what is *there*. Then, we must point it out to them: "Hannah, I notice you are leaving spaces between your words. That made it so easy to read. Thanks!" or, "Did you know I could read every word in your paper? I didn't have to guess once," or, "I see you've discovered periods. Great! Tell me about periods and how you know just when to use them."

Gentle, gradual encouragement is among the most effective of all teaching strategies. We have more or less abandoned this approach in much of our formal instruction, but most of us, if we think about it, instinctively

Stressing neatness instead of content is an ever-present danger. Many of us were carefully taught the opposite during our school days. But especially in early childhood, all attempts at writing should be celebrated rather than corrected!

Bea Johnson (1999, 33)

know the power of a teacher who believes absolutely in our capability. Picture a father cheering on his eleven-month-old daughter as she learns to walk. "That's it! Come on! One more step. You can do it! Yes! Good! Move your feet—that's it. Come on—I'll catch you! You can do it!" We need this image in our heads as we teach writing. We need to notice the little things (not just the big milestones) and put them to work to encourage our young writers, who are often doing much more than they get credit for.

The father in our scenario knows that correctness is a goal for later; exploration is the right goal for now. How surprised we would be to hear him say, "*No*, Martha, not *toe* first—*heel* first, remember? Do it the way I showed you. No, I really can't call that walking, not *real* walking. It's just kind of stumbling along. I'm afraid I can't give you credit for that. Oops, you fell—well, five points off." Sound ridiculous? How much more ridiculous is it than setting our expectations for young writers too high too soon?

HOW TRAITS LOOK EARLY ON

Keep in mind that such things as voice, vocabulary growth, fluency, or expression of ideas show up in oral storytelling and in picture writing long before students begin to produce conventional text. So we must learn to *listen* for the traits even before we see them printed on a page. Next, we must learn to look for hints of the traits in even the earliest text, including pictures—then in letter play, letter strings, word strings and finally—oh, joy—that first full sentence. Here are just a few things you might look and listen for in young writers' work—and in their responses to literature, too:

IDEAS

Little close-up details: veins in leaves, wings and legs on insects, expressive faces

Signs of movement (e.g., a person or animal running)

Multiple pictures that tell a more complex story

Any message—no matter how delivered—that makes sense to you, the reader

Ability to retell a story (here, the child is making the meaning)

Ability to recognize another writer's point or message

ORGANIZATION

Balance on the page—good use of white space

Balance within pictures: proportion, sizing, two sides that match

Use of a title (an early form of a beginning)

> It's been a good thing that babies don't understand the concept of "clumsiness" or else they'd never learn to walk.
>
> Alan Ziegler (1981)

> When children can sit down and put their thoughts on paper quickly and easily, they are fluent writers *even if they make errors*. If the teacher is always correcting the students' spelling and punctuation errors, the children will stop guessing and trying. This will lead to dull writing with students afraid to use words they can't spell.
>
> Bea Johnson (1999, 33)

> As a society, we allow children to learn to speak by trial and error. But when it comes to reading and writing, we expect them to be right the first time.
>
> Donald Graves and Virginia Stuart (1987)

Coordination of text with illustrations

Layout that works and that's pleasing to the eye

More than one detail or events put in order (e.g., through multiple pictures)

Ability to predict events in a story (grasping the concept of organization)

Ability to see how a picture and text go together (e.g., What extra information does the picture give you?)

Ability to choose one beginning or ending over another

Ability to group "like" things (by shape, color, size, etc.)

Use of "The End," often the earliest form of a conclusion

VOICE

Originality and expressiveness—in color, shape, style, choice of images, choice of labels, choice of topics

Expressiveness and emotion—what do you see on characters' faces?

An image, a moment, an idea that makes you *feel* something

Love of life, love of writing/drawing

Enthusiasm, exuberance

Playfulness

Ownership (you can tell it belongs to *this* child, and no other)

Pleasure in hearing strong voice in the writing of others

WORD CHOICE

Use of *words!* (They might be single letters, letter combinations or letter strings at first, but in the young writer's mind, these are words)

Words that show action, energy, or movement (expressed orally or in writing)

Words that describe

Words that convey feelings

A passion, a love, for new, unusual, or fun-to-say words

Words that stretch *beyond* the child's spelling capabilities

Words that help you see, feel, understand

Expressed curiosity about new words

SENTENCE FLUENCY

Letter strings that translate into sentences

Word grouping that imitates sentence patterns

Sentence sense (an ear for what a sentence is)

That first whole, complete sentence!

Use of multiple sentences

Two or more sentences with even *slightly* different beginnings

A knack for putting words together in pleasing patterns

A willingness to try new sentence forms—breaking out of patterns into variety (Compare *"I like my dog. I like my cat. I like school,"* with *"I like cats and dogs. But I do love my cat the most. Do you like school? Me too."*)

CONVENTIONS

Left-to-right orientation

Top-to-bottom orientation

Spaces between words or lines

Association of letters with sounds

Letters that appear upright on the page

Letters that face the right direction

Readable spelling

Use of punctuation (whether placed correctly or not)

Distinction between capitals and lowercase (whether used correctly or not)

Use of end punctuation

Use of a title

Awareness of margins

Use of *I (capitalized)*

Ability to spell own name

Interest in environmental print

Any of these lists can—and should—be expanded as you notice other features of young children's writing. Keep track. Reward each step by noticing how far young writers have come.

IDEAS FOR TEACHING TRAITS TO BEGINNERS

Here are ten general ideas for teaching traits to beginning writers.

Idea 1: Don't Worry About Numbers—Yet

Wait a minute, you're saying. I *have* to worry about numbers because I have to worry about grades. Fair enough. We'll get to that level of assessment in Chapter 12—assessment for you, for parents, and for your school or district. For now, let's talk about communicating with the most important audience for assessment: students.

The key to good assessment that communicates *to young students* is observing signs of growth and change—not putting numbers on their performances. (Plenty of time for that beginning in third or fourth grade.) For younger writers, describe what you see, as clearly as you can, using language that makes sense to them, but do not worry about whether it's a 2 or 3 or 4—or for that matter an A, B or C or an E (excellent) or N (needs work). Numbers are most effectively used with students who can begin to understand the meaning *behind* those numbers. If we say to a primary writer, "Well, Bill, this piece of writing is about a 3 in ideas, but we're going to work on getting you up to a 4 or 5," we can't expect this to be anything but gibberish to Bill. It makes much more sense to say, "Bill, a while ago I had trouble sometimes reading your work without your help. But now I am recognizing some letters, and even some words. I can understand your writing even when you're not there to read it to me. This is *so* exciting."

Consider Jack's paper (Figure 11.3) on his dog. Don't think about numbers as you look at it. Instead, ask yourself, What do I see here? What do I hear? What are the little early signs of *ideas* and *voice*?

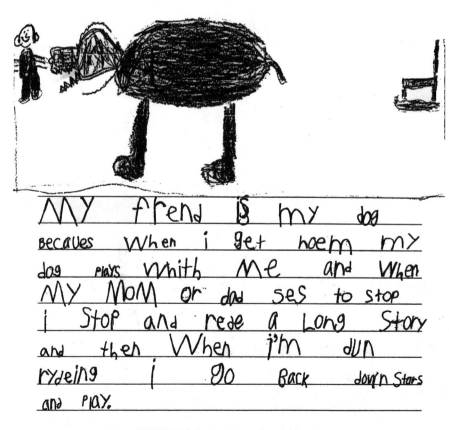

MY frend IS my dog
BeCaues When i get hoem my
dog plays whith Me and When
MY MoM or dad ses to stop
i Stop and rede a Long Story
and then When i'm dUn
rydeing i go Back down Stars
and play.

FIGURE 11.3. "My Friend Is My Dog"

To begin with, consider the choice of topic: a dog who's a loyal friend—someone to share good times with. That's a nice beginning. Then notice the amount of detail this young writer manages to weave into this very short piece: he looks forward to seeing his dog when he comes home; when things get too rough, mom or dad suggests a story time; then the play resumes! That's a lot to tell in a few lines, and it gives us a clear picture. The illustration has great character (notice the size of the dog, who's important and powerful)—which is simply a form of voice. Jack looks happy, too, don't you think?

Kean's piece (Figure 11.4, grade 1) is highly audience-oriented. It has a sincere, heartfelt tone ("I relly like Sam"). Both "very" and "really" are early ways of injecting voice. But even better is Kean's willingness to share a secret. Psst—come closer: "I ustu bit his finggers." Direct connection to an audience is the very foundation of voice.

Lincoln, also a first grader, writes very lovingly of his brother Nick (Figure 11.5). "He plays a lot if hes not bisey." We have to be delighted with this line, imagining Nick making time for Lincoln, and noting how much Lincoln appreciates it. He generously refers to him as the "faveis" [favoritist]. But the last line is best of all: "His kindnis gits biger avre day." Wouldn't you love to have a friend say that about you? We need to tell Lincoln just that.

In Figure 11.6, Michael, grade 1, writes of his great grandfather, who fought in World War I. This piece shows great fluency through expanded writing, and much attention to detail: Great Grandfather is 101 years old! He's kind to all, and "play's carfly with" Michael—a beautiful image. Nice sentence rhythm at the end: "He is about seven feat. that's tall." That's voice, too. Notice the size of the period at the end—that's all he's going to

FIGURE 11.4. "Sam Is My Friend"

My faverit brauther is nick   he

hase bene the faveist in the female.

He plays a lot if hes not bisey. His

kindnis gits biger avre day.

FIGURE 11.5. "My Favorite Brother Is Nick"

write for now. This young writer is very aware of conventions; his inventive (temporary) spelling is excellent, capturing virtually all important sounds. He has spacing between words, complete sentences, and numerous apostrophes—many placed correctly, some experimental. He is learning. Look at those capital "I's." So much for a young editor to take pride in here. What do you suppose will happen to his work if we comment only on those things he does correctly?

Jimmy, in grade 2, has an advantage: he is composing on a word processor. And as the example in Figure 11.7 shows, the relative ease and playfulness of this method of writing encourages him to write more and to experiment with conventions. Jimmy had a small amount of editing help. Remarkably, though, much of the editing is his own. Although he needs some help tying

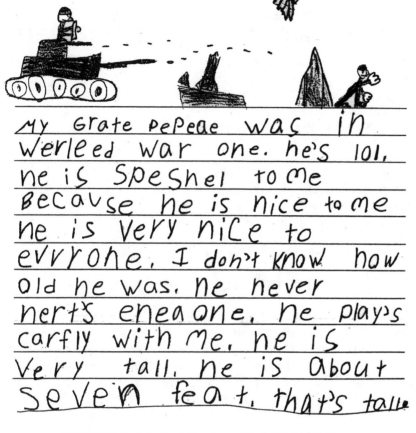

My Grate PePeae was in
werleed war one. he's 101,
ne is speshel to me
Because he is nice to me
ne is very niCe to
evvrone. I don't know how
old he was. ne never
nerts eneaone. ne play's
carfly with me. ne is
very tall. ne is about
Seven feat. that's tall.

FIGURE 11.6. "My Great Grandpapa Was in World War I"

ideas together (which will undoubtedly come with practice), the length and complexity of this text are impressive. He has given some thought to time machines and the perils of actually using one: you might just find yourself back with *T. rex.* Notice the word choice, too: "strange object . . . dials and gadgets . . . The next second . . . a magical lizard . . . offered . . . deal with."

Nicholas is a confident first-grade writer, and his confidence fills his writing (Figure 11.8) with voice. He uses his experience masterfully to fill his paper about the library with rich and personal details. This is not on-the-surface writing. We get right inside Nicholas's head. What a treat it is when a young writer shares so much of his thoughts and feelings!

To appreciate the amazingly sophisticated sentence fluency of this piece, read it aloud. How many different ways does this writer find to begin? Does he hear a strong sense of rhythm? You bet. "When I go . . . First I'm greeted . . . Then, it's up to me . . . Luckily, she is patient." This is beautiful writing—and quite remarkable from a first grader. We cannot

As Tim got up, he saw a strange object under his bed.

It was covered with buttons, dials and gadgets of all shapes and colors.

He turned the biggest dial to number 7.

The next second he was 3000 years later in the future. He put his card inn the slot, and Tim knew that the machine wouldn't give it back until tomorrow.

Tim heard a voice. He saw a lizard standing in front of him. "Good day!" he said.

It was a magical lizard.

"I just ate something," it said. "Would you like a dish?" "No", he said.

"I should get my card and gift by tomorrow."

The lizard offered Tim a nice warm place to sleep.

The next day he got them. He said, "let's find the time machine!"

But he could not find it. He needed help.

He took away some branches, and suddenly he found it!

He turned it on. He went to the past. He saw cave men. He was with dinosaurs. "A T-rex! AAAAAAAAAAA!"

He quickly turned on the time machine. He was home.

"Hi, Mom hi Dad."

I'm not going to deal with strange machines ever again.

FIGURE 11.7. Jimmy's Word-Processed Composition

expect all first graders will attain this level of skill and grace. Nicholas writes with some ease, and has begun experimenting with a wide range of conventions, including paragraphing, hyphens, dashes, commas, apostrophes and exclamation points. How very much of the conventional world his young writer's eyes have taken in. Not all first graders yet have this repertoire of skills from which to draw, but we can enrich their worlds with samples of good writing, and we can read to them often with care and expression. We might surprise ourselves with how far we can take them.

Jocelyn shows wonderful fluency for a young writer in an expanded story of a cat and dog on a shopping trip. Look for the moments of voice in Figure 11.9. It may remind you of some of your own shopping adventures! In addition, this particular piece shows remarkable control of many conventions and excellent experimenting with inventive (aka, temporary) spelling. Notice the ellipses (ate them in the store . . . then called a taxi), as well as the quotation marks and exclamation points ('this is disgusting!!!'). The inventive spelling shows a sharp ear for sound: *seriel, grocry* (this is how most of us actually pronounce it), *cupbord, somthing.* In addition, many words are spelled with conventional accuracy: *taxi, disgusting, opened, melted, jokes, uncles, shopping*—not to mention *ice cream sandwiches* (did she look at the label on this one?). The ending is wonderful, with the cat and dog doing what most of us do at the end of a long shopping day—swapping stories till they grow punchy.

Some of the best writing is spontaneous. One example appears in Figure 11.10, a notice one of the students wrote on the chalkboard one day

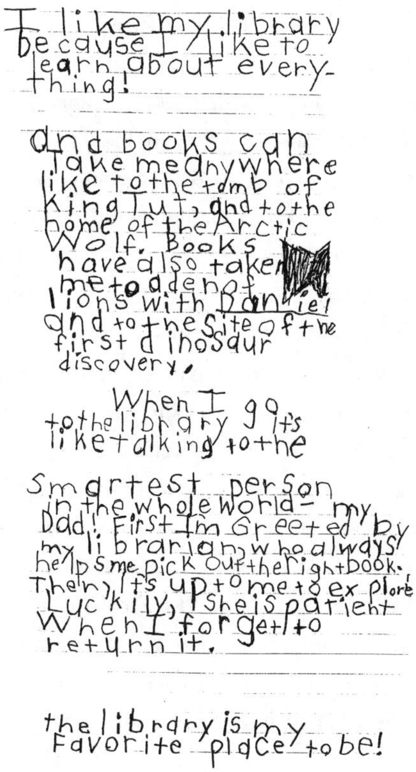

I like my library because I like to learn about every-thing!

and books can Take me anywhere like to the tomb of King Tut, and to the home of the Arctic Wolf. Books have also taken me to the hot lions with Daniel and to the Site of the first dinosaur discovery.

When I go to the library it's like talking to the

Smartest person in the whole world— my Dad! First Im Greeted by my librarian, who always helps me pick out the right book. Then, it's up to me to explore Luckily, she is patient When I forget to return it.

the library is my Favorite place to be!

FIGURE 11.8. "I Like My Library"

when I was visiting a second grade class. They were studying beetles, and one escaped, prompting a class-wide search. This child seized the writing moment, as you see.

In Figure 11.11, we see an extended, very voicy reflection by Megan, grade 3. This is a fascinating piece. First, ask yourself, What does it mean to be old—in the eyes of a young child? Perspective is everything. When my six-year-old best friend's brother turned 20, we thought it was all over; he was no longer one of "us." By comparison, Megan is quite mature in her thinking, but notice the power of numbers; as soon as she puts a figure with her definition, she is afraid she's offended *someone.* Suppose her reader meets her definition of "old"? And the remainder of the paper is spent comforting, reassuring the audience that it is OK, it is all right, you're a kid: "Say it kid, kid Ok maybe not a kid but like a teenager." Whew. That's a relief.

Leah, a second grader (Figure 11.12), is inspired to write to the Tooth Fairy when her tooth is lost and she's concerned about the consequences. Letters, as noted earlier, are a powerful means for developing voice—as this one clearly illustrates. Like any good business letter, it comes right to

Catdog Shopping

One day my cat and my dog were hungrey so they
went to the cup bord to get somthing to eat but
there was no cat or dog food in the cupbord and so
they wint to the catdog shopping mall. They went to
the grocry store and first they went to ial 8 and
they looked at all the catfood and dogfood and they
said "this is disgusting!!!" so they went to ial 4 to get
some sereil but all of the boxes of seriel were opened
so they could not buy any seriel, and so they went
to ial number 1 for ice cream sandwiches. they put
the ice cream sandwiches in ther cart but the ice
cream sandwiches melted and so they went back to
ial 1 and got more ice cream sandwiches and they ate
them in the store . . . then they called a taxi and on
the way home they told jokes about their mothrs and
uncles and the dog laffed so hard he fell off the seat
and then they were home and they went in the
house.

Jocelyn, Grade 1

FIGURE 11.9. "Catdog Shopping"

the point, too. Notice in particular the postscript; Leah seems to reflect that it may not be a wise move to lie to the Tooth Fairy—best to come clean with the whole story.

Perspective is the foundation for "Jamey The Cat" (Figure 11.13), too. Second grader Veronica has had some help with her editing, but has also done much of it herself, via computer, and it is work to be proud of. Even more

Beetle on the lose! Alis Marty. If you find,
call Emily or Kelsey.

(Beetle on the loose. Alias Marty. If you find, call Emily or Kelsey.)

Grade 2

FIGURE 11.10. "Beetle on the lose!"

OLD

I think you get old when you are 60. If you are 60 it is ok because it is fine you you should be happy about it. You will probably get married and you will have grand kids. Or maybe even kids your self. Love your family and friends and grand kids. Don't think you are too old for any thing. Be happy and cheerful and go to church every Sunday. Take vacations and get a job probably. So don't be scared of beining old. Well I'am not scared of being old but maybe you are. Like I was saying, old is not bad and it doesn't mean any thing bad either I'am 8 and I'am not scare of bein 10 but kind of scared about being 60. I can't stop saying old is not BAD! Actually you should be proud of being old. Think of your self as a kid. Say it kid, kid. Ok maybe not a kid but like a teenager. You're a teenager not old.

OLD

By: Megan

FIGURE 11.11. "OLD"

impressive, though, is her take on point of view. Her teacher, an artist, has told the class how different the world can look, depending on who you are and where you are. Veronica's understanding of this concept is quite profound, as she adopts the role of a cat who is loving, yet a little resentful that her friend Sarah gets all the fun; revenge is afoot—a most sophisticated and subtle ending.

When a piece is as clean as Veronica's, it is easy to see the ideas, the voice, and the organizational structure. When conventions are less under control, we need to look a little harder, but it is worth it, for so often, the ideas are there, waiting to be discovered, like violets in the shade. Tiffany (Figure 11.14) imagines herself as a beautiful gift: a wedding dress—with matching "tights." The voice in this piece truly shines. You can hear Tiffany's sense of joy and wonder as she envisions the pageantry—and the romance of marrying "her feansas tucsitow." It takes patience at times to read primary writing—but look what we'd miss if we did not take the time.

Tony, a special education fourth grader (Figure 11.15), has an abundance of information to share on his new baby sister, Sarah. His word choice is excellent: She "gurgles" and "scrunches her face up and looks as cute as Mrs. Stenson does when she sings." That is truly vivid imagery. If we focus on this part—and less on Tony's spelling—we give him a reason to make the conventions stronger. The message must be, "Your writing spoke to me." When Baby Sarah "screms" or grabs Tony's finger and "squs et so tite," we feel that squeeze, too; that's clarity, word choice, and voice. If we tell Tony

Dear Tooth Fairy,

I don't have a tooth right now because
my dog ate my tooth.

So my point is, I lost my tooth, my
dog ate it, so do still get money?

Your still beliver,

Leah

P.S. I don't know if my dog really ate it
but I really lost it.

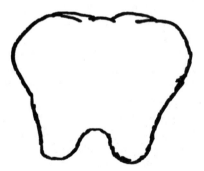

FIGURE 11.12. "Dear Tooth Fairy"

his spelling needs work, we waste our breath telling him the one thing he
already knows. On the other hand, Tony is a strong writer in *everything but*
conventions—only maybe he doesn't suspect. Wouldn't it be a shame if we
did not share this information?

Andrew's work shows how much can happen even with writers who are
just entering the sentence stage—and who are often more comfortable with
single words. In Figure 11.16, Andrew (a kindergartner) tries his hand at a full

"Jamey The Cat"

My name is Jamey. I am a cat. I like this window sill. I can see a lot from here. Sarah is outside. She is having a picnic with a friend. I love Sarah. I love outside. But I can't go outside now. I've been fixed. That means I can't have kittens anymore. I didn't want kittens anyway. They are a lot of hard work. My nails were pulled out too. If I go outside I will get clawed till I die. So I don't go outside. I'd like to, but I don't. I love Sarah, but I want to picnic too. When Sarah comes home I'm not letting her pet me!

By Veronica
Grade 2
St. Wilfrid

FIGURE 11.13. *"Jamey the Cat"*

sentence: "Mr. Bear is loving." He gets just the first consonant of the last word, but never mind. He'll be filling in the blanks in no time. He shows plenty of imagination with his grocery list (Figure 11.17): peanut butter, bread, and honey; and even more with his "To Do" list (Figure 11.18): eat, play, [watch] TV, [go to the] park, [ride my] bike, read, and draw. He is bursting with ideas; a list gives him a simple, coordinated format for expressing them.

Notice how much information second grader Connor packs into his piece "My Winter Vacation" (Figure 11.19). The voice is strong, yet very controlled and sophisticated for so young a writer: "I had to have an IV; it was very annoying." Indeed. There's word choice brimming with nuances of meaning. Then there's good old Aunt Helen, who provides Connor with an exceptionally thorough history book. We can only hope that this teacher has told Connor how much voice and life lives and breathes within his work. How do you suppose Truman Capote wrote as a second grader? I like to think he might have sounded something like Connor, worldly wise with some very waggish overtones.

By the way, for simple trait-based scoring scales you can use for classroom assessment and for sharing students' progress with parents, see the end of this chapter.

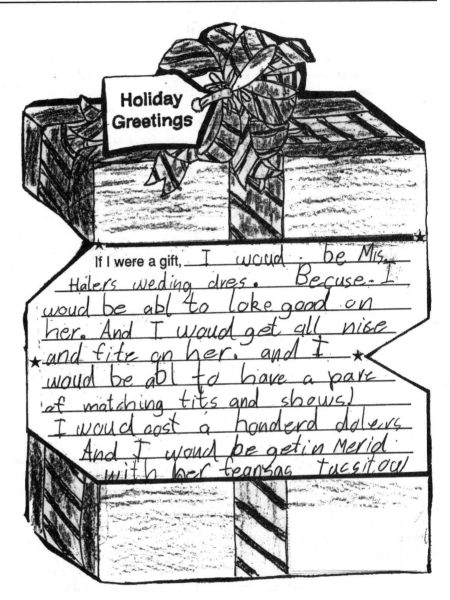

FIGURE 11.14. "If I Were a Gift"

Idea 2: Building Awareness With Language

If we are not going to use numbers with students, how do we create a "scoring guide" that primary or beginning writers can use? Simple. Remember the lesson from Chapter 10, that scoring guides do not all look alike? Some are checklists, for example. They could also be lists of writers' questions—and this form serves our purpose here well.

If we take the top end of our scoring guide and reshape it without any numbers, we have a list of goals that we can turn into important writers'

Baby Sarah
By Tony

My sister Sarah grgls a lot and some times whin she grgls she scuchis hwr face up and looks as coat as mrs. Stenson does whin she songs.

Sarah is realy coat to and she sleps a lot. she always falls aslep when shes eating. She also grabs my freger and squs et so tite it feels like she's triing to bet me up!

She screms a lot to. One time she scremed so loud I could hir al the way down stais! Sarah slepes mostly all night but some times she wakes up.

Grade 4

FIGURE 11.15. "Baby Sarah"

questions. These questions show young writers, in a simple but clear way, how to begin thinking about their writing, without the threat of judgment or formal evaluation.

You can have students help you add to this list, if you like. Add new questions, or reword others. Many teachers make individual trait posters of them with large print (so much easier for young eyes).

THINKING LIKE A WRITER
IDEAS

What is my *message?*
Is my *message* clear?
Do I have enough *information?*

ORGANIZATION

How does my paper *begin?*
Did I tell things in a good order?
How does my paper *end?*

FIGURE 11.16. Andrew: "Mr Bear is loving"

FIGURE 11.17. Andrew's grocery list

VOICE

Do I really *like* this paper?
Does this writing sound like *me?*
How do I want my reader to *feel?*
My favorite part is _____

WORD CHOICE

Have I used some words I really *love?*
Can my reader tell what my words *mean?*
Have I used any *new* words?
My *favorite* word in this paper is _____

SENTENCE FLUENCY

Did I use *sentences?*
How *many sentences* did I use?
How many *different ways* did I begin my sentences?
Did I use some *long* sentences?
Did I use some *short* sentences?

FIGURE 11.18. Andrew's "To Do" list

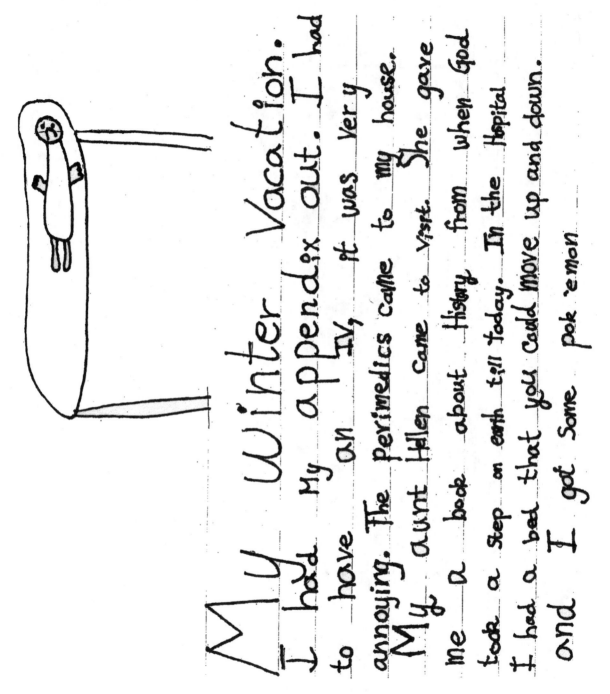

FIGURE 11.19. "My Winter Vacation"

CONVENTIONS

Did I leave *spaces* between words?

Does my writing go from *left to right* on the page?

Did I use a *title?*

Did I leave *margins* on the left and on the right?

Did I use any *capital* letters? Why?

Did I use *periods?* How about *question marks?*

Did I do my *best* on spelling?

Could another person read this?

This is a long list, but remember: You can introduce *one trait at a time* and *one question* at a time. Don't rush. Use your own writing as a model, and ask yourself these same questions as you go. Then, as you read aloud from favorite literature, ask the questions with your students about books or other things you read. Let students know from the first that you value their opinions as evaluators. In this way, you teach students to ask these questions of *themselves* as they write. And that is the goal.

Idea 3: Focus on Ideas and Voice First—Then on Conventions

THE POSTCARD RESPONSE

Think about receiving a postcard in the mail. Your friend Irene is vacationing in the "Hibrides." She tells you of the glorious scenery, the remarkable bargains on woolens, and the indescribable taste of salty fish and crisp potatoes at the end of a hard day hiking through the heather. What is your response? "Oh, Irene, Irene—that is *not* the way to spell Hebrides!" Surely not. More likely you think, "Irene! You sound relaxed. You sound *young.* No wonder you wanted to buy those expensive new walking shoes; hope your arches are holding up. Bring me back some smoked salmon."

It is mostly with students that we tend to think in conventional terms first. By high school, if the conventions are not in place, we sometimes get a little concerned—even desperate. But at primary level, we can afford to wait. In fact, we do ourselves and our students a good turn if *we do* wait. If we do respond as we would to a postcard from a friend—to the voice and ideas first—this gives students a clear message: "You are an interesting person, and I can hardly wait to read what you have to say. Write more. Write again so I can write back to you."

When we focus on conventions exclusively or even first—with no comment on the content—we say to students: "What you had to say wasn't very interesting. It didn't spark a single idea or question in my mind. In fact, right now what interests me most is your spelling here . . . and the absence of a period over here . . . Perhaps another time when I'm not so obsessed with spelling I can pay attention to what you have to say."

Evaluation is embedded in all we do. Every time we make a choice—cereal or toast for breakfast, the black skirt or the black pants . . . each decision involves evaluation. We're all pros at it.
Jane Fraser and Donna Skolnick (1994)

Teachers who habitually try to mark every error in a paper, no matter the cost to themselves, may wind up unintentionally giving their students two very negative messages: first, that they really do not care what students say, they only care that they say it correctly; and second, that they consider teaching writing a great burden and a thankless task.
Maxine Hairston (1986)

In both reading and writing, errors have meaning. . . . Work in spelling research suggests that mistakes made by young writers may not be mistakes at all, but rather, can be considered part of children's growth pattern as writers.
Charles Chew (1985)

Not long ago, a teacher I worked with did a presentation on 6-trait writing for her district. At the end, she invited anyone interested to visit her class and observe her teaching or talk with her students. One participant took her up on it. The day of the visit, the guest—isn't it the way of things?—sat down next to one of the teacher's most challenged writers, and asked to read a piece of her work. The student agreed happily, and at the end, the visitor, to be helpful, quietly pointed out some conventional problems: "Did you know this word was misspelled? Also, you left a word out—right here? And here—see?—a period is missing." The student writer didn't miss a beat: "Yes, I know, but right now I'm working on getting all my *ideas* down—and then later I'm going to do all the editing." The visitor was impressed: "I did not know," he said, "that children so young could understand the process of writing so well." They understand because this teacher has not abandoned conventions, but simply put them in their rightful place—as a support for ideas.

Idea 4: Help Students Think Like Writers

Use writer's vocabulary routinely to talk about students' writing. *Never* miss an opportunity to point out a moment of voice, a small indication of detail, however tiny. Remember Nikki's picture in Fig. 11.1? When you get a piece like this, it's a great opportunity to sneak in some trait language (think writers' language) that helps shape your student's thinking: "Nikki, you have really taken a close look at spiders! Wow. You noticed they have eight legs and multiple eyes. That's detail! And this bat—I love his toes and the hollow ears. Look at this smile on his face. That's what I call voice!" Then perhaps Nikki will think, "I'm a person who takes a close look at things. My writing has detail. My writing has voice."

With your comments, you plant a seed, from which will blossom an amazing flower—if you nurture it. Talk about details, beginnings, transitional phrases, favorite words, endings. Make these words and phrases part of your students' writing vocabulary. This way, you give them a tool for thinking about writing—and understanding it.

Remember, students understand writers' vocabulary *long* before the traits show up in their *own* writing. We underestimate them if we fail to recognize this. In various primary classes where I have shared favorite books and asked for students' responses, I have loved the sophistication of their thinking: "It has voice!" "She speaks right to you!" "It paints pictures in your mind!"

In one first grade class, I asked the students (as I often do with students of any age), "What kind of books do you like best?" Without hesitation, a student in the front row jumped up and cried, "*Hard* books! We are tired of easy books with words we already know. We want to learn new things."

Idea 5: Read and Celebrate Literature

If you love to read aloud (and what teacher of writing doesn't?), you already have at your command the most powerful means available for teaching the traits to beginning writers. Think of the books you love most to read aloud.

Chances are, many are strong in details and imagery (ideas), feelings (voice), word choice or fluency. Many likely have catchy beginnings or surprise endings—both good for teaching organization. Or maybe they're full of surprises, so you can invite your students to make predictions that may or may not come true—also good for teaching organization. Here are just a few examples.

Who can surpass William Steig (1977) when it comes to word choice? In *Amos and Boris* we can savor every luscious syllable in his description of friendship between the intrepid, seafaring mouse, Amos, and his benevolent and courageous friend Boris, a whale:

> *Boris admired the delicacy, the quivering daintiness, the light touch, the small voice, the gemlike radiance of the mouse. Amos admired the bulk, the grandeur, the power, the purpose, the rich voice, and the abounding friendliness of the whale.*

Who better to learn word choice from than someone who relishes and reveres language as Steig does? Students will find meaning in words they didn't know they knew. That's the power of a master who can make meaning clear from text and phrasing.

Try a word picture from Faith Ringgold's (1991) magical tribute to a child's imagination, *Tar Beach.*

> *I will always remember when the stars fell down around me and lifted me up above the George Washington Bridge.*

We literally see and hear the hushed whisper of falling stars when those words are read aloud. We feel ourselves float. What do you see and feel? You might sketch a picture. It's one way to sense the power of ideas.

Consider the possibilities in these opening lines from Petra Mathers's (1991) enchanting tale *Sophie and Lou.*

> *Sophie was shy—so shy she did her shopping during the lull hours, so she wouldn't have to talk to anyone. Every Wednesday the Book-Mobile parked in front of the supermarket, and every Wednesday Sophie almost went in. But the librarian was so tall!*

What will become of someone so shy she is afraid of tall people? Make a prediction. Predicting as you go is an important organizational skill.

Try writing an ending to a story that really has none, such as Hannah and Henry Hoose's *Hey, Little Ant.* Will the boy squish the ant—or will the ant's argument prevail? Students can decide, then draw a picture or write an ending.

As you read, ask students to tell you what they picture (ideas), what they feel (voice), what expressions they notice (word choice). Ask them to listen for the rhythm or, sometimes, to say the words back and hear the beat (fluency).

In using books with primary writers, you can follow up by asking them to draw pictures, write letters to the author, pretend to be a character, ask questions, talk in groups about the book, write a similar story using the book as a model—or any of a dozen other things. But it's also important to

From my own experience I realize that the literature I heard, rather than read, as a child resonates again and again in my memory whenever I sit down to write. . . . vocabulary and a sense of rhythm are almost impossible to "teach" in the narrow sense of the word. So how are children expected to develop a sense of rhythm or a wide vocabulary? By being read to, alive, a lot!

Mem Fox (1993, emphasis in original)

realize that just reading aloud is often enough. When you share a book, you say, "I love books. I love to read." And when you ask students, "Listen for the voice in this piece," or "See if you can pick out one favorite word," or "Tell me what you picture [ideas] as you listen to this story," you are enriching their listening by helping them see what gives each book its special power.

FAVORITE BOOKS FOR PRIMARY

Here are some of my other favorite read-aloud books to use with primary/beginning writers:

Animal Dads by Sneed B. Collard III: Ideas, word choice, organization

Beast Feast by Douglas Florian: Word choice, fluency

The Big Box by Toni Morrison: Ideas, voice, fluency

The Blushful Hippopotamus by Chris Raschka: Ideas, voice

The Crocodile and the Dentist by Taro Gomi: Ideas, organization

Dear Mr. Blueberry by Simon James: Ideas, organization

Fables by Arnold Lobel: Ideas, word choice, voice

Fish Faces by Norbert Wu: Organization

From Head to Toe by Eric Carle, Organization

Great Crystal Bear by Carolyn Lesser: Fluency, ideas

Hey, Little Ant by Phillip and Hannah Hoose: Ideas, voice

I Am the Dog, I Am the Cat by Donald Hall: Voice

Insectlopedia by Douglas Florian: Word choice, fluency

Julius, the Baby of the World by Kevin Henkes: Voice

Look Once, Look Twice by Janet Marshall: Ideas, organization

My Little Sister Ate One Hare by Bill Grossman: Voice, organization, fluency

My Painted House, My Friendly Chicken and Me by Maya Angelou: Ideas

No, David! By David Shannon: Ideas, voice, conventions (easy print and words for young readers)

Old Black Fly by Jim Aylesworth: Fluency, word choice

Our Wet World by Sneed B. Collard III: Ideas, fluency

Pete's a Pizza by William Steig: Ideas, organization, word choice

Piggie Pie by Margie Palatini: Voice

Rotten Teeth by Laura Simms: Organization, ideas, voice

Seasons by John Burningham: Ideas, organization

Snowballs by Lois Ehlert: Organization, fluency

Something Beautiful by Sharon Dennis Wyeth: Ideas, voice

Stellaluna by Jannell Cannon: Good for word choice, fluency, ideas fluency, voice, conventions—highly original layout

Toad by Ruth Brown: Word choice

Today I Feel Silly by Jamie Lee Curtis: Voice, ideas

The Twits by Roald Dahl: Voice

Verdi by Jannel Cannon: Ideas, organization, word choice

Where the Wild Things Are by Mauric Sendak: Ideas, organization

Whoever You Are by Mem Fox: Ideas, voice, fluency

Wild Child by Lynn Plourde: Fluency, word choice

Wilfred Gordon McDonald Partridge by Mem Fox: Ideas, organization, voice

CHOOSING BOOKS

These are only a few suggestions, of course—your school library is over-flowing with dozens of other possibilities. I'm often asked how I know which trait to use a book for. Honestly, after so many years of working with students on traits, it seems to me that I start leafing through a book and it just shrieks, "Fluency! Use me for fluency!" or whatever. But, here, as closely as I can identify them, are the qualities I look for:

Books for ideas: Is it very clear? Does it have one central idea or an easy-to-follow story? Interesting details? Glorious images? Does it make "movies" flow through your mind?

Books for organization: Does it have a powerful beginning? A strong or sur-prising conclusion? Is everything clearly linked to one main idea: bears, insects, whales, oceans, etc.? Does the book follow a pattern that student writers could imitate in their own writing?

Books for voice: Will I LOVE reading this book aloud? Will I enjoy reading it more than once? Can I hardly *wait* to share it? Would I give it as a gift? Does it make me laugh or cry?

Books for word choice: As I skim through, do I notice words or phrases I'd like students to know? Words I love myself? Are the words challenging without being *too* technical or difficult? Is meaning clear from context? Does it contain some words likely to be new to students? Are everyday words used in creative ways?

Books for fluency: Does it read like poetry? Are sentences highly varied in length and structure? Does it have a nice flow when read aloud? Does it have repeated rhythms or choruses where kids could chime in?

Conventions: Does the book use a wide range of conventions so I could point some out to students? Does it make unusual use of any conven-tions—capitals, exclamation points, quotation marks, etc.? Is the layout (how it's presented on the page) unusual or striking?

GO FOR STRENGTH—AND BE SURE YOU LOVE IT

Writers do not sit down, of course, and say, "Well, today, I think I'll write a book that's strong in voice." That just happens. But books, like any writing, have relative strengths, so when you're choosing books, go for the strength. Read what you like because you'll enjoy it more and you'll read better. If you don't read with expression and passion, you might as well forget the whole thing; and reading with passion is hard if you find the book boring.

So don't take anything from my list or anyone else's that you don't just love. And remember: You can use *any* book for more than one trait. If it's strong in voice, it probably has strong ideas and word choice, too.

THINK BEYOND BOOKS

You can, of course, use many forms of writing to teach traits with primary writers—just as you can with writers of any age. As you explore together maps from the zoo or amusement park, a bus schedule, a brochure from the veterinarian's office, a poster from the dentist's office, a mystery story, a movie review from the local paper, a description of a program in *TV Guide*, an advertisement for computers or clothing, or whatever, talk about, really *talk* about, whether the writer makes ideas clear (Does this make sense?), how the writer begins (Would *you* keep reading?), whether the piece has voice (Does this hold your attention?), which words you like or dislike, which you understand or do not understand, which pieces are stories (narrative), which are informational pieces (expository), which are meant to convince you (persuasive), and which paint word pictures (descriptive). Young writers learn the language of writing with ease, and once they have the language, thinking like writers becomes second nature.

Idea 6: Reward an Adventurous Spirit and View "Mistakes" As Experiments

A professional diver will practice for months or years, entering the water tens of thousands of times. We do not look upon all these early dives as "mistakes" that the diver has made; we look on them as practice. This is what primary students are doing all the time. They are practicing, trying things out, testing new ideas.

Children who write before they read become better writers than those who don't.
Bea Johnson (1999, 1)

Today or next week or the week after, they may not copy all the print in their environment perfectly, but they will come ever closer. Meanwhile, we can continue to read from the best and most exciting literature we can dig up, and we can fill their world with a wealth of wonderful words that are fun to say and to think with—and therefore are worth copying and using: *festival, dilapidated, ego, quake, reverie, fortuitous, serendipity, ludicrous, legend, cauldron, stellar, flick, bedevil, malevolent, skitter, flummoxed, decry, rhythm, crisp, delectable, writhe, lantern, facility, spicy, lexicon, candle, slang, Brigadoon, linger.* We can help children see, hear, and feel (yes, some words do feel different on the tongue) the magic within words—a magic that comes to life in Tina McElroy Ansa's (1994) story of her early fascination with words.

> *I asked [my mother] as a little girl why we didn't eat oatmeal, because people at my school, on cold mornings, would have a bowl of oatmeal. My mother made an ugly face and said, "I can't stand oatmeal. It multiplies in my mouth." And I recognized how wonderful her use of that word was, because I immediately started feeling this oatmeal multiplying in my mouth.*

(p. 18)

As students write, we can stretch our vision to look beyond "mistakes," to find the hidden power within a growing repertoire of skills: A new discovery in conventions? Quotation marks? Apostrophes? Terrific. Notice, applaud, celebrate. Fret over meticulous placement later. The same curiosity that drove the child to copy these mysterious marks in the first place will drive him or her to decipher their meaning. Too often we trust our own didacticism more than we trust that curiosity.

We can reward differences, too. Voice is individuality, so every time a writer allows herself to be lost in the crowd, a little bit of individuality is lost. To stand out, to stand alone, takes courage. We must reward students who dare to speak with strong voices. Reward them with recognition and appreciation. When your students have completed an assignment, you can say, "Do you know what I loved most about your essays on marine life? Each one was different. No paper was exactly like any of the others. As I read them, it was as if I could hear every single writer's voice, speaking right to me."

Idea 7: Write—and Talk About It

As a writer, you can show your students the whole process, even if they are still experimenting, just dipping in a toe to test the waters. Primary students may not be ready for full-blown revision of a written work (for many it's still too slow, too tedious), but they can learn what revision is before they begin to do it themselves. You can show them.

A friend one day received a faulty bill from the electric company and wrote them a rather angry letter—which she shared with her first and second graders. They were delighted! After all, adrenaline produces voice. That night, she reflected and decided to tone her letter down. But wait—here was an opportunity. She shared her revision with the class, telling them why she had revised the letter and asking them if they could hear the difference. Indeed they could, and though they were more than a little disappointed to have the original fiery version set aside, they could easily understand the reason for the change. "I shared lots of revisions with them that year," she told me. "Guess what? By the end of the year, some of my students were saying 'You know, I think I need to revise this.' Now understand, I never asked them to revise. I wouldn't do that with first and second graders. I don't require revision at this age. They just wanted to do what they had seen me doing."

That teacher was modeling more than revision, of course. Her example also said, "Writing is important. Writing is a way of making things happen." In addition, by sharing her writing with her students, she helped them feel that their opinions and suggestions were important. She asked for specific feedback: "Does my second letter sound more polite than the first?" She also showed them how the writer can control what happens in a response group.

> Writing with real honesty takes tremendous courage. Such writing should never be taken for granted. Writers of all ages often find they lack the nerve to write honestly.
>
> Ralph Fletcher (1993)

> We want to help children learn how to reread or "resee" their work. Above all, we want them to have a growing sense of options available to them during composing. . . . What we demonstrate [through our own revision] is not so much how to revise as a certain stance toward the world, a sense of our intentions, and how we listen to ourselves when we write.
>
> Donald Graves (1994)

"KASHA"—MY MODEL FOR REVISION

I use modeling with younger writers—just as I do with writers of all ages through adult. One of my favorite stories to use with beginning writers is a harrowing experience that occurred when I was about seven years old. I begin with a single statement, and invite the student writers to be a writing group for me by asking questions that will encourage me to fill in the blanks—what Barry Lane calls "digging for the potatoes." Here is my opening statement:

I was terrified of Kasha.

These are the questions students most often ask:

- How old were you?
- Where were you?
- Who is Kasha?
- Is Kasha human?
- Why were you afraid? What will Kasha do?
- Where was your mom? Why didn't she help you?
- What happened?
- Did you get hurt?

I answer these questions—briefly—and then use the answers to create a rough draft. So you can know, too—Kasha was a Russian Wolfhound who ran roughshod over our neighborhood when I was a small child. Since Wolfhounds are often very gentle, no one could explain his behavior, but perhaps he'd been mistreated. He attacked numerous people, some of whom required stitches. He also attacked a quarter horse pastured across from us, but was no match for her, and never repeated that performance. Lack of a leash law kept Kasha from being tied at home, and those of us under four feet tall learned to keep a sharp eye out for this renegade. Without warning, he attacked his owner with exceptional viciousness one day, and the owner shot him (I usually do not share this unhappy ending with students unless they ask, and then I do tell them the truth of what happened). We (the children in my neighborhood) did not mourn him.

Kasha very nearly attacked me during one of our white-out blizzards, and I was saved by a neighbor's dog who, though certainly no fighter, was extremely courageous and buffaloed the horrifying Kasha into running for home. Maybe Kasha was just a bully after all.

Usually, after setting the stage by answering a few questions, I begin my actual modeling by sharing three possible leads. I write these on the overhead, reading them aloud as I go, realizing that students cannot necessarily read all the words I am writing. But they will hear the leads—and I will repeat them when I'm done, so they can choose a favorite:

- I want to tell you a story about a scary thing that happened to me when I was seven.

- Kasha was the meanest, most terrifying monster for miles around, and one day I found myself only 20 feet from him.
- Are you frightened of dogs? I used to be. I will tell you why.

Students usually, but not universally, choose lead #2, and this gives us a good opportunity to talk about why. It's also a chance to talk about what a lead is. Then I can go on to a short draft. I'll make it simple, deliberately leaving out a few details:

> Kasha was the meanest, most terrifying monster for miles around, and on one terrible day I found myself only 20 feet from him. I did not know what to do! I thought he might attack me. So I stood very still for a long time. My feet got cold. My hands got cold. Finally, it was over, and I went home.

This draft is pretty skimpy in comparison to the information I have already given students orally, and they usually recognize the difference (what's in my mind vs. what's on the page). I ask them if I have left anything out. They will often say,

- You didn't tell how scared you were.
- There's nothing about the blizzard.
- Your story doesn't tell how you got away.
- Your story doesn't really tell what happened.
- You didn't make Kasha seem as scary as when you told it.
- You left out the part about Buff.

Using their comments, I write a revision on the overhead. It goes something like this:

> Kasha was the meanest, most terrifying monster for miles around, and on one terrible day I found myself only 20 feet from him. Snow was falling hard and fast. I knew my mom could not see me, even though I was close to home. The wind was blowing hard, so she could not hear me either. I was scared Kasha would jump on me, or maybe bite right through my mittens or jacket. I did not know what to do, so I stood very still, hoping he would go away. He growled low in his throat and I could see his yellow fangs. I tried not to cry. Suddenly, there was a flash of golden fur, and my brave friend Buff, a golden retriever, hurled himself at Kasha. I was so surprised! I had never seen Buff fight. He was so gentle! But he scared Kasha, all right. The big monster took off howling through the snow. Buff jumped on me and licked my face. We walked home together.

Students can see immediately how their questions and comments have made a difference. If they can hang in there for one more revision—perhaps the next day—I'll play with the ending. I think it needs work. Too "happily ever after" for me. Do you agree? The ending I want to use is this:

Buff got lucky that day. If Kasha had stuck around, he might have killed both of us.

Buff was a true hero, you see, in that he stood no chance against Kasha at all. Buff was just a big old teddy bear of a dog. But he was brave, and I think my story needs to bring that out.

A lesson like this can go on as long as students maintain interest. For instance, I have no title yet. That makes for another lesson (on another day, of course):

- Buff and Me
- Kasha
- The Monster
- The Day I Got Scared
- The Bully of the Neighborhood

Asking for students' opinions gives them practice in making choices and lets them know I value their help as a response group for my writing. It also engages them in the thinking and planning part of the writing process, and allows them to see drafting and revision unfold before their eyes. Of course, they won't have a strong sense of process after one lesson. I'll have to model my writing again and again. Each time, they'll get a little better at being advisors.

PAINLESS REVISION

Primary students can do a form of revision that is not only relatively painless but that also teaches them that revision is more than "fixing it." It is not editing, not correcting; it is truly "seeing it again."

Ask students to describe something important in their lives. They can do their descriptions in the form of a picture or written text. Then ask them to close their eyes and "see it again" just for a moment. Take another look. Is there anything you didn't see the first time? Touch it. How does it feel? Take a moment to tune in to the sounds that fill that time and place. What do you hear? Do you smell anything? (It's amazing how smells provoke memories.) Then, open your eyes. Look again at your description. See if there is one detail that you forgot the first time and that you'd like to add now. One is enough, though some young writers have more to add.

As Donald Graves (1994) reminds us, adding information is developmentally one of the first tasks young revisers learn. Playing with chronological order comes a little later, along with making insertions and moving information, learning to structure details around a main idea, and, finally, deleting information, which is developmentally one of the most difficult tasks. This should not surprise us. Don't most of us, as writers, feel a kind of reverence toward our own printed text? Even if we do not love what we have written, we love the fact we are "finished." Boy, that feels good.

Adding on is a very natural part of young children's writing. It can be regarded as an early form of revision or as part of drafting, for there is no clear division between the two.

Lucy McCormick Calkins
(1994, 99)

Idea 8: Respect the Many Forms That Writing Can Take

Primary students, in particular, need a variety of ways in which to express themselves, including pictures, dictation, oral storytelling, labeling, and planning. Notice the expressiveness (a story about to happen) in this young writer-artist's cat picture (Figure 11.20).

Pictures, as we've seen, reflect the beginnings of ideas (details), voice (emotion, playfulness, individuality, and humor), and organization (format and balance). Further, children who are not quite ready to create extended text (they may not yet have the concentration, ability to form words, or fine motor skills to make writing relatively simple) can dictate stories or simply tell them to others. In their telling, we hear the vocabulary, voice, sequencing, and development of ideas that they have no means yet to project through standard text. The point is that these things are part of their thinking and imagination, so why not encourage a "writing" form that lets them show that thinking in action?

Young writers can also help you plan your writing or a sample of class writing. For instance, let's say you have someone visit the class to talk to students about birds of prey. Together, you compose a thank-you letter, with students helping you decide how to begin, what to say next, which details are important and which not, what sort of voice or tone the letter should have (formal? friendly?), how to close, and so on:

Dear Mr. Martini:

Thank you for bringing Sara the hawk to visit us! We love her. It was fun learning about where hawks live and how they hunt. I think we will notice hawks for sure from now on. When will you bring Amanda the barn owl to visit? We promise to be very quiet and not frighten her. Thank you again for coming to our class.

Mr. Ross's Second-Grade Class

FIGURE 11.20. "Fat Cat on the Prowl"

Idea 9: Give Primary Writers Editing Tasks They Can Handle

DO TEACH *CONVENTIONS*

Teaching conventions is not the same thing as *correcting* conventions—or assessing conventions, for that matter. Just because we wait a bit before expecting conventional correctness is no sign we must wait *even a minute* to begin teaching and talking about conventions. Anyone who works with primary writers for just one day will be struck by how much they notice and how quickly they begin to include in their writing exclamation points, quotation marks, ellipses, semicolons, and parentheses—not always correctly placed, mind you, but present. We can take advantage of this curiosity by filling their environment with plenty of print to borrow from, and by continually asking students, "Have you noticed this mark in your reading? Can you find one somewhere in this room? Why do you suppose writers use this? What does it show?"

Begin as simply as you need to. I like to start with a treasure hunt. You can use any text at all for this. Choose a piece that is at least one paragraph long and that shows a variety of conventions; it is NOT essential that the students be able to read this page. Then invite them, each with a partner, to engage in a conventions treasure hunt. They must put their finger right on the convention as you name it. Once they've correctly identified a convention (e.g., quotation marks), ask them to tell you why writers use it (e.g., to show people are speaking). It helps to have a list ready to go. Here are some I've used, but you could make your own:

- Capital letter
- Period, question mark, comma, semicolon, exclamation point, etc.
- Any proper name
- Any simple word (How many times does it appear?)
- Italics
- Ellipses
- Parentheses
- Quotation marks
- Margins
- Titles or subtitles

Or—Insert one or two mistakes in your copy. See who can find them.

I played this conventions treasure hunt game with first graders not long ago and because they were so exceptionally good at finding everything I could name, I told them I'd give them my conventions "challenge"—*ellipses*. One girl in the front row put her finger immediately on the ellipses and raised her hand. When I asked if she could explain how ellipses are used, she said sure. She stood up before the group. "Ellipses," she explained, "are when you . . . [and her voice drifted off for a time, then resumed] . . . pause in your thinking—like that." Not bad. We wrote *ellipses* (the word and the convention) on the board and everyone practiced making the little dots. I have no doubt that for that group of first graders, the day's writing was filled with pregnant pauses.

Among the most successful spelling teachers I've seen was kindergarten teacher Sally, who began each day with a reader/writer circle in which up to three children were invited to name one word they would like to add to the class spelling dictionary (of which they all had copies in their desks). One child might choose "music," and the whole class would work on sounding it out. "What do you hear first? *M-m-m-m-m-* What do you think the first letter might be?" Then, when they'd made their best guess, Sally would print the correct version (sometimes the same, sometimes very close) on a big card, with letters two or more inches high, and the group would talk about how close they had come. The correct version was hung in the room for all to see, and also went into personal dictionaries. By the end of the school year, their spelling was remarkable for kindergartners—and they had generated the entire list themselves.

You can also ask students to do very simple editing tasks:

- Putting their names on papers
- Checking to see if their names have capital letters
- Putting the date on each paper
- Giving a paper a title

Even very beginning writers can do these things, and they will feel like independent editors if you call it editing. Later, as skills grow, you can add to this editing checklist:

- Capital letter to begin each sentence
- Period, question mark, or exclamation point at the end
- Capital on each name
- Using words and sentences to tell a story
- Making sure your picture goes with your words (if you have a picture)
- Writing a beginning to your paper
- Writing an end to your paper

When students begin writing simple sentences, create simple editing practice that invites them to "track down" errors. Make a game of it. It's like "Finding Waldo," only you're finding "Mr. Mistake." Be sure that each sentence you give them (1) is a complete, short sentence, and (2) contains *only one* error. Do as many of these as your students have concentration for. Two or three are good; five or six are better. Remember, students only learn to edit by editing, and it is much more fun to practice on the work of others. So, use a sample like this on the overhead. Notice that the first sentence is correct; this allows students to compare that sentence to the others—each of which contains one error.

The cat ate my fish. (Correct version)

- The cat ate my fish
- The ct ate my fish.
- the cat ate my fish.
- The cat my fish.
- The cat eat my fish.

You can see how this works—the number of possibilities is endless. But of course, you don't want to work one sentence to death. Move on with a new example each day, but keep at it. *One error at a time.* That way, students develop that proofreader's eye early on. Let students correct the text first, using the Copy Editor's Symbols for Beginning Writers (Figure 11.21). When they've finished, ask them to check their text with a friend. Then, have them tell you how to fix the text so you can do it on the overhead for everyone to see. The process should be fast, lively, and interactive. No worksheets. Just a group of editors, talking and editing.

Idea 10: Keep It Simple

YOU DO NOT ALWAYS NEED TO HOST A "WRITING EVENT"
For beginners, it's a comfort to know that brief, manageable assignments are sometimes acceptable. Beginners also enjoy interesting shapes on which to write. My friend Arlene Moore, who teaches a K–1 combination, gave her young writers 3" x 5" paper suitcases on which to write me short messages: What I should be sure to pack as I travel around the country talking with teachers and students. Their recommendations included these—most of which I've followed:

- A snake so no one will steal your stuff
- A book to read
- Earrings to make you beautiful
- Roses for all the teachers you meet
- A charge card
- Plenty of chocolate so you won't get hungry

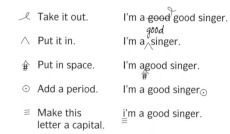

FIGURE 11.21. Copy Editor's Symbols for Beginning Writers

- Pictures of your children so you won't get lonely
- Clothes, so you won't need to run around in your underwear

CRITERIA FOR CHARTING GROWTH

This section includes two very simple scales you can use to chart young or beginning writers' growth. The first (Figure 11.22) is intended for *very* beginning writers: those who are writing primarily through pictures, scribbles, letter play, letter strings and beginning words that may include first and last sounds only.

The second scale (Figure 11.23) is for those writers—still beginners—who are more advanced: those who are writing complete words and sentences, even short paragraphs—up to multiple paragraphs.

Writers more advanced than this, those who are writing one- or two-page essays, and those who would consistently score at the "Accomplished" level on the higher scale, are ready for assessment on the scale presented in Chapter 3. The scales presented in this chapter are for those students who would likely receive many 1s and 2s on the more advanced scale, and who therefore need a way of showing success, of showing what they *can* do—not just what isn't in place yet. For each scale, performance is defined at three levels: Exploring, Developing, and Accomplished.

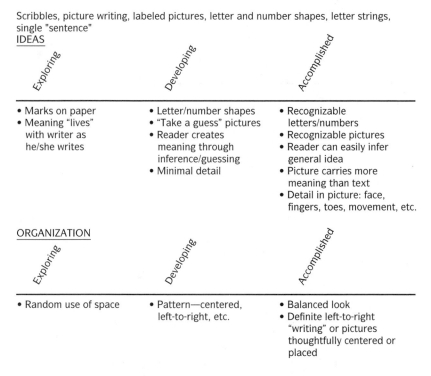

Scribbles, picture writing, labeled pictures, letter and number shapes, letter strings, single "sentence"

IDEAS

Exploring	Developing	Accomplished
• Marks on paper • Meaning "lives" with writer as he/she writes	• Letter/number shapes • "Take a guess" pictures • Reader creates meaning through inference/guessing • Minimal detail	• Recognizable letters/numbers • Recognizable pictures • Reader can easily infer general idea • Picture carries more meaning than text • Detail in picture: face, fingers, toes, movement, etc.

ORGANIZATION

Exploring	Developing	Accomplished
• Random use of space	• Pattern—centered, left-to-right, etc.	• Balanced look • Definite left-to-right "writing" or pictures thoughtfully centered or placed

FIGURE 11.22. Early Beginning Writers

VOICE

Exploring	Developing	Accomplished
• Bold lines • Use of color • Voice expressed through dictation	• Pictures show mood/feeling • Exclamation points or periods • BIG LETTERS • Multicolor pictures	• Recognizable as "this child's piece" • Unique flavor, style • Expressive pictures • Expression of feeling in text

WORD CHOICE

Exploring	Developing	Accomplished
• Scribbles • No real letter/number shapes *yet*	• Recognizable letter/number shapes • Borrowing from environmental print • Labels • Letter strings—may be hard to read without writer's help	• Easy-to-read letter/number shapes • Some recognizable letter string words • Variety of words

FLUENCY

Exploring	Developing	Accomplished
• No letter/word strings yet • Dictates sentences to go with writing	• Letter strings suggest beginning sentences: ilpdg • Not translatable without help • Dictates multiple sentences	• Letter strings form readable sentences: i l k t p l w m d g (I like to play with my dog.) • Dictates a whole story or essay

CONVENTIONS

Exploring	Developing	Accomplished
• No recognizable conventions yet • Can point to conventions in environment	• Places punctuation randomly in text • "Scribbles" imitate look and shape of text • Writes name on paper • Writes one or two readable words	• Borrows conventions from print • Uses title • Uses name and spells it correctly • Writes several or more readable words • Periods placed correctly

FIGURE 11.22. Early Beginning Writers (continued)

Readable words, sentences ⟶ Multiple paragrahs

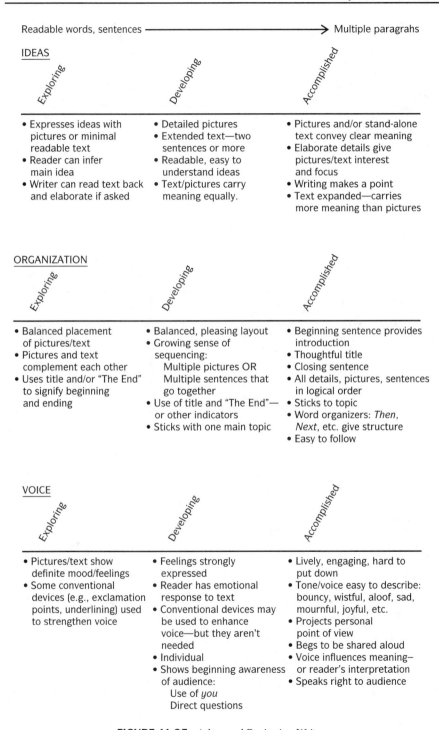

IDEAS

Exploring   *Developing*   *Accomplished*

- Expresses ideas with pictures or minimal readable text
- Reader can infer main idea
- Writer can read text back and elaborate if asked

- Detailed pictures
- Extended text—two sentences or more
- Readable, easy to understand ideas
- Text/pictures carry meaning equally.

- Pictures and/or stand-alone text convey clear meaning
- Elaborate details give pictures/text interest and focus
- Writing makes a point
- Text expanded—carries more meaning than pictures

ORGANIZATION

Exploring   *Developing*   *Accomplished*

- Balanced placement of pictures/text
- Pictures and text complement each other
- Uses title and/or "The End" to signify beginning and ending

- Balanced, pleasing layout
- Growing sense of sequencing:
  Multiple pictures OR
  Multiple sentences that go together
- Use of title and "The End"— or other indicators
- Sticks with one main topic

- Beginning sentence provides introduction
- Thoughtful title
- Closing sentence
- All details, pictures, sentences in logical order
- Sticks to topic
- Word organizers: *Then, Next,* etc. give structure
- Easy to follow

VOICE

Exploring   *Developing*   *Accomplished*

- Pictures/text show definite mood/feelings
- Some conventional devices (e.g., exclamation points, underlining) used to strengthen voice

- Feelings strongly expressed
- Reader has emotional response to text
- Conventional devices may be used to enhance voice—but they aren't needed
- Individual
- Shows beginning awareness of audience:
  Use of *you*
  Direct questions

- Lively, engaging, hard to put down
- Tone/voice easy to describe: bouncy, wistful, aloof, sad, mournful, joyful, etc.
- Projects personal point of view
- Begs to be shared aloud
- Voice influences meaning– or reader's interpretation
- Speaks right to audience

FIGURE 11.23. Advanced Beginning Writers

<u>WORD CHOICE</u>

Exploring *Developing* *Accomplished*

Exploring	Developing	Accomplished
• Uses recognizable words • Uses nouns, verbs and modifiers • Often labels pictures • Uses words correctly in most cases	• Uses words to prompt feelings or create pictures in reader's mind • Uses variety of words • Stretches for new words	• Vivid, expressive language • Memorable phrasing • Minimal repetition • Vocabulary extends beyond spelling ability • Striking, unexpected phrasing: (e.g., I was *panukstriken*)

<u>FLUENCY</u>

Exploring	Developing	Accomplished
• Writes at least one complete simple sentence (may not be punctuated correctly)	• Writes more than one sentence • Writes complete or close-to-complete sentences • Favors patterns: e.g., I love my dog. I love my school. I love my mom • Creates text that is easy to read aloud	• Writes up to one or two paragraphs or more • Writes complete sentences • Occasional compound/ complex sentence • Varies sentence lengths and/or beginnings • Text sounds very fluent when read aloud

<u>CONVENTIONS</u>

Exploring	Developing	Accomplished
• "Plays" with conventions • Liberally sprinkles text with punctuation marks • Attempts phonetic spelling • Most words readable • Grammar correct on most sentences	• Experiments with wide range of conventions • Uses periods, question marks, exclamation points correctly • Uses capitals on *I*, names, beginnings of sentences • Includes margins • Spelling correct on most words of four or fewer letters • Attention to placement of title, name, date, etc. • Sometimes uses paragraphs	• Uses wide range of conventions correctly, easily • Text *easy* to read • May use commas, quotation marks, parentheses • Uses capitals correctly and consistently • Starts paragraphs in right places • Neat margins • Careful placement of title, name, date, etc. • Spelling correct on most one- or two-syllable words • All spelling readable • Grammar correct in most cases

FIGURE 11.23. Advanced Beginning Writers (continued)

GIVE IT TIME

Some children pick up a pencil and begin creating meaning through text at a remarkable early age, because for them writing is totally natural. Similarly, some children will, almost from the first day, write much the way they speak, gracing every line with that truest of voices which flows like water when the writing is an extension of self. As Gloria Wade-Gayles (1994) declares, "Writing simply is. In the same way that being alive is about breathing, being alive for me is about writing. . . . Writing simply is. It is an expression of my 'who-ness'" (p. 103).

We must allow primary writers to express their "who-ness" while their belief in the power of writing is strong. It stands to reason they will not all reach milestones of achieving readable spelling, correct spelling, knowledge of terminal punctuation, skill with capital letters, ability to form complete sentences, and so on at the same time. We know this intuitively, yet we (as parents and as teachers) often become anxious when a child seems to fall behind others. What's wrong? we ask.

In most cases, not only is nothing wrong, but something is very right. That something is that the child is adventuring, playing with language in his or her own way, finding the child's own path to learning. A reading specialist once told me about the importance of filling the classroom with books and other printed materials because young readers were hungry for print. "So this is a way to encourage them?" I asked. She shook her head. "It isn't a matter of encouraging them," she explained patiently. "You can't *stop* them. I'm just providing the tools and getting out of the way."

You can't stop children from writing, either, if the tools are there. Then we can let them create at their own pace and in their own way, not looking for or demanding "correctness" too soon. We can remind ourselves that much experimenting is essential in any task, from cooking to diving, and perhaps we can relax and enjoy their learning. You learn to eat before you learn to cook, and though I have no evidence to prove it, I'd be willing to bet that people who enjoy eating make the best food.

REFLECTING ON CHAPTER 11

1. Sometimes we put a great deal of emphasis on early mastery of correctness in writing. What are the forces at work that urge us toward this position?

2. What is the worst thing that could happen if we focused less on correctness at primary level and more on content and voice? What is the best thing?

3. It is important for teachers of all grades to write with their students, but why might this be especially important at primary level?

4. What are some signs that a student writer is ready for assessment on the higher level scoring scale shown in Chapter 3? Do you see any samples of student writing

in this chapter that seem to show that "readiness"? How do you know? Is grade level a good indicator?

ACTIVITIES

1. Collect four or five samples of primary writing—or use samples from this chapter. Score them on one of the writing scales in Figures 11.22 and 11.23 on one or more traits. Discuss the results.
2. Model for your colleagues or your class a lesson on writing, revision, or editing that you might use with primary writers.

LOOKING AHEAD

In Chapter 12 we examine communicating with students in the language of the traits and converting trait scores to grades. We also look briefly at grading issues, and share some thoughts on student response groups.

12

COMMUNICATING:
Through Comments, Conferences, Peer Review, & Grades

It is the work I am grading, not the student. It is work that can be shown to the student, to colleagues, to administrators; it is work that relates directly to the quality of the reference that would be given for the student when that student applies for more advanced courses or for a job.

Donald M. Murray (1985, 143)

The giving of marks and the grading process are overemphasized, while the giving of useful advice and the learning function are underemphasized.

Paul Black and Dylan Wiliam (1998)

I tell people all the things I like about their piece—how wonderful the atmosphere is, for instance, and the language—and also point out where they got all tangled up in their own process. We—the other students and I—can be like a doctor to whom you take your work for a general checkup.

Anne Lamott (1995, 153)

While being critiqued, do make notes of what people say about your story, even if it seems stupid. It may make sense later.

Ursula K. LeGuin (1998, 155)

LANGUAGE MAKES ALL THE DIFFERENCE

A few years ago, I was both amused and distressed to hear Grant Wiggins tell a large group of conference attendees about a new teacher who was saying farewell to her students after what had seemed a highly successful term. One of the students, Wiggins explained, paused to whisper a question she'd been too timid to ask earlier: "You've written this on so many of my papers, but I don't understand. What is 'va-goo'?" Va-goo (vague) all too often describes *us* as we try to clarify our expectations for students. In this chapter, we will talk about four important ways of communicating with student writers about their performance: through comments, conferences, peer review, and grades.

COMMENTS

Can you recall the most **positive** thing anyone ever said to you about your own writing? It might have come from a teacher or, perhaps, a friend, colleague, parent, child, editor—anyone. A comment that inspired you and gave you confidence.

Now, turn the tables. Try to remember the most **negative** comment you ever received on your work—one that momentarily bumped you off the path or perhaps even stunned you, stopped you short.

Here are two examples from my personal experience. In a class on using writing to think, I had written a poem about moving to Oregon to get married. I'd left my mother distraught and in tears, my father sullen and angry (he thought I was too young to marry or to move so far from home), and we hauled our pathetic cache of belongings, my love and I, in a U-Haul truck that didn't do hills. The Rockies were a challenge. My poem was personal and profoundly emotional, and I felt nervous sharing it aloud. Later, I felt happy I had shared it when the teacher wrote, "The way words move through you, through your pen. I envy that, *love* that." I saved her words and today have them taped inside a drawer because they gave me both encouragement and courage itself. (Thank you, Elaine.)

In 11th grade, I spent five days writing an essay on *The Great Gatsby*. I didn't know nearly enough about life to appreciate the book at that time, but like many 16-year-olds, I thought classics were supposed to be dull, and anyway, I'd worked hard on my essay, particularly the symbolism involving light. I received only one comment, written at the end: "Your most irritating habit is your relentless, *persistent* misuse of the semicolon. Please revise!" Relentless? Persistent? What an angry man to envision me plotting the strategic placement of semicolons to create maximum annoyance (I wasn't that clever)—not to mention the startling phrase "*most* irritating habit." Apparently, out of my vast array of annoying habits, this was the one—this semicolon thing—that provoked him most. He ended with "Please revise!" but I think what he really meant was "Please revise your*self*. Write differently. Write something else, for some*one* else, or at least, write some*where* else."

I have often asked other teachers to recall positive or negative comments, and am startled to learn how long some comments have stayed in their minds:

TEACHERS RECALL THE GOOD TIMES . . .

Good clear thinking. You always develop your ideas completely and show remarkable insight.

Appears to be from personal experience. Very moving.

You have a special way with words!

You have a creative soul!

You made me want to keep reading—even at 11 pm.

This sounds so much like you I had to keep looking over my shoulder to see if you were in the room.

I like the way you wrote this sentence. It makes me feel I'm right there with you.

I like your use of the word *flamboyant*. I can picture Irene perfectly.

I like the way you write. You say what you have to say, and then quit.

Continue with this—I want to know more about this experience. How did you resolve the tension? More, more!

Very convincing. I began this paper believing one thing, and though you haven't totally turned me around, you have really made me think.

Beautiful sentence rhythm. I could use this to *teach* fluency. It's that good.

You told me you couldn't write. You can. This proves it.

Thank you for sharing your poem. It spoke to me.

You took a technical, hard-to-penetrate idea and made it reader-friendly. I felt like an insider. Thanks!

. . . AND THE NOT SO GOOD TIMES

I can't believe what I see here. There is nothing of worth, except that the documentation is perfect. It is only the documentation that boosts this paper to a D–. *[Boosts?]*

Ugh!

I think you may have it in you to write competently, but not brilliantly.

Don't get cute.

In looking at this paper again, I believe it is even worse than I originally thought.

Reading this has depressed me more than I can say.

I do not have time to read this much. Please be more concise.

You simply don't know how to write.

This is basically verbal vomit.

No one would read this who was not paid to read it.

Lay off the exclamation points. This isn't that exciting.

What in the *world* are you trying to say? Just spit it out.

You will never, ever be an author.

You missed the point completely. F.

This could not possibly be your best effort.

Do the world a favor. Don't write.

I do not believe you wrote this. This is not your work.

Dialogue doesn't work. It sounds stilted, phony. *No one* talks this way.

Your writing reminds me of a porcupine—many points leading in meaningless directions.

One teacher's comment came in the form of a gesture: Her teacher shredded her paper and returned it to her in a paper bag. It takes only seconds to create a lifetime memory. We must think before we write.

Is Anybody Listening, Though? Actually, Yes . . .

While some of the preceding comments seem bitter and rancorous, *most* teacher comments are, from teachers' perspectives at least, well-intentioned. Sometimes, though, good intentions are not enough to bridge the communications gap. As the weeks tick by and we note no major changes in writing skill, we may wind up wondering whether anyone is even listening. As the samples below show clearly, student writers usually *are* responding to our comments, but often not in the way we had imagined or hoped.

When the teacher wrote "Needs work," students responded this way:

Kind of rude. Work on what?

I learn nothing from this comment.

I feel discouraged.

This is so harsh. It makes me feel hopeless.

I have to ignore this or I'll wind up hating the teacher.

When the teacher wrote, "You need to be more concise," students responded this way:

I'm confused. What do you mean by "concise"?

I'm not Einstein. I can't do everything right.

What do *you* do to make *your* writing concise? I can't picture it.

I thought you wanted details and support. Now you want concise. Which is it?

When the teacher wrote, **"Be more specific,"** students responded this way:

You be specific.

It's going to be too long then. What happened to concise?

What do you *mean?* Specific *how?* About *what?*

Maybe you need to read more closely. Maybe it's *you* not paying attention.

When the teacher wrote, "You need stronger verbs," students responded this way:

I lack verby power.

I *knew* it. I should have used the thesaurus.

This is confusing. How would different verbs help?

I don't know any other verbs. Give me some examples.

It's my choice, not yours.

I'm confused. Guess I'll just write the way I want.

Research by Maxine Hairston (1986) confirms that these responses are not isolated examples but are, in fact, typical of students who feel overwhelmed by the impossibility of it all, who simply shrug and give up, or who adapt a defensive, defiant stance, showing their contempt for all that English teachers regard as so important.

> Children, like adults, learn best in a supportive context.
> Lucy McCormick Calkins (1986)

Curiously, most marginal comments offered by teachers are not intended in a mean-spirited way at all but are meant only to help. It might seem on the face of it that one of the best ways to help a budding writer is to point out what he or she is doing wrong. Yet the truth is that this usually *doesn't* help; it hurts. Sometimes, it hurts a lot.

Getting Specific

What *does* help is to point out what the writer is doing well and to help the writer build on that. There's a trick to writing good positive comments, though. They must be truthful, and they must be very specific. It's one thing to say, "Good job, John." That's not negative, but it's very general. You should know that it can, and often does, sound very phony. Think of a four-year-old who is showing off his new bike-riding skills to a father who's engrossed in the stock market report. "Look at me, Dad! Look at me!" the four-year-old shouts over and over. Dad maintains a running commentary—"Great, son, just great!"—without ever looking up. No one appreciates this mindless kind of approval. To show that you actually read the paper, you need comments like these:

- Your examples were enough to convince me that chocolate-covered marshmallows are not a good idea. I'm giving them up!

- Voice! I could hear in this piece your sense of horror at the idea of freeze-drying a cat, but some amusement, too. You really know how to connect with an audience.
- So penguins can "launch" themselves. No kidding? I can picture it, and I *love* picturing it!

As author/teacher Tommy Thomason (1998) tells us, "Praise works when it tells writers specifically what they did well. This motivates writers to keep on writing, to take chances, and to work even harder on areas where they have demonstrated their success" (29).

What If You Don't Like the Paper?

Sometimes it's tough. Maybe you don't like the paper much, or there isn't that much there. Don't give up. Look within. There's nearly always a moment of voice. Just a *moment*—that's enough. Seize it. Take time to comment. Make sure the student knows you noticed. Find a word or phrase you enjoyed—just one; a detail that stood out; an opening that shows improvement over others or an ending that surprised you; one transition that helped connect ideas; one sentence beginning that made the reading smooth; one line that needs no editing at all. If you look hard you will find *something*. Make a very big deal of it. Next time, there will be another something to reward your efforts.

Is It Ever OK to Make Suggestions?

> I genuinely believe it is possible to find something good in each piece of writing, and I think you'll find it becomes an acquired skill that is central to being a constructive critic.
>
> Barry Lane (1993, 126)

Of course! It's essential. Emphasizing the positive does not mean we give up all intervention, coaching, and teaching. It simply means controlling that intervention so we do not try to take on all things at once and overwhelm students. In his excellent and thorough book *The English Teacher's Companion*, teacher Jim Burke (1999) likens good teaching to his experience learning to play tennis (80). For several years, he explains, he just mindlessly batted the ball around the court, and though he spent hours a day doing this, no serious improvement occurred—until his parents hired a coach. Now he had an "expert" who could observe, offer suggestions at appropriate times—and offer encouragement, too. Follow the lead of Jim's coach. Pace yourself. Along with pointing out strengths, offer *one or two* suggestions: *Think about connection between your title and the writing; Try starting your sentences with words other than "There is" or the pronoun "I" and see if this doesn't give your writing some power; In our next conference, let's brainstorm together some alternatives to the word "special"; Remind me to show you how I cut one of my paragraphs from 150 to 75 words—I think it will help you understand what I mean by "concise."* Step by step. Little victories build writers. Barry Lane suggests dividing constructive criticism into three categories:

- Questions—Things the writer did not answer or just things you're curious about

- Comments—including praise
- Concerns—Passages that confused you or potential problems the author may wish to pay attention to (Lane, 1993, 126)

CONFERENCES

Must We?

The very word *conference* can be horrifying to teachers who are already pressed for time. This is often so because they think that

1. They must ask all the questions and control everything that happens during the conference (much like an orchestra conductor).
2. They must use the conference as an opportunity to "fix" the writing (sometimes a big task).

These are myths, and reflect an overblown vision of what a conference is. It's a chat. That's all. I like Tommy Thomason's analogy (in *Writer to Writer: How to Conference Young Authors*, 63–64) to the two neighbors talking gardening. One is a veteran gardener, one a novice. The veteran might answer a question one day about when to plant lettuce. Another day he offers a suggestion on how to keep the flowers from falling off the tomato plants. But never does he take over the garden himself, examine every plant—or give a lecture on "All About Gardening." And if he did, then next time he appeared at the fence, the novice gardener might feel a sudden need to have his teeth drilled. Like the veteran, we conference best when we stop by to "talk writing" for a moment.

Successful conferences are

- Short and focused—they do not try to "cover" everything
- Student-oriented, so the writer has a chance to talk
- An opportunity to work on *one* writer's problem—not the whole world of writing

Students who know the traits well are often more comfortable in a conference because first they're not starting from ground zero—they already know a lot about what makes writing work; and second, they have writers' language to use in forming opening questions:

- I need help with my lead.
- I don't know if I have one main idea—or two.
- Have I said enough about this to make my argument convincing?
- I think this is too wordy, but I don't know how to cut it.
- This has no voice. What do I do?

Shorter is Better

A conference tends to make a student writer feel special, and this, even more than what is said, is the special contribution the conference makes to writing instruction. A conference also offers, for the student who is shy about asking a question in class, a quiet and safe moment in which to receive help on a particular problem. It also offers the instructor an opportunity to give personal, individual attention, however short-lived that might be. In *Free to Write*, Roy Peter Clark (1987) talks about the value of a short conference that focuses simply on where the writer is in the process and the most important problem or obstacle that writer faces—and that's it. End of conference. This don't-drag-it-out approach comes from his experience as a journalist watching city editors deal with dozens of reporters in 30- to 60-second intervals: "City editors learn these techniques or die" (36–37).

Students walking away from a writing conference are frequently overwhelmed with information. It's important to teach them to learn how to listen to their own internal critics . . .

Barry Lane (1993, 109)

A student should come away from a conference *not* with a polished, ready-to-go draft, but simply with an idea of where to go next or, at the very least, a clear sense of a useful writing question to answer: Should I think about a different beginning? Can I make it shorter? Do I have enough support for my allegation that home schooling works?

A Chance to Be Heard

Tommy Thomason (1998) emphasizes the importance of "helping writers talk out problems they are having or verbalize their plans for the piece" (32). So often students feel no one listens—really *listens* to them. One minute of good listening can be worth twenty minutes of canned writing advice, however conceptually sound. So while you listen, really tune in; do not spend time thinking of the next strategic question you will ask. Take in the writer's thoughts and take your cue from there. Also, let students know ahead of time that the conference will be an opportunity for them to ask questions; get them to write their questions on a small piece of paper or note card, if you wish. You may want to practice this with the whole class first, asking everyone to write one question, then quickly responding to ten or so. This modeling can get them into the questioning spirit—and will encourage them to expect a chat, not a seminar. A conference is not meant to hold you for life. It's meant to help you work through one writing problem, and that's a lot.

If children don't speak about their writing, both teachers and children lose. Until the child speaks, nothing significant has happened in the writing conference.

Donald H. Graves (1983)

In addition, do not allow yourself to feel overwhelmed. Here are two more myths you can dispel immediately:

1. You need to read EVERYTHING every student writes. Actually, it may not even be helpful to do this. Often, we read the paper because we aren't sure what else we're supposed to be doing. But the paper as a whole may not be ready for sharing. It may be much more useful to read just the lead or just one paragraph about a main point or a main character.
2. You need to confer with EVERY STUDENT DAILY. Oh, please. Could *anyone* do this and live to write about it? And really—don't you think this would pressure students, too? You can ask students to schedule conferences

so that those who most need help will receive it most often. Also consider group conferences, focusing on a main issue: finding a topic, how to begin, searching for details, keeping it short enough, developing a character, shaping an argument, using comparison-contrast effectively, finding a thesis so your writing is more than a long list of facts, and so on. Group conferences that run once or twice a week may last five or ten minutes; you can afford to take more time because you're working with more students at once.

DON'T JUST STAND THERE—DO SOMETHING

Questions are good, especially when they come from students *to* us. But questions are not the only way to conduct a conference. Following are some useful things you can *do* with students (especially those needing some direct help) in less than two minutes:

- Brainstorm three possible leads (or endings)
- List 10 transitional words
- Brainstorm five possible titles
- Identify together the main idea of the piece
- Point out a detail that really works because no one else thought of it
- Brainstorm six alternatives to a tired word or phrase
- Rewrite a wordy or jumbled sentence in three different ways
- Show how a semicolon works
- Show how commas come inside quotation marks
- Brainstorm six alternatives to "said"

You can undoubtedly think of others. The point here is that questions like "Where will you go next with this writing?" are provocative for skilled writers, but often too broad to be helpful or meaningful to those who need more direct intervention. These students don't *know* where they're going—or sometimes, where they've been. They don't even know what you mean by a question like this. They need some sleeves-rolled-up instruction that gives them one—just *one*—practical skill they can take into revision land and work with right now.

PEER RESPONSE GROUPS

On September 23, watching ABC's *Good Morning America,* I heard Charlie Gibson interview actor John Lithgow and ask him what he considered to be the most satisfying part of his career. Smiling, Lithgow replied that it was his years on Broadway. "Why?" Charlie wanted to know. Why not television or films? Because, Lithgow explained, on Broadway, you play right to an audience. That's when you find out if you can act. Response groups are like that—a chance to play to an audience. And so, potentially, one of the most valuable and rewarding parts of the writing process. Peer review can be a waste of time, though, if it's little more than a social hour, and often it disintegrates into this if students do not know what to do during the time they meet and share their writing. When peer response groups are not working, it's often for one of the following reasons.

1. **No Writer's Vocabulary.** If students have no language for thinking about voice, leads, transitions, details, fluency, and phrasing, then "I liked your paper, Jim" may be the only comment that occurs to them.

2. **Weak Listening Skills.** When students have a directed task—such as paraphrasing, giving their impression of the main point, telling what they see or feel, or noting those words or phrases which spoke to them in particular—they learn to listen actively, to truly take in the reader's text, respond to it, and think about it. But someone must provide this direction, and it should be the writer, not you, who says what kind of response will be most useful. You can model this and offer suggestions, though.

3. **Roles That Are Unclear.** We often assume, because it may seem obvious to us, that students know precisely what to do in a peer response group. Often, this is far from the case. No one is sure who should read first or whether they must read the whole piece. Should listeners take notes or just pay attention? Should the writer show the piece to the group or only read it aloud? What kinds of response should listeners give? Should they say whether they like it? Should they score the piece analytically? These questions need to be answered before writing groups meet.

Making the Process Work for Students

Here are some suggestions to help deal with some of the issues that block the effectiveness of peer groups.

TEACH STUDENTS THE LANGUAGE OF THE SCORING GUIDE
We must give students the tools they need to make comments like, "It really surprised me when your grandmother eloped with the taxidermist—what a character she was!"

READ ALOUD OFTEN
As teachers we tend to be very visual in our response to text. Students are, too. What we see with our eyes (messy scribbles, neatly processed text dressed up with graphics) often belies the truth of what is deep inside a piece of writing. We must hear it to know. Encourage students to respond to literature as writing, too. Though it's fine to discuss plot, theme, structure, and author's purpose, it's also important to ask, "How does this writer achieve these things? Does the introduction pull you in? Why? Does the voice and tone fit the audience? How do you know? Will people still read this a hundred years from now?"

KEEP THE TIME FRAME WORKABLE
Peer review is, by nature, a reflective activity, and we must respect that. On the other hand, allowing too much time can make students feel pressured to say more than they have to say, and soon the conversation drifts to unrelated topics.

Try this (adjusting if the timing does not work for you): Put students into groups of three. This allows each reader to have two listener-responders. Set up a time frame for students, and let them know that while they will have ample time to make comments, peer review will not go on forever. They will need to stay focused and on task, and to make comments that are to the point.

Ask students to take a minute or so to decide who will go first, second, and third. Then, give each student three minutes to read his or her work; it is not necessary to read the whole piece (unless it fits comfortably within this time limit). Readers can be selective about what they choose to share, and they should be selective if the piece is very long. Allow responders about two minutes each to give a focused, clear, concise response to the reader's piece. This means that, given groups of three, the whole process will take just over twenty minutes. This is about right. It allows you time, as an instructor, to set the process up and to discuss at the end how things went, both of which are important.

DISTINGUISH BETWEEN PEER EDITING AND PEER REVIEW
In peer review, listeners seldom see a writer's text. There is no need. They are not correcting the text. They're asking, How does the writing play to the ear and to the imagination? They may tell what they picture in their minds or how the text makes them feel. In most cases, the writing is still in process, and the writer is still experimenting and revising, so editing is neither appropriate nor desirable.

In peer editing—a very tricky process to manage well—writers work together to proofread a text and correct faulty punctuation, spelling, grammar, paragraphing, capitalization, and so on. This is a completely different experience and should be handled separately. (See Chapter 7 for more suggestions.)

DEFINE ROLES CLEARLY
Make sure both readers and responders understand very well what their roles are and what is expected of them.

THE WRITER'S ROLE
Students frequently believe that the role of the writer is first to subject listeners to a rapid, low-volume, monotone reading of the text, then to sit passively by as responders give any sort of feedback that suits them. This reminds me of the way strangers often greet each other when they first meet: "How's it going?" "Fine. And you?" "Great, thanks." No real questions are being asked; no real answers are being given. It's a polite waste of time.

Give your response group process some clout and purpose. First, the writer should give the text the best interpretive reading possible, keeping in mind that it is fine to select just a portion—just the lead or conclusion or just one descriptive paragraph. Second, the writer should let listeners know what kind of response would be helpful.

For instance, a writer may want to know what reader-listeners expect upon hearing a particular lead or whether a certain word or phrase works. It might be helpful to know what kind of voice listeners hear or what they think of a particular character. Is Mara's persuasive essay on wetlands convincing, or does it just restate the obvious? Do listeners learn anything about the giant squid from Brad's story "Night Terror"? Is it realistic enough to be terrifying, or just clichèd science fiction? What do listeners picture on hearing Tia's expository piece about the invasion of fire ants in the South? The listeners' role is made ever so much easier by knowing what *kind* of response will be useful to the writer.

THE RESPONDER'S ROLE

Help responders understand that they are not responsible for choreographing the revision of the piece; that is the writer's job. As responders, their job involves listening attentively, with every sense in tune. What do they see, hear, smell, or feel as the writer shares a piece? How do they react emotionally? These questions should be going through their minds as they listen, even if they do not share all this information with the writer. If the writer does not ask for specific feedback, responders can say, "What kind of response would be most helpful to you right now?"

> Even very young children can listen and look for one colorful word or the most exciting sentence or a line that has interesting sounds or the scariest phrase.
> Marjorie Frank (1995, 140)

Model the Process

Read a piece of your own writing, and let students be a writing group for you. Let them know what will be helpful to you as a writer. You might—

- Ask students to listen to three or four possible leads, and to tell you which one would most likely keep them reading.
- Read two versions of a paragraph and ask which has more voice.

Another useful response involves asking listeners, "What words, phrases, or images caught your attention? Tell them back to me."

DON'T APOLOGIZE

Perhaps it's a cultural thing, but so often we feel compelled to apologize for weaknesses, real or perceived, in our performance. Nowhere do we do this more often or more vocally than in preface to our own writing. "Remember," we say, "this is just a rough draft. I wrote this when I was recovering from knee surgery, and the computer was down. I had a sprained thumb, I had to use a crayon on butcher paper, and the neighbor's dog was howling." See what this does to an audience? It says to them, "Never mind the text; pay attention to *me*. I am very insecure here." Most audiences will leap to the rescue, eager to make the writer feel better. Is that the kind of response we want, though?

When you model peer review for students, just plunge in. Later, after they've had a chance to respond, you can point out to them how you just began to read, no apologies, and tell them, "You do this, too. Be brave. Dive in and read your text with confidence, assurance, and voice so that the feedback you get will be more about your writing and less about you."

SHOW STUDENTS WHAT NOT TO DO

Ask a volunteer to read aloud a short piece of writing: the writer's own or one you provide (e.g., "Redwoods"). Then illustrate the kinds of responses that do not work: staring at the ceiling, laughing inappropriately, making a negative remark ("How could *anyone* write with such a flat voice?"), or telling the writer what and how to revise ("You need to tell what the Redwoods looked like, where you hiked, what you saw and the things you did"). Ask your volunteer to let you know how each kind of response makes him or her feel. Then talk about it as a group.

Suggestions for how to fix something may be valuable, but should be offered respectfully. Even if you're sure you see just how it ought to be changed, this story belongs to the author, not you.
  Ursula K. LeGuin (1998, 154)

HELP STUDENTS "READ" THE AUDIENCE

You don't have to share your writing aloud more than once to discover that you learn more from the audience's immediate reaction—facial expressions, body language, laughter, groaning, sighing, gasping—than from almost any comments they can offer. Help students learn to read these responses, too, and to use them. Ask, "Was the audience engaged? Why or why not? Did they laugh where you thought they would? Did they go ceiling grazing midway through? If so, what does that tell you?"

MAKE IT REAL

Many teachers feel more comfortable with a rule that says, "Each responder will make one positive comment prior to offering other kinds of feedback." This *can* work, provided that the comments are heartfelt and the writer does get his or her most important questions answered. In some ways, however, it seems a little formulaic. First, we'll say something nice to put the writer at ease; then we'll slam her with the necessary criticism to ensure improvement.

To begin with, it is not up to the listener to assess, rank, or otherwise weigh positives and negatives. Prior to revision, that's the *writer's* job. More important, our responses to writing do not have to be couched in positives and negatives unless we choose to structure them in those terms. And why would we? Our first impression is more likely to occur in terms of asking ourselves, What do I *see* (if anything)? What do I *feel* (if anything)? Why not share those immediate and highly useful responses?

A student said one day in response to a piece I'd written on a very tense, confrontational family Thanksgiving, "Your family seems very argumentative. *Very.* When you talked about staring into the candlelight reflecting off your mother's blue glass plates, I thought you were trying to escape. I used to do that." She was quite right, though I had never before thought of myself as "escaping." This response meant much more to me than if the student had said, "I enjoyed your description of the candlelight reflecting on the plates." A compliment makes us feel good for a moment; an insight keeps us thinking for hours—sometimes forever.

BEGIN WITH "I"

We can teach students to frame negative responses in positive terms, to make them less painful for writers; when you start with "I," you shift the focus from the writing to you and your response, a much less accusatory position. For instance, *"Your imagery* is weak" can become *"I could not get a clear picture of the dining room in my mind."* Or, *"Your argument lacks support"* can become *"I was confused about how a flat tax rate would affect people earning over forty thousand dollars."*

GRADING

Do We Honestly Need Grades at All?

To some educators, grades seem old-fashioned, cumbersome, and hopelessly out of sync with new approaches to assessment. Even educators who still advocate use of grades will admit that, for many purposes, there are better, more thorough methods of measuring and recording student achievement. A very well designed portfolio system, for instance, that offers multiple opportunities not only for diverse, thoughtfully assessed performance across a range of skills but for reflective self-assessment as well, provides a richer and more complete picture of what a student can do than reams of test scores. Similarly, a teacher's narrative record of student performance, if sufficiently detailed, can provide a wealth of information no report card can hope to match.

As Barry Lane tells us, "For a writing teacher who believes in encouraging revision, graded papers are nothing less than a curse. Low grades discourage and high grades imply that a piece is done. Even worse, students begin writing to improve their grade instead of finding out what they have to say" (1993, 129). Donald Murray (1985) calls grades "the terminal response," meaning that once a grade is assigned to a piece of writing, it virtually dies, for the student will not look at it again.

In his book *Punished by Rewards,* Alfie Kohn (1993) talks openly about the naïveté of those who believe we can motivate students to strive for excellence with a simplistic carrot-stick, A-to-F grading system. A student's inner world, he assures us, is far too complex to permit this. When grades dominate the classroom environment, Kohn holds, students tend to

1. place minimal value on things learned, and to care only about the grade earned;
2. become dependent on the reward, allowing themselves to be controlled by the threat of the grade; and
3. become unwilling to take any risk, however promising, which might jeopardize their GPA.

Kohn also cites the research findings of John Condry (1977), who concluded that people motivated only by the offer of immediate rewards "seem to work harder and produce more activity, but the activity is of a lower quality, contains more errors, and is more stereotyped and less creative than the work of comparable nonrewarded subjects working on the same problems" (pp. 471–472).

What Do Grades Mean to Students?

Ask *students* what grades mean, and you're likely to get some startling answers. We may think of an A, for instance, as a sign of success. But many students will tell you that As are mostly for parents (or for pre-college records)—and sometimes translate into money, the right to drive the car, or other tangible rewards. They are not always intrinsically rewarding; they're simply the gateway to something else. Think C means average and F means failure? Think again. Many students will tell you that the *worst* grade to receive is a C because while an F means you didn't try or didn't care (this can even be a badge of honor), a C indicates you did your best but *still* failed—and that's depressing.

> When I first began to teach, I was a tough grader right from the first day. . . . My students didn't realize I was terrified they might rise up and attack me. I put them in their place with grades.
> Donald M. Murray (1985)

What's more, though many of us hate admitting this, grades have no universal meaning beyond the most general level. In a workshop one day, I asked teachers to define what "B–" meant to them. Here are just some of their intriguing, diverse answers:

- You tried hard, but it needed work
- Good job! Just needed that little something more.
- Close to what I expected—almost!
- Average work. It's what used to be a C.
- 80–82%—it's pure mathematics.
- I tried to like your work, but I couldn't.

Being Consistent

Given these diverse responses to grades, can we ever hope to achieve consistency, clear definition of performance goals, and all-around fairness? We can. Indeed, we must. By connecting grades to criteria, we say to students, "We will define what we mean by various levels of performance, and we will apply those definitions as consistently as human nature will allow." It isn't a perfect system. How can it be when we are talking levels of quality, and not rights or wrongs? But the more we read and write ourselves, and the more we practice assessment with our students, the more consistent our scoring becomes, and the more we draw students into our interpretive community.

Some ways of making grades work for us include these:

- Grading a *body of work*, rather than individual pieces of writing.
- Connecting letter grades to explicit written criteria (i.e., basing grades at least partially on earned scores) in order to increase consistency and give the grades more meaning.
- Inviting students to participate, as appropriate, in determining how grades will be assigned.

HOW AND WHAT TO GRADE

If you grade a body of work, you will give students a better picture of their overall strengths and weaknesses.

Barry Lane (1993, 128)

Certainly student achievement (performance, that is) will be at the heart of most grading systems. But should other factors be considered as well? What about effort or attitude? Let's consider these factors one at a time.

Achievement

I do not, however, grade on potential, talent, improvement, effort, motivation, intention, behavior, personality, weight, height, sex, race . . . I grade on accomplishment, subjectively, I admit, but to the standards I feel are appropriate to the course.

Donald M. Murray (1985, 143)

If we grade on achievement, we tell students, in effect, that those who attain a higher level of writing proficiency will receive higher grades. To many people, this seems a fair approach to grading, and I agree. After all, demand for high-level achievement is a reality of life, both in and out of the classroom. Writers whose work no one wants to read do not get published, nor do they get hired as journalists, technical writers, communications specialists, or editors. Performance counts everywhere, not just in school. Having said that, we must determine what kinds of achievement we wish to measure and how we will go about it.

Much of this book is devoted to defining and promoting a performance assessment approach that judges the quality of students' writing based essentially on final products. For many teachers, this is enough.

However, achievement could also include performance on foundational writing tasks, such as spelling tests, analytical scoring of someone else's work, or editing.

In addition, creative assessors might look at such things as

- The student's ability to self-assess and defend that judgment in an essay
- The student's ability to both assess the work of others and defend that judgment in writing or orally
- Full participation in the writing process, from coming up with an original topic to presenting (publishing) the writing in some way
- Skill in coaching other writers through peer review or in one-on-one conferences

These and other questions can form the basis for assessing not only a student's understanding of the process of writing itself but also his or her ability to become an independent writer. One caution, though: Good process skills do not guarantee fine writing. For this reason, I prefer an assessment method that combines process with product. Keep a running record of analytical trait scores; then note participation with careful observation and use this factor to separate the B– student from the B+ student.

Effort

Effort is an intangible commodity, hard to measure and even harder to recognize. One teacher may define effort as "completing and turning in all homework on time," while to another it means "making a positive contribution to the classroom." The first definition is not so nebulous as the second, but still, such differences lead to inconsistency in grading. Furthermore, haven't we all known people whose specialty was making the next to impossible look easy? And haven't we, honestly, valued and sometimes even envied this capability? Imagine the difference in Fred Astaire's career had he lurched across the stage, huffing and puffing. Would anyone then have said, "Boy, that Fred Astaire is some dancer! What an *effort* the guy makes!" We don't want huffing, really; we want good dancing that looks effortless even when we know it's not.

Keep in mind, too, that assertiveness can look a lot like effort. The student who is forever asking a clarifying question or seeking additional writing advice is often judged to be highly motivated. This may be a correct perception, but what of the quiet or shy writers who would love to have a fraction more of our attention but are too withdrawn to ask for it? Who knows how much effort it takes for those writers just to share their writing in a group, to undergo assessment, or to compose pieces they know other eyes will see.

Suppose, then, that we do not grade on effort. It's only fair to ask, What about the student who really *is* making an effort but simply cannot succeed? What, other than effort, will rescue this student from failure?

Instead of rewarding the effort, which provides a hollow, unsatisfying kind of victory, why not reshape the task to better fit the student's skill? Change the assignment; let the student choose another topic or approach this topic in another way. Allow the student to dictate part of the piece or to flesh out a story with illustrations. If editing is involved, simplify the task by asking the student to search out fewer errors or fewer kinds of errors. Lengthen the time allowed to complete the assignment, or provide more support with a revision checklist or a good listener who will help the writer identify strengths in the text. In other words, let's find a way to help writers succeed with the business of writing. Then we won't hear ourselves saying to students, via artificially inflated grades (which fool no one, least of all students), "I see that you cannot make it as a writer. But you seem like such a good person, here are some points for trying." It is, I believe, condescending and disrespectful to inflate performance scores. Students know when they have done a good job and when they need to work harder. Let's not demean them by pretending we see things differently.

> The student deserves the teacher's respect, and deserves a grade that indicates how that work measures up. The student is not rewarded for potential, for effort, for commitment; the student is rewarded for accomplishment, for producing writing that stands up to a reader's critical eye.
>
> Donald M. Murray (1985)

Attitude

I write virtually every day, but I do not feel positive and open about it every day. Once when I was working on a piece on economics (far from my favorite topic), the computer "ate" a large chunk of the chapter I had been struggling with for two weeks. On that day I wanted to be Mad Max—just for an hour—but of course computers are not yet sufficiently advanced to experience pain, so all this energy was wasted. I certainly would not have been happy to be visited just then by someone with a clipboard and checklist, assessing my attitude.

Keeping at it when you don't feel like it (even if you're kicking and screaming all the way) is my definition of good attitude. But then, another teacher-assessor will look for a cheery disposition, a lengthy journal, visible and complicated evidence of prewriting, willingness to try a new topic or new form of writing, lack of fear when reading aloud, or willingness to write more than others want to write. The point is, can we really define good attitude or recognize it when it confronts us—any more than we can recognize effort? We can probably make some good educated guesses, but in the end, we will all be left with our personal definitions. This means—bottom line—that we should reward effort separately with an appreciative smile and lavish praise. But we should not figure it into our grades.

TRANSLATING ANALYTICAL SCORES INTO GRADES

The following are a few suggestions for those teachers who plan to use the six-trait scoring approach as part of their total assessment plan.

1. Do not assess everything. We want to gather just enough information to make confident grading decisions and no more. We know that one or two samples are not enough. When we assess somewhere between four and six samples of writing, though, we see a *body* of work; then we are probably approaching a level at which we can feel confident that our assessment is meaningful.

Students, with your help of course, can be selective about what is assessed. During a given grading period, if you are focusing on business writing or technical writing, you might ask students to select two to three samples of each form that they feel are worthy of going all the way through the writing process; others remain "practice drafts"—good for developing skills, but never assessed. Normally, practice revision, free writing, journals, and beginning drafts would not be assessed, either (except in the sense that the teacher may check to see that they are done).

If you do a complete autopsy on every piece, your writers will perish from too much pruning.
Marjorie Frank (1995, 104)

2. Score those traits that are most relevant. You do not need to assess all six traits each time, though you can if this kind of "full picture" approach makes you more comfortable. Consider, though, that in a piece of technical writing, ideas, conventions and word choice may be more important than, say, fluency. A student who is explaining how to tie a fly must think about detail and organization, while one who is telling the story of a narrow escape from fire will likely focus most on organization and voice. Assess what you have taught first. Then, once your students know all the traits, assess what best fits the purpose and content of the piece.

3. Do not *grade* individual pieces of writing. If you stick to numbers, it is fairly simple at the end of the grading period to total points earned and to grade accordingly (more on this in a moment). If you use letter grades, you can never be sure your students are interpreting them accurately—unless, of course, you are willing to define, in writing, the precise meaning of *each grade* (that's 12 levels of performance, A through F, assuming you do not give grades of A+). Is it worth the effort? A grade adds no new information. Students who know the traits know that if they're receiving 4s and 5s, they're doing well. Scores of 1 and 2 mean much revision is needed. There's never any mystery.

4. Remember: A "5" is not an "A." By the way, with five letter grades and five numbers on the scale, it is very tempting to make a direct translation: 5=A, 4=B, and so on. Resist this temptation, for it will lead to *grossly inaccurate assessment*. Remember that a letter grade is a holistic summary of how a piece of writing works overall: ideas, organization, conventions, voice—the works. A 5 in, say, *ideas* does not equal an A. That 5 represents achievement in one highly specific, focused area, whereas the A is far more global in its implications. Further, as we have seen, letter grades are defined quite differently teacher to teacher.

5. Give students the option to revise. In many classrooms, students who are unsatisfied with the formal assessment on any piece of writing have the option to revise and thereby raise their scores. This option not only reinforces the value of revision but also says to students, "Assessment is not a final judgment. It is an impression based on current performance." That puts things into perspective.

6. Make students partners in the record-keeping process. Let students know as they go along how they are doing in terms of total points earned and total points possible. This ensures that final grades will not be a surprise. It also allows those who wish to work toward a certain grade to plan accordingly. Let students know ahead of time what percentages of total points earned will be required for an A (90%? 94%?), a B, and so on. These percentages are arbitrary, which is another way of saying that they are up to you.

7. Allow students time to self-assess during the revision process. This early assessment, student directed, is not for the purpose of grading, but rather to set up a plan for revision—prior to the teacher's assessment of the piece.

8. Base grades on points earned out of points possible. To figure out a student's actual grade, *begin* by computing a percentage based on points earned out of points possible. First, determine the total possible points a student *could* earn in a grading period if he/she received the highest possible scores on each trait assessed.

Let's say a teacher scores six assignments, and scores all six traits each time. Each assignment would be worth 30 points (6 traits x 5 points = 30). The total points a student could earn, if she got a 5 on every single trait

Students are graded on practically everything they do every time they turn around. Grades generate anxiety and hard feelings between students, between students and teachers, between students and their parents, and between parents and teachers. Common sense suggests they ought to be reduced to the smallest possible number necessary to find out how students are getting along toward the four or five main objectives of the program, but teachers keep piling them up like squirrels gathering nuts.

Paul B. Diederich (1974)

every single time would be 180 (30 points per assignment x 6 assignments = 180 total points possible).

Let's say that a given student—call her Connie Consistent—receives scores of 3 on every trait every time. (This rarely happens, but just suppose.) Her total points will be 108 (3 points per trait x 6 traits per assignment x 6 assignments). You don't have to be a rocket scientist to see that Connie's percentage score will be 60%. We compute this percentage by *dividing points earned by points possible.*

For Connie, if we divide 108 (points earned) by 180 (points possible), we get 60%. Now logic tells us that with all those 3s, Connie's grade *should* be somewhere in the vicinity of a C, but the percentage says low D! Oops. Not comfortable. Why doesn't this work out? If this were a geography test with 180 questions, it *would,* and Connie's 60% would be a borderline passing score. But it's not a geography test where we're dealing with actual numbers, one point per question; it's a scoring scale, a continuum.

Picture that continuum for a minute, stretching out with a *range* of 1s, a *range* of 2s a *range* of 3s and so on, and you'll see that a score of "5" or whatever (name any score) is really only an *approximation.* So, in other words, a 4 is not really a 4.0. Sometimes when we give a score of 4, we're thinking, "Well, it's a 4, but just barely," so if we graphed it on our scale it might be, say, a 4.1. Other times we might think, "Well, I could almost go 5 on this—it's *so* close," so if we graphed that score, it might be a 4.9. (See Figure 12.1 to see how this works.)

Similarly, Connie's 3s aren't really 3s in the 3.0 sense. She doesn't nail that precise spot on the continuum every single time she earns a 3. If we could *really* measure that precisely (which we can't because we're only human, which is why we give her an approximation score of 3), we'd see that sometimes she's really a 3.9 (almost a 4), and sometimes she's a 3.1 (just hanging on by the fingernails). But nobody (that I know anyhow) wants to get *this* precise with analytical scoring. Too troublesome by far. Just reading about it is probably giving you a headache without trying to do it. So here's how to get round it.

The 4-6-8-10 Rule

First, just go ahead and compute the percentage, dividing points earned by points possible. Then, think 4-6-8-10. For any percentage of 90% or more, add 4%. For 80% to 89%, add 6%. For 70% to 79%, add 8%, and for 60% to 69% (or anything lower than this), add 10%. (See Figure 12.2 for a summary of how to compute these totals—and *don't* let the math scare you. It's a piece

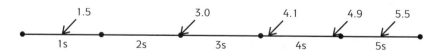

FIGURE 12.1. Placement of scores along a continuum

of cake.) These additional percentage figures were determined by examining numerous student scores and computing the resulting percentages. They are arbitrary figures, but they will make your percentages match the grades you feel are appropriate, given the actual scores a student earns. *If you do not use them,* know that your students will have to obtain *extremely* high scores to receive respectable grades. By the way, in case you're concerned, you are *not* giving the student extra points by adding in these percentages; you are not *giving* the student *anything.* You are simply making up for the fact that measurement on a continuum is by nature slightly imprecise, so we have to adjust it to make it fit our grading system. (Notice, by the way, that scores right on the fringe—60%, 70%, etc.—are adjusted by a factor of 1. This is so that a student who received, say, 69% as a total would not wind up outscoring the student who received 70%. The adjusted scores are shown in Figure 12.2.)

The 4-6-8-10 Rule

This simple-to-remember rule will help you convert any percentage to a score that allows you to assign a fair grade to a student:

✓ For scores over 90%, add 4% to the total.
✓ For scores over 80%, add 6% to the total.
✓ For scores over 70%, add 8% to the total.
✓ For scores over 60%, add 10% to the total.

Note: For scores right on the edge (60, 70, 80, 90), add one additional percentage point, for reasons that will be obvious in the following conversion chart. Remember, *figure out the basic percentages first*—then refer to this chart for a percentage you can convert to a letter grade.

Conversion Chart

Add 4%	Add 6%	Add 8%	Add 10%
90+4+1=95%	80+6+1=87%	70+8+1=79%	60+10+1=71%
91+4 =95%	81+6 =87%	71+8 =70%	61+10 =71%
92+4 =96%	82+6 =88%	72+8 =80%	62+10 =72%
93+4 =97%	83+6 =89%	73+8 =81%	63+10 =73%
94+4 =98%	84+6 =90%	74+8 =82%	64+10 =74%
95+4 =99%	85+6 =91%	75+8 =83%	65+10 =75%
96+4 =100%	86+6 =92%	76+8 =8%	66+10 =76%
97+4 =101%	87+6 =93%	77+8 =85%	67+10 =77%
98+4 =102%	88+6 =94%	78+8 =86%	68+10 =78%
99+4 =103%	89+6 =95%	79+8 =87%	69+10 =79%

You will notice that without adding the one additional percentage point, a score of, say, 89% would convert to 95%, while a score of 90% would convert to 94%. That doesn't seem fair! So, we have added on "bonus" percentage point to those scores right at the turning points of 60, 70, 80 and 90.

Students who receive percentage scores of 97% or higher, actually wind up over the 100% mark. We simply look on this as "extra credit."

FIGURE 12.2. Using the 4-6-8-10 System

If all this sounds complicated, trust me, it's not. Let's peek in on Connie again, and you'll see at once how easy it is. Notice that if we add 10% to Connie's original 60%, she comes up with a total of 70%, which is then adjusted to 71%, or a low C (a minimal C). This is a fair grade for a student who earns ALL 3s during the grading period. Also note that if Connie were to receive even *eight* scores of 4 during the same period (28 three's and only 8 four's out of 36 tries), it would affect her grade by quite a bit. In this case, her total score would be 116, not 108. Thus, her original percentage would be 116 divided by 180, or just over 64%. Adding our 10% to tweak the figures, Connie would have a respectable 74%—moving into more solid C territory. And that feels about right. All this is based, of course, on a 90% for an A, 80% for a B, and so on, kind of system.

Differential Weighting

This system is precisely the same as the total points method except that certain traits are weighted for certain assignments. For instance, if you decided that the trait of ideas was especially important in an assignment on the Holocaust, you might weight that trait by a factor of 3, making it worth 3 x 5, or 15 points total. For a business letter, you might weight conventions and presentation similarly.

COMMUNICATING WITH PARENTS

Parents are used to letter grades. Now, suddenly, here you are with numerical scores, continuums, scoring guides, strengths and weaknesses, and the rest. How do you explain it all?

Perhaps the best way, if you have the luxury of a little time, is a mini–training session in which you summarize the six traits and even have parents attempt to score a paper or two. You might even, if you're very brave, ask them to write a short paragraph and assess their own writing (as our sixth-grade teacher Elaine describes in Chapter 9). Nothing brings the traits so vividly into focus as looking at your own work!

Writing Goals

Explain that students will be learning the six traits as writing *goals* and that this process will take time. Some papers that are sent home may be drafts in process, and not everything needs to be edited. Tell them that it will be helpful if they are *listeners* rather than editors for a time, hearing their students' writing (*not* correcting it, though) and responding as if to a letter from a friend.

Parents who know the traits can interpret numerical scores as well as students can. Students who are receiving scores of 4 and 5 on most assessments are going to wind up with a grade of A or B; students who are receiving primarily 1s and 2s may have lots of work to do on revision just to achieve a passing grade. Emphasize, however, the possibility of raising scores by spending extra time on revision—or, if you like, by writing a new piece. Grades become final only when we make them so. We can always allow opportunities for change.

REFLECTING ON CHAPTER 12

1. Why are grades so important to so many of us? What factors influence that importance?
2. Which would you prefer to receive, a good letter grade or an expansive, thoughtful comment on your writing? Why? Which would tell you more?
3. Are grades addictive? Explain.
4. As a writer, do you enjoy sharing your work in a group? How does it make you feel? What kinds of feedback do you most like to receive? What kinds do you least like? Have you ever communicated those preferences to listeners in a very open way? What happened? Or (if you have not done so) what do you think might happen if you did?
5. What is the most positive comment you have ever received in response to your writing? How did it influence you? What is the most negative comment? How did that influence you? Share comments with your study group or class if you feel comfortable doing so.

ACTIVITIES

1. Share a brief piece of writing with your class, asking them to be a response group for you. Or, if you are a student, share a piece of writing within a response group. Discuss the results. What kinds of responses were most helpful? What difference does it make when the writer takes control of the response group?
2. For fun, act out a "bad response group" scenario, doing some role playing to illustrate the kinds of responses you find least helpful.
3. Come up with a grading system that you think is fair that incorporates the six traits but may not be based solely on the six traits. Explain why you think your system is fair.
4. Compose an argument for maintaining or for doing away with grades. Defend your position using your own experience and that of at least two other people. Hold a debate in your class or study group on this topic.
5. Compose a brief letter to parents outlining how their students' work will be assessed using the analytical scoring method and what they can do to help.

LOOKING AHEAD

The Epilogue presents some closing thoughts on the evolution of language to its present state—which some describe as a state of mediocrity. We'll consider whether that's true, and offer some final comments.

CLOSING THOUGHTS FROM STUDENTS' WRITING

- How could I be related to some guy who told fish stories I didn't even want to hear?
- Sorry—sometimes I trail off from the herd . . .
- Death: It changes lives.
- Hawaii is like a big island.
- My parents are having their vowels redone.
- I was the Valid Victorian of my class.
- I thought I was going crazy, but now I know it was only sinuses.
- He had one of those tiny, stuffy, gives-you-a-headache-no-matter-what cars.
- Well, bon voy ash, dudes!

REFLECTING AND BELIEVING

I believe the ultimate in education is reached when learners—both students and teachers at all levels—take charge of their own learning and use their education to lead rich and satisfying lives.

Regie Routman (1996, 147)

What is needed is a culture of success, backed by a belief that all pupils can achieve.
Paul Black and Dylan Wiliam (1998)

When my students and I discover uncharted territory to explore, when the pathway out of a thicket opens up before us, when our experience is illuminated by the lightning life of the mind—then teaching is the finest work I know.

Parker J. Palmer (1998, 1)

Not long ago, in one of my workshops, a teacher stood up to comment upon what she saw as a decline in the general standards and expectations regarding our language. That decline is everywhere, she alleged: on television, in the newspapers, in our printed literature, and in students' work. "Why do we tolerate mediocrity?" she cried, and there was deep anxiety in her voice.

This question is not going to go away. Many people perceive a growing slackness in the way we view writing, and often this slackness is associated with students' ability (or inability) to write conventionally correct text. It is also associated with the continual changes in our language, changes which now occur at a breathtaking rate and that require us to shift our dictionaries and thesauruses to electronic media just to keep pace.

For some people, this change will probably never feel comfortable; indeed, it may always be perceived as vaguely threatening. They may feel, along with John Simon in *Paradigms Lost,* that "language, for the most part, changes out of ignorance" (McCrum, Cran, and MacNeil, 1986, p. 346). Partly, perhaps. But that is far from the only reason for change. Language changes also through imagination, through creative borrowing, and through need. We may take on words from another culture just because we like their sound: *kangaroo, billabong, mate, jumbuck,* and *boomerang* from Australia; or *voodoo, tote, juke, banana, bad-mouth, nitty-gritty, high five, banjo, okra,* and *jam session* from African cultures. Think how our language is enriched by our passion for borrowing: *cupola, balcony, piano, pizza, balloon,* and *volcano* from Italian; *paragraph, alphabet, school,* and *thermometer* from Greek; *canoe, toboggan, chipmunk, pecan,* and *kayak* from Native American; *shampoo, pepper, panther,* and *ketchup* from Asian cultures; *physician, milieu,* and *poetry* from French; *hamburger, pretzel,* and *kindergarten* from German; *ski, knife, happy,* and *egg* from Scandinavian.

As we change culturally and technologically, our language must expand to let us talk about who we are and where we're going. No one needed to talk of cyberspace, interfacing, computer hackers, modems, or virtual reality fifty years ago, but these terms are part of our common language now—and more are coming. It's all a matter of perspective, though. The words *education* and *dedicate* were new (and suspect to some) in 1531, when Sir Thomas Elyot published *The Book Named the Governour,* said to be "the first book on education printed in English" (McCrum et al., 1986, p. 93). Poor Sir Thomas actually felt pressed to apologize for his use of the trendy new *maturity,* a word he admitted seemed dark and obscure, but one with which, he assured readers of his book, they would soon feel right at home.

Not so many years ago, in the early 1700s, we had no English dictionary to refer to at all, and were it not for writers like Shakespeare, Milton and Sir Francis Bacon, our current dictionaries might be impoverished, pathetic little things—but early lexicographers borrowed heavily from these lords of word choice, and so now we are drowning in language—more than some of us can use. Conventions are ever in flux, too, shifting to suit our needs and to match our invention. Wedidnotalwayshavespacesbetweenwordsorpunctuationeithernottomentionparagraphingallofwhicharenewonthescene, and all of which—it must be admitted—make our processing of text far easier. Don't you think?

Changes in language are not just about the addition of new words or innovations in conventions, though. We continually change in the whole way in which we speak. Speech has become, especially in recent decades, both more rapid and more direct. In 1850, Nathaniel Hawthorne wrote *The Scarlet Letter,* a work which critic Arnold Bennett (quoted in the 1993 Barnes and Noble edition) called "as near to perfection as is granted a man to bring his achievements." It is a fascinating text, which continues to be studied and puzzled over by many high school students. Near the end of the story, Hawthorne writes, "Arthur Dimmesdale gazed into Hester's face with a look in which hope and joy shone out, indeed, but with fear betwixt them, and a kind of horror at her boldness, who had spoken what he vaguely hinted at, but dared not speak" (p. 204).

Hawthorne's writing is eloquent, even reverent, in the way it caresses language, carefully laying down word upon word. But does it speak to us now? Students frequently find it dull and tedious. They lack the patience (and the time) it takes to decipher text written at this slow pace and level of complexity. We can belittle their ignorance or lack of taste, but then we have to ask ourselves, "Would this book stand a chance of becoming a best seller today? Would we *ourselves* read it if it were not an established classic? Could Hawthorne seriously compete with Stephen King, Robert B. Parker or John Grisham?"

Here's an even more intriguing question: Would Hawthorne *himself* write this way now—if he could have lived in both times—or might he write something more like this: "Arthur was filled with hope and joy at Hester's words, but he knew his eyes revealed a growing sense of fear. How brave she was. Suggesting even now that she could and *would* be part of his life, no matter what the cost. He had *thought* of them together, certainly, even wondering if she could read his thoughts. But unlike Hester, he had *never* had the courage to speak of it."

Some people may find it presumptuous to be editing Hawthorne, but it's kind of fun (therapeutic, even)—and anyway, I do so only to suggest that the rhythms of language and the word patterns to which readers respond change constantly. And this is something of which successful writers would do well to be aware. It was only back in 1963 (far after Hawthorne's time) that Eric Enholm was teaching "Basic Story Structure," which he took to include "incident . . . meetings, interchanges, episodes, encounters, purposes, scene difficulties, suspense points, dramatic points, actions . . . preparations, lines of progress . . . character objectives . . . conclusive acts, plot steps, sequels, stories, patterns, furtherances, [and as we might expect] hindrances" (6–7). Only "when these items with their definitions and rules of procedure are known and mastered," asserts Enholm, can we be sure of a good play, novel, or story. Well, if this is *"basic,"* heaven deliver us from "advanced story struc-ture," which is likely to prove fatal to anyone lacking Hawthornian strength. (And remember, this is only one trait—*structure*. It probably gets worse.)

In philosophical opposition to the Simonesque fear of change is the belief that we keep ourselves and our language alive with new infusions. In 1919, H. L. Mencken wrote in *The American Language*, "A living language is like a man suffering incessantly from small hemorrhages, and what it needs above all else is constant transactions of new blood from other tongues. The day the gates go up, that day it begins to die" (McCrum, Cran, and MacNeil, 1986, p. 47).

Having said all this, though, let's return for a moment to that agitated teacher's essential question: Why do we tolerate mediocrity? First, let me say I am not convinced that we do. Though many student writers struggle, I personally encounter students every year whose writing both moves and teaches us. Some of that work appears in this book. And much of it is stunning. You will not see it in the newspaper, probably, because as a reporter told me once, "Kids writing well? That's not news. People want to hear about the *problems.*" Baloney. The much-guarded secret that countless American students write somewhere between functionally and brilliantly is definitely newsworthy. Certainly it would be reassuring to parents desperate for their children to succeed in college or at the work place. It would be emotionally life-saving to teachers grading papers at 11 pm and wondering how else they can help their students "get it."

For the sake of argument, however, let's acknowledge that not *all* our students are achieving in writing at a level we can feel good about. In that case, my response to the question is simply, Let's *not* tolerate mediocrity, not for a moment. But let's also not kid ourselves that intolerance alone will be a powerful weapon. Intolerance breeds only disdain, not student improvement. Strong instruction from confident teachers who are themselves writers has always been—and continues to be—our best hope. So, instead of simply criticizing, let's help them do it. If you're an observer of today's educational scene, get involved. Volunteer. Coach. Read to kids. Be a writer and share your writing. If you have children in school, read to them and listen to their writing. Talk with your child's teacher about the criteria he/she uses to score or grade work; suggest (as gently as you like) that those criteria be handed out in written form. If you're a teacher, don't give up. Read to your students. Write with them and share your writing. Show them how you edit a piece of work. Ask for their opinions. Criteria can and will help you. They speak to kids in language that makes sense—and suggest to students that they are capable and worthy critics, which they are.

Meanwhile, let's also be very, very careful about how we define mediocrity. Surely, we want our language to expand and to demand new things of us. As beautiful as it is, we do not wish to write or think in the language of Hawthorne, nor that of Chaucer or Milton or Shakespeare, except for those suspended periods of time when we work very hard to penetrate that old English syntax and pull out the meaning. This language is our history, and we will always treasure it as such, but the harder, leaner, more rhythmic beauty of Truman Capote, Maya Angelou, Alice Walker, Norman Mailer, Joseph Heller, Anne Tyler, Toni Morrison, and E. Annie Proulx speaks to us equally:

> *The bay crawled with whitecaps like maggots seething in a broad wound. A rough morning. Quoyle jumped down the steps. He would drive. But walked first down to the dock to look at the water. The boat charged against the tire bumpers. The waves pouring onshore had a thick look to them, a kind of moody rage.*
>
> *(Proulx, 1993, p. 197)*

"The bay crawled with whitecaps . . . The boat charged . . . a thick look . . . a kind of moody rage"—we love the richness of that language. It's fierce and full of fight. It has echoes of Shakespeare, Hawthorne, Melville, and Dylan Thomas. It isn't any of them. It is Proulx's own voice, but enriched by a multitude of other voices which have no doubt resounded in her head at one time. We can revere what has gone before and still create our own text.

In addition, I am vehemently opposed to defining mediocrity solely as conventional imperfection. While I believe passionately in teaching and promoting correct and intelligent use of conventions, this vision of writing skill as correctness is too small, too confined. Let's use it, though, just for a moment. Let's say we have as *one* of our goals the teaching of conventions and editing skill. How do we go about this?

First, we teach *ourselves* conventions, not just as they were taught to us but as they are *now* used by the best editors of our time. Write to publishing houses; get copies of their editorial rules. Check *The Chicago Manual of Style, The MLA Style Manual, UPI Stylebook, Elements of Style, Woe Is I, Write for College, Write to Work,* and other current and reliable handbooks. Read from them routinely and quote from them, too. Provide students with extensive, frequent practice in editing text of all kinds: poetry, fiction, informational text, technical pieces, journalistic reports—and your own writing!

Scour newspapers, novels, journals, advertisements, pamphlets, and other sources both for creative use of conventions and for mistakes. Ask your students to do the same. Question students about the reasons behind conventions. Why do we spell things consistently? Why is much of our spelling not phonetic? Why do we need punctuation? What issues of layout and formatting will become critical over the next ten years? Ask them to think. No one can memorize conventional rules; there are simply too many. The only logical, reasonable way to teach them is to learn the reasons behind them so they make sense and become, like rules of the road, almost instinctive. And, of course, to have multiple resources handy and to refer to them often. Finally, do not edit for your students except to teach or illustrate. They will learn only what they do.

Now, let's expand the vision. More than about mediocrity in punctuation, I am concerned, as a teacher, about mediocrity in thinking, reasoning, shaping text, and sharing ideas. Let's teach our students to identify the issues and questions that are worth writing about, whether for personal or socially significant reasons. Let's teach them to find information and to share their findings, not by piling up detached facts like logjams but by sifting, examining, synthesizing, and condensing. Let's help them see that all good writing has purpose: to teach, to provoke, to trouble, to question, to delight, to persuade or to entertain. The writer who knows a topic and audience well can choreograph their interaction like a well-timed dance. We can put this power into students' hands. Let's teach them to analyze the volumes, the acres of writing over which they will travel, to know what is good, to respond to the voice, and to dig for the ideas at the heart. Let's teach them also to analyze their own work, to examine their journey as writers, to be demanding of themselves, not because we say so but because they know what they're capable of and will accept no less.

Why do we tolerate mediocrity? I cannot imagine. We do not have to. We have right here, in our power, the means to take our students to a new height and vision.

Finally, *believe*. Believe that just 'round the bend is a new piece of writing to surprise and delight you. Never fear being too readily impressed. Never be ashamed of your unabashed joy at a student's success, however humble; it is the greatest gift you can give a new writer who longs for someone to love the words on the page. Believe that as a teacher, you are doing the most important work anyone can do—opening doors to new thinking. As Parker J. Palmer reminds us, no innovation, no reform movement, no amount of restructuring and no set of standards will "transform education if we fail to cherish—and challenge—the human heart that is the source of good teaching" (1998, 3). Believe that every time you listen thoughtfully to your students' work, share your own writing (good or bad), express your sense of joy in discovering a new, fine piece of literature, or help a student writer hear a moment of voice in his or her writing, which just a second ago that writer did not know was there, you are making a difference. For you are.

REFERENCES

Anderson, Richard C., Elfrieda H. Hiebert, Judith A. Scott, and Ian A. G. Wilkinson. 1985. *Becoming a Nation of Readers.* Washington, D.C.: U.S. Department of Education.

Angier, Natalie. 1995. *The Beauty of the Beastly.* New York: Houghton Mifflin.

Ansa, Tina McElroy. 1994. In "Tina McElroy Ansa." Rebecca Carroll, *I Know What the Red Clay Looks Like: The Voice and Vision of Black Women Writers.* New York: Crown.

Aronie, Nancy Slonim. 1998. *Writing From the Heart: Tapping the Power of Your Inner Voice.* New York: Hyperion.

Atwell, Nancie. 1987. *In the Middle: Writing, Reading and Learning With Adolescents.* Portsmouth, NH: Boynton/Cook.

Atwood, Margaret. 1996. *Alias Grace.* New York: Bantam Doubleday Dell.

Ballenger, Bruce. 1998. *The Curious Researcher.* New York: Allyn and Bacon.

The Big Red One. 1980. Film produced by CBS/Fox Video. Directed by Samuel Fuller.

Black, Paul and Dylan Wiliam. 1998. "Inside the Black Box: Raising Standards Through Classroom Assessment." *Phi Delta Kappan* (October), pp. 139–148.

Blake, Gary and Robert Bly. *The Elements of Technical Writing.* 1993. New York: MacMillan.

Bradbury, Ray. 1992. *Zen in the Art of Writing.* New York: Bantam Books.

Bragg, Rick. 1997. *All Over But the Shoutin'.* New York: Random House.

Brandt, Ron. 1993. "On Teaching for Understanding: A Conversation With Howard Gardner." *Educational Leadership* 50 (September), pp. 4–7.

Brown, John Seely. 1991. "Research That Reinvents the Corporation." *Harvard Business Review* (January–February), pp 102–111.

Brown, Ruth. 1996. *Toad.* New York: Dutton Children's Books.

Burke, Jim. 1999. *The English Teacher's Companion.* Portsmouth, NH: Heinemann.

Calkins, Lucy McCormick. 1994. *The Art of Teaching Writing,* rev. ed. Portsmouth, NH: Heinemann.

———. 1986. *The Art of Teaching Writing.* Portsmouth, NH: Heinemann.

Cappon, Rene J. 1991. *The Associated Press Guide to News Writing:* New York: Prentice-Hall.

Charlton, James, ed. 1992. *The Writer's Quotation Book.* New York: Penguin.

Chew, Charles. 1985. "Instruction Can Link Reading and Writing." In *Breaking Ground: Teachers Relate Reading and Writing in the Elementary School.* Edited by Jane Hansen, Thomas Newkirk, and Donald Graves. Portsmouth, NH: Heinemann.

Chicago Manual of Style, The. 14th edition. 1993. Chicago: University of Chicago Press.

Chin, Beverly Ann. 1996. Personal interview with author. Boston, MA, NCTE Conference, March 21.

Cisneros, Sandra. 1989. *The House on Mango Street.* Toronto: Random House.

Claggett, Fran. 1996. *A Measure of Success.* Portsmouth, NH: Heinemann.

Clark, Roy Peter. 1987. *Free to Write: A Journalist Teaches Young Writers.* Portsmouth, NH: Heinemann.

Clarke, William. 1829. *The Boy's Own Book.* New York: Charles S. Francis.

Collins, James L. 1998. *Strategies for Teaching Struggling Writers.* New York: The Guilford Press.

Condry, John. 1977. "Enemies of Exploration: Self-Initiated vs. Other-Initiated Learning." *Journal of Personality and Social Psychology* 35: 459–477.

Conlan, Gertrude. 1986. "'Objective Measures of Writing Ability." 1986. In *Writing Assessment: Issues and Strategies.* Edited by Karen L. Greenberg, Harvey S. Wiener, and Richard A. Donovan. White Plains, NY: Longman.

Conroy, Pat. 1995. *Beach Music.* New York: Doubleday.

Crichton, Michael. 1988. *Travels.* New York: Random House.

Dahl, Roald. 1988. *Matilda.* New York: Viking Kestrel.

Diamond, Jared. 1997. *Guns, Germ, and Steel.* New York: W. W. Norton & Company, Inc.

Diederich, Paul B. 1974. *Measuring Growth in English.* Urbana, IL: National Council of Teachers of English.

Edwards, Pamela Duncan. 1997. *Barefoot: Escape on the Underground Railroad.* New York: HarperCollinsPublishers.

Elbow, Peter. 1986. *Embracing Contraries.* New York: Oxford University Press.

Enholm, Eric. 1963. *Basic Story Structure.* St. Petersburg, Florida: Bayside Publishing Company.

Fitch, Janet. 1999. *White Oleander.* New York: Little, Brown and Company.

Fletcher, Ralph. 1993. *What a Writer Needs.* Portsmouth, NH: Heinemann.

Fox, Mem. 1989. *Night Noises.* New York: Harcourt Brace & Company.

Fox, Mem. 1993. *Radical Reflections.* New York: Harcourt Brace.

Frank, Marjorie. 1995. 2d edition. *If You're Trying to Teach Kids How to Write . . . you've gotta have this book!* Nashville, TN: Incentive Publications, Inc.

Fraser, Jane, and Donna Skolnick. 1994. *On Their Way: Celebrating Second Graders As They Read and Write.* Portsmouth, NH: Heinemann.

Galler, Barbara Ann. 1995. Curriculum. Issaquah, WA.

Gardner, Howard. 1993. "Educating for Understanding." *The American School Board Journal* (July), pp. 20–24.

Gayles, Gloria Wade. 1994. In "Gloria Wade-Gayles." Rebecca Carroll, *I Know What the Red Clay Looks Like: The Voice and Vision of Black Women Writers.* New York: Crown.

Gerson, Sharon J. and Steven M. Gerson. 1997. *Technical Writing: Process and Product.* Upper Saddle River, NJ: Simon and Schuster.

Graves, Donald H. 1999. *Bring Life Into Learning.* Portsmouth, NH: Heinemann.

———. 1983. *Writing: Teachers and Children At Work.* Portsmouth, NH: Heinemann.

———. 1994. *A Fresh Look At Writing.* Portsmouth, NH: Heinemann.

Graves, Donald H., and Virginia Stuart. 1987. *Write from the Start: Tapping Your Child's Natural Writing Ability.* New York: NAL Penguin.

Hairston, Maxine. 1986. "On Not Being a Composition Slave." In *Training the New Teacher of College Composition.* Edited by Charles W. Bridges. Urbana, IL: National Council of Teachers of English.

Hawthorne, Nathaniel. [1850] 1993. *The Scarlet Letter.* New York: Barnes and Noble.

Heard, Georgia. 1995. *Writing Toward Home.* Portsmouth, NH: Heinemann.

Hegi, Ursula. 1994. *Stones From the River.* New York: Simon and Schuster.

Hillocks, George, Jr. 1986. *Research on Written Composition: New Directions for Teaching.* Urbana, IL: ERIC Clearinghouse on Reading and Communications Skills.

Hoose, Phillip and Hannah Hoose. 1998. *Hey, Little Ant.* Berkeley, CA: Tricycle Press.

Huot, Brian. 1990. "The Literature of Direct Writing Assessment: Major Concerns and Prevailing Trends." *Review of Educational Research* 60 (Summer), pp. 237–263.

Johnson, Bea. 1999. *Never Too Early to Write.* Gainesville, FL: Maupin House Publishing, Inc.

Keillor, Garrison. 1989. *We Are Still Married.* New York: Viking Penguin.

King, Janice M. 1995. *Writing High-Tech Copy That Sells.* New York: John Wiley & Sons, Inc.

Kohn, Alfie. 1993. *Punished by Rewards.* New York: Houghton Mifflin.

Korda, Michael. 1999. "Editing Explained." *Sky Magazine* (September), pp. 106–112. Reprinted with permission from Michael Korda. 1999. *Another Life.* New York: Random House.

Kuralt, Charles. 1990. *A Life on the Road.* New York: Putnam's.

Lamott, Anne. 1995. *Bird By Bird.* New York: Bantam Doubleday Dell Publishing Group, Inc.

Lane, Barry. 1996. "Quality in Writing." *Writing Teacher* 9 (3), pp. 3–8.

———. 1999. *Reviser's Toolbox.* Shoreham, VT: Discover Writing Press.

———. 1997. *Writing As a Road to Self-Discovery.* Shoreham, VT: Discover Writing Press.

———. 1993. *After THE END.* Portsmouth, NH: Heinemann.

Lederer, Richard. 1994. *More Anguished English.* New York: Dell.

Lederer, Richard and Richard Dowis. 1995. *The Write Way.* New York: Simon and Schuster.

Lederman, Marie Jean. 1986. "Why Test?" In *Writing Assessment: Issues and Strategies.* Edited by Karen L. Greenberg, Harvey S. Wiener, and Richard A. Donovan. White Plains, NY: Longman.

LeGuin, Ursula K. 1998. *Steering the Craft.* Portland, OR: The Eighth Mountain Press.

Levy, Steven. 1995–1996. "The Year of the Internet." *Newsweek* (December 25, 1995–January 1, 1996), pp. 21–30.

Lunsford, Andrea A. 1986. "The Past—and Future—of Writing Assessment." In *Writing Assessment: Issues and Strategies.* Edited by Karen L. Greenberg, Harvey S. Wiener, and Richard A. Donovan. White Plains, NY: Longman.

McCammon, Robert R. 1991. *Boy's Life.* New York: Pocket Star Books.

McCourt, Frank. 1999. *'Tis.* New York: Scribner.

McCrum, Robert, William Cran, and Robert MacNeil. 1986. *The Story of English.* New York: Viking Penguin.

McMurtry, Larry. 1985. *Lonesome Dove.* New York: Simon and Schuster.

Mailer, Norman. 1984. *Tough Guys Don't Dance.* New York: Random House.

Mathers, Petra. 1991. *Sophie and Lou.* New York: Harper.

Microsoft Corporation. 1994. *Concise User's Guide.* Redmond, WA: Microsoft Press.

Mohr, Marian M. 1984. *Revision: The Rhythm of Meaning.* Upper Montclair, NJ: Boynton/Cook.

Morrison, Toni. In Murray, Donald M. 1990. *Shoptalk.* Portsmouth, NH: Heinemann.

Murray, Donald M. 1982. *Learning By Teaching.* Portsmouth, NH: Bounton/Cook.

———. 1990. *Shoptalk.* Portsmouth, NH: Boynton/Cook.

———. 1984. *Write to Learn.* New York: Holt, Rinehart and Winston.

————. 1985. *A Writer Teaches Writing.* 2d ed. Boston: Houghton Mifflin.

O'Connor, Patricia T. 1996. *Woe Is I.* New York: G. P. Putnam's Sons.

————. 1999. *Words Fail Me.* New York: Harcourt Brace & Company.

Palmer, Parker J. 1998. *The Courage to Teach: Exploring the Inner Landscape of a Teachers Life.* San Francisco: Jossey-Bass Publishers.

Paulsen, Gary. 1994. *Winterdance.* Orlando: Harcourt Brace & Company.

————. 1989. *The Winter Room.* New York: Dell.

————. 1992. *Clabbered Dirt, Sweet Grass.* New York: Harcourt Brace Jovanovich.

————. 1993. *Dogteam.* New York: Delacorte Press.

Proulx, Annie. 1999. *Close Range.* New York: Scribner.

————. 1993. *The Shipping News.* New York: Simon and Schuster.

Purves, Alan C. 1992. "Reflections on Research and Assessment in Written Composition." *Research in the Teaching of English* 26 (February), pp. 108–122.

Quammen, David. 1996. *The Song of the Dodo.* New York: Scribner.

————. 1998. *Wild Thoughts From Wild Places.* New York: Scribner.

r.w.t. Magazine for Writing Teachers K–8. San Antonio, TX: ECS Learning Systems Inc.

Rice, Scott, ed. 1996. *Dark and Stormy Rides Again.* New York: Penguin Books.

————. 1992. *It Was a Dark and Stormy Night: The Final Conflict.* New York: Penguin Books.

Ringgold, Faith. 1991. *Tar Beach.* New York: Random House.

Robinson, Barbara. 1972. *The Best Christmas Pageant Ever.* New York: Harper & Row.

Romano, Tom. 1987. *Clearing the Way: Working With Teenage Writers.* Portsmouth, NH: Hienemann.

————. 1995. *Writing With Passion.* Portsmouth, NH: Boynton/Cook.

Routman, Regie. 1996. *Literacy At the Crossroads.* Portsmouth, NH: Heinemann.

Sachar, Louis. Keynote address: Author's Luncheon. Florida Reading Association. Orlando. October 16, 1999.

Sagan, Carl. 1980. *Cosmos.* New York: Random House.

————. 1995. *The Demon-Haunted World.* New York: Random House.

Sebranek, Patrick, Verne Meyer, Dave Kemper, and John Van Rys. 1996. *School to Work.* Lexington, MA: Heath.

Sebranek, Patrick, Dave Kemper, and Verne Meyer. *The Write Source Handbooks for Students.* Wilmington, MA: Great Source Education Group.

Shaughnessy, Mina P. 1977. *Errors and Expectations.* New York: Oxford University Press.

Smith, Frank. 1984. "Reading Like a Writer." In *Composing and Comprehending.* Edited by Julie M. Jensen. Urbana, IL: ERIC Clearinghouse on Reading and Communication Skills.

Steele, Bob. 1998. *Draw Me a Story.* Winnipeg, Manitoba, Canada: Peguis Publishers.

Stegner, Wallace. 1992. "Thoughts in a Dry Land." In *Where the Bluebird Sings to the Lemonade Springs: Living and Writing in the West.* New York: Random House.

Steig, William. 1971. *Amos and Boris.* New York: Puffin Books.

————. 1987. *Abel's Island.* Toronto: Collins.

Stiggins, Richard J. 1996. *Student-Centered Classroom Assessment.* 2d ed. Columbus, OH: Merrill Education/Prentice-Hall.

Strickland, Kathleen and James Strickland. 1998. *Reflections on Assessment.* Portsmouth, NH: Boynton/Cook.

Strong, Richard, Harvey F. Silver, and Amy Robinson. 1995. "What Do Students Want?" *Educational Leadership* 53 (September), pp 8–12.

Strunk, William, Jr. and E. B. White. 2000. *The Elements of Style*, 4th edition. Boston: Allyn and Bacon.

Tatalias, Ellen. 1996. "Doublespeak Assignment." New Tripoli, PA.

Thomas, Dylan. [1954] 1962. "Reminiscences of Childhood." In *Thought in Prose*. 2d ed. Edited by Richard S. Beal and Jacob Korg. Englewood Cliffs, NJ: Prentice-Hall.

Thomas, Lewis. 1979. *The Medusa and the Snail*. New York: Penguin.

Thomason, Tommy. 1993. *More Than a Writing Teacher*. Commerce, TX: Bridge Press.

———. 1998. *Writer to Writer: How to Conference Young Authors*. Norwood, MA: Christopher-Gordon Publishers, Inc.

Thomason, Tommy and Carol York. 2000. *Write on Target: Preparing Young Writers to Succeed on State Writing Achievement Tests*. Norwood, MA: Christopher-Gordon Publishers, Inc.

Tredway, Linda. 1995. "Socratic Seminars: Engaging Students in Intellectual Discourse." *Educational Leadership* 53 (September), pp. 26–29.

Twain, Mark. 1965. *Huckleberry Finn*. New York: Harper & Row.

Wade-Gayles, Gloria. 1994. In Rebecca Carroll, *I Know What the Red Clay Looks Like: The Voice and Vision of Black Women Writers*. New York: Crown.

Wasserstein, Paulette. 1995. "What Middle Schoolers Say About Their Schoolwork." *Educational Leadership* (September), pp. 41–43.

Welty, Eudora. 1983. *One Writer's Beginnings*. New York: Warner Books.

White, E. 1985. *Teaching and Assessing Writing*. San Francisco: Jossey-Bass.

Wiggins, Grant. 1992. "Creating Tests Worth Taking." *Educational Leadership* (May), pp. 26–33.

Will, George. 1995–1996. "Oh, What a Revolution." *Newsweek* (December 25, 1995–January 1, 1996), p. 136.

Winokur, John. 1990. *W.O.W.: Writers on Writing*. Philadelphia: Running Press.

Wolcott, Willa, with Sue M. Legg. 1998. *An Overview of Writing Assessment: Theory, Research, and Practice*. Urbana, IL: National Council of Teachers of English.

Ziegler, Alan. 1981. *The Writing Workshop*. Vol. 1. New York: Teachers and Writers Collaborative.

Zorfass, Judith, and Harriet Copel. 1995. "The I-Search: Guiding Students Toward Relevant Research." *Educational Leadership* (September), pp. 48–51.

INDEX